IPO

A GLOBAL GUIDE

Third Edition

Also by Philippe Espinasse:

Non-fiction:
IPO Banks: Pitch, Selection & Mandate (2014)
Cornerstone Investors: A Practice Guide for Asian IPOs (2018)

As joint author:
Study Manual for Paper 15 Sponsors (Principals) and Paper 16 Sponsors (Representatives) of the Licensing Examination for Securities and Futures Intermediaries (with Syren Johnstone, 2013)

As a co-author:
The Hong Kong IPO Guide 2013 (2012)
The IPO Guide 2012 (2012)

Fiction:
Hard Underwriting (2015)
The Traveler (2016)

IPO

A GLOBAL GUIDE

Third Edition

PHILIPPE ESPINASSE

HKU
PRESS
香港大學出版社

Hong Kong University Press
The University of Hong Kong
Pokfulam Road
Hong Kong
https://hkupress.hku.hk

ISBN 978-988-8754-00-7 (*Paperback*)

British Library Cataloguing-in-Publication Data
A catalogue record for this book is available from the British Library.

10 9 8 7 6 5 4 3 2 1

Printed and bound by Suncolor Printing Co., Ltd. in Hong Kong, China

For Christelle, Gabriel, Camille, and Maëlle

Contents

Figures and tables

Preface

This book was first published in 2011 and last updated in 2014 (as a paperback version). It is now a good time to print a third edition.

Much has changed in the intervening period. Market activity has continued unabated, including, surprisingly, throughout the COVID-19 pandemic (although not across all jurisdictions). Equity underwriting fees in 2020 reached an unprecedented US$13.2 billion, topping the previous record in 2009 by some 40%. The Chinese markets, and Hong Kong's in particular, continue to lead the issuance charts and dominate IPO volumes, alongside the New York Stock Exchange, while "elephant" deal, billion-dollar IPOs, which were something of a rarity only ten years ago, have now increasingly become commonplace. In late 2019, Saudi Aramco raised almost US$26 billion on the Tadawul (the Saudi stock exchange) in what was then the world's largest-ever IPO. What was even more remarkable was that this offering was completed exclusively domestically, without an international tranche. At the time of writing (in the second quarter of 2021), while a planned Hong Kong IPO of up to more than US$34 billion by fintech issuer Ant Financial had been postponed, there was talk that it could be relaunched, setting yet another record.

Special purpose acquisition company (SPAC) issuance has experienced a strong revival, and particularly in the US, while much of the equity issuance around the world is now by corporates that are active in the internet, IT, fintech, and biotechnology industries. Many of the companies from such sectors are also not yet at the stage when they are profitable businesses, even when they can generate significant levels of turnover and cash-flow, and often achieve multi-billion US dollar IPO valuations, something that stock exchanges and investors have had to learn to work with.

Another development has been the advent of direct listings (sometimes known as disintermediated IPOs), although these remain rather marginal, compared with the more traditionally marketed and underwritten deals.

Market regulators have also become much more demanding and more aggressive, imposing, on occasion, unprecedented and very sizable fines on IPO sponsors, in particular in connection with shortcomings pertaining to the latter's due diligence investigations. I have been personally involved in a number of such cases as an expert witness, both on the prosecution and defence sides, and in particular in Hong Kong.

The second edition of this book was much expanded to reflect the then new listing environment. It featured chapters on business trusts in both Singapore and Hong Kong, as well as on listing requirements (and a detailed case study) for Malaysia, on account of its status as one of the most active markets in Southeast Asia at the time. Some 25 recent examples of transactions were added throughout to illustrate topical issues, while a similar number of new definitions resulted in an expanded glossary.

Likewise, this new edition has been the subject of a complete and detailed revision throughout, and also includes new information addressing some of the more recent, above-mentioned market developments. Some topics, such as spin-off offerings, SPACs, listing requirements, due diligence, and others have also been further expanded while, as before, some 15 additional IPOs have been included as examples, to illustrate various aspects of new offerings.

However, and as always, while I have taken care to cross-check facts and information, I still caution readers working on actual new issues to seek current regulatory, corporate finance and advisory, legal accounting, and tax advice, as may be appropriate.

My blog is available online, and now includes well over 350 of my articles that have, for the most part, featured in a variety of financial and general publications, such as the *South China Morning Post*; *L'Agefi*; the *China Economic Review*; Dow Jones and the *Wall Street Journal*; the *Nikkei Asian Review*; and Euromoney's *GlobalCapital*. I still actively appear in interviews in print media, online, on TV, and on the radio to comment on new offerings, of which many are used as examples and case studies herein.

I have published other books, too, including the new study guide for candidates taking IPO sponsor licensing examinations in Hong Kong (jointly with Syren Johnstone); one more particularly focused on how investment banks pitch for business, and on how they are selected and mandated by companies and their shareholders; as well as another that addresses cornerstone investors, in particular in the Asian markets of Hong Kong, Malaysia, and Singapore.

Lastly, whether you are a prospective IPO candidate, an equity issuer, an equity capital markets professional, an investment banker, a private equity practitioner, an investor, or a journalist, I am always keen to hear from you. Please do reach out to discuss remarkable transactions, changes in market practice (whether pertaining to documentation, valuation, or marketing techniques), or regulations.

I trust you will enjoy this new global guide. IPOs remain one of the most fascinating, and least understood, aspects of the financial markets. Hopefully, I will have further unveiled some of their enduring mysteries.

Philippe Espinasse
Hong Kong, April 2021

Acknowledgements

There are a number of people without whom this book would never have come to light. Not all of these can be publicly acknowledged; however, I would like to thank in particular (and in alphabetical order), Kasia d'Aquino, Yves Bodson, Laurence Borde, Christiaan Brakman, Donald Bryden, Jorge Calvet, François de Carbonnel, Yin Yee Chan, David Charters, Shu-Ching Jean Chen, Datuk Paul Chong, Amadea Choplin, Helena Chung, Fabio Coelho Neto, Lara Czysnok, Jacques-Henri David, Sébastien Desarbres, Charles Egersperger, Christelle Espinasse, Jacques Espinasse, Mark Fischer, Caroline Fong, Cecilia Fong, Lord Freud, Laurie Gavitt-Smith, Aidan Goddard, Thierry Gougy, Therese Grunder, Piers Higson Smith, Ho Mei Peng, Maxime Holder, George Kwok Lung Hongchoy, Anthony Hopson, Elaine Humphries, Takashi Kasagami, Su Mi Kim, Teresa Ko, Joan Lew Kwan, Paul W. Lai, Didier Lamarche, Paul S. Lau, Lorraine Li, Mark Lidiard, Joanne Lim, Herald van der Linde, Wendy Lui, Jasper Moiseiwitsch, Juan Muro-Lara, Delano Musafer, Doris Ng, Marshall Nicholson, Anthony Power, Julian Proctor, Alistair Reid, Swastayan Roy, Datuk Ganen Sarvananthan, Tina Sen, Jeremy Stoupas, Kelvin Teo, Charles Vacher, Saskia van Steensel, Julian Waldron, Josh Wymard, Ralph Ybema, Tony Yue, and Maggie Yun Zhou. With special thanks also to Robert L. Rosen for reading through, and making very helpful suggestions on, the chapters on financial information, comfort and disclosure letters, as well as legal opinions, for the second edition of this book.

I would also like to thank the staff (and former staff) at Hong Kong University Press, in particular Winnie Chau, Michael Duckworth, Clara Ho, Dawn Lau, Christy Leung, Christopher Munn, and Yasmine Hung.

Introduction to the first edition

I remember vividly the first initial public offering I worked on as a young and eager investment banker in 1994. I had joined what was then the largest investment bank in London as a graduate trainee with the 1991 intake. I spent the early years of my career writing briefing notes and working in the debt capital markets department, executing long-dated mortgage debentures and sterling-denominated bond issues for property developers, co-operative societies, and brewers in the north of England. I longed for transactions that had a more international flavour and had just transferred to the equity capital markets (ECM) team, where people seemed to be permanently flying to exotic locations such as Argentina or India, living a champagne lifestyle, and flying first-class to pitch to banks, oil majors and media companies.

After only a few weeks, most of my new colleagues decamped to join a rival firm on absurdly high guaranteed remuneration packages, and I found myself, alongside a handful of other bewildered bankers who had been left behind, tasked with executing the IPO of a relatively small issuer from Sweden. The company's headquarters were located about one hour outside Göteborg, and I became accustomed for a number of months to being picked up at home by a chauffeured car, once a week at 4:30 a.m., to catch the early morning flight at Heathrow. The issuer was a textile retailer specializing in underwear and similar apparel for middle-aged women. The company was owned by a couple of private equity investors focused on the Nordic markets, and the CEO and the CFO were two stout men of a certain age, with no experience whatsoever of capital markets. That was just as well, as I had never worked on an IPO myself. We were, however, fortunate in having a talented research analyst who had taken part in the pitching process (something that would be unthinkable nowadays). I have fond memories of helping to organize site visits for the syndicate of banks, of accompanying a dozen alpha males dressed in pinstripe suits to tour downtown shopping malls in small provincial Swedish communities, frightening housewives away from the shops, and of trying to understand the intricacies of product display, supply arrangements, and point-of-sale technology. I recall training the senior management for their roadshow presentations and having great difficulty in getting them to master the pronunciation of the word "lingerie". I also remember doctoring the pre-deal research report to make it more "punchy"; spending much longer than was necessary to choose the picture of the attractive and (dare I say it?) scantily clad model that would figure on the cover of the prospectus; marvelling at what appeared at the time to be an unlimited expense account when on the road with management; and flying on a private jet to Stockholm for the closing dinner because the managing director in charge of the transaction wanted to sleep in his own bed in London that evening. How things have changed!

Following the "dot com" crisis, the collapse of Enron, Arthur Andersen and the more recent credit crunch, going public will never be the same again. In most markets, research analysts have now been banished for good from corporate finance departments and can no longer shape and spin the stories that help win IPO mandates. In turn, ECM bankers are no longer permitted to lend a heavy hand to research analysts' reports to entice institutions to pile into hot issues. Risk factors now sometimes account for a quarter of prospectuses, and comfort letters from accounting firms come in various versions to limit their liability in what have become litigious jurisdictions. Companies no longer need to seek listings on the New York Stock Exchange to raise ten-figure proceeds, and (who would have guessed it only ten years ago?) issuers from mainland China now regularly top the lists of the world's largest IPOs. Corporate governance and compliance have become a major focus of regulators in the financial industry. Complex, new valuation methodologies have been introduced alongside the familiar price-to-earnings and price-to-book ratios. Largely unheard-of categories of institutional investors have made their mark, such as sovereign wealth funds and hedge funds, both of which are now price leaders, major players, and participants in new issues.

All the same, the process of coming to market still remains a daunting one, particularly for those who have never worked on an international IPO (by which I mean an IPO that is marketed to a reasonably wide universe of investors, both retail and institutional, as well as domestic and international). A large number of parties need to be appointed and seamlessly coordinated, and many different and unfamiliar tasks must be simultaneously conducted. Executing an international IPO can take months and can cost large amounts of money. It is easy to get lost within the jargon and the myriad rules and regulations that govern the various aspects of listing a company's shares for the very first time. It is also easy to get things wrong, which could prevent an issuer from tapping investors for more funding for years to come.

This book looks beyond the theory and is intended as a guide to conducting international IPOs for entrepreneurs, corporate management teams, private equity and venture capitalists, market practitioners, and students in finance. Guides issued by stock exchanges tend to focus primarily on listing criteria, while those published by legal advisers, consultants and audit firms usually only address that part of the issue process related to their particular area of expertise. Books on equity capital markets more generally also often include a plethora of mathematical formulas or lengthy academic studies of the performance of, or anomalies associated with, past offerings. By contrast, my approach has been a purely practical one and is based on my experiences of working as an ECM banker on the origination and execution of a variety of transactions across some 30 different countries.

While the book is global in its outlook, I have included many examples from IPOs undertaken by issuers from the BRIC countries (Brazil, Russia, India, and China), in addition to the US, the UK, and continental Europe. At the time of writing, the third-largest IPO on NASDAQ over the previous two years was by a Chinese issuer. Over the same period, the second-largest IPO on the New York Stock Exchange was by a Brazilian bank, and on the London Stock Exchange by an Indian energy company. The Asia-Pacific region in particular is the one that now exhibits the largest deals, highest transaction volumes, and number of new listings, so it is only natural to convey developments in that fast-growing part of the world. The second-largest ever IPO world-wide (US$22.1 billion) was, after all, made by a bank from mainland China in 2010 (as was the third-largest ever IPO, in 2006, with the fourth-largest flotation made by an insurance company listed in Hong Kong in 2010, and the fifth-largest by a Japanese telecommunications company in 1998). Asia has also been at the forefront of innovation, introducing (and sometimes successfully adapting from the US) products such as real estate investment trusts (REITs), business trusts, and listed infrastructure funds, which Europe has only more recently embraced.

I have examined in detail how investment banks are organized, how they work with each other, as well as with their corporate, institutional and other clients, and with third-party advisers. I have also included tips, real-life examples and case studies, and attempted to address all the practical aspects and building blocks associated with bringing a business to market. These include documentation, legal, accounting and corporate governance issues, valuation considerations, as well as a detailed analysis of marketing aspects. The processes of dual-track IPOs, pre-IPO investments and appointing cornerstone investors—as well as institutional investment styles, public and employee offers, pre-deal research, investor education, roadshows, bookbuilding and order solicitation, pricing, allocation, listing, and price stabilization—are explained plainly and simply. Lastly, I have also included in the appendixes detailed checklists for due diligence, issue expenses and prospectuses; sample forms for investor education and order indication; details of initial listing requirements for major stock exchanges around the world; and an extensive glossary with definitions of more than 550 industry terms, as well as an index for easy reference.

More perhaps than in other industries, however, regulations do change frequently and individual circumstances do very much matter, so I would, in all cases, caution readers to consult their investment banking, legal, accounting, and other advisers, as well as the relevant stock exchange listing groups when considering any capital raising, sell-down and listing.

Conducting an international IPO is the culmination of years of hard work for management teams and corporate shareholders, and can bring many rewards, both financially and in successfully funding and implementing ambitious business plans.

At the same time, it makes companies more accountable and vulnerable to market forces. Mastering the process and understanding its building blocks are key to making the most of what a flotation can offer. I hope this insider's guide will help travellers plot the course and navigate through this exciting journey.

Philippe Espinasse
Hong Kong, March 2011

About the author

Philippe Espinasse spent almost two decades working as a senior investment banker, including as a managing director, head of equity corporate finance, and head of equity capital markets. Throughout his prior banking career, he has successfully completed more than 140 corporate finance transactions and has marketed to issuers, and/or executed, capital markets offerings across some 30 jurisdictions.

Philippe lives in Hong Kong, where he now writes and works as a consultant and independent expert, in particular in connection with litigation and arbitration cases. He has also been honorary lecturer in the Faculty of Law of the University of Hong Kong (Department of Professional Legal Education) for a number of years. He is the author of *IPO Banks: Pitch, Selection and Mandate* (Palgrave Macmillan, 2014) and *Cornerstone Investors: A Practice Guide for Asian IPOs* (Hong Kong University Press, 2018), and a co-author of the English/simplified Chinese character *Hong Kong IPO Guide 2013* (LexisNexis, 2012) and *IPO Guide 2012* (LexisNexis, 2012). Philippe is the joint author, with Syren Johnstone, of the study manual for IPO sponsor examinations in Hong Kong (Hong Kong Securities and Investment Institute, 2013). His first book, *IPO: A Global Guide* (initially published by Hong Kong University Press in 2011), has also been translated in simplified Chinese characters. He is the author of two fiction thrillers, *Hard Underwriting* and *The Traveler*, both published by P&C Books, in 2015 and 2016 respectively.

He has contributed regular columns to *GlobalCapital*, the *Nikkei Asian Review*, Dow Jones Banking Intelligence, the *South China Morning Post*, and France's leading financial daily *L'Agefi*. His articles have also been published in the *Wall Street Journal*, on the website of BBC News, and in the *China Economic Review*. Philippe has been interviewed by, or has featured in, a variety of publications, including Bloomberg, Singapore's *Business Times*, the *China Daily*, *The Edge Singapore*, *FinanceAsia*, *Financial News*, the *Financial Times*, the *Hong Kong Economic Journal*, the *International Financing Review*, *Le Monde*, Reuters, *Quartz*, and *Treasury Today*, among others. He has been a keynote speaker at a number of events and conferences and has also appeared on Bloomberg Television, CNBC, BBC World News Television, the

BBC's World Service radio, Australia Broadcasting Corporation radio, and Hong Kong's RTHK 3.

Visit Philippe's blog and website at www.ipo-book.com.

1
Defining the parameters

1.1 Going public

Going public—offering shares for the first time to third-party investors—is probably one of the most important decisions that can be made during the life of a company. For shareholders of family-owned businesses, it can provide a welcome source of liquidity for their holdings. But it also opens up their affairs to the scrutiny of outsiders. Through a flotation, entrepreneurial ventures can find an unparalleled source of capital to support their development. Investors buy initial public offerings (IPOs) because they offer them the opportunity to build a sizeable position in a stock, something that would in most cases be more costly and take a long time to achieve in the secondary market. Most companies coming to market for the first time also exhibit some form of IPO discount, which makes them more attractive relative to their listed peers.

There are a variety of reasons for listing a company in an IPO on a stock exchange, but these generally come down to two: selling down one or more stakes in the business, and raising additional equity capital.

1.1.1 Primary and secondary offerings

In technical terms, the raising of new money in an equity capital markets (ECM) transaction is called a "primary offering", whereas a sell-down—whether by a government in a privatization or by long-term shareholders in a business that has, until now, remained in private hands and is now coming to market to generate liquidity (perhaps as a result of an inheritance)—is described as a "secondary offering". Often, both are combined, so that one or more existing shareholders choose to reduce their holdings, while new funds are raised to enable the business to grow. In certain markets, such as in the UK or in Hong Kong, a primary offering is called an "offer for subscription" since new shares are issued by the company for subscription by investors, whereas a secondary offering is, quite logically, called an "offer for sale".

Most of the time, raising new money is an easier exercise, particularly if the issuer exhibits attractive characteristics, for example, if the market can clearly see that the new funds will help finance development. By contrast, selling down one or more shareholdings in a company is sometimes viewed with suspicion by investors, especially when no remaining stakes are retained by the sellers after listing. For example, investors would probably be wary of a private equity investor exiting in full in an IPO, not only because the investor would be seen to be trying to maximize its exit price at all costs, irrespective of how the shares may trade in the aftermarket, but also because its interests would no longer remain aligned with those of new investors, post-listing. A private equity investor in such a position may therefore prefer to wait until a later date to fully cash in on its investments, perhaps through one or more further sell-downs.

Similarly, investors will often be concerned when an IPO is solely structured through an offer for sale, with no proceeds being raised as part of the deal. A good example of this is the US$1.5 billion equivalent IPO of car manufacturer Aston Martin on the London Stock Exchange in 2018. It took the form of a 100% secondary offering, which, alongside other factors, in my view contributed in the ensuing months to the issuer losing much of its stock exchange value.

Rather confusingly, the term "secondary offering" is also sometimes used to describe a follow-on transaction for a listed company, irrespective of whether new money or old shares are issued or sold. In addition, the term "primary equity" (or "primary equity market") is commonly used to describe the new equity issue market (including IPOs), whether the offerings consist of new or old shares, while the secondary market often describes that for the trading of shares, once they have become listed, in what is also known as the "aftermarket".

1.1.2   Other reasons for going public

Other reasons for going public can include the prestige and recognition attached to the status of a listed company, raising the profile of the business, or achieving optimal liquidity for the shares so that they can be more easily traded. In some cases, issuing new shares and listing in an IPO is a practical way to reduce the level of gearing that a company has accumulated over the years, perhaps as a result of conducting a costly acquisition, and with which it has been burdened. This is likely to become more prevalent following the recent credit crunch and COVID-19 pandemic, as some corporates find it difficult to obtain bank financing.

A business may want to re-focus on its core activities and spin off or de-merge a division in a newly listed company. For example, in 1995 Sandoz, the Swiss pharmaceuticals group, listed its specialty chemicals subsidiary in a US$1.4 billion equivalent international IPO in Zurich. The business was, at that time, renamed Clariant to give it a new, stand-alone identity. Clariant subsequently developed as a new chemicals group with the acquisition in 1997 of the chemicals business of Hoechst, with further sizeable acquisitions in 2000, 2006, and 2008, while Sandoz itself merged with Ciba-Geigy in 1996 to form Novartis. Another example of a spin-off is the US$3.1 billion equivalent listing in 2014 in Hong Kong, through a fixed single investment trust, of HK Electric Investments and HK Electric Investments Ltd. The assets of the trust were spun off from Hong Kong-listed Power Assets Holdings to create a separate, vertically integrated power utility with a focus on the generation, transmission, distribution, and supply of electricity to the islands of Hong Kong and Lamma. Spin-offs will be discussed in greater detail in Section 1.1.3. Examples of such transactions are also provided in the case studies in Appendix 1.

A company can also opt to list on more than one stock exchange, for example because it has become so large, or so global in nature, that this may be a way to more easily access investors around the world, so that they can trade the shares in their own time zones. For example, Prudential, the British insurance company, conducted secondary listings for its shares in Hong Kong as well as in Singapore, in addition to its primary listing on the London Stock Exchange (LSE), at the time of its attempted acquisition of AIA (the Asian arm of AIG) in early 2010. The reason for this was to be able to more easily target and tap Asian investors in a global rights issue, in order to raise funds for the acquisition.

Similarly, a business may have evolved in such a way that there has been a significant geographical shift in the company's activities, so a second (or even a third) listing may be a way to more closely align where the company carries out its activities with where its shareholders are located.

In some cases a company may even decide to de-list from one stock exchange and to re-list on another to try to achieve more recognition from investors, more active trading in its shares, and better sell-side research coverage. One reason for this can be because the new stock exchange is larger, or has higher daily trading volumes, which may also ultimately result in a higher valuation for the business. It is believed that, in 2007 Want Want, a Taiwanese food manufacturer, de-listed from the Singapore Exchange (SGX) and, after a corporate re-organization, subsequently re-listed its shares on the Stock Exchange of Hong Kong in 2008 precisely for this reason. Similarly, Hainan-based Sihuan Pharmaceutical, which manufactures heart drugs in China, also chose to de-list from the SGX in 2009 and to re-list in Hong

Kong in October 2010 in a US$741 million equivalent IPO on similar grounds.[1] Kohlberg Kravis Roberts's (now known as KKR & Co. Inc.) transfer of its listing from the Amsterdam stock exchange to New York in July 2010 followed the same logic, although in this case other considerations also applied. These are said to have included succession planning at the top level in the US, as well as potential tax considerations.[2] Indeed, sales of shares by a founder in a listed buy-out firm were expected to attract a higher rate of capital gains tax (as compared to 15% at the time) pursuant to a bill discussed in the US Senate, so this may perhaps also have influenced the timing of KKR's IPO and new listing in the US. Other private equity firms in the US, such as Carlyle and Apollo Global Management, also subsequently listed there.

Another factor for a re-listing can be because, historically, a market has seen listings from companies in a particular industry sector, and will attract investors and research analysts more likely to understand the company's business, thereby often resulting in a higher valuation and better pricing for the IPO. This includes Nasdaq in the US for technology or internet companies (although in recent years significant businesses in that industry, such as Twitter, instead chose to list on the New York Stock Exchange (NYSE)); or the London Stock Exchange (LSE) in the UK, the Toronto Stock Exchange (TSX) in Canada or the Australian Securities Exchange (ASX) for companies in the minerals or mining sector. At the time of publishing the first edition of this book, the LSE had agreed to acquire the TMX Group, the parent company of the TSX, although that transaction was ultimately not completed.

1.1.3   Spin-off transactions

Spin-off transactions deserve a special mention. Essentially, a spin-off occurs when a listed issuer decides to seek a separate listing for one of its businesses, either on the same stock exchange or on another listing platform (in the same country or abroad).

This carve out can perhaps be made on a geographical basis for companies that are active internationally (e.g., the IPO in Hong Kong of Langham Hospitality in 2013 involved the spin-off of Great Eagle's Hong Kong hotel assets, while the parent company retained such assets in other countries); or it can concern a particular line of business (as was the case, also in Hong Kong, with the IPO of BOC Aviation, an aircraft leasing business, by Bank of China in 2016).

A number of important considerations must be taken into account in the case of a spin-off IPO. The main reason for this is that, in such cases, the parent company itself is also a listed entity.

As an example, in Hong Kong, all issuers planning for a spin-off must first submit proposals to the exchange for approval. In addition, the proposed spin-off entity must satisfy all the requirements of the listing rules for listing applicants, including the quantitative and other listing criteria. Further, a stock exchange will not normally consider spin-off applications within a number of years of the listing of the parent (in Hong Kong, this period of time is three years), since the original listing of the parent company will have been approved on the basis of that company's portfolio of businesses at the time of the flotation, and the expectations of investors at that time would have been that the parent would continue to develop such businesses.

For a stock exchange to consider approving a spin-off listing, it must also be satisfied that the parent will, after the spin-off, retain a sufficient level of operations and sufficient assets to support its separate listing status (and therefore continue to be able to satisfy its own listing requirements).

In addition, there should be a clear delineation between the business(es) retained by the parent company and the business(es) to be spun off, including independence of business operations (with minimum continuing connected transactions between the spun-off company and its parent, or the shareholders of the parent company); independence of directorship and management (i.e., a majority of directors and senior management cannot overlap); and independence of administrative capability (in other words, the parent and the spun-off company must have their own administrative teams, and be managed and operated independently, without relying on each other).

There should also be clear commercial benefits, both to the parent and spun-off company, which should be elaborated upon in the listing document, and, importantly, no adverse impact on the interests of shareholders of the parent resulting from the spin-off.

Further, shareholder approval of a spin-off may be required in cases where the assets, profits, revenue, market capitalization, or number of shares of the company to be spun off represent a significant percentage (typically 25% or more) of those of the parent.

Finally, to further protect the interests of the parent, the shareholders of the latter may in some jurisdictions (such as Hong Kong) be provided with an assured entitlement to shares of the spun-off company under the IPO, either pro rata, by way of a distribution *in specie* of existing shares in the spun-off company (which is rather infrequent), or of a preferred application in any offering of new shares by that company (which is more generally the case).

1.1.4   Duties and drawbacks associated with listing

Conducting an IPO can bring many advantages, but there are also drawbacks to becoming a public company. It is generally a costly exercise, both at the time of listing as well as over the long run because of the additional disclosure required to maintain a listing and to keep new shareholders abreast of corporate developments. Investor relations require not only a high level of transparency, which can give competitors, suppliers, or customers an edge, but also a significant commitment by the management in time and resources to meet the expectations of the market.

Lastly, in extreme cases, a flotation can result in attracting unwanted shareholders (such as Bernard Arnault's LVMH taking an initial 14.2% stake for a reported US$2 billion in luxury leather goods company Hermès in France in October 2010) and even ultimately mean a loss of control over the business for the original shareholders. This could result from a takeover bid, to which listed companies are obviously vulnerable once the majority of their capital falls into public hands. Or it may happen because raising new equity from third parties, thus diluting existing shareholders, may be the only solution to rescue a business riddled with debt accumulated on its balance sheet. Some corporate structures, however, such as dual- or multiple-class shares and weighted voting rights, real estate investment trusts (REITs), or business trusts, can enable legacy shareholders to raise equity capital and maintain effective control over a listed business while avoiding some of the dilution issues that come with the listing of shares on a stock exchange.

1.2   Listing requirements, equity story, and liquidity

Regardless of where, and how, a company decides to proceed with an international IPO, a number of factors always apply.

1.2.1   Listing requirements

The company must first satisfy the thresholds laid out by the relevant regulator or stock exchange on which it has chosen to list. These vary, but will often include a minimum track record for the business (most of the time, at least three years of operations); a minimum amount of turnover, cash-flow, or net profit, or a combination of these, either based on the latest financial year or an average over several years; or a minimum market capitalization upon IPO. Waivers can sometimes be granted, or there may be special provisions under the listing rules particularly for minerals, exploration, or project companies, as well as for certain internet, fintech, or biotechnology issuers. The accounting standard for the accounts in which the company reports, to be included in the prospectus published at the time of the IPO, as well as for disclosure on an ongoing basis thereafter, will also be specified (although nowadays, most issuers, with the exception of the US, will likely report their financials under the IFRS standard).

Other common listing criteria include continuity in ownership or management, or in the type of business carried out by the company over a specified period of time. The stock exchange or regulator may also specify some requirements relating to the share capital of the company. For example, it may be a requirement that all the shares have the same voting rights. And, clearly, such shares should also be freely transferable.

Some countries also allow different classes of shares with different characteristics, values, privileges, or voting rights to be issued. For example, Warren Buffett's Berkshire Hathaway, which is listed on the NYSE in the US, has both Class A and Class B common stock. A share of Class B common stock has the rights of 1/1500th of a share of a Class A common stock, except that a Class B share has 1/10,000th of the voting rights of a Class A share (rather than 1/1,500th of the vote). In addition, in this particular case, the Class A common stock is convertible at any time, at the holder's option, into a Class B common stock (but not the other way around) at the rate of one Class A share for 1500 Class B shares. Both Class A and Class B shareholders are entitled to attend the Berkshire Hathaway annual general meeting (AGM).[3] Facebook is another company listed in the US, on Nasdaq, that has a dual-class share structure, designed to retain control for legacy shareholder Mark Zuckerberg after the company's IPO in 2012. As another example, Chinese e-commerce Alibaba reportedly decided in 2014 to list its shares in the US, rather than in Hong Kong, because the latter trading platform and its regulator, the Securities and Futures Commission, were not prepared to accommodate a share structure giving voting power to founder Jack Ma and other historic shareholders above and beyond that available to minority shareholders investing at the time of the IPO, as well as in the aftermarket. (Alibaba, however, subsequently also listed in Hong Kong as the rules there were eased, while retaining its US listing.) As a last example, "boutique" investment bank Moelis & Company's founder Ken Moelis structured its share capital in a way such that he could retain 96.6% of voting rights following the firm's listing on the NYSE in 2014.[4]

In the past, and particularly in the case of privatizations, the capital of some issuers was restructured to include a "golden" or "special" share, enabling governments to restrict shareholdings by foreign investors by retaining a single share with special attributes and powers. This was first introduced in the UK in the 1980s, probably in connection with the privatization of British Telecom, but quickly spread all over the world, from France to Portugal to Turkey, and as far as Malaysia, Canada, and Jamaica. Golden shares were especially popular for companies in industry sectors considered as "strategic" or sensitive, for example the manufacturing of armaments or of nuclear facilities. The use of special shares was contested by the European Commission during the struggle between Portugal Telecom and Spain's Telefónica for the control of Brazil's mobile telecommunications operator, Vivo, in the first half of 2010.[5] Golden or special shares are now most unlikely to be a consideration for issuers in an IPO, although there are still restrictions in certain countries (and particularly in South and East Asia) on the foreign ownership of companies operating in certain industry sectors.

To minimize both cost and embarrassment, a company's ability to satisfy minimum listing requirements should obviously be ascertained at the outset— ideally, before the start of the execution of any transaction, unless there are clear grounds for seeking an exemption from one or more of the listing criteria. It is believed that, in late 2013, Malaysia's Securities Commission did not allow the proposed listing of a company that operated the LEGOLAND and KidZania theme parks to proceed on Bursa Malaysia on the grounds that it did not have a sufficiently long track record since its inception. In addition, a stock exchange will often require a minimum number or spread of public shareholders upon listing— typically, a few hundred to a few thousand (e.g., 300 shareholders for the Main Board in Hong Kong, and 100 for the second board, GEM). This is generally achieved through an offering to retail investors. In addition to, or sometimes instead of, these requirements, and to achieve good liquidity in the shares, the listing candidate will also be asked to put (and, importantly, to maintain) a proportion of its share capital in public hands at the time of, and after, the IPO (the "free float" not owned by the controlling shareholders or parties acting in concert with such shareholders). This is generally in the order of 25%, but can sometimes be a smaller proportion for very large companies.

Summaries of several principal initial listing requirements for the main boards of some of the largest stock exchanges around the world are included in Appendix 8.

1.2.2   The investment case

Any candidate for listing must have an attractive business, or what investment bankers call an "investment case" or an "equity story". A company might, for example, have an attractive equity story because it is the leader, or one of the leaders, in a fast-growing sector, because its compound annual growth rate (CAGR) in sales or margins is higher than that of its competitors, because the business generates a significant level of cash-flow on a recurring basis, intends to pay attractive dividends to its shareholders, or perhaps because it offers a unique exposure to a new sector that investors have not yet had an opportunity to buy into. Whatever the reason, there has to be a clear angle to "position" the company, including relative to those seen as its peers. Its performance should be sustainable and it should also offer good visibility for the future. Failing this, the response from investors to the IPO will generally be lukewarm, or the company's aftermarket performance will, over time, certainly be disappointing, as was demonstrated by the "dot com" crash in early 2000.

Importantly, the growth of a company should also be assessed on a consistent, like-for-like basis. For example, in the case of a retail company, growth within existing stores, rather than just growth by adding new stores to the company's portfolio, is a key consideration.

Accordingly, in this respect, equity capital markets are quite different from debt capital markets. In the case of the former, the importance of the story is paramount, whereas for the latter, it is the strength of the credit of an issuer that matters most, that is, its ability to pay the interest, and to repay the principal due under a bond (or similar) issue.

While listing a business simply to monetize assets can, and indeed has been, achieved, particularly in a bull market (the high-profile IPO of Aston Martin, which I have already discussed, being a case in point), it is key to have an original and attractive long-term business model to be able to tap the market on an ongoing basis and, ultimately, achieve growth in the share price. This is also true for fund companies, for example, infrastructure funds, real estate investment trusts (REITs), or business trusts. For these, it is important not only to have a clear focus—in terms of region, industry sector, or real estate segment, or a consistent investment theme—but also to ensure that the assets making up the funds are actively managed to achieve a "total return proposition", both through organic growth and growth via acquisitions.

A company whose assets are solely or substantially composed of cash or short-dated securities is not normally considered as suitable for listing, except perhaps in the case of securities brokerage businesses.

Since the difficult precedents set by Eurotunnel in 1987 and Euro Disney in 1989, raising equity in the public equity capital markets for project companies (i.e., companies at a very early stage of development and which may not generate substantial profits for a considerable period of time) often became a challenging proposition, although this is obviously changing with internet and biotechnology issuers. Institutional and retail investors alike often become wary of over-optimistic projections, cost overruns, and construction deadlines. However, projects where significant returns are well above average, or can be guaranteed, for example by governments (this was the case with the Macquarie Korea Infrastructure Fund, or MKIF, which listed in a US$1.01 billion equivalent IPO on South Korea's KRX in 2006), have successfully been brought to market. In Australia, there have been many IPOs of such companies, in the infrastructure sector in particular, both as a result of clever structuring and marketing (including co-investment by the lead banks) and because of the significant domestic pension and superannuation sector there, which is particularly hungry for stable, yield-based returns. Again, one of my former employers, Macquarie Bank, is probably the best-known serial issuer of such listed funds, which have over the years comprised a variety of assets, ranging from property to airports, toll roads, tank farms, and green energy assets, among others.

1.2.3   Strategic investors

The profile of a company being listed in an IPO can sometimes be raised with the inclusion of one or more strategic investors, often coming on board at a relatively early stage during the execution process. These can, for example, be corporates in the same line of business as the company or in a complementary line of business and taking a minority stake in the capital of the issuer. Or they can be private-equity investors, or even investment banks. In recent years, it has in fact been relatively common for IPOs of Chinese companies on the Stock Exchange of Hong Kong to attract investment banks as strategic investors. These investment banks use their own balance sheets, sometimes to help secure the mandate to lead the IPO, and with a view to crystallizing a significant capital gain over time, after the company has started trading as a listed entity.

Investments by strategic investors are generally subject to a lock-up, that is to say, they are prevented, either pursuant to a contract with the company or by stock exchange regulations (or both), from selling their stakes in the company for a period of time after the IPO, most commonly six months to a year. Strategic pre-IPO investments can be carried out in a number of ways. They can take the form of a straightforward investment in ordinary shares, or—perhaps more commonly—can be by way of other securities, such as bonds convertible into shares or convertible preference shares. Such investments are generally made at a significant discount to what will be the valuation of the company at IPO, to reflect the early stage of an investment in what is, as yet, an unlisted business. In some cases, such investments can even be made at nominal value, thereby resulting in significant capital gains upon exit. Price re-adjustments to pre-IPO investments made closer to, or even after, the launch of the IPO, however, are often frowned upon by regulators, for example in Hong Kong. Similarly, special rights that represent an unequal treatment of shareholders (e.g., director nomination rights, anti-dilution rights, or prior consent for selected corporate actions) are often not allowed to survive the listing of the company.

The terms sheets for such investments also often include a number of conditions, as well as indemnity and termination clauses. Stock exchanges generally have rules to govern the use of pre-IPO commitments, particularly pricing formulas, the maximum size of such investments relative to the share capital of the company; or board representation. This information should in any event be disclosed in the prospectus for the IPO.

Strategic pre-IPO investments are distinct from pre-IPO commitments by cornerstone investors (described in more detail in Chapter 2, Section 2.12.7) in that cornerstone investors generally come in at a much later stage, commit to paying the IPO offer price as do other investors, and do not therefore have the benefit of a discount. They are, however, guaranteed sizeable allocations at an early stage in the marketing process for providing early momentum and demand leadership. In some jurisdictions (but not all), they also have to abide by lock-up rules.

1.2.4 Going-public convertible bonds

On occasion, a company or its shareholders may seek to raise funds in the public markets prior to the issuer actually being ready to float in an IPO. In such cases, the company may choose to issue a going-public bond, convertible into the shares of the company once it becomes listed. Alternatively, the shareholders may issue a bond exchangeable into shares of the company upon listing. Such a structure is a fairly rare occurrence and most pre-IPO convertible bonds are unlisted, private transactions, but there are a number of precedents: some, for example relating to early privatization attempts in Turkey, go as far back as the early 1990s.

More recently, in 2006, Angara Mining, a UK producer of gold in Siberia, issued a two-year US$50 million bond listed on the LSE through Nomura and URALSIB Financial Corp. with a 7% coupon, convertible into its shares upon listing. In the event that listing did not happen within a specified timeframe, the bonds were to be redeemed at 140% of their principal amount as a penalty, together with accrued interest. The pre-IPO convertible bonds (the first ever issued by a UK company in the public markets) were successfully placed with a small group of institutional investors.[6] In the end, however, the bonds were redeemed.

In Asia, also in 2006, Golden State Environment, a waste-water treatment company in mainland China, raised, through Merrill Lynch, US$150 million in a privately placed, seven-year going-public convertible bond with a 6% coupon, stepping up to 9% after two years so as to encourage an early listing. Like the Angara Mining bonds, redemption upon maturity was at a premium to par.[7]

Other examples from that same year include a US$130 million two-tranche pre-IPO convertible offering for Greentown China Holdings, a leading property developer in mainland China, led by JPMorgan; and a US$3.5 billion pre-IPO Islamic bond (*sukuk*), listed in Dubai and convertible upon listing, for Dubai Ports World, a leading company in international marine terminal operations and logistics, which was led by Barclays Capital and Dubai Islamic Bank.[8]

Glencore, the world's largest commodities broker, which is incorporated in Switzerland, issued in December 2009 a US$2.2 billion going-public convertible bond to investors including BlackRock, Government of Singapore Investment Corporation (GIC), and private equity firm First Reserve Corp., giving the company a pre-conversion equity value of US$35 billion, equivalent to nine times its 2009 EBITDA. Glencore subsequently conducted in 2011 a multi-billion-dollar IPO, with a dual listing on the LSE and in Hong Kong.

1.2.5   Special purpose acquisition companies (SPACs)

Special purpose acquisition companies (SPACs) are shell or blank-cheque companies that undergo an IPO and are listed with a view to acquiring a business or company at a later stage. They are sold on the basis of the experience of the management team, and enable that team to use the proceeds of the SPAC's IPO to invest in the business or company. SPACs became widespread in the US after 2000 and are essentially a US phenomenon, although a handful were listed in Europe, including Liberty International Acquisition Company, which listed in Amsterdam in a €600 million IPO in 2008.[9]

In 2019 and 2020, SPACs experienced something of a revival amid considerable investor demand for such vehicles. In 2019, one in four IPO offerings in the US were by SPACs, together raising US$13.6 billion through 59 IPOs, according to SPACData. This trend continued the following year: in the first nine months of 2020 alone, there were 104 SPAC IPOs in the US, raising around US$40 billion, with the total reaching US$79 billion for the year, as noted in the *Financial Times* on 23 January 2021. In the first three weeks of 2021, there were 57 SPAC IPOs in the US, raising US$15.7 billion, according to Refinitiv. As of April 2021, a number of stock exchanges (including the LSE, France's Euronext, Hong Kong's HKEx, Indonesia's IDX, Bursa Malaysia, and Singapore's SGX) were actively considering amendments to their listing rules to allow IPOs by SPACs. Most of the SPACs issued outside of the US, however, have so far been listed in Amsterdam.

In the first quarter of 2021, SPAC IPOs were being prepared by, among others, Garth Ritchie, one of the highest paid executives at Deutsche Bank until his departure in July 2019; Gary Cohn, a former senior partner at Goldman Sachs, who also served as Director of the US National Economic Council and as chief economic adviser to President Donald Trump in 2017 and 2018; and Tidjane Thiam, a former chief executive officer of Credit Suisse. There were, however, doubts on the part of some market observers (including David Solomon, the chief executive officer of Goldman Sachs) as to whether the "SPAC craze" could be sustainable. As of April 2021, issues raised by the Securities and Exchange Commission (SEC) in the US about the accounting treatment of warrants issued, and liability risk of forward-looking disclosures by SPACs, as well as "investor fatigue", had forced a number of issuers to put their plans for SPAC IPOs on hold.

SPACs usually take the form of a combination of ordinary shares and warrants and can trade either as a unit or with the shares and warrants separately quoted. All (or the vast majority) of the proceeds raised in the IPO of a SPAC are held in a trust, and there is a specified period of time, usually 12 or 18 months, following the IPO for the management of the SPAC to sign a letter of intent to conduct, or effect, a merger or acquisition (often, but not always, of a start-up company). Failing this, the SPAC is dissolved and the money returned to its shareholders. The shareholders of a SPAC must also generally vote to approve such merger or acquisition, after which the SPAC effectively becomes a "normal" company, and full disclosure is made of the target business when seeking approval. In this regard, SPACs are different from the blind-pool companies listed in the US in the 1980s and 1990s.

SPACs often have a particular focus in terms of industry or geographical coverage. For example, a SPAC may target the acquisition of a business in China, reflecting the experience of its management team. Management teams are often unpaid but receive a proportion of the equity upon IPO, typically 20%, in addition to purchasing warrants prior to the IPO. According to the law firm Proskauer, at the end of 2020 some 200 SPACs were actively seeking business combinations.

In effect, SPACs are relatively similar to rounds of private equity funding, except that, for the issuers, they are much more efficient and can be conducted over a much shorter period of time. Conversely, the funds raised must be put to use more quickly, as failing this they must be repaid. The companies that SPACs buy, however, can be of varying quality and SPACs can also exhibit high levels of costs. It is not unusual for SPACs to ultimately only spend about two-thirds of the amount they have raised to effect an acquisition, having spent the balance as operating expenses. In addition, the share prices of many SPACs subsequently fall in the aftermarket, and/or post-acquisition (or merger), even though investor demand for them remains considerable, perhaps pointing to the market participants investing in some of these structures, or companies acquired, often being of sub-par quality.

1.2.6   Stand-alone business and insider ownership

A listed company should be able to operate independently and should own its key operating assets as well as the contractual and intellectual property rights necessary to the conduct of its business. Where such assets (or rights) are held by another (usually a related or connected) company or individual (say, the parent company, or a director of the latter), they must be transferred to the listing candidate and an appropriate group re-organization should be carried out, except where such related-parties arrangements are conducted on normal commercial terms, and on a continuing basis—for example, where the listing candidate rents its head office from a controlling shareholder at market rates. In such cases, however, specific waivers usually need to be obtained from the relevant stock exchange or regulator, although these are usually only granted for a limited period time (generally up to three years), after which an alternative solution must generally be found. Fair value should also be paid as consideration for any transfer of assets to avoid unfortunate legal and tax consequences. Where a group re-organization is implemented, care should also be taken at the same time to optimize the company's tax efficiency.

Investors also look for companies where the interests of the management are aligned with theirs. Appropriately incentivizing a number of senior management insiders through stock options or a similar scheme is generally well received by the market. This will be discussed in greater detail in Chapter 3, Section 3.8.

1.2.7   Liquidity and transaction size

Lastly, and irrespective of the minimum listing criteria defined by the stock exchange, it is essential that the business—and therefore the market capitalization and free float—is large enough to prevent the company from becoming an "orphan stock", a company with no trading liquidity or investor following, after the IPO. There are two closely related reasons for this. First, larger, and therefore more widely held, listed companies typically achieve higher trading volumes. While there will generally be a spike in the average daily trading volume (ADTV) in the first days or even weeks following any IPO, for smaller companies, such ADTV will often trickle down to a much lower level once the initial interest has subsided among investors. Secondly, listed stocks that achieve a high ADTV are regularly followed by sell-side research analysts, employed by brokers and investment banks, as well as by buy-side researchers, working for institutional investors or hedge funds. This, in turn, contributes to generating interest, and therefore further liquidity, in these securities.

For the most part, smaller companies are not researched (or at least not as well researched) by analysts, and often exhibit a much lower market liquidity. This can hinder further capital-raising exercises, as the amounts to be raised will invariably represent high multiples of the ADTV and will therefore not be easily absorbed by the market.

What should be the ideal minimum size for a company to conduct an IPO? This varies from market to market. Some brokers and boards of stock exchanges even specialize in mid- or micro-caps or smaller capitalization companies. As a general rule, however, the larger, so-called "bulge-bracket" investment banks (those firms that regularly dominate the IPO league tables) will typically set a minimum market capitalization threshold of around US$250 million to US$400 million equivalent (with an average free float or typical IPO size of about US$50 million to US$100 million). Below this minimum, an IPO becomes not only much more challenging to distribute but also, importantly, not a profitable enough exercise for the lead brokers. Smaller IPOs are obviously feasible, particularly if the company posts strong growth or offers very clear visibility to investors, or if the lead bank is appointed on a sole basis. Smaller brokers with lower overheads and a different corporate and institutional client base naturally have lower thresholds.

It should be noted that investment banks generally have no such minimum size criteria for follow-on transactions, that is, for ECM offerings for companies that are already listed. This is because the amount of preparation work necessary for their execution is greatly reduced. Block trades of existing shares often require minimal documentation beyond a simple sale and purchase agreement and, perhaps, placing letters. Even when a prospectus is required in the case of a fully marketed offering, the precedent documentation created at the time of the IPO and available as a result of ongoing filings with the regulator or stock exchange makes placements easier and much faster to execute.

In recent years, there has been a trend among some stock exchanges, particularly in Asia, to increase the threshold for the size of the companies they seek for listing on their platforms. In 2012, Singapore's SGX increased the size of the minimum market capitalization (which pretty much doubled, from S$80 million, about US$64 million at the time, to S$150 million, then equivalent to around US$120 million) and amount of profit required of candidates for listing on its Main Board. Under this makeover, the minimum consolidated pre-tax profit for listing on the SGX's Main Board was S$30 million (US$24 million) for the latest financial year. Previously, issuers could secure listing there with yearly profits as low as S$1 million, provided that the three-year cumulative figure reached S$7.5 million.

More recently, in 2018, Hong Kong's HKEx raised the minimum market capitalization for new listings from HK$200 million (about US$25 million) to HK$500 million (US$64 million). Back in the early 1990s, the minimum market capitalization for listing in Hong Kong was just HK$100 million. At the time of writing, in the first quarter of 2021, HKEx was also suggesting, through a market consultation, a significant increase in the minimum profit requirement for companies listing on its Main Board.

1.3   Selecting the optimal listing location

Selecting the optimal listing location is not an easy task for a board of directors, and many considerations need to be taken into account. In some cases, stock exchanges only allow listings of companies of a certain nationality. For example, for a long time, the Stock Exchange of Hong Kong only allowed companies incorporated in Hong Kong, the People's Republic of China, the Cayman Islands, and Bermuda to list in Hong Kong. This prevented many companies from listing there, unless they carried out an extensive restructuring exercise. The policy has recently evolved to allow listings in Hong Kong by issuers from a variety of other countries (see Appendix 8), even if the overwhelming majority of issuers now listing on HKEx are mainland Chinese companies and, to a lesser extent, companies from Hong Kong itself. Experiments with international listings in Hong Kong have generally been disappointing, often resulting in a number of cases in lower trading volumes and poor share price performance. Similarly, only companies incorporated in India can list on that country's BSE and NSE stock exchanges. However, more often than not, issuers nowadays, particularly those that manage their business on a global basis, can choose from several possibilities when it comes to listing their shares in an IPO.

However, listing shares without offering stock for sale at the same time—perhaps through a "backdoor" listing by purchasing a listed shell company; by way of introduction if the company already has a sufficient spread of public shareholders; or by establishing a level 2 sponsored American depositary receipt (DR) programme in the US (see Chapter 2, Section 2.15.3.2)—is unlikely, in most cases, to achieve initial significant trading volumes or to generate much investor interest. Again, and despite its large size, Prudential is a case in point: it achieved trading volumes in Hong Kong and Singapore representing only a small fraction of those on its primary listing in the UK after listing on these Asian stock exchanges by way of introduction in 2010.[10] Similarly, the listing by way of introduction of mining

Brazilian giant Vale in Hong Kong that same year also resulted in poor liquidity,[11] as has also been the case with the listing there in March 2014 of Japanese fashion retailer Fast Retailing, which owns brands such as UNIQLO, Theory, and Princesse tam.tam.

There have, however, been a handful of successful listings in the US without bona fide IPOs in which no shares were offered to investors. These will be discussed later (see Chapter 4, Section 4.2). They, however, remain the exception, rather than the rule.

1.3.1 Choosing the right listing location

Other than for companies where there is an obvious, natural anchor market, a practical way to decide on a listing location can be to list, analyse, and grade a variety of factors in a matrix. The following example examines the case of a large European consumer goods company, with significant activities in Asia (see Table 1). Each line assesses how major listing considerations are matched across various listing locations. For example, in the case of this European company, listing on Euronext (in Amsterdam, Brussels, Dublin, Lisbon, London, Oslo, or Paris) or on the LSE would better match the location of its headquarters than a listing in the US or in Asia. One "tick" identifies those listing locations that partly satisfy each criterion; those with two ticks meet the requirement; and those with three ticks fully meet the relevant consideration.

Most major markets nowadays will generally have a solid corporate governance framework, a good degree of transparency, and the rule of law with an independent judiciary system. In addition, most countries have now also adopted the IFRS accounting standard. The clearing, trading, and settlement infrastructure will vary, particularly in the case of emerging markets, but generally there are no major material differences.

Listing on a well-regulated and transparent exchange with comprehensive listing requirements will often attract better classes of investors, a deeper pool of funds, better liquidity, and wider sell-side research coverage. It may also ultimately lead to a better valuation being achieved than by listing on a less strictly regulated exchange, even though, at first glance, this may appear to be an easier and less demanding market on which to list.

1.3.2 Domicile and country of incorporation

The location of group headquarters and the country of incorporation are straightforward but key considerations, and take into account the time zone in which

	Euronext	New York Stock Exchange	Nasdaq	London Stock Exchange	Stock Exchange of Hong Kong	Singapore Exchange	Tokyo Stock Exchange
Location of headquarters	✓✓✓	✓	✓	✓✓	✓	✓	✓
Country of incorporation	✓✓✓	✓	✓	✓✓	✓	✓	✓
Profile and prestige	✓✓	✓✓✓	✓✓	✓✓✓	✓✓	✓	✓✓
Match with geographical profile of revenues	✓✓	✓	✓	✓✓	✓✓	✓✓	✓
Index considerations	✓✓	✓✓	✓	✓	✓	✓✓	✓
Peer group compatibility	✓✓	✓	✓	✓	✓✓	✓✓	✓
Achievable and sustainable valuation multiples	✓✓	✓✓	✓✓	✓✓	✓✓✓	✓	✓✓
Acquisition currency	✓	✓✓	✓✓	✓	✓✓✓	✓✓	✓
Initial listing requirements	✓✓✓	✓	✓	✓✓✓	✓✓	✓✓✓	✓
Ongoing listing requirements	✓✓✓	✓	✓	✓✓✓	✓✓	✓✓✓	✓
Accounting and GAAP*	✓✓✓	✓	✓	✓✓✓	✓✓✓	✓✓✓	✓
Listing fees and costs	✓✓✓	✓	✓	✓✓	✓✓	✓✓✓	✓
Access to key institutions	✓✓	✓✓	✓	✓✓✓	✓✓	✓✓	✓
Access to retail investors	✓✓	✓	✓	✓	✓✓✓	✓	✓✓
Research coverage	✓✓✓	✓✓	✓	✓✓✓	✓✓	✓	✓

* GAAP = generally agreed accounting principles
✓ = partly meets requirement; ✓✓ = meets requirement; ✓✓✓ = fully meets requirement

Table 1
Examples of listing considerations across various stock exchanges

senior management operate. They should ideally match the listing requirements laid out by the relevant exchange.

1.3.3   Profile and prestige

The profile and prestige that can be achieved by listing on a particular stock exchange typically derive from the market capitalization, average size, and number of companies listed in that market, especially peers. Listing on a large or prestigious market, however, is not necessarily a guarantee of success. In 2000, the French media company Vivendi Universal (as it was called at the time) listed its shares on the NYSE, in addition to its home listing in Paris, to facilitate its merger with Seagram and enhance its profile. It decided, however, to de-list from the NYSE a few years later in 2006, following the low trading achieved on that market, which represented less than 5% of total shares traded in both 2004 and 2005,[12] and because of demanding ongoing disclosure requirements and the resulting high costs associated with maintaining a listing in the US. The highly litigious business environment in the US (where class-action lawsuits are allowed) can also be a concern for some issuers. Vivendi nevertheless re-established an unlisted, less onerous level 1 ADR programme in the US in late 2008 (see Chapter 2, Section 2.15.3.1).[13]

Similarly, companies such as AXA from France, OTE (the Hellenic Telecommunications Organization) from Greece, and Allianz, Daimler, Infineon Technologies, and Deutsche Telekom from Germany also followed suit with de-listings from the NYSE in 2010. Allianz had earlier announced in 2009 its intention to also de-list from the LSE, Borsa Italiana in Milan, NYSE Euronext (as it was then known) in Paris, and the SIX Swiss Exchange in Zurich. BASF, Bayer, and E.ON—all German companies—had earlier also chosen to voluntarily de-list from the NYSE in 2007.[14]

1.3.4   Matching the profile of revenues

Matching the geographical profile of a company's revenues with a particular listing location is an interesting proposition. In the first half of 2010 the cosmetics company L'Occitane—incorporated in Luxembourg but with French origins— decided to list in Hong Kong, rather than in Paris on NYSE Euronext, because the largest proportion of its turnover at the time of listing, and probably an even larger proportion of expected sales, were in Asia.[15] A case study of the IPO of L'Occitane is included in Appendix 1. Only a handful of companies have to date taken a similar decision. In 2011, Italian fashion company Prada and luggage-maker Samsonite (incorporated in Luxembourg) both chose to conduct their IPOs in Hong Kong.

However, the additional pressure on management servicing a listing in such a distant time zone must be carefully considered. As noted earlier, the vast majority of companies listing in Hong Kong are, in any event, from China, rather than from international jurisdictions.

1.3.5 Index considerations

Another criterion that can be taken into consideration is the likelihood of the company being included in relevant market indices, for example the DAX in Germany, the IBEX in Spain, or the TOPIX and NIKKEI 225 in Japan. The composition of indices is reviewed regularly (often on a semi-annual or quarterly basis), and generally on the basis of market capitalization, free float, or trading volumes. For larger, and particularly liquid, companies, this can be relevant since inclusion in a significant, highly followed index means automatic, passive buying of their shares by institutional investors benchmarked to index performance. There is also clearly an element of prestige associated with the fact that a company can claim to be a member of the Footsie, CAC 40, or Hang Seng indices. For example, Essar Energy, an Indian energy company listed in May 2010 in a billion-dollar IPO on the LSE, was subsequently included in June 2010 as a constituent of the prestigious FTSE 100 index.[16] A case study of the IPO of Essar Energy is included in Appendix 1. As another example, Agricultural Bank of China (ABC) was included in the Shanghai SSE 50 and SSE 180 indices shortly after the start of trading of its A shares in its US$22.1 billion global (A and H share) IPO, resulting in significant buying by passive index funds in mainland China. This reportedly helped support the share price in the immediate aftermarket, allowing the exercise in full of the over-allotment option for the A share portion of the offering and ABC to claim the title of the largest ever (at the time) global IPO on a world-wide basis.[17] Similarly, Russian telecommunications company MegaFon secured inclusion in the MSCI Russia index less than a month after its US$1.7 billion IPO in Moscow in November 2012, reportedly attracting in the process some US$300 million of index-driven demand.[18]

1.3.6 Valuation considerations

Valuation, and the existence of a group of companies against which the issuer may be benchmarked, is also an important issue. While this is often a major area of focus for issuers and their shareholders, it should not be looked at in isolation. A significant number of foreign companies proceeded with secondary listings on the Tokyo Stock Exchange (TSE) in the 1980s and in the early 1990s after considering the very high P/E ratios typical of that market at the time, only to achieve low trading levels there, with many of these corporates choosing to de-list in later years, after having also spent considerable amounts of time and money to comply with Japanese ongoing listing and disclosure requirements. For example, voluntary de-listings from the TSE include those by Telefónica in 2011; AEGON, Deutsche Telekom, and UBS in 2010; BNP Paribas in 2009; Alcatel-Lucent, Barclays, Bayer, Boeing, BP, and Société Générale in 2008; Henderson Land, Volkswagen, and Westpac in 2007; and DaimlerChrysler, Deutsche Bank, and National Australia Bank in 2006.[19]

Indeed, the number of international companies that remain listed in Tokyo nowadays can be measured in single digit terms (only two, as of April 2021), even if the TSE and Japanese government recently expressed interest in attracting more international companies, in particularly against the background of the political situation in Hong Kong in 2019 and 2020. In other words, the Japanese equity markets pretty much remain the exclusive preserve of domestic issuers (although international institutional investors on the other hand, as opposed to equity issuers, remain very active in that market, alongside their Japanese counterparts).

It may perhaps make sense for a high-growth technology company to try to obtain a higher offer price by listing on Nasdaq or the NYSE, given that market's industry focus, and irrespective of its country of incorporation, provided it can fulfil the listing requirements. But in the end, achieving and, most importantly, sustaining a high valuation are more a function of the intrinsic characteristics of a listing candidate than of the average multiple for a given market, provided there is enough liquidity in the counter. As an example, increasingly many Chinese internet companies will nowadays choose to list in Shanghai or Hong Kong instead of (or perhaps, in some cases, in addition to) the US markets.

1.3.7 Initial and ongoing listing requirements

A listing candidate should obviously be able to fulfil both initial and ongoing listing requirements, which include being able to produce and publish accounts in the accounting standards required by the relevant regulator (typically nowadays IFRS) or exchange at prescribed intervals. For example, this can entail the annual filing by certain foreign (i.e., non-US) issuers of Form 20-F with the Securities and Exchange Commission (SEC) through the Electronic Data Gathering, Analysis, and Retrieval (EDGAR) system in the US. Disclosure can also prove demanding and costly in the long run. This may require segmentation of revenue, profits or assets, certification of financial statements, or disclosure of management compensation; it may also include local regulations, perhaps pertaining to the composition of the board, the requirement to set up board committees, or rules on internal financial controls. For example, the Sarbanes-Oxley legislation for companies listed in the US introduced, among other things, certain potential personal civil and criminal liabilities for chief executive officers (CEOs) and chief financial officers (CFOs). This prompted some non-US companies to shy away from listing in the US and others to seek a de-listing from the NYSE or from other exchanges there (see also Section 1.3.3).

Most large stock exchanges now have a smaller market or "second board", in addition to the "main board", for fast-growing companies at an early stage of development to list. Such second boards often have more flexible listing requirements, although generally at the expense of liquidity and research coverage. Indeed, many companies listed on second boards often exhibit a low level of trading activity and following both by sell-side research analysts and investors. Examples of these second boards around the world can be found in Appendix 8.

There has also been a recent trend whereby stock exchanges seek to somehow facilitate requirements for listing on their platforms (e.g., as noted earlier, it is now possible to list companies with weighted voting rights in Hong Kong, and listing requirements there have been eased for internet/new economy or biotechnology companies). At the same time, however, requirements for the oversight of listed issuers by IPO sponsors have been considerably strengthened, with heightened obligations to conduct adequate due diligence, and probe in a large amount of detail the business affairs and financials of listing candidates. This has on occasion resulted in very high fines and other penalties being imposed on investment banks in certain jurisdictions. I have personally been involved in a number of cases involving such disciplinary proceedings, in Hong Kong in particular. As more companies get access to public equity markets, executing IPOs nowadays has at the same time certainly become a more demanding and significantly more complex exercise than was the case previously.

1.3.8   Targeting investor types

While institutional investors are increasingly global in nature, each market has its own rules and characteristics. Understanding these can help a company make the appropriate choice when it comes to achieving the desired investor mix. For example, in the case of a heavily oversubscribed public offer, the rules of the Stock Exchange of Hong Kong require an automatic "claw-back" of shares from institutional to retail investors. In cases where the retail tranche, which is generally set at only 10% initially, becomes subscribed more than 100 times, 50% of the IPO will usually be automatically allocated to retail investors (see Appendix 8). Such claw-back is compulsory, whether high-quality institutional investors have placed orders or not. As a result, the registers of Hong Kong-listed companies often include at the outset a high proportion of retail shareholders. Australia and Japan are examples of other countries with a high retail investor bias in IPOs. By contrast, the rules in Singapore do not provide for such claw-back provisions, and retail tranches there are generally in the order of 5% to 10% only. Accordingly, liquidity in the Singapore primary equity market is more driven by institutional investors. As another example, for listings on Bursa Malaysia, companies that derive more than 50% of their net profit from Malaysia are required by law to reserve, as part of their IPOs, 50% of their free float to ethnic Malay (*Bumiputera*) investors under a separate tranche at the behest of the Ministry of Trade and Industry (MITI). The Indian IPO market, for example, is also one where issuers have less flexibility when it comes to allocating new issues to investors.

1.3.9 Research coverage

Lastly, as we have seen, the likelihood of a company becoming actively covered by research analysts should also be taken into consideration. This is, in part, determined at the time of the IPO. The syndicate of banks should include enough houses with good research capabilities to allow for reasonable initial coverage, both prior to the launch of the offering (where permitted) and after the initial embargo or "blackout" period for research publication has expired, but also on a continuing basis. It is therefore important to identify research analysts who actively follow peer companies, as well as sector and country analysts who are "ranked" highly by institutional investors in independent surveys, such as the Greenwich, Peter Lee, Extel, or Institutional Investor surveys. Obviously, relatively close proximity to where management is located will facilitate coverage and communication.

1.3.10 Dual and multiple listings

What about listing in multiple locations? There may be good, or sometimes "political", reasons for this. In 1999 Amadeus GTD, the global travel distribution company initially listed in Madrid in a US$900 million equivalent IPO led by UBS Warburg (with Merrill Lynch as junior partner), proceeded with secondary listings in Paris and Frankfurt immediately after, reflecting the nationality of its shareholders at the time (Iberia, Air France, and Lufthansa, with Continental Airlines selling its stake in the business in the IPO). Amadeus GTD was subsequently privatized by private equity investors, restructured, and floated again in 2010 under the name Amadeus IT Holdings S.A. in a €1.32 billion IPO in Spain led by Goldman Sachs, JPMorgan, and Morgan Stanley.[20] In 2012, hospital owner and operator IHH Healthcare listed in both Malaysia and Singapore in the first-ever simultaneous dual listing in two ASEAN countries. Part of the business, Parkway, had previously been listed in Singapore, while one of IHH Healthcare's home markets is Malaysia and the company was also at the time controlled by Malaysian sovereign wealth fund Kahazanah Nasional Berhad. Accordingly, there were good reasons for securing listings on two trading platforms rather than on a single one.

Listing requirements for secondary listings on most (but not all) stock exchanges are usually less onerous than those for a primary listing. However, dual (or indeed multiple) listings generally only make sense for extremely large corporates. Even in these cases, most of the trading in the shares will generally occur on what is perceived by investors to be the home or anchor market, with often rapid "flow-back" of shares from the secondary market to the home market. In some cases, as previously mentioned, this becomes so extreme that it is uneconomic to maintain the secondary listing or listings, and ultimately necessary to de-list the shares from these exchanges altogether. Japanese broker SBI Holdings, which listed depositary shares in Hong Kong in 2011—becoming the first-ever Japanese company to list in the special administrative region—in addition to its existing listing in Tokyo, announced in March 2014 that it had decided to relinquish its listing in Hong Kong, on account of the low trading volumes achieved there.[21] It should be noted that de-listing is not necessarily a straightforward exercise in some markets. It is a complex process in the US and Japan (in the US, de-registering from the SEC is even more difficult), particularly while a minimum number of local, including retail, shareholders remain. For example, Magyar Telekom, the Hungarian telecommunications company 59.5% owned by Deutsche Telekom and which was also listed on the Budapest stock exchange, announced its intention to de-list from the NYSE in mid-2010.[22] However, it was reported at the time to be facing some difficulties in effectively implementing this decision since more than 5% of its registered equity was traded on the NYSE, with a de-listing being only possible below that crucial threshold.[23]

In addition, undertaking further capital raising for companies listed on more than one stock exchange can be a cumbersome exercise, especially when rights issues are conducted. For example, different jurisdictions may have different rules for whether rights can trade separately and for how long, as well as different settlement methods. This is addressed in greater detail in Chapter 4, Section 4.3.2.

1.3.11 Tickers and codes

Once listed, a company is generally assigned a "ticker". This unique symbol often comprises three or four letters, or numbers, and serves to quickly identify the stock on trading screens, for example, KO for Coca Cola or WMT for Walmart (previously known as Wal-Mart) in the US or 5.HK for HSBC in Hong Kong. A listed stock is also assigned other, longer, alpha numerical codes, generally an International Securities Identification Number (ISIN), which comprises 12 characters, a Stock Exchange Daily Official List (SEDOL) code of seven characters in the UK and Ireland, or the first six characters of a CUSIP (Committee on Uniform Security Identification Procedures) alphanumeric code, which is used to identify issuers and trades in securities in North America. More examples of tickers, ISINs, and CUSIPs are provided in the case studies in Appendix 1. Other codes can also be used in other countries, such as a Valor number (incorporated in the Swiss ISIN number) to identify listed securities in Switzerland, or a Wertpapierkennnummer (WKN), which does the same in Germany. In Asia, obtaining a ticker with "lucky" numbers (for example including several "8" digits) can be highly prized by some issuers. It can also allegedly encourage certain retail investors to buy the stock.

1.4   The IPO corporate management team

From the standpoint of the issuer, lead banks, and third-party advisers, it makes sense to appoint a dedicated IPO corporate management team. The size of such a team will vary from company to company, and from deal to deal, but selecting a small number of individuals fully dedicated and committed to the IPO throughout the duration of the transaction not only ensures continuity, but also provides a focal point for enquiries from all parties appointed to execute the offering. The team can be retained for a number of months, and sometimes up to a year or more. It can also help prepare the company for forming an investor relations (IR) department following the listing (see Chapter 4, Section 4.2.5).

The CEO or the CFO should not necessarily form part of this IPO management team—they already have enough on their plate running the day-to-day business of the company—but should instead remain on call for important due diligence meetings, and to help resolve thorny issues. They will obviously become very much involved towards the later stages of the deal during the marketing phase, the roadshow, and pricing. In the initial stages, however, and with the exception of high-level due diligence meetings focused on the company's strategy, their participation on a regular basis will probably be limited to fortnightly steering committee meetings.

Seasoned, mid-level executives are ideal to act in what is in effect a coordination role. Some may have experience of capital markets, as ex-investment bankers, IR specialists, or market practitioners in a selling or research capacity. Those with a legal background, particularly ex-securities lawyers, are also well suited to discussing the drafting of the prospectus with other advisers, as well as negotiating the various agreements that will evidence underwriting arrangements.

In some markets, such as in Hong Kong, the prospectus will need to be published in more than one language, in this particular case, in both English and Chinese. Language skills should therefore also be taken into consideration, where relevant.

Once the IPO management team is chosen, one or more investment banks should be selected and appointed to lead the transaction, some in more than one role.

1.5   Who does what in an investment bank?

Investment banks are complex organizations, with a variety of divisions, departments, and teams. A number of areas will be involved in any IPO, at various stages throughout the transaction.

1.5.1   The banking side

Broadly speaking, some investment bankers are "within the Chinese wall", that is to say, they have access and can discuss confidential information not generally known to the market with their corporate, government, or institutional clients. These include bankers working on mergers and acquisitions, either with a country or an industry sector focus, as well as those dedicated to corporate finance or the raising of capital for their clients, either in the form of equity, debt, or hybrid capital, such as convertible or exchangeable bonds. In an IPO, in addition to equity specialists, some debt capital markets bankers may also be involved if the issuer has a strong yield bias, for example in the case of a REIT, a business trust, or an infrastructure fund. To simplify, I will refer to bankers within the Chinese wall as the "banking" side of the firm.

1.5.2   The markets side

Others are "outside the Chinese wall" (or on the "markets" side of the bank) and focused exclusively on market activities, that is, researching, selling, or trading equities, fixed income, commodities, currencies, or derivative products, with extensive back office and operations departments for the administration and settlement of trades. Research analysts, described in greater detail in Chapter 3, Sections 3.1, 3.2, and 3.4, follow a particular type of security, often with an industry sector, regional, or country focus; they discuss with, and recommend investment ideas to, investors, and publish reports on individual (or groups of) stocks. Salespeople are tasked with selling securities in their area of focus to certain institutional investors, and are supported in their selling efforts by research analysts. By contrast, traders or market makers buy and sell securities in the financial markets either on behalf of clients served by salespeople, or for the account of the bank itself (in the case of proprietary traders). Sales traders talk directly to clients to promote new investment ideas and also provide market execution. Their clients are institutional investors (e.g., pension funds, asset managers, mutual funds, insurance companies, charities, hedge funds, or sovereign wealth funds), other banks (including proprietary trading desks and private banks), treasury departments of companies, or high net-worth individuals.

In some cases, the terms "investment bank" or "investment banking" only refer to the banking side of the business rather than to both the banking and markets side of a firm.

There is an inherent conflict of interest between both sides of the Chinese wall in an IPO in that, while investment banks try to achieve the best value for their corporate clients (the issuers) in an IPO or other ECM transactions, they also serve their institutional (and, for some, retail) clients in the secondary market. The objectives and interests of these clients are at the opposite of those of new equity issuers, that is, to pay as little as possible for the securities on offer. Such conflicts of interest are managed in ECM departments and equity syndicate desks under the supervision of compliance departments, where both sides of the equation are taken into account, resulting in the company and the selling shareholders issuing and selling shares at the best price that the market can pay, following an extensive marketing exercise targeted at investors.

1.5.3 Other areas within the investment bank

All investment banks also have support departments dedicated to the analysis and control of risk and credit, as well as legal and compliance departments, to ensure that contracts entered into by the bank do not breach laws, regulations, or internal guidelines, that regulators and other authorities are kept abreast of relevant developments, and that the Chinese walls between the various departments are properly maintained and strictly enforced. Compliance departments also run "control rooms" to check pre-deal and other research reports published by the bank, so as to manage political or other potential issues.

Also involved in IPOs are the investment banks' corporate communications departments, found in most sizeable firms. Although during the execution of a transaction they will usually simply be tasked with providing a "no comment" response to enquiries from the media, they may on occasion be called on to help defuse or resolve issues concerning the issuer, its business, or the IPO process itself, perhaps arising as a result of investigations by a particularly inquisitive (or biased) journalist. In addition, they will help promote a bank's credentials and involvement in a particularly successful transaction after the IPO, and also lobby for the bank and its issuer clients to receive some of the many industry awards presented by the financial press. For example, the US$2.1 billion IPO of hospital owner and operator IHH Healthcare in both Malaysia and Singapore in 2012, which I have already mentioned, was named "Best IPO in Asia" and "Best deal in Malaysia" by *FinanceAsia* magazine; "Best IPO in Asia" by *Asiamoney*; "Best deal in Malaysia" by *The Asset*; and "Best capital markets deal in Malaysia" by *IFR Asia*.

Investment banks have dedicated committees to decide on new business they take on and, crucially, on the level of fees they will charge for such business. These generally meet regularly (often weekly) at larger banks. Other committees, generally called underwriting or commitment committees, are also convened in an IPO, as well as for other ECM transactions. Typically, they will meet prior to a transaction becoming "public", that is, just prior to the publication of pre-deal research (when allowed); at the time of determining the price range for the IPO; and prior to the pricing and actual underwriting of a deal. Such committees will generally include senior representatives from both the banking side and "permanent insiders" (for compliance purposes) from the markets side, as well as senior legal and compliance staff and people from the risk management and credit departments. On particularly difficult transactions, when lengthy negotiation may become necessary with the issuer, for example at the time of pricing, the underwriting committee may need to be convened several times at short notice, often by way of conference calls. Some investment banks have a variety of committees for the approval of transactions, both of a global and regional nature, and addressing issues such as reputation, economics, ethics, execution, and other factors. These (and the related terminology) obviously vary from one firm to the next.

It should also be noted that, in most jurisdictions, client-facing investment banking staff need to hold relevant licences with local regulators. Such licences are often granted after the bankers or brokers have sat and successfully passed professional examinations, which typically take the form of one or more multiple-choice tests, such as the "Series 7" examination in the US. In addition to securities licences, staff involved in the corporate finance execution of an IPO sometimes need other qualifications, for example to be eligible to act as a Principal or Representative to sponsor new listings in Hong Kong. Depending on the experience of the candidate, this normally requires prior transaction experience, as well as taking dedicated examinations or attending a "refresher" course. It should also be noted that such individuals are often few in number at any particular bank, so the bankers who can actually "sign off" on execution matters pertaining to an IPO are usually high in demand because of their qualifications—and also particularly busy. The flipside is that they are inevitably the ones "on the spot" in the event of a regulatory enquiry, when unforeseen problems arise with a new issue, or when fraud has been alleged on the part of a company, certain members of its management, or shareholders.

1.5.4 Outside the investment bank

Most large investment banks generally have separate private banking (or wealth management) and asset management arms, which are treated at arm's length by the banking and markets areas, although some private banks (such as Credit Suisse, Deutsche Bank, HSBC, Barclays, or UBS) also have specialist, in-house groups of dedicated bankers, servicing their own clients for mergers and acquisitions (M&A) or capital-raising transactions.

See Figure 1 for a high-level diagram of the various departments (or divisions) both within and outside an investment bank involved in an IPO.

1.6 Investment banking business titles

Business titles in investment banks look grand. They are often confusing to people not working in the industry. There are slight variations from bank to bank, but career progression and equivalents between titles are generally fairly easy to follow and understand.

1.6.1 Entry level and beyond

Irrespective of the department or area of the bank in which one works, a fresh university graduate will typically start as a graduate trainee, analyst, or business analyst. This is not to be confused with research analysts, who research and publish reports on listed companies to support sales efforts of securities to institutional investors. However, an analyst could be employed in a research department as a junior research analyst or research assistant. As is common at UK, US, or Japanese firms in particular, analysts are often hired on campus as part of a large intake of new hires once or twice a year. Well-structured summer internships, often including rotation among various departments, as well as a mixture of on-the-job training and in-house academic courses, are a good opportunity to spot talent early, and a high

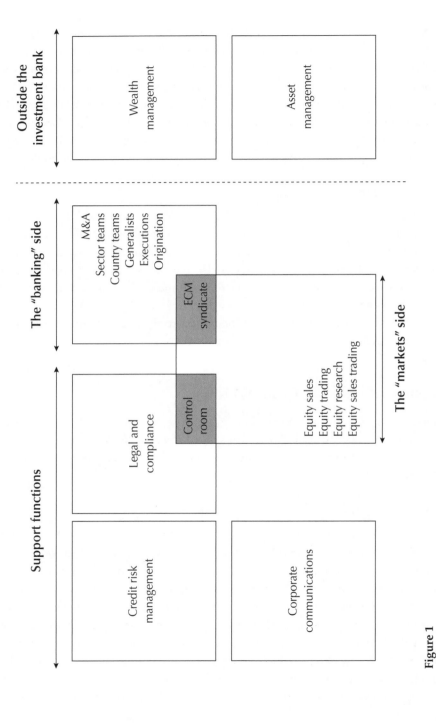

Figure 1

The main departments of an investment bank involved in an IPO

proportion of fresh graduates will often have spent some time in a summer job in an investment bank before being recruited into the entry programme.

Front office, entry-level staff normally work very long hours (often up to 100 hours per week on a regular basis) and generally spend much of their early years drafting and putting together presentations to pitch for new business (see Section 1.9.2) and writing minutes of meetings with clients. I spent a considerable amount of time as a graduate trainee writing briefing notes for the then chairman of S.G.Warburg, Sir David Scholey, on the clients he was meeting around the world. This involved reading through annual reports and management files and enquiring about current marketing initiatives and transactions with colleagues throughout the firm. It was a demanding and time-consuming but ultimately formative exercise.

Entry-level staff are usually promoted to the level of senior analyst or associate after one or two years. At this stage, in the US in particular, it was common for junior investment bankers to leave to study for an MBA, and then re-join the industry after a couple of years, although these days, many entrants to investment banks already have a master's degree (or more) on their CV. They will remain at this level, sometimes becoming senior associates in the process before promotion to the rank of manager, senior manager, or, more frequently, associate director or vice-president, again for a few more years. Starting from such levels, investment bankers gradually take on more marketing responsibilities, pitching to prospective (or existing) clients for new business, in addition to executing transactions.

1.6.2   The senior ranks

The next level up is director or senior vice-president, often followed by that of executive director. Again, employees will generally stay a few years in each role. Importantly, it should be noted that the title of director or executive director does not indicate any board membership or affiliation. Accordingly, these titles are generally followed on business cards by the name of the department in which the individual works.

The most senior levels are managing director, sometimes senior managing director, and, for some investment banks that have retained such a structure, there may also be a partnership level. For example, Goldman Sachs has managing directors and more senior partner managing directors. The Australian investment bank Macquarie has both managing directors and division directors at the same level, depending on the country or region in which they work, whereas its higher, de facto partner rank is (somewhat confusingly) the executive director level. At S.G.Warburg, the highest level was that of director. The primary responsibility of front office managing directors is the origination of new business.

Lastly, there will often be a further senior layer with several vice-chairmen, chairmen, or presidents, often without defined team leadership responsibilities (although they may be affiliated to a particular division or group), but dedicated to senior client coverage or to ensuring senior representation for the firm.

1.6.3   Head titles

There are many "head" titles in investment banks. There are country heads (e.g., head of China investment banking), product heads (e.g., head of M&A, head of ECM—all of which can have global, regional, sub-regional, or dedicated country or sector responsibilities), heads with sub-product responsibilities (e.g., global head of equities, then global head of cash equities, followed by head of Asia cash equities, with further sub-heads for Hong Kong, Singapore, etc.), heads of product origination and heads of product execution, heads of industrial sectors (e.g., head of telecoms, media and technology, which may include several sub-sectors, all of which would each have their dedicated head). In fact a head may often have a very small (or sometimes no) team reporting to him or her. Global heads, as the name indicates, have world-wide responsibility, with various local or regional teams reporting to them, and are generally the most senior bankers within an investment bank. These should not be confused with local or regional heads of a global business, for example, head of Singapore global debt capital markets, who have a much narrower scope of responsibilities. Again, the terminology varies from one firm to the next.

In a further twist, some banks have a generic title structure, with different, equivalent titles in various regions, reflecting local market practice. For example, HSBC investment bankers are assigned a numbered grade indicating seniority, irrespective of their marketing title. Other investment banks, in the Asia-Pacific region in particular, also have similar arrangements. As noted earlier, managing directors in Asia at Macquarie were equivalent to a division director in Australia. This can all be rather tricky to grasp, particularly when several investment bankers from the same bank, with different title structures, are working on the same IPO (or pitching to a prospective issuer).

The key is to remember that investment banking is a particularly specialized and very compartmentalized world. A successful managing director in an investment bank may only have nine or ten years of working experience (although more generally this will be at least 12 years); in most cases, this would be inconceivable in an industrial company. To put things in perspective, Goldman Sachs announced in 2010 the appointment of 321 new managing directors and 110 partners across the whole firm,[24] in addition to its already many existing managing directors, the list of which, now no longer available on its website, and set out in several columns, covered a number of pages.

It should be noted that the first or second quarter of the year often sees a significant turnover among investment banking staff as many employees join competitors following the payment of annual bonuses. This is true in particular for research analysts and salespeople but more generally applies across the board; it has continued despite the new remuneration policies introduced after the recent credit crunch and sub-prime debacle in the US, involving increased fixed salaries and deferred payments and claw-backs for the variable component of compensation.

Table 2 summarizes the levels for career progression for investment bankers, as well as equivalents between investment banking titles.

1.7   The IPO banking team

Investment banks appointed in a leading role will normally give issuers a little bound book that includes a list of working parties at the outset of an IPO. Several versions will be issued as the execution of the transaction progresses, and it is generally the responsibility of one of the more junior bankers at one of the lead banks to keep this document up to date. For each of the banks involved, this will often include dozens of names spread out across a variety of teams, demonstrating the extent of the commitment made by the firm towards the execution of the offering. Many of the investment bankers listed will, however, have a very defined and time-sensitive role in the transaction. Some of them, and many others not listed in the list of working parties, the issuing company will actually never see. In fact, the investment banking team that remains dedicated to the IPO throughout the deal will probably be fairly light, even in the case of a very large offer or privatization.

1.7.1   Senior management

Starting with investment bankers within the Chinese wall, there will often be one or two very senior names, perhaps the chairman or chief executive officer of the bank, or the global or regional head of investment banking, under a "senior management" heading. These will invariably hardly ever get involved in the transaction. They may appear briefly at the pitching or at other crucial stages, and may perhaps show up at a roadshow presentation and at the closing dinner. They may perhaps also appear as signatories of letters sent to the management of the company, and/or its shareholders in an effort to get their firm appointed in certain additional roles for

Thereafter	President (of region, country, team or department) Chairman (of region, country, team or department) Vice-chairman (of region, country, team or department)	
After 1–3 years	Partner managing director Senior managing director Executive director	
After 1–3 years	Managing director Division director	
After 1–3 years	Executive director	
After 1–3 years	Director Senior vice-president	
After 2–4 years	Associate director Vice-president Senior manager Manager Associate manager Senior associate Associate	← Optional MBA
After 1–3 years	Senior analyst	
Entry level	Graduate trainee Business analyst (BA) Analyst	

Table 2
Career progression and equivalents between investment banking business titles

the transaction (which, obviously, may result in additional league table credit or remuneration).

1.7.2   The core execution team

Sometimes a core or dedicated transaction team will be highlighted. It will probably include a managing director (although managing directors in investment banks are primarily dedicated to the origination of new mandates and to business development, as we saw earlier) or an executive director, together with a mid-level and a junior executive. They will either be generalist or execution bankers, sometimes with a dedicated country, industry sector, or product (in this case, an ECM) specialization. Some investment banks, such as UBS, Morgan Stanley, or Bank of America (previously known as Bank of America Merrill Lynch), actually have dedicated teams (often known as equity corporate finance teams), specializing in the overall execution of IPOs, and of equity offerings or capital markets transactions generally, and who remain involved from start to finish. Sometimes, such a team will have a particular bias towards work on transaction documentation and legal issues and a different name, for example, "special execution" at Goldman Sachs. Wider country teams, with local language capabilities, or industry sector teams, with a particular expertise on how to approach the valuation of the business, may also be involved either throughout the deal or appear from time to time during the execution of the transaction.

1.7.3   The ECM team

Members of the ECM team will be involved at key stages in the transaction. ECM teams are generally primarily responsible for the origination of ECM business, which includes IPOs, primary and secondary equity offerings, block trades, convertible and exchangeable bond offerings, REITs, business trusts, and infrastructure funds, as well as for the later stages of the execution of such transactions. Accordingly, their first involvement will be at the pitching stage, in an effort to secure a lead mandate for the firm that employs them. Depending on how the bank is set up, they will often leave the day-to-day management of the transaction and documentation to a dedicated IPO or equity corporate finance investment banking team, but will gradually become more involved as the transaction progresses towards the marketing stage, when contact with investors is initiated, and until the start of trading and beyond. Crucially, they will be responsible for targeting and often, in coordination with the equity syndicate desk, contacting institutional investors in a pre-IPO fund raising or cornerstone investor round. They will also liaise with the equity sales teams around the world to ensure wider contacts are established with investors at the appropriate time and that feedback is obtained from them, and acted upon. They will be instrumental in managing the pre-marketing or pre-deal investor education (PDIE) process and the order-gathering, also called "price discovery", or bookbuilding, as well as for the pricing, allocation, and stabilization of the offering. Because of this hybrid role, ECM teams, while technically within the Chinese wall, are often set up as joint ventures for cost and revenue purposes between both the banking and markets side of investment banks. In summary, their focus is more particularly on market, rather than corporate finance, or general execution matters.

1.7.4   The equity syndicate desk

Key team members within the ECM team are those on the equity syndicate desk (naturally, with a dedicated local or regional and global head), whose role is to liaise with the equity sales teams around the world, as well as with other investment banks to ensure coordination. They are generally not involved in the origination of new ECM business (or perhaps only superficially, and the issuing company will probably not see much of them until the later stages of the offering). Another important role of the syndicate desk (or team) is to coordinate investor education and the building of the investor book of demand. In addition, they will often be tasked with sounding out a select group of investors about their interest and views on pricing, prior to the launch of follow-on ECM transactions. The syndicate team is sometimes actually physically located within the markets side of the bank, even though it is within the Chinese wall for compliance purposes. It will therefore often sit on the trading floor, but within a dedicated enclave, with access physically closed to salespeople and traders. Increasingly, many investment banks, especially US houses, have now formally moved this function to their equities departments. I have worked at firms that used both models, with syndicate bankers either sitting within the ECM department or alternatively on the trading floor.

1.7.5   The in-house roadshow coordinators

Most of the larger investment banks will also have one or more dedicated roadshow coordinators, generally either part of, or working closely with, the ECM team and the equity syndicate desk in particular. Their role is to take charge of the logistics associated with management roadshows, in particular travel arrangements and the hiring of venues for group presentations, for new issues, or as part of investor conferences organized by the bank. For smaller transactions, they will often coordinate the entire roadshow themselves, but on more complex offerings, or for offerings led by several investment banks, a third-party consultant will sometimes be appointed. In such a case, their role will be to liaise with such consultants to ensure in particular that the meetings arranged by their bank are correctly reflected in the schedule. This can be quite a stressful role because the roadshow schedule can change frequently and at short notice, so as to adapt to the locations of major investors that may commit substantial amounts of money to a transaction.

1.7.6   The legal and compliance teams

Also within the Chinese wall is an in-house legal team, which is involved in the negotiation of the various engagement letters and legal agreements. Legal teams within investment banks are often part of larger compliance departments, which, aside from liaising with regulators and other authorities, also look closely at the relationship between both sides of the Chinese wall. In an IPO in particular, they will be in charge of establishing contact with, and for liaising between, the ECM team and the research analysts. At many houses, investment bankers cannot even speak to research analysts unless a legal or compliance officer is also in attendance. Another role of legal and compliance departments can be to assist in regulatory enquiries, or even litigation. In this respect, it should be noted that all the major investment banks now have in-house personnel dedicated to litigation. I have worked with a number of them in my role as an independent expert witness.

1.7.7 The research analysts

In most IPOs, other than in the US, Canada, and Japan, where research distribution is prohibited, even for offerings by issuers from other countries, "pre-deal" research is published on the company to be floated, so as to present institutional investors with a synopsis on the company that is more "user friendly" than the offering circular or prospectus published by the issuer. Research analysts, who are outside the Chinese wall for compliance purposes, are also responsible for PDIE—that is, travelling around the world to meet with institutions to discuss the merits of the issuer, following the publication of their pre-deal research reports, and gather investors' views on valuation. In smaller IPOs, there will generally only be one research analyst involved from any investment bank. But in larger transactions, such as privatizations, or in IPOs of companies that have a business encompassing several distinct areas, such as conglomerates, more than one research analyst may be involved in the offering process. For example, when I worked on the US$1.4 billion equivalent IPO of MTR Corporation in 2000 in Hong Kong, a company that runs the metro system there, but is also a major property developer, the equity research team for the transaction included both property research analysts (with a particular emphasis on the Hong Kong market), and analysts specializing in transportation stocks. Sometimes, both a research analyst with a country focus and another with an industry sector focus are involved.

1.7.8 The equity sales teams

Also on the "markets" side are equity salespeople. These can form a fairly large global group, generally based where the institutional investors they serve are located, or organized according to the nature of such institutions. For example, some salespeople may only have hedge funds as clients; others may have sovereign wealth or pension funds. To ensure coordination, one or more "deal captains" are generally appointed for each IPO from within the senior salespeople to liaise with the ECM team and ensure that selling efforts are consistent and well targeted. Sometimes, the deal captain changes from deal to deal to enable several executives to gain experience in such a role. Some investment banks also have one or more salespeople particularly dedicated to ECM transactions, who may be permanent insiders for compliance purposes, and who therefore will most closely liaise with the syndicate desk. Indeed, at some firms, the head of syndicate can be a senior salesperson (or, perhaps more commonly, a former salesperson).

1.7.9   Other areas

At banks that have a wealth management or private banking arm, these are often systematically contacted, at arm's length, by the bank's (or indeed other banks') ECM team(s) to generate high-net-worth investor demand for IPOs.

As outlined in Section 1.5.3, corporate communications departments within investment banks are sometimes involved in IPOs, most particularly in the case of particularly high-profile or "sensitive" transactions, such as privatizations. They will also usually be involved after the deal to help increase the lead bank's profile in the media and win further IPO and ECM business, and also to win coveted industry awards granted by financial magazines.

Lastly, and something generally rarely seen by the issuing corporate, will be back office teams, in charge of the administration and settlement of trades for the shares allocated to investors under the IPO and located outside the Chinese wall. This can be a complicated and extensive exercise, involving large amounts of money (as well as foreign exchange transactions and/or regulatory issues) and significant volumes of stock, tight deadlines, and sometimes unfamiliar procedures, as was, for example, the case with the first international IPOs by Chinese issuers, or that by the first issuer (a pharmaceutical firm) to come from Croatia after the war in former Yugoslavia in the early 1990s. In cases where an IPO is listed on two or more stock exchanges, or involves the simultaneous sale or issue of depositary receipts (although this is rare nowadays), this can, on occasion, be a rather daunting task.

1.8   Bank roles and the pecking order

There is a significant amount of confusion among the public, the media, and even the investor community about the various roles that an investment bank can have in an IPO. Accordingly, it is worth clarifying here who does what, and the implications, for a given investment bank, of being appointed to a particular role.

1.8.1   Deal sponsors

In most IPOs, one or more banks are responsible for liaising with the regulator and/or stock exchange and for "sponsoring" the corporate on its listing. This role, which probably originated in the UK and is common in those countries that broadly follow the same execution model as the UK for IPOs (such as Germany, Hong Kong, or Singapore), is a fairly administrative one and largely involves due diligence, helping the issuer to navigate the listing rules, and helping with the drafting of the prospectus and the negotiation of its contents with the regulator or exchange. The terminology varies from market to market—"sponsor" in Hong Kong, "lead underwriter" in Tokyo, "issue manager" in Singapore, "principal adviser" in Malaysia, or "nominated adviser" (Nomad for short) for the Alternative Investment Market (AIM) in London. The main requirement is that the bank has experience of, and is qualified, to undertake this role. This generally involves a recent history of past IPOs where the bank has acted in this capacity and a minimum number of qualified personnel with the requisite experience, for example in Hong Kong, known to be qualified as Principals or Representatives. As in Hong Kong with Principals, in mainland China, any lead broker underwriting an IPO must have at least two executives acting as "sponsors" within the firm, each of whom must sit and pass a test on underwriting regulations. Such executives cannot work on more than two IPOs simultaneously. The sponsor should also be independent from the issuer, and confirmation to that effect is generally required to be made to the exchange. This role does not involve marketing or selling shares in the IPO.

A sponsor (or equivalent) can be just that, and some boutique investment banks with no research or securities distribution capabilities do act, and get remunerated for acting, solely in a sponsor capacity. In some rarer cases, accounting firms, lawyers, or consultants may even act in such a role, provided that they meet the requisite qualifications laid out the regulator. Some banks are perfectly qualified to sell an IPO on a global basis to investors. But because they are perhaps new to a particular market, or have not recently been involved in stock exchange listings in a particular jurisdiction, they may not necessarily be qualified to act as a sponsor, or at the very least to act as a sponsor in a sole capacity. Accordingly, another house as a joint sponsor may perhaps need to be appointed, which is also the case when the other sponsor is not independent from the issuer, for example, if it is part of the same group of financial companies. More often than not, however, the lead bank appointed to market and distribute the IPO will also act as the sponsor. Sometimes, several lead banks may be appointed in a lead role, with only one or two of them acting as sponsor.

It is finally worth noting that in recent years there has been increasing pressure on the part of regulators with respect to the duties discharged by IPO sponsors. In particular, regulators have handed out heavy fines to a number of sponsor firms as a result of failures in the quality of their due diligence work. In certain markets, such as in Hong Kong, this has even included suspending the ability of such firms to sponsor IPOs there for up to a year (although they could still market and underwrite deals). The standards of work pertaining to inquiries into a prospective issuer's business are now very demanding indeed, and it is generally no longer possible for such firms to rely, or even commonly delegate part of their work to third parties. Sponsors are now expected to probe, and even on occasion, question, in an increasing amount of detail, the work carried out by legal advisers, experts, and even reporting accountants.

1.8.2   Global coordinators

Next is the role of global coordinator. The role and title were first coined in the UK in the 1990s. Again, this is often combined with the role of sponsor. As with sponsors, more than one bank can act in this capacity, as joint global coordinators (JGCs), generally on larger IPOs. Sometimes, but more rarely, banks can also be appointed in a co-global coordinator capacity, although such a term might be perceived, unlike a joint role, as not being on an equal footing. The responsibilities of a global coordinator are made clear in the title—this is a coordination role, tasked with helping to bring together the various parties involved in the transaction. Almost systematically, a global coordinator will also be a bookrunner and a lead manager, although not necessarily the other way around, which I will discuss in Section 1.8.3. A global coordinator is also often entitled to an extra share of the fees or *praecipium*, sometimes spelt as *praecipuum* (generally 0.25% or 0.50%), deducted from the gross fees (or, more commonly, part of the gross fees) payable by the issuer and/or selling shareholders.

In practice, the role of global coordinator is less meaningful these days as syndicate structures have become streamlined. Appointing one or more JGCs made a lot of sense when a large number of banks were selected to join a syndicate for the underwriting of an IPO, in particular when several sub-syndicates were set up to distribute regional tranches, as was the case in the 1990s. Nowadays, a single syndicate is generally appointed to distribute most IPOs, and banks are free to sell stock to investors pretty much globally, subject obviously to the licences they may hold. In addition, the average number of banks appointed in a syndicate has now been markedly reduced, generally to a single-digit number—although a recent trend for Chinese IPOs in Hong Kong has been to appoint a very large number of houses to underwrite and distribute new listings. For example, no fewer than 28 bookrunners were mandated on the multi-billion-dollar IPO of Chinese pork producer W.H. Group in 2014, a record for a flotation in the city. This practice creates a number of issues and often results in unnecessary complications in terms of communication and execution, as well as in poor-quality books of demand being assembled by these brokers and banks. It also blurs the messages that are communicated to potential investors, as a result of the very large number of firms involved in the transaction.

The system of a single, global syndicate was devised for the very first time for the £5.4 billion follow-on privatization of British Telecom in 1993 (BT3), which was led by S.G.Warburg, with a total of 11 global managers appointed from around the world to distribute the offering globally, breaking away from the previous system of using ring-fenced regional syndicates.[25] A good example of the use of regional tranches is the US$1 billion IPO of Spanish bank Argentaria, now part of Banco Bilbao Vizcaya Argentaria or BBVA, also in 1993, which included a dual listing in Spain and on the NYSE, with a Spanish retail and institutional tranche for 60.7% led by Argentaria's investment banking arm, Argentaria Bolsa (now merged with Banco Bilbao Vizcaya, or BBV); a US tranche for 14.3% led by Morgan Stanley; a UK and Ireland tranche for 12.5% jointly led by S.G.Warburg and Banco Santander; a continental European tranche for 8.9% led by UBS; and a Rest of the World tranche for 3.6% led by Merrill Lynch, with many of the above banks also acting in more junior roles in some of the other tranches in the IPO, in addition to the one for which they had been appointed as bookrunner. For example, S.G.Warburg also acted as co-lead manager in the continental European tranche, while UBS had a similar role in the UK tranche.[26]

Regional syndicates continued to be used until well after the mid-1990s, most particularly in privatizations, but they have now completely disappeared, with the exception of dedicated tranches for Japanese public offerings without listing (POWLs), which I will discuss in Chapter 2, Section 2.14.5.

1.8.3   Bookrunners

Most important is the role of bookrunner. Again, there can be more than one bank appointed in such capacity, as joint or, more rarely, as more junior co-bookrunners. A bookrunner can also be (and often is) a sponsor, global coordinator, and lead manager. However, not all lead managers (and more rarely sponsors) manage also to be appointed as a bookrunner. This is considered the key role in any IPO, as it involves controlling the book of demand, that is, maintaining the list of orders placed by institutional investors in the IPO and, most importantly, deciding on the allocations of stock to such investors. While, in theory, allocations should be made in an independent fashion, and having regard to the perceived quality of each investor (e.g., taking into account whether an investor has a long-term investment horizon), every investment bank is keen to allocate more stock to its best institutional investor clients. Being a bookrunner ensures this and, although not necessarily willingly, enables banks to allocate sizeable amounts of stock to those investors that effectively pay them significant commissions in the secondary market. Investors will therefore almost invariably place orders with a bookrunner, even more so in a "hot" deal that is heavily oversubscribed and, therefore, is likely to see both demand heavily scaled back through the allocation process and an increase in the share price when the stock starts trading. In the US in particular (although this is increasingly becoming commonplace in other markets), a distinction is sometimes made between "active" bookrunners (in practice, generally the banks that also act in a sponsor and global coordinator capacity and who are therefore fully involved in all phases of the transaction) and "passive" bookrunners, who, as the name suggests, are not significantly involved in the execution and marketing of the transaction, although their status and remuneration still place them above those of other firms appointed to join the syndicate of underwriters. Such terminology is informal—it is not something that will be found in an offering circular or underwriting agreement—but nevertheless describes well the roles that bookrunner banks can play in an offering. In a syndicate that includes a large number of bookrunners (say, more than six), those that are not also sponsors and/or global coordinators will inevitably have a relatively passive function in the deal.

Allocations can lead to considerable negotiation (and very late nights!) when various bookrunners are appointed on the same IPO, each bank being obviously keen to favour its own investors that have placed orders in the book of demand. Banks at the bookrunner level will sometimes have written arrangements in place to govern how they will work with each other on a particular transaction. Such memoranda of understanding (MoUs) or "rules of engagement" will generally cover their respective roles, economics, appearance, entitlement to investor meetings, hosting arrangements for roadshows, bookbuilding, pricing, allocation, and stabilization issues, as well any advertising arrangements post-IPO. Previously, such arrangements were the subject of lengthy telexes, documents or PowerPoint presentations, but nowadays they will often be set out in the form of an email. They will be superseded by the sale and purchase or underwriting agreement once executed.

Depending on the size of the IPO, it often makes sense for an issuer to appoint more than one lead bank as JGCs and joint bookrunners. The amount of fees paid remains the same irrespective of how many banks are ultimately appointed in such roles (the pie is just divided into more portions) and it is also useful to create an element of competitiveness, both for corporate finance execution and for marketing, among the houses tasked with leading the offering. At the same time, appropriately motivating the brokers responsible for leading the transaction is also an important consideration, and issuers should avoid going overboard. Some governments did so in early privatization IPOs in Southeast Asia, when numerous bookrunners were signed up to manage a transaction, resulting in much posturing, unnecessary arguing, diluted fees, and ultimately a loss of motivation and efficiency. As mentioned above, such a trend is now firmly (and unfortunately) surfacing again for certain IPOs by mainland Chinese issuers in Hong Kong. Conversely, enough houses should obviously be appointed in a lead role for multi-billion-dollar IPOs, such as those for the top commercial banks from mainland China. The leading Asian insurer AIA appointed four JGCs and joint bookrunners, and a further seven additional bookrunners in a more junior capacity in its IPO (estimated at the time to total US$15 billion, and which ultimately reached US$20.4 billion after exercise of a 20% upsize option, pricing, and exercise in full of the over-allotment option) in October 2010.[27] Again, in such a case, the bookrunners not at global coordinator level are not really expected to work actively on the execution of the transaction, except beyond the actual marketing phase of the deal.

1.8.4   Lead managers

Below the role of bookrunner is that of lead manager. Again, a lead manager is often also a bookrunner, and sometimes also a global coordinator and sponsor, but not always. Lead managers may also (although rarely nowadays) be entitled to a *praecipium* deducted from the gross fees (or, usually, part of the gross fees), as are global coordinators. When a lead manager is also a bookrunner, there is not too much to distinguish its particular role. When it is not, then it simply means that it is slightly higher in the pecking order than more junior banks in the syndicate, and that it is usually entitled to somewhat higher fees. In effect, a lead manager without a bookrunner title is just a glorified senior underwriter. It can also be included in lead manager league tables, although what really matters, as mentioned above, is to be appointed as a bookrunner and increasingly also as a JGC and/or sponsor. If not a bookrunner, a lead manager will probably find it difficult to effectively sell shares in an IPO to institutional investors for the reasons outlined earlier.

1.8.5   Junior syndicate members

Moving down the syndicate ladder, one or more banks, depending on the size of the IPO, may be appointed as co-lead managers. This is a junior role, where banks are not generally expected to contribute much to the sale of the securities on offer. Their responsibility centres more on the publication, where allowed, of pre-deal research—which is also carried out by banks appointed in all of the above marketing roles—and, to some extent, on conducting investor education on the back of such pre-deal research. Accordingly, the main criterion for appointing co-lead managers should be their respective capabilities in equity research and, most particularly, in the country and industry sector pertaining to the issuer. This can often be ascertained by looking at annual independent investor surveys ranking research analysts, which I will discuss in Chapter 3, Section 3.1. It can also be the case that investment banks unsuccessful in being appointed for the top roles after pitching (perhaps in a so-called "beauty parade") are given a co-lead ticket by way of compensation, although not all the bulge-bracket banks are willing to take on junior roles, because they can be time consuming and the fees are usually modest. Junior syndicate members typically do not participate in due diligence, (although a dedicated meeting or call might, on occasion, be arranged specially for them, see Chapter 2, Section 2.5.4), nor actively in the negotiations for underwriting arrangements.

Co-lead managers may also sometimes be among the relationship banks of the issuer and therefore find their way in the syndicate as a result of, for example, their corporate banking or lending activities. Nowadays, co-lead managers are most of the time not paid on the basis of the amount of stock they underwrite and sell, but more by way of a fixed sum for contributing to publishing pre-deal research on a company. This amount varies from region to region, from deal to deal and from bank to bank, and can be anywhere from US$150,000 to US$500,000 equivalent per co-lead manager for a given transaction. If anything, however, this amount has gradually been reduced over the years. Generally, a bank acting in such a role will have a threshold in dollar terms for these fixed fees, below which it will not participate in the underwriting syndicate. Sometimes, senior co-lead managers can be appointed above the co-lead manager level. Their role is similar but they can be given a slightly higher underwriting amount or fees in the transaction, normally for conducting more pre-marketing meetings, above and beyond the slightly fancier title.

The most junior level in a syndicate is that of co-manager, in cases where banks are not expected to contribute to research (and even less to sales efforts) and often paid a token amount for putting their name to the deal. Relationship banks of the issuer, obviously not among its main bank relationships, will sometimes be appointed to this role. Nowadays, few banks are actually appointed in this capacity given the lack of expected (and actual) contribution from co-managers.

Rather confusingly, "co-manager" is also a generic term used mainly in the US for banks not at the bookrunner or lead manager level. In Singapore, and in some other markets such as the UK, junior syndicate members such as co-lead managers and co-managers are often called "sub-underwriters" instead. This is partly because the term "lead" in "co-lead manager" may imply additional responsibilities and liabilities, for example under Singapore law, which is often why junior syndicate members there prefer to use another title, and also not to appear on the cover of the prospectus. The term sub-underwriter is also used in markets such as Australia, although in that jurisdiction in a more literal sense, with such banks assuming part of the risk underwritten by other houses.

In the US only, banks can also be appointed to underwrite an IPO as major bracket underwriters, sub-major bracket underwriters, or simply as underwriters depending on how much they each underwrite. Other banks may be appointed as part of a selling group (or as placing agents) and are paid the selling concession on orders they bring in (typically from retail investors), but not management or underwriting commissions.

Table 3 illustrates how a syndicate of eight banks may be organized in a (relatively large) international (non-US) IPO. Some banks, and in this example probably too many, appointed in the lead roles combine several responsibilities, while a few others have a simple, well-defined junior position in the syndicate. Further examples are provided in the case studies set out in Appendix 1.

Obviously, league tables can be drawn up for each (or a combination) of these roles. Investment banks have long mastered the art of "cutting" league tables across ECM roles, regions, industry sectors, types of ECM transactions and timeframes to ensure that they appear in a favourable light or lead position. Junior investment bankers in ECM departments spend much of the first years of their careers devising such league tables for inclusion in pitching materials.

1.8.6 Receiving banks

In addition to banks selling to institutional investors, in most jurisdictions, commercial banks with retail investor clients also need to be appointed as receiving banks. This is because in some markets retail investor demand can be very high, for example in Japan, Australia, or Hong Kong. More generally, it is because a minimum spread of shareholders is compulsory under the listing rules and a retail offering is

	Bank A	Bank B	Bank C	Bank D	Bank E	Bank F	Bank G	Bank H
Sponsor	✓							
Global coordinators	✓	✓						
Bookrunners	✓	✓	✓					
Lead managers	✓	✓	✓	✓				
Senior co-lead manager					✓			
Co-lead managers						✓	✓	
Co-manager								✓

Table 3
An IPO syndicate with a sole sponsor, two joint global coordinators, three joint bookrunners, and four joint lead managers

the only practical way to attain the number of 500 (in Singapore), 300 (in Hong Kong), or 2,200 (for Nasdaq in the US or for the First Section of the exchange in Tokyo) shareholders required by the stock exchange for listing. It should be noted, however, that not all stock exchanges require such a spread of shareholders to be achieved—sometimes a minimum free float expressed as a percentage of capital is the only requirement (see Appendix 8 for initial listing requirements for a variety of major stock exchanges around the world).

1.8.7 Independent advisers

Sometimes, issuers may appoint an independent adviser in an IPO advisory capacity to help them navigate this complex process, and to "keep the lead banks honest". ABN AMRO Rothschild, the erstwhile joint venture between the Dutch bank and the Franco-British investment bank used to specialize, in addition to some underwriting roles, in such assignments (for privatizations in particular) prior to the acquisition of ABN AMRO by The Royal Bank of Scotland in 2007. Firms such as Rothschild (following the dissolution of the joint venture with ABN AMRO), Lilja & Co, or Moelis & Co are also known for acting in this capacity. Such advisers are often boutique firms with no research, distribution, or trading capabilities—and therefore no conflicts of interest. Or they can be fully fledged investment banks not otherwise involved in the IPO, or even (more rarely) consultants. Their role may or may not be disclosed to the lead banks or to the public at large.

When an independent adviser is appointed to help on an IPO, it is a good idea to make the appointment at the outset of the transaction and, in any event, prior to the lead banks themselves being appointed. Such an adviser may be able to save an issuer substantial amounts of money, effort, and time by helping on the request for proposal (RFP) and negotiation processes for the fee and expenses payable to the banks and other advisers, as well as with a number of other issues pertaining to the offering. Readers may want to refer to my book *IPO Banks: Pitch, Selection and Mandate* for more information on independent advisers, RFPs, beauty parades, and the appointment of investment banks in connection with an IPO.

1.8.8 Appearance and other roles

Appearance is an important issue for investment banks, that is to say the way and order in which their names are listed on the cover of prospectuses, and subsequently in "tombstones" recording the "bare bone" facts of a deal or press announcements. Appearance can be subject to much discussion and negotiation. Traditionally, the bank with the most senior role always appears in the top left position. When several lead banks are on an equal footing, alphabetical order will generally be used, and this may even be mentioned underneath the names so that no confusion can exist in the minds of investors or the public. Banks may also appear, for example, in alphabetical order for global coordinators, as well as in reverse alphabetical order for bookrunners, again, this being made clear below the names. If several banks are listed on the same line (or in a "cascading" fashion) but do not appear in alphabetical order, then the bank that appears "out of order" in the top left generally has the most senior role in the line-up. This may be because it underwrites a larger amount of stock than do the other banks and/or has a greater involvement in the whole process. It may also be because it is entitled to a larger share of the fees, which, in practical terms, generally amounts to the same. It has now become uncommon for the names of junior syndicate members to appear on the cover of prospectuses, although this will often still be found in the "underwriting" or "plan of distribution" sections of such documents. For banks appointed in the more junior roles in an IPO, involvement will remain limited to the equity syndicate desk, research analyst and, perhaps, a handful of salespeople to conduct pre-deal investor education calls.

Although not necessarily part of the syndicate for an IPO per se, companies listed in the UK must appoint financial advisers and brokers on a retainer basis. This is the case whether companies are admitted to list on the main board of the exchange or on the secondary market (AIM). Such financial advisers and brokers are often (but not always) appointed as global coordinators and bookrunners for subsequent equity transactions. In Hong Kong, firms known as compliance advisers must be appointed by issuers for a full financial year following their IPO (a period that may be extended at the request of the regulators) and must also be qualified to act as IPO sponsor. The case study of the IPO of L'Occitane in Hong Kong in 2010, set out in Appendix 1, includes an example of appointment of a compliance adviser. There is usually not a lot of money to be made when working in that capacity, so this role is usually the preserve of smaller or specialist firms, rather than that of bulge-bracket houses (except where there may perhaps be "strategic" reasons for them to act in such capacity).

Generally, global coordinators, bookrunners, and lead managers are appointed at the outset of a transaction. However, some of these roles may be decided later on, for example just prior to the bookbuilding stage, to reward those banks that have pulled their weight at the preparation or corporate finance stage, completed a particularly extensive PDIE exercise, or brought on board cornerstone investors. In April 2010, the financial group from mainland China, Agricultural Bank of China, appointed (in this order) Chinese investment bank CICC, Goldman Sachs, Morgan Stanley, Deutsche Bank, JPMorgan, Macquarie Capital, and its own investment banking arm, ABC International, as joint bookrunners of its US$12 billion H share IPO in Hong Kong. At the end of June 2010, following the completion of investor education and the naming of cornerstone investors, it announced that CICC, Goldman Sachs, Morgan Stanley, and ABC International (in that order) had also been named as global coordinators for the transaction, entitling them to a higher proportion of the reported US$200 million in fees payable on the offering (estimated at the time of launch). In the event, the fees for the IPO were slashed by about 30% upon closing to a reported US$142 million, as it was said that the issuer took the view that a number of discussions with, and the successful appointment of, certain cornerstone investors had taken place without much involvement from the lead banks.[28] Deciding final titles nearer completion of the transaction is also a trend that is becoming increasingly frequent in the UK, especially where independent advisers are involved. This is something that generally infuriates investment banks since it introduces a major element of uncertainty to their mandates (and potential fees!). However, in most IPOs, the roles and titles of the various lead banks will be made clear at the outset of the offering.

1.9   Pitching for the lead roles

Often, a company that is planning to conduct an IPO will have gone public with its plans, or will have been approached by one or more investment banks pitching to lead the transaction. The banks will have explained the process in some level of detail, attempted to put a value on the company using a variety of methodologies, and also presented their credentials to convince the issuer that they are best placed to be appointed in the most senior roles in the offering.

There is much creativity on the part of investment banks when it comes to pitching for new business. Management are wined and dined (although the budgets for such entertainment are much lower nowadays than they once were), invited to conferences hosted by the banks, or given the opportunity to meet senior strategists who will give their views on where the markets are heading. Relationships will be built at all levels throughout the company—junior bankers will liaise with their counterparts, while the more senior managing directors will focus on chairmen, CEOs, and CFOs. In the past, investment banks have even commissioned short films or videos to illustrate their enthusiasm for working on a particular transaction. Short clips or letters with testimonials of satisfied CEOs are also not uncommon, and can be effective in conveying a bank's credentials. Some pitching teams for IPOs of textile retailers have on occasion even turned up fully clad in clothing produced by the issuer! As another example, I worked on a major IPO in the healthcare sector, in connection with which an American investment bank submitted its pitchbooks in individual doctors' briefcases, complete with painted red crosses and syringes glued to their sides!

Before the late 1990s and early 2000s and the ensuing dot com craze, much use was made of research analysts in pitching. Research analysts specialize in stocks from a particular region, country, or industry sector and talk daily to institutional investors, so they are, in many ways, best placed to convey the views of the market. However, this also creates conflicts of interest between the banking and markets side of investment banking firms (see Section 1.5.2). Nowadays, most research analysts never participate in pitches (and when they do, this will perhaps be a side conversation, or they will be asked to leave the room after conveying their views). Their assessment of IPO candidates through pre-IPO research is done completely independently. ECM teams and investment bankers from within the Chinese wall can no longer (in theory) influence research analysts when it comes to writing their reports. Research teams now need to come to their views on their own, and to give a factual and fair assessment of the businesses on which they write reports. In addition, no price targets or recommendations (such as "buy" or "accumulate") can be included in pre-deal research reports issued in connection with IPOs.

1.9.1   Key attributes of a lead bank

Even though research analysts are no longer involved in drumming up new IPO business, appointing a lead investment bank (or banks) with strong research capabilities is still an important consideration, since research analysts remain involved in a major way in the new issue process through the publication (where allowed) of pre-deal reports and investor education. Research analysts involved in an IPO will also have a head start and be best placed to continue coverage of a company, after it has become listed. Another important criterion in appointing lead banks is obviously a track record of successfully conducting similar transactions, both in terms of industry sector and geographical location. No issuer wants its lead banks to reinvent the wheel, or to itself act as a guinea pig because they are lacking experience in certain areas. Strong capabilities in selling and trading similar securities across a number of jurisdictions is also a must. A lead bank should be able to provide support to the company after the IPO, through research, trading, and corporate broking activities, and/or, for example, through the organization of thematic investor conferences.

Lastly, investment banking is, at the end of the day, a people's business, and the issuer should work with bankers it can trust and with whom it has developed a relationship based on mutual understanding. Importantly, it should be noted that the bankers pitching for new business may not necessarily be the ones working on a particular deal, so it is also important for a listing candidate to identify the individuals who will primarily be responsible for working on its IPO, and who will lead the execution of the deal. As noted earlier, senior and seasoned bankers may well deliver a very impressive pitch, but this is unlikely to benefit the issuer if they are subsequently never to be seen again working on the deal. It can also pay to talk to past issuers to get their views on how the process was managed, how they would perhaps do things differently a second time around, and which firm(s) really did a good job.

The number of banks that are appointed in a lead role, as well as other houses to be chosen as part of a syndicate, depends largely on the size of and, ultimately, the amount of fees available to be paid for the transaction. In a smaller deal, one lead bank with perhaps a couple of co-lead managers to provide research coverage will often suffice, and the overall quantum of commissions will necessarily be limited. Appointing too many banks in such circumstances will simply mean less money for each of them, which may not be conducive to adequately motivating them. In a multi-billion-dollar IPO, extensive coverage of all segments of the institutional and retail investor communities will be required, and there will be more fees to be split among a larger group of underwriters. In such a case, appointing several banks in the lead roles will ensure broad marketing as well as a healthy level of competition in their marketing efforts. In some markets, a popular combination for transactions of an average size is the appointment of a mix of lead banks, for example an international house as well as a domestic bookrunner. In this case, both houses will often have complementary domestic as well as international distribution capabilities.

1.9.2 Requests for proposal

A practical way for a company that is planning to go public to control the pitching process, perhaps with the help of an independent adviser, is to issue a request for proposal (RFP) to a number of banks, setting out issues on which their views are sought. This can help comparison across a significant spectrum of banks on a fair basis, and selection of one or more lead banks for the transaction. Investment banks that decide to reply to the RFP are not being paid for doing so (conversely, I am aware of a couple of instances when issuers in mainland China asked for prospective lead underwriters to pay an "entry fee" to participate in the pitching process, although these are extreme cases), and this can also provide the company with a wealth of information in preparation for the flotation. RFPs can also specify conditions laid out by the company for participating in the IPO, such as an expected contribution on the part of the lead banks to expenses associated with the offering. For example, investment banks may not be reimbursed for their legal or out-of-pocket expenses, or these may be subject to a cap. Banks may even be asked at that stage to agree to other key terms and conditions pertaining to the offering—later to be detailed more fully in their mandate letters and in the sale and purchase and underwriting agreements. As I explain in greater detail in my book *IPO Banks: Pitch, Selection and Mandate*, an RFP process is also in effect a great opportunity to successfully negotiate a number of elements of the IPO with prospective lead banks. Once the senior underwriters have been appointed, they are to a significant extent in control of the process and negotiating with them becomes much more difficult.

Investment banks often have extensive graphics and presentations departments and are used to responding to RFPs at very short notice. Often responses will be sought within a week, perhaps two at most. However, it is usually best to give investment banks enough time to work on a quality submission. RFPs can be issued in many languages—it is not uncommon for them to be issued in Chinese or Korean to some bankers working in the Asia-Pacific time zone. ABC reportedly sent an extensive RFP of 35 pages in length to a group of more than 20 banks to pitch for one of the lead roles in its US$12 billion H share IPO in April 2010; this was in addition to another group, reportedly of ten banks, to lead the A share portion of its global offering, giving them barely a week to respond over an Easter bank holiday weekend.[29] Many investment banks will actually re-use parts of earlier or recent pitches, given their high level of ECM activity and the similarity between most RFPs. Some of the larger investment banks will even make regular use of outsourcing firms, often physically located in India, for the most commonly used parts of pitches or to help compile statistics. This can include trading multiples for comparable companies, or brief descriptions of potential acquisition targets in the case of M&A transactions. It also frees up junior personnel from working on the most "mechanical" aspects of pitches to concentrate on more value-added areas.

It is fairly common for RFPs (at least for larger IPOs) to be split into two parts: a written presentation and, subsequently, an oral presentation for those banks shortlisted after the initial stage. The written submission for an IPO will generally include, in a specified format, a maximum number of pages including or excluding appendices, the language to be used, or a minimum font size, and some or all of the following:

- an assessment of current and forecast market conditions, on a global basis, as well as for the country and industry sectors relevant to the company;
- an assessment of current and forecast primary equity market conditions, including a pipeline of disclosable new issues, perhaps highlighting comparable, similar, or competing offerings;
- a summary of the equity story and market positioning for the issuer as it would be marketed by the bank, together with possible concerns that may be raised by investors as well as potential mitigating factors suggested by the investment bank;
- an attempt at valuing the business, explaining the various methodologies used, and those likely to be favoured by investors. The issuer may sometimes include selected forecast financials in the RFP so that all the banks can attempt a valuation on a comparable footing. This may also include specifying recommendations for the capital structure of the company upon IPO, perhaps including the use of a special dividend;
- a recommendation as to which stock exchange(s) to list on, if not specified;
- a summary of the execution process, together with any anticipated execution issues, and the bank's ideas on how best to resolve these;
- the main issues that will be the subject of due diligence on the part of the investment banks and other relevant advisers;

- a list of documents that will be required for the transaction, together with suggestions for third-party advisers to be appointed in connection with the IPO;
- a proposed timetable for the transaction;
- details of the bank's proposed transaction leader and execution team, along with their respective experience;
- the proposed offer structure and marketing strategy for the IPO, including jurisdictions in which investors of various types will be targeted, and into how many tranches the global offering should be divided;
- a proposed structure (and, perhaps, names of potential participants) for the syndicate of banks that will lead the offering;
- the bank's recommended approach for research coverage for the company, together with details, coverage, and rankings of its research analysts that would be assigned to research the company;
- a list of target investors, together with likely demand expected from such investors. This may also include identifying investors for a pre-IPO or cornerstone round, and may sometimes be split between bottom-up and top-down demand estimates;
- details of how price ranges were determined for recent IPOs led by the bank and of where such IPOs were ultimately priced relative to their price ranges;
- the use of price stabilization for the offering;
- proposed fees for the IPO and a schedule of likely expenses (and, perhaps, the bank's willingness to absorb some of the latter, if not already specified in the RFP);
- details of any research, investor relations (including the hosting of investor conferences), and trading and market-making capabilities that may be provided by the bank to support the stock in the aftermarket; and
- credentials for the investment bank, perhaps including league tables in specified formats and for a given period of time; and, importantly, a track record of recent, relevant IPOs led in the jurisdiction(s) considered, with their share price performance at set intervals, as well as in the industry sector of the issuer.

In addition, banks are also often asked to state that they would have no conflicts of interest with participating in the proposed IPO. Certain confirmations of a legal or regulatory nature may also be requested.

It is not uncommon for ECM pitches or responses to RFPs to run into hundreds of pages, particularly as extensive credentials designed to impress the prospective issuer are recycled from earlier presentations. Accordingly, issuers and their shareholders may wish to specify a clear format (including a maximum number of pages) for these as submissions will necessarily need to be reviewed and assessed over a short period of time, so as to maintain momentum for the proceedings and keep banks under control. RFPs and ECM pitches are invariably put together over long hours by the more junior investment bankers; much of their role in the first few years of their careers actually consists of drafting and writing such presentations, before they are given the opportunity to meet with corporates to execute transactions and, ultimately, participate in business development efforts by themselves, pitching to potential clients.

1.9.3   Oral presentations

Oral presentations by a shortlist of houses generally follow the written submission and provide a forum for clarifying issues and physically identifying personnel from each investment bank primarily responsible for the running of the transaction. The most commonly adopted format is for a bank to make a 25–30-minute presentation, to be followed by a question-and-answer session for up to the same duration. Seeing the banks in sequence over a couple of days offers a good opportunity for immediate comparison between various houses, and the exercise is usually quite telling.

It is usual to give a more junior role in the syndicate to at least some of the banks that are ultimately not selected for the lead roles in the offering, although some of the larger houses are often reluctant to take on co-lead tickets and prefer instead to focus all their efforts on winning and executing transactions in a lead role.

1.10   Formally engaging investment banks

Investment banks are, most of the time, formally contracted through the signing of a formal engagement or mandate letter. Each bank has its own format, so a neutral format must be drafted when more than one bank is appointed. Investment banks that are active in primary equity markets work with each other all the time, so their legal departments are well aware of each other's sensitivities or peculiarities. Initial drafts are generally provided to issuing clients by the investment banks themselves, although it may often be preferable for issuers (especially when working with independent advisers) to write the first draft to facilitate initial negotiations.

Mandate letters can be fairly detailed, and run over several pages. They cover the engagement of the investment bank for the duration of the transaction, until the signing of the underwriting and sale and purchase agreements following the pricing of the IPO. Several clauses, such as those dealing with confidentiality and indemnity, survive the termination of the engagement. Mandate letters record the roles in and titles under which each lead bank is appointed, the fees to be paid by the client, and, often, how such fees are to be split among the banks, as well as arrangements regarding the reimbursement of expenses. Mandate letters also include clauses on access to management and to information pertaining to the company; confidentiality and the sharing of information between departments and subsidiaries of the bank; and record keeping. They also commonly include liability and indemnity clauses. In addition, they make clear under what circumstances, and how, the mandate can be terminated, for all the banks involved, or perhaps for only one or some of them.

Mandates for IPOs are often granted on an exclusive basis, but this generally does not prevent issuers from adding other banks to the syndicate in a senior or similar role at a later stage. Indeed, the letter may even make express reference to such a possibility. In some (although rare) cases, banks can be granted exclusivity or a right of first refusal on subsequent transactions for a period of time. In the past, a single form of mandate letter was commonly used for all the lead banks, irrespective of their role(s) in the transaction. Increasingly, a separate mandate letter is often drafted to contract banks acting in a sponsor capacity, whose role can be distinct from those involved in marketing the shares (accordingly, one bank acting in both roles may perhaps end up signing more than one engagement letter for the transaction). Sponsor banks may also be paid fixed fees, whereas those acting in a global coordinator or bookrunner roles will usually be paid on the basis of a percentage of the proceeds raised under the IPO. Under the new IPO sponsor rules that came into force in Hong Kong in October 2013, sponsor banks cannot be paid on a "no deal, no fee" basis, and must therefore be remunerated irrespective of the completion of an offering.

As IPO mandates can take time to negotiate, some banks have opted for a shorter format, with standard terms and conditions appended to the letter. This should obviously not preclude an issuer from negotiating the entire engagement letter, including the so-called standard terms, which form an integral part of the engagement.

In some cases, no mandate letter is signed at the outset and, indeed, some investment banks actually do not like to sign immediately engagement letters. There is simply an informal, sometimes vague, understanding about the terms of the engagement; this may not even include a final agreement on fees or the more senior roles in the syndicate until the last few weeks of the transaction. Some banks take the view that the best way to secure a mandate is to start working on it, and to negotiate details of the conditions of their appointment at a later stage. Prior to the new IPO sponsor regime in Hong Kong, this was not uncommon, especially with issuers from mainland China. In such a case, however, there is always a risk that the bank may end up footing the bill (or at the very least part of the bill) for expenses incurred by it and its own advisers in the event that the IPO is not completed, or abruptly pulled. It is generally best for all parties to proceed with a comprehensive mandate letter for the lead banks at the start of the execution process, so that the structure and terms of the deal and the capacities in which the banks are contracted remain unambiguous. This is prudent and will best cater to all eventualities.

1.11   How investment banks get paid

There are basically two ways investment banks get paid on an IPO.

First, gross fees are charged to the issuer and to any selling shareholders as a percentage of the issue size, and deducted from the proceeds realized in the IPO. Secondly, brokerage is often charged to investors as a percentage of the value of the stock allocated to each of them in the offering. Brokerage can, however, be optional in some transactions, whereas fees are always charged to issuers and/or sellers (as appropriate): on occasion these can be very low indeed for prestigious follow-on and/or privatization transactions where league table credit can be deemed as important as, if not more important than, actual deal revenues. Goldman Sachs reportedly quoted much lower fees than its rivals did when bidding for the mandate to lead the US$23.1 billion IPO of General Motors in the US in the summer of 2010.[30] Similarly, some government sell-downs in India (although not IPOs) have been conducted on commissions as low as 0.02%![31] In September 2013 in the UK, the UKFI, HM Government's department tasked with managing shareholdings it owned in bailed-out banks, negotiated the sale of a 6% stake in Lloyds Bank (equivalent to more than US$5.3 billion) at no cost to the taxpayer, the banks only being entitled to brokerage fees they charged to institutional investors. In addition, the UKFI also negotiated for 25% of such investor fees to ultimately be paid to the government under a negotiating arrangement with the underwriters.[32] However, this was only possible because the executives in charge at the UKFI were themselves former investment bankers (some of them were former colleagues of mine), and therefore knew how far they could "push the envelope" while still getting the results they wanted.

IPO fees charged to issuers vary from market to market and also depend on the size of the transaction. They have been gradually falling over the last few years in Europe (except on AIM in the UK, as well as on other "second boards", where they often remain relatively high owing to the relatively smaller size of IPOs on these platforms) and across most of Asia to about 2.00% to 3.50% of issue proceeds. However, they still remain particularly high in the US, typically up to 6.50% or even 7.00% (except for the more competitive billion-dollar IPOs of internet giants, for which a significant effort on remuneration is deemed necessary to secure a senior role), although many issuers there do not reimburse banks for their legal and out-of-pocket expenses as a result of this. Examples of fees charged on IPOs across various markets around the world are included in the case studies set out in Appendix 1.

Brokerage on an IPO, when charged to investors, is generally in the range of 0.25% to 1.00%. On top of the gross fees, corporates are sometimes also charged a documentation or advisory fee, commonly in the order of several hundred thousand US dollars, or the equivalent in the currency of issue, by the bank acting as sponsor.

Negotiating fees is part of business life, but at the end of the day one gets what one pays for. It may perhaps be preferable to pay slightly higher fees and to receive the full attention of a lead bank (or banks) than for an issuer to squeeze commissions as much as possible and see its offering become just another IPO on the firm's mandate list. What should really matter more to both issuers and vendors is the amount of net proceeds they ultimately receive from an IPO rather than how much the banks effectively charge to lead and manage the process. In addition, issuers and their shareholders should be wary of dividing the fee pool among too many houses, and therefore of diluting their earnings, which may result in their not receiving the full attention they deserve on the part of their lead underwriters.

There are various ways fees can be structured, and they may also include an incentive element. For example, an issuer may be charged a base, fixed percentage of, say, 2.00% of gross proceeds, with an additional variable component amounting to a further 0.50%. This can be entirely discretionary, with the issuer deciding at the time of pricing (or maybe even later) whether to pay the extra amount, and to which banks, depending on whether they have delivered on their claims or promises. This can also be a guaranteed amount, although the issuer may perhaps keep the identity of the recipients flexible, depending on their respective performance, and allocate this as it thinks fit. It can also be paid according to previously agreed criteria. Generally, the main criterion will be the final offer price, with perhaps a stated ratchet with higher fees paid as the offer price increases, although such an arrangement is rather uncommon. Conversely, it can also be based on the level of over-subscription achieved in the global, institutional, or retail offering (although there could be distortions owing to order inflation), or it can depend on whether certain pre-identified investors have placed orders, or on any other criteria agreed between the issuer and the lead banks. Two of the case studies described in Appendix 1 include examples of incentive fees.

While understanding gross fees charged to the issuer or brokerage is easy, the issue of how investment banks allocate IPO fees among each other is a rather complex matter, which requires explanation.

1.11.1 Components of the gross fees

Traditionally, gross fees for ECM transactions are split into three components: a management commission, an underwriting commission, and a selling concession. Historically, the split between such components has been 20/20/60. Management and underwriting commissions, which are effectively charged for dedicating the banks' resources to the transaction, as well as for underwriting the deal, are paid on fixed amounts underwritten by each bank. By contrast, the selling concession, which is charged for actually selling the offering to investors, is paid on variable amounts allocated to each bank, based on its final book of demand. Under such an arrangement, since the lion's share of the fees is paid on the basis of allocated demand, it is not difficult to understand why banks aspire to be appointed as a bookrunner in any ECM transaction.

In some cases, banks underwriting a transaction may pass on some of their underwriting exposure to other banks (or, indeed, investors) by entering into an individual sub-underwriting arrangement and by paying them a separate sub-underwriting fee. This is quite common in some jurisdictions, such as Australia.

I have mentioned earlier that global coordinators (and, more rarely nowadays, lead managers) are also sometimes paid extra fees in the form of a *praecipium*. This can be deducted either from the gross fees prior to any 20/20/60 split (in which case the *praecipium* obviously represents a higher amount) or, much more commonly, from the management commission only as a percentage of the 20% cut from the gross fees.

Traditionally, the management and underwriting commissions were available to account for unreimbursed expenses and stabilization losses. With the introduction of fixed or guaranteed economics for the more junior syndicate members, this is, in practice, generally no longer the case for co-lead and co-managers.

Table 4 illustrates how the various components of the fees are calculated. The amounts for the management and underwriting commissions per share are multiplied by the number of shares underwritten, whereas those for the selling concession (also on a per share basis) are multiplied by the number of shares allocated. To keep things simple, I have not included details of any *praecipium* in this example.

Offer price: US$1.80 per share
Total offering: 225,000,000 shares

Gross fees: 3.00%, equivalent to US$0.054 per share
- 20% management commission = US$0.0108 per share
- 20% underwriting commission = US$0.0108 per share
- 60% selling concession = US$0.0324 per share

Bank	Underwriting (shares)	Allocation (shares)	Management commission (US$)	Underwriting commission (US$)	Selling concession (US$)	Total commissions (US$)
A	150,000,000	200,000,000	1,620,000	1,620,000	6,480,000	9,720,000
B	50,000,000	20,000,000	540,000	540,000	648,000	1,728,000
C	25,000,000	5,000,000	270,000	270,000	162,000	702,000

Table 4
A simple worked example (without a *praecipium*) for the calculation of the various fee components

In addition, such amounts can increase after the start of trading, depending on whether all or a portion of the over-allotment option (if any) has been exercised. This will be discussed in greater detail in Chapter 4, Section 4.1.

1.11.2 US market practice

The selling concession can also be the subject of further twists, especially under market practice prevailing in the US. Equity offerings in the US typically use what is called a pot system, whereby the bookrunner is the only member of the syndicate that can solicit orders from institutional investors. The system was devised to avoid the same investors receiving multiple calls from syndicate members to sell them shares in the same transaction. Investors can, however, choose to designate a portion of the selling concession to other members of the syndicate. How this works in practice is as follows. Generally, a proportion of the selling concession is shared on a fixed, guaranteed (or pre-agreed) basis among all the syndicate members, usually in proportion to underwriting amounts and irrespective of actual sales made. The remainder of the sales credit is "designated" or allocated to syndicate members by investors in what is called a jump ball system ("jump ball" is a basketball term). The split between the fixed and jump ball portions of the selling concession varies, but is usually around 30/70, although in practice, pretty much all of the jump ball portion gets paid to the bookrunner. In some transactions, the system can be 100% jump ball, which in theory appears more fair to all the banks in the syndicate in that it puts everyone on the same footing but invariably results in the banks below the bookrunner level receiving no or very few designations for their sales efforts.

The example in Table 5, using the same parameters as the example in Table 4, shows how fees would be allocated under a typical US pot system. In this case, the selling concession is split 30% as a fixed portion, payable on the number of shares underwritten, and 70% as a variable component, which is paid based on designations by investors. Total fees payable by the issuer remain the same under both systems.

1.11.3 Designations and split orders

For international equity offerings outside the US, market practice is somewhat different. Orders can in theory be placed by institutions with banks other than the bookrunner, although, as in the US, syndicate members not at the bookrunner level do not really have a fair shot at generating orders as investors are generally advised to place orders with the bookrunners to secure allocations. Sometimes designations of part of the selling concession (as in the US) are allowed, in which case syndicate members are often given a period of up to 48 hours after the closing of the book to "chase" designations of sales credits from investors. In addition, split orders, that is, an investor placing more than one order with two or more banks, may (or, more rarely, may not) be allowed, depending on the rules that have been laid out by the lead banks in the transaction.

1.11.4 Fee caps

Both inside and outside the US, the bookrunners are sometimes capped as to the proportion of selling concession that they can receive. For example, the bookrunners may be capped at 75% or 80% of the selling concession, allowing the remaining 15% or 20% to be made available on a competitive basis exclusively for payment to the more junior syndicate members, so as to encourage their sales efforts.

1.11.5 Fees and re-allocation between tranches

When separate institutional and retail syndicates of banks are involved, the rules generally provide for the re-allocation of stock between the syndicates depending on investor demand generated in each tranche. As previously mentioned, sometimes this can be done by way of fixed claw-back triggers, such as in Hong Kong (indeed, Hong Kong is the only jurisdiction of which I am aware that provides for such

Offer price: US$1.80 per share
Total offering: 225,000,000 shares

Gross fees: 3.00%, equivalent to US$0.054 per share
- 20% management commission = US$0.0108 per share
- 20% underwriting commission = US$0.0108 per share
- 60% selling concession = US$0.0324 per share, of which 30% is fixed, based on underwriting amounts, and 70% jump ball

Bank	Underwriting (shares)	Designated jump ball sales credits (shares)	Management commission (US$)	Underwriting commission (US$)	Selling concession 30% fixed (US$)	Selling concession 70% jump ball (US$)	Total commissions (US$)
A	150,000,000	200,000,000	1,620,000	1,620,000	1,458,000	4,536,000	9,234,000
B	50,000,000	20,000,000	540,000	540,000	486,000	453,600	2,019,600
C	25,000,000	5,000,000	270,000	270,000	243,000	113,400	896,400

Table 5
The same worked example, using an institutional pot and jump ball fee system

mandatory claw-back triggers under the listing rules). Alternatively, this can be made at the discretion of the lead banks. When a claw-back (or a claw-forward, which is the reverse mechanism) happens, part of the fees may follow stock, and move from one tranche to the other, depending on local market practice or the provisions laid out in what is called an inter-syndicate agreement, which I will discuss in some detail in Chapter 3, Section 3.10. For example, management and underwriting commissions may be paid to banks underwriting stock in the initial tranche, but the selling concession may "move across" to the banks in the other tranche if stock has been re-allocated in a claw-back (or claw-forward) mechanism.

1.11.6 Pre-agreed and guaranteed economics

Such complexities notwithstanding, it is now very much common practice for the lead investment banks to pre-agree at the outset how the fees will be paid among themselves, which may even include brokerage charged to investors. When several banks are involved on the same footing, a straight equal split is generally the norm. Conversely, one or more banks may receive a higher proportion of the fees as decided by (or negotiated with) the issuer. Sometimes, banks are added in a senior role later in the transaction, with lower fees carved out for them. Such pre-agreement on the split of gross fees does not, however, extend to how allocations of stock are made to investors. This is only logical as allocations should in truth (at least for the institutional portion of the offering), reflect the quality of the book of the demand, rather than an economic arrangement among the underwriters. Accordingly, there remains an element of competitiveness to be able to reward a bank's institutional investor clients with stock, irrespective of how the bank is paid at the end of the day.

A major part of the marketing that banks use to pitch for, and win, ECM mandates revolves around how they have "outsold" other houses appointed in the same role in previous transactions. Therefore, even though joint bookrunners may be paid the same, receiving a higher allocation based on one's order book remains an important outcome for investment banks on any ECM offering.

I mentioned earlier that co-lead managers, or co-managers or sub-underwriters, are now usually paid a fixed fee or "guaranteed economics", in the case of co-lead managers specifically for publishing pre-deal research. Since they do not run the book of demand, they therefore generally do not contribute to selling efforts and do not receive allocations of stock. There are, however, ways in which the more junior members of a syndicate may be incentivized (perhaps beyond the pre-agreed economics) to contribute to the marketing of an IPO, above and beyond research. These can, for example, include:

- keeping the size of the overall syndicate small, so as to ensure meaningful underwriting amounts for all participating banks;
- structuring the fees to reward selling efforts, so that the majority of commissions are paid on actual shares placed with investors, rather than reward passive underwriting; this is generally the case in any event, but does not really work in practice given the constraints imposed by the bookrunner system;
- as mentioned above, capping the share of the bookrunners' selling concession to a certain level (perhaps 75% or 80%) so as to ensure that a meaningful proportion of the fee pool always remains available for the more junior members of the syndicate;
- mentioning the names of co-lead and co-managers on the cover of the prospectus to create more visibility for them with investors; and
- allowing global access to institutions, rather than ring-fencing sales efforts within a particular region, which is now also the norm for most IPOs—or indeed limiting access to certain institutional investors to some of the banks only.

1.11.7 IPO expenses

In addition to paid fees, investment banks are often reimbursed by issuers for their out-of-pocket expenses, which include travel, hotel, communications, printing, and so on, as well as for the fees of their own legal advisers. In the past, an estimate of such expenses was made and deducted from IPO proceeds, and the expense account finalized at a later stage. This is now very rarely the case, and expenses are charged by investment banks to issuers either at regular intervals throughout the transaction or, more commonly, in one go after the offering has been completed. What happens in practice is usually that one of the senior banks collates all the information from the other syndicate members (more precisely, from the firms whose expenses the issuer and/or selling shareholders have agreed to reimburse) to simplify the process. In some cases, particularly for very prestigious, large, or privatization mandates, expenses incurred by banks may not be reimbursed at all. In extreme cases—ECM offerings in South Korea are notorious for this—the investment banks are actually asked to contribute to part of the issuer's own expenses in order to participate in the transaction. For example, in the US$1 billion IPO of Chinese issuer Shanda Games on Nasdaq in 2009 (a case study for which is included in Appendix 1), the underwriters had agreed to reimburse the issuer for up to an estimated US$6 million in expenses in connection with the IPO. This appears to be a particularly high number until one realizes that, in this particular transaction, the gross fees received by the underwriters were estimated in the offering circular to be US$65 million.[33]

In any event, it may often be a good idea for an issuer to cap the lead banks' out-of-pocket expenses, perhaps to a maximum of, say, US$50,000 or US$75,000 per bank (excluding the cost of legal advisers), to prevent abuses. Expenses of banks below the level of bookrunner, which are usually not significant in any event, are traditionally not reimbursed.

1.11.8 Trading fees

Lastly, and not strictly part of the IPO fees themselves, come the trading fees. Since volumes are often very high in the first few days or even weeks of trading for newly listed stocks, banks generally earn considerable trading fees from institutional investors buying and selling shares in companies that have just been the subject of an IPO. The bookrunner banks on the deal are obviously best placed to capture the lion's share of such trading business as they are aware of which institutions received allocations in the offering and may therefore potentially be interested in topping up (or, indeed, selling some of) their holdings in the aftermarket.

2
Getting ready

2.1 Navigating the maze—the working parties on an IPO

In addition to investment banks, a number of other parties must be appointed to execute an IPO. For all such third-party advisers, several fixed quotes to pay for their services will usually be obtained before appointments are made. It is now rare to pay legal or other advisers by the hour for an IPO, except perhaps for very small transactions.

2.1.1 Legal advisers

Most important are the legal advisers. There are generally "two sides" of legal firms in a primary equity transaction. Broadly speaking, one firm, or one set of firms, advises the issuer and another, the underwriters. Each side can comprise a number of different firms, depending on the nature of the transaction.

The legal firm advising the issuer generally—and always in the US—takes the lead role in drafting the offering circular. It also conducts due diligence into the affairs of the issuer, and advises on listing rules, as well as on the negotiation of the various agreements entered into by the company, both with the banks and other parties. This may for example include a deposit agreement if some global or American depositary shares (GDSs or ADSs respectively) are to be issued. The legal firm also often issues due diligence reports and legal opinions and, if required and if the offering is to be sold to onshore US investors in particular, a disclosure letter.

The legal firm advising the underwriters has a similar role. Traditionally, however, it does not have primary drafting responsibility for the offering circular but generally drafts the underwriting and other agreements, as well as the guidelines for the publication of pre-deal research (where allowed). Although in most markets the sponsoring bank is responsible for communicating with the listing authority or regulator, in the US the legal advisers to the issuer are also tasked with liaising with the Securities and Exchange Commission (SEC) to negotiate the contents of the registration statement.

It is important for the company and the lead banks to decide at an early stage how the US market will be approached. One option (for a non-US issuer) is for ADR certificates evidencing the shares to be listed there, in which case a specific set of rules and standards are observed and the legal advisers to the issuer will liaise with the SEC, even though the issuer remains the "owner" of the document. Alternatively, the issuer can opt to list on a stock exchange outside the US, but retain access to investors in the US pursuant to an exemption from registration for the re-sale of securities there. In practice, this allows the banks to market in the US to large institutional investors only, and to forfeit the option to sell shares to the US public or retail investors, or to smaller US institutions, as would be the case with a local US listing.

This generally entails the banks selling in the US, through a private placement pursuant to Rule 144A of the Securities Act of 1933 (as amended), only to qualified institutional buyers (QIBs), which number several thousand and include most US institutions with assets under management above US$100 million. Alternatively, an issuer can decide not to offer stock in the US at all. This, however, still enables the company to target offshore US institutions under Regulation S (Reg. S) of the Securities Act of 1933 (as amended).

How sales in the US are made is a key decision as the level of disclosure is more demanding in the case of a Rule 144A private placement than for a Reg. S offering: this applies especially to financial information, as will be described in more detail in Section 2.6.

In addition, the US federal and (typically) New York State law arm of the legal firm, or an entirely separate US legal firm if the appointed lawyers do not advise on matters of US law, needs to be involved. It is also customary in the case of a Rule 144A private placement for US legal advisers to deliver to the underwriters a disclosure (or 10b-5) letter, basically confirming that no material information pertaining to the issuer and its affairs has been omitted from the prospectus. This letter is an important component of the due diligence defence for the underwriters, in the event of disciplinary proceedings on the part of the regulators or litigation.

In addition to US law (where necessary), both the issuer and the underwriters need to seek advice as to the local jurisdiction where the company is incorporated, and where the shares will be listed, assuming obviously this is not in the US. For example, in the case of an investment bank involved in an IPO in Hong Kong of a mainland Chinese company with a Rule 144A private placement in the US, legal advice will need to be sought at least as to Hong Kong law, the laws of the People's

Republic of China (PRC law) and US federal and New York State law. In addition, many Chinese issuers are actually incorporated in the Cayman Islands or, more rarely, in Bermuda, so legal advice in respect of these jurisdictions may also be required. It therefore generally makes sense, where possible (and is often better value), for both the issuer and the underwriters to use large legal firms specializing in capital markets law, with a variety of international offices and lawyers and able to provide a "one-stop-shop" service, rather than to involve several legal firms on each side.

Legal advisers specializing in other jurisdictions may also need to be involved to advise on selling restrictions, that is, on the latest regulations on the sale of securities to institutional investors under private placements in a variety of countries where the shares will be offered. Large, one-stop-shop international legal firms are generally also able to advise on such restrictions for the most common jurisdictions: these include "magic circle" firms such as Allen & Overy, Clifford Chance, Freshfields Bruckhaus Deringer, Linklaters, and Slaughter and May in the UK, or "white shoe firms", said to include firms such as Cleary Gottlieb Steen & Hamilton, Cravath, Swaine & Moore, Davis Polk & Wardwell, Latham & Watkins, Shearman & Sterling, and Sullivan & Cromwell in the US. However, such advice may need to be sub-contracted to other local legal firms for some countries. For example, this may on occasion be the case for some provinces in Canada, or perhaps, where required, for Saudi Arabia or the United Arab Emirates. As mentioned above, legal advisers involved in IPOs generally provide a fixed quote—and charge accordingly—for providing advice on a transaction. Cases where legal advisers charge by the hour other than for providing punctual advice on a topical issue or for micro- or small-cap deals are now rare. I personally haven't been involved in an IPO where this was the case.

What matters most when appointing legal advisers and, indeed, any other advisers in an IPO is to identify an experienced partner within the firm who will drive the transaction on behalf of the client. Such a partner will preferably have previously worked on capital markets transactions in the same country and in the same industry sector. While IPOs for general industrial companies usually do not require much prior industry knowledge, this is different for transactions in the financial sector, the mining industry, or for issuers from telecoms or pharmaceutical or healthcare groups. It therefore pays to appoint someone who already has some level of knowledge about, or understanding of the business in which the company operates. Choosing experienced senior associates is also key since they will invariably be in charge of most of the drafting work. Another key issue is to identify at the outset what each law firm will be providing in terms of legal opinions, due diligence reports, and disclosure letters (if any). Their respective scope of work is therefore best decided and agreed prior to the start of the transaction to avoid misunderstandings down the line. Such information is also essential in order for each of the firms of legal advisers to provide a realistic and accurate fee quote.

Examples of the various legal advisers appointed on transactions around the world can be found in the case studies included in Appendix 1.

2.1.2   Auditors

The issuer must also appoint, or in most cases will already have appointed, a reputable firm of auditors, or reporting accountants, as they are called in the UK. Often, issuers coming to market for the very first time will change their auditors, or appoint alongside their existing auditors one of the better known "big four" firms (i.e., Deloitte, EY [previously known as Ernst & Young], KMPG, and PwC) or one of their local affiliates.

Their role is, among other things, to draw up audited accounts according to the generally agreed accounting principles (GAAP) required by the regulator or stock exchange for the relevant period (typically nowadays IFRS). This is generally for at least three years (although it can, more rarely, be five years in some countries), but, depending on the timing of the IPO in relation to the company's year end, it may also be necessary to include accounts for an interim period, either quarterly or half-yearly accounts, together with accounts for the comparable stub period in the previous year. This is because stock exchanges generally require the publication of interim accounts to be made before a certain period after the year end has expired and also because the annual accounts generally go stale for comfort purposes by the auditors after a period of 135 days has expired (see Section 2.8.2). Such interim accounts will generally not be audited, but will be subject to a review by the reporting accountants.

Accountants are also required to provide the issuer and the underwriters with comfort letters in which they will source, cross-check, or re-compute pretty much all the financial information included in the prospectus with the company's existing records. This also includes narratives rather than just the financial accounts and generally takes the form of letters addressed to the issuer and to the underwriters (or senior underwriters on behalf of the syndicate) in which the various procedures that have been performed are explained, and to which a copy of the prospectus is appended, showing the checks that have been made. Comfort letters are explained in greater detail in Section 2.8.

2.1.3   Property valuers

For companies in the property sector, or for real estate investment trusts (REITs), or often simply corporates with substantial property assets (above a certain threshold and depending on the nature of such assets, for example, whether they are for own use, or constitute investment property, or assets held for sale or development), property valuers, such as Jones Lang LaSalle, Cushman and Wakefield (which acquired DTZ in 2015), CB Richard Ellis, Knight Frank, or Colliers International, must be appointed to carry out an independent valuation of the assets, and their report is also included in the prospectus. This valuation is generally conducted on an open-market basis, and follows the format prescribed by the relevant regulator or stock exchange, which itself often follows the rules of the local institute of surveyors. The report includes details of the properties that are the subject of the valuation, their address, description, use, leases, age, details of tenants, and so on. The valuation must also be recent, generally not more than three or six months prior to the time of listing. The property valuers enter into an engagement letter with the issuer and agree to publish their report in the prospectus. The report is reviewed and commented upon by the issuer, lead banks, and the various legal advisers involved in the transaction. In some jurisdictions, certain conditions exist for a firm of property valuers to be able to act in such a role in an IPO, so these should be carefully reviewed prior to any appointment, or the firm should demonstrate that it is qualified to do so to avoid any issues down the line.

2.1.4   Specialist consultants and experts

Companies that come to market in an IPO can fall into a variety of industry sectors. In some cases, other specialist consultants may be called upon to act as experts and provide reports that will be published in the prospectus to assist investors in having a better grasp of a company's business. This can also be a requirement on the part of the stock exchange and/or regulator for issuers from certain industry sectors. Again, such reports often have to follow a prescribed format, or at the very least certain rules on disclosure. For example, they may provide information on market size and market shares, or on commodity or raw material prices.

For mining companies specifically, this typically sets out the amount of their estimated resources and reserves, generally pursuant to one of the standards issued by the Australasian Joint Ore Reserves Committee (JORC), South African Code for the Reporting of Exploration Results (SAMREC), or Canadian Code for the Valuation of Mining Properties (CIMVAL). Investors and research analysts that specialize in mining stocks are very familiar with such reports, which is why disclosure by mining companies will normally follow one of these international and well-recognized standards.

Such consultants may also include those specializing in oil or gas assets; or shipping or traffic consultants in the case of companies in the transportation sector. Examples of such consultants are provided in the case studies in Appendix 1.

In the US, the SEC has issued industry guides for the disclosure of information for businesses active in certain industry sectors, including real estate companies. For example, guidelines for the disclosure of oil and gas operations are referred to as Guide 2; statistical disclosure by bank holding companies are referred to as Guide 3; and those for the description of property by issuers engaged or to be engaged in significant mining operations are referred to as Guide 7. Other stock exchanges usually also have similar guidelines for expert reports and related disclosure, which are generally available for consultation on their respective websites.

2.1.5   Remuneration consultants

Where it is decided to set up an employee share ownership programme (ESOP) prior to, or in connection with, an IPO, specialist remuneration, also called human resources or HR and performance consultants, are sometimes engaged by issuers to help design such schemes, having regard to prevailing local regulations, market practice, tax constraints, and the characteristics of the company's workforce (this will be described in more detail in Chapter 3, Section 3.8). While investment banks can also generally advise on ESOPs, consultants such as Towers Watson, Hewitt New Bridge Street, or Aon Rewards Solutions, among others, can assist in setting up such programmes, including across multiple jurisdictions and tax regimes, and varying levels of seniority among employees.

2.1.6   Roadshow consultants and financial PR firms

It may be necessary to appoint roadshow consultants for large IPOs marketed around the world, when multiple bookrunners are appointed and when the issuer has a sufficiently large senior management office to allow for two or even three teams to travel simultaneously on a roadshow to meet investors. Roadshow consultants such as Media Tree or Imagination specialize in handling the complex logistics associated with air travel, booking hotels and conference rooms, arranging luncheon presentations for wide audiences, as well as inter-city limousine transportation. This can become quite complex as IPO roadshows are by nature dynamic and changing exercises. Investment banks have to remain flexible about where management will travel, depending on investor interest expressed during the investor education phase. While management invariably visit the main financial centres (unless prevented to do so, for example, during the recent COVID-19 pandemic), it may on occasion become necessary to arrange at short notice a trip to Abu Dhabi, Kuwait, or Qatar if there is the likelihood of an investor there placing a US$100 million order in the IPO book. Most large investment banks have in-house roadshow coordination teams. But when multiple bookrunners are involved it can become necessary to outsource this to a neutral provider to avoid petty politics between equity capital markets (ECM) teams. In such a case, investment banks agree in advance which banks will host the various group meetings, with perhaps a senior representative from one bank introducing management at one of the larger venues, and another senior representative from another bank handling a question-and-answer session, and vice versa in another location. Representatives of each of the lead banks usually travel together with management, thereby also perhaps taking advantage of the opportunity to market further corporate finance ideas and business to a (relatively) captive audience over a couple of weeks.

Given the many changes that occur in roadshow schedules in the last few weeks of an IPO, and because of the global nature of the marketing for larger transactions, roadshow consultants need to be well versed in rapid turnarounds and in working in multiple time zones. They may also be asked, for example, to arrange dinners for a large party at popular venues or any other similar or related services. Only a handful of firms specialize in this highly stressful business. Some of the IPO case studies included in Appendix 1 include details of the itineraries and estimated costs for their roadshows, the latter as disclosed in particular in their prospectuses and regulatory filings.

Alongside roadshow consultants, an issuer may find it useful to appoint a financial public relations (PR) or communications firm such as Citigate Dewe Rogerson, iPR Ogilvy & Mather, Hill+Knowlton Strategies, Taylor Rafferty, WATATAWA, Artemis Associates, or Weber Shandwick to help develop its image and promote its investment case to the wider world. Since what can be communicated (and to whom) is highly regulated, and in particular restricted, at the time of an IPO, this needs to be done in close consultation with the legal advisers to ensure consistency with the contents of the prospectus. This may involve the creation, or the update of, a company website, perhaps with the help of a website consultant. It is also quite common for significant advertising campaigns, sometimes with appropriate disclaimers, to coincide with the final stages of an IPO to increase exposure in the media and to the general public.

A practical way to manage the PR process effectively is to identify at an early stage the various events that the issuer may attend, or in which it may participate, together with third parties. This may include trade conferences, result announcements, or any other events held in the ordinary course of business. What is then published or commented upon at those events should be carefully vetted in advance by the legal advisers. Management and all the parties involved in an IPO should also be briefed through so-called publicity guidelines at the outset of the transaction by the company's legal advisers (usually, although not always, the legal advisers to the issuer) on what may (and mainly may not) be disclosed about the company and on the policy for dealing with media enquiries.

An issuer may perhaps also find it useful to work with a financial communications firm following its listing in an IPO to help it organize non-deal roadshows and assist in promoting, on a continuing basis, its business to both the sell-side (in particular, research) and buy-side communities. This can be particularly beneficial in difficult times, or against the background of challenging market conditions, when greater visibility is required, and clear, consistent, and (hopefully) positive messages need to be relayed to research analysts and institutional investors.

2.1.7   Designated market makers

Technically not really involved at the time of the IPO, and solely for those companies listing on the NYSE or the NYSE American (formerly known as NYSE MKT LLC) in the US, one or more independent equity specialists, called "designated market makers" or DMMs since October 2008,[34] may need to be appointed. DMMs are US broking firms responsible for establishing a market and for providing liquidity in given stocks listed on the NYSE or the NYSE American, where prices are set by auction. They effectively work as auctioneers, matching buyers and sellers, resolving imbalances that may exist in the trading of a particular stock and helping to maintain an orderly market. A DMM may need to trade for its own account and sometimes regardless of profitability, in order to achieve this. When listing on the NYSE, between three to five DMMs are generally interviewed in New York, prior to one firm being appointed to act in such a role. There are strict rules for both their interview and appointment. There are no designated market makers on Nasdaq, where several official market makers are required to quote two-way prices for a given security. For example, in the case of a level 2 ADR programme, that is, a listing on Nasdaq without a concurrent offering of stock, a price must be obtained from three or four market makers before the listing can become effective.

2.1.8   Depositary banks

The issuer must appoint a depositary bank in the case of offerings of global depositary shares (GDSs), commonly listed in London or Luxembourg (or in Singapore), or of American depositary shares (ADSs), either listed or unlisted, in the US. The depositary bank effectively issues and redeems certificates, usually denominated in US dollars, that evidence shares in the company and ensures payment (normally in US dollars) through a custodian of dividends to the owners of these certificates. Appointing a depositary bank is generally not a costly exercise for the issuer: this is effectively paid for by institutions trading the GDSs or ADSs, and depositaries will often heavily subsidize and contribute to the costs of creating the depositary receipt (DR) facility. Thanks to recent disclosure rules in the US, information on such subsidies is now publicly available in regulatory filings. For example, Brazilian bank Banco Itau received US$11.9 million from The Bank of New York Mellon in connection with its ADR facility, while Taiwan's telecoms operator Chunghwa Telecom was paid US$10 million by JPMorgan Chase. At the other end of the scale, India's Sify Technologies obtained about US$124,500 from Citibank.[35]

GDSs nowadays are often issued by corporates from countries with restrictive foreign exchange regulations or offering substantial foreign-exchange risk exposure to investors, in effect emerging markets.

The benefits of establishing a DR facility for a company that is already listed on a major stock exchange are debatable. In the US, various "degrees" of DRs exist and an ADR facility may even be established, if there is a market for it, separately from any capital-raising exercise by a corporate, and without its involvement. Some DR facilities are also very illiquid. I will discuss DRs in greater detail in Section 2.15. Many large commercial banks offer depositary bank services, for example The Bank of New York Mellon, Citi, JPMorgan, Deutsche Bank, or HSBC.[36]

2.1.9   Financial printers

I have already mentioned earlier the prospectus that is published by an issuer and distributed to investors in connection with an IPO. A financial printer, such as Bowne or RR Donnelley, who both have offices in most major financial centres, must therefore be appointed to typeset and print what can often be a lengthy and bulky document. While the initial draft is normally produced by the legal advisers to the issuer on common commercial software (at least for IPOs above a certain size; often the lead investment bank itself will be drafting this document on behalf of the issuer for smaller transactions), as the document becomes more complex and as more parties contribute to its contents, it is often more practical to switch to a third party to handle the typesetting, input multiple detailed overnight amendments, and distribute printouts (or nowadays, more commonly, soft copies) to what will become an increasingly large number of recipients. The use of dedicated, password-protected websites has considerably facilitated the logistics of distribution in recent times.

Most members of the core execution team (and generally the more junior ones), together with legal advisers and the accountants, invariably find themselves spending several nights "at the printers" prior to the publication of the preliminary (and, more rarely these days, the final) offering circular to iron out the last details of the document. Printers often have a variety of well-appointed meeting rooms with catering facilities and are able to host large groups involved in the drafting of documents. They can also, particularly in the US, conduct the required electronic filing of registration statements on the SEC's Electronic Data Gathering, Analysis, and Retrieval (EDGAR) database. Lastly (and importantly!), financial printers are also well known for being generous with corporate gifts (although perhaps less so these days, given the increasing regulatory oversight) and hospitality, so are generally popular with investment bankers.

2.1.10 Translators

In some jurisdictions—Hong Kong for example—it is a legal requirement to have prospectuses published in more than one language. In Hong Kong, all IPO prospectuses must be made available to investors in both English and Chinese. In such a case, certified translators are used when the initial draft is near completion to produce the version required in the other language. The translators are also asked to produce a certificate for accuracy, even though all versions of the document are, in any event, thoroughly reviewed by all the relevant parties. Many of the largest financial printers such as Bowne, RR Donnelley, or Merrill Corporation/ IFN Financial Press now also provide (or can sub-contract) quick and efficient translation services.

2.1.11 Share registrars and transfer agents

In most markets the issuer needs to appoint a share registrar and transfer agent, which is often, but not always, a bank, to maintain a record of the public shareholders in the company to establish authenticity of ownership, ensure the accurate payment of dividends, and offer shareholders the opportunity to take up their rights in the event of a rights issue. It is also the responsibility of the share registrar to process and ballot applications from retail investors (which can involve complex calculations and also significant logistics) and to dispatch share certificates to applicants' allocated shares in an IPO. Computershare is an example of a well-known share registrar, originally from Australia but now active in more than 20 countries.

2.1.12 Receiving banks

Receiving banks have already been briefly discussed in Chapter 1, Section 1.8.6. When, as is often the case, an IPO involves a retail offering, receiving banks, usually one or more large commercial banks, must be appointed to manage the application process by members of the public. Unlike institutional investors (who pay for the shares their receive in an IPO under a simultaneous delivery versus payment (DVP) arrangement), retail investors generally pay in advance for the amount for which they apply, and are reimbursed, without interest, for the different between the price paid by them and the final offer price, as well as for the balance between that amount and the amount they actually receive as an allocation. Retail offerings themselves can be effected through a variety of application methods: at bank branches, over the internet, or even, such as in Singapore, through automated teller machines (ATMs).

2.1.13 Stock exchanges

Last but not least, an issuer will normally be required to enter into a listing agreement with the relevant stock exchange, whereby it commits to abide by the initial and ongoing listing requirements and to pay the required listing fees. This is not always the case, though: for example, in Hong Kong, a listing agreement is only required for investment companies listing on the exchange. Short profiles of stock exchanges around the world and of their respective initial listing requirements are provided in Appendix 8.

2.1.14 Market research firms, advertising agencies, and call centres

In very large IPOs only, and particularly in privatizations, such as in the 1980s and 1990s, when billion-dollar equity offerings were untested in most jurisdictions, other than perhaps in the US and Japan, it was common to commission market research firms to gauge the public's interest in a transaction. This took the form of qualitative market research, where retail investors' attitudes towards the issuer (or the IPO, or both) were assessed, often through the use of focus groups. This also involved quantitative market research to test the attractiveness of various incentives. Such incentives could come in a variety of ways: straight discounts, bill vouchers for utility stocks, free or bonus shares (perhaps one free share for 10 shares held), deferred instalments for the payment of shares, or a combination of these. All of the above were used, often with great success, particularly in the early privatizations in the UK in the late 1980s and 1990s.[37]

In addition to market research, it was common to advertise such high-profile IPOs and subsequent, secondary offerings through TV, press, and radio promotional campaigns. Some of us may perhaps still remember the "BP. Be part of it" campaign for the £7.25 billion follow-on privatization of the energy company; the "Tell Sid" campaign for British Gas; the British Telecom third privatization commercials starring Maureen Lipman and promoting the virtues of "tranches" in the early 1990s in the UK; or the "Hello boss!" campaign by MTR Corporation in Hong Kong in 2000. Advertising agencies were therefore at the time also part of the working groups for these new issues. They sometimes still are nowadays, although generally not with such responsibilities or on such a large scale.

Since the public might have questions about the application process, dedicated hot-lines were also made available to explain the procedures to become a public shareholder, where to place an order for the shares, and how to pay for them. For this reason, call centres were often also contracted, although the detailed script used to answer queries from potential applicants is normally drafted by the banks and the legal advisers, both acting on behalf of the issuer. Nowadays, this has pretty much disappeared. It may perhaps be used again for large-scale privatizations in countries that have yet to go through such a process, but IPOs five or ten times the size of the major privatizations launched 20 or even 10 years ago are now regularly brought to market without any shareholder incentives, nor advertising campaigns, let alone call centres to help steer the public through the complexities of the new listing process. Advertising campaigns can also be rather costly, particularly when television is involved (with new media such as the internet, campaigns nowadays may achieve a wide reach at lower prices, although these come with their own issues, such as compliance with securities rules regarding the dissemination of information in what is a truly global medium). The IPO market has come of age.

A template to assist issuers, independent advisers, and investment bankers compute estimates of fees and expenses for the various advisers to be appointed in connection with an international IPO can be found in Appendix 3.

2.2   Strengthening the board

An IPO is often the time when the corporate governance arrangements of a company must be, and are, reviewed. Corporate governance guidelines were introduced in the Cadbury report in the UK in 1992,[38] following the corporate abuses that arose as a result of the collapse of Robert Maxwell's media empire. In 2002, a former S.G.Warburg investment banker, Sir Derek Higgs, was commissioned by the Labour government in the UK to chair a review of the role and effectiveness of non-executive directors, resulting in the publication in 2003 of a report that bears his name.[39] Many recommendations made in the report have now been widely implemented and adapted around the world.

2.2.1   Independent and non-executive directors

Major stock exchanges now require that independent, non-executive directors (or INEDs) (generally at least two or three, or a certain percentage of all board members, typically one-third) be appointed on the board of a listed company. Sometimes, for companies not incorporated in the place of listing, it is also a requirement, for example in Singapore, that at least some of the independent non-executive directors be locally based or local nationals or residents.

One or more of the independent, non-executive directors are additionally sometimes required to have certain professional qualifications or, at a minimum, accounting or financial management experience. Leading investment banks can, most of the time, suggest lists of names and even help to arrange interviews with prospective candidates, as can the Institute of Directors or its local affiliates.

In addition, although this does not specifically apply to INEDs, it is increasingly required on the part of listed companies that a certain proportion of gender diversity be achieved within their boards of directors.

2.2.2   Board committees

In addition to independent, non-executive directors, it is often also a requirement for listed companies to set up board committees. These include, at a minimum, an audit committee tasked with oversight of financial reporting and disclosure and generally composed solely, or mostly, of non-executive and independent directors (one of whom will also chair that committee). At least one or more of the members of the audit committee are often also required to have certain professional expertise. For example, this may include a Certified Public Accountant or CPA qualification, which is a requirement in Hong Kong. For non-US companies listing in the US, the requirement to set up board committees mirrors what is required in their home jurisdictions, whereas US companies are actually required to set up such various board committees.

A remuneration committee can also be established to set up a remuneration policy to attract, reward, and retain executive directors and senior management, balancing their interests with those of shareholders and of the company. Again, such a committee should be composed of a majority of independent, non-executive directors (and chaired by one).

Lastly, a nomination committee can also be set up to discuss the procedures and policies for, as well as the appointment of, directors. As for other committees, this should include a majority of independent, non-executive directors, one of whom will act as chairman.

Other committees (e.g., a risk committee, an investment committee or a committee overseeing the issuer's environmental, social, and corporate governance [ESG] activities) may also be established, depending on the specifics and business of the company. Irrespective of whether these are formal requirements, such changes to the structure of the board of the company constitute in any event good practice, and transparent corporate governance is always appreciated by investors. Nevertheless, and even accounting for the addition of independent and non-executive members, a board of directors is often best kept to a manageable (and, ideally, relatively small) size. Independent, non-executive directors can be appointed for several terms, although there is usually a limit as to how many times their mandate can be renewed. Good practice generally dictates that INEDs will need to relinquish their responsibilities after a period of nine years on the board of a company (unless their sitting on the board for a longer period can be justified), although I am aware of examples of INEDs who have acted in such a role for the same company for more than 25 years, which is obviously an extreme, and probably undesirable, outcome.

2.2.3   Directors' responsibility and insurance arrangements

Directors should be briefed by the legal advisers to the issuer at the outset of the transaction (if already appointed) to enable them to understand the potential criminal and civil liabilities that may apply to them in connection with the IPO. A number of these relate to the contents of the prospectus, since false or misleading statements (or indeed the omission of material information) may trigger legal proceedings on the part of disgruntled investors. The directors of a company applying to listing should thoroughly review and, where necessary, also seek legal advice on, the prospectus and offering circular. They should also be given ample time to do so.

Unfortunately, it is often the case that INEDs are appointed at a late stage in connection with an IPO and not given sufficient time to review transaction documentation. This is obviously a concern given the responsibilities (and potential legal consequences) that come with such a role.

In addition, it is common for companies that are contemplating an IPO (and indeed, most listed companies) to have director and officer (D&O) insurance arrangements in place. These insure the directors and senior management against liability arising from negligence, default, breach of duty and (more rarely) fraud.[40] Most of the large non-life insurance companies can provide coverage and write relevant policies.

2.2.4   Local representatives

A minimum number of authorized representatives generally need to be appointed to serve as the main point of contact for the stock exchange with the company. Often these are directors, although the company secretary, or secretary to the board, can sometimes also act in this capacity. For corporates not incorporated in the country of listing, or whose headquarters are located in another country, most stock exchanges will also generally require the presence of senior management locally, often in the form of two or more executive directors.

For example, in Japan, listed foreign companies whose main market is the Tokyo Stock Exchange (TSE) are required to appoint a local Officer Responsible for Handling Information (ORHI). The ORHI, who plays the role of liaison for investors in Japan, as well as with the TSE, must be selected among executives or officers fluent in Japanese. Conversely, the TSE requests foreign listed companies whose main market is not the TSE to designate a Corporate Information Handling Officer (CIHO) to remain in contact with the TSE and enhance timely disclosure. The CIHO can communicate with the TSE in Japanese or English, and is also generally in charge of corporate disclosure in the home country.[41]

Other stock exchanges in Asia, such as Hong Kong's HKEx or Singapore's SGX, also have requirements for local directors or local representatives to facilitate communication and the handling of enquiries. In the case of HKEx, the corporate governance adviser (see Chapter 1, Section 1.8.8) can also fulfil such a role on behalf of the issuer (which, more often than not, will be a company from the PRC).

2.3   The IPO timetable

The timetable for an IPO depends, in part, on the degree of sophistication of the issuer and on management's familiarity and experience with capital markets. A frequent issuer of publicly traded fixed income instruments, perhaps through a Euro Medium Term Note (EMTN) programme, will already be well versed with the level of disclosure required by a stock exchange and in working with legal advisers and accountants on similar transactions. The company will also generally have good management information systems in place to enable the in-depth analysis required to draft an offering circular. Similarly, a listed group that decides to spin off one of its subsidiaries or a division in a flotation (see Chapter 1, Section 1.1.3) will generally find it comparatively easier to bring another such corporate entity to market.

2.3.1   Availability of financial information

Most of the time, the timetable for an IPO is first and foremost dictated by the availability of the company's accounts for publication in the disclosure document to be filed with the regulator or exchange. In addition, if a company has undergone recent changes in its business, or carried out material acquisitions or disposals in the recent past, it may be necessary to re-compute historic accounts on a pro forma basis, as if the business as it stands today had been in existence in the past few years (typically for a period of up to three years). This may generate a considerable workload for the financial management team and the auditors, particularly if the acquired or sold business is spread across a variety of jurisdictions. For additional information on pro forma accounts, please see Section 2.6.

2.3.2   Due diligence, drafting, and prospectus review

The average company probably needs the best of six, and sometimes up to nine, months, or even longer, from the start of the process to the first day of trading, to execute an IPO. Companies with extensive manpower resources are obviously able to achieve a listing in a shorter space of time. Broadly speaking, the IPO process includes preparation time, comprising due diligence and documentation, and subsequently a marketing phase to investors.

At first, the bulk of the time consists of due diligence carried out on the business by the various advisers, in compiling the financials, and in the drafting and negotiation of the prospectus and other required documentation. This can take several months.

Once it reaches a relatively advanced stage, the draft prospectus can be sent to the regulator or, depending on the market, to the stock exchange for review. In the UK, prospectus review is undertaken by the Financial Conduct Authority or FCA (previously, such review was undertaken by the UK Listing Authority [UKLA]). The FCA is therefore distinct from the London Stock Exchange (LSE). In the US, this review is undertaken by the SEC rather than by the New York Stock Exchange (NYSE) or Nasdaq. Similarly, in Malaysia, it is the securities regulator, the Securities

Commission Malaysia (known in Bahasa Malaysia as Suruhanjaya Sekuriti) that reviews prospectuses, rather than the local stock exchange (Bursa Malaysia). In other markets, such as Hong Kong or Singapore, the prospectus is reviewed by the stock exchange itself (in Hong Kong, the Securities and Futures Commission, or SFC, used to review prospectuses alongside HKEx but now delegates this role to the exchange). The review process can be extremely short as some exchanges or regulators adopt a rather open disclosure regime, and refrain from commenting much once the minimum prescribed information has been disclosed. By contrast, other exchanges or regulators insist on drilling down deeply into the business of the issuer and asking for numerous clarifications to be made and included in the document, sometimes resulting in several hundred questions being sent to the issuer through the sponsor banks or, in the US, through the legal advisers.

The review process generally takes between four and six weeks in the EU and between six and eight weeks in the US. The review process for prospectuses in Hong Kong has recently been shortened under the new regime for IPO sponsors to about three weeks, from 10 or 12 previously, provided that the listing document the exchange receives is in "substantially complete" form.[42] In most other markets, between one to two-and-a-half months are needed for this process, at the end of which, often following a committee meeting or hearing, a letter is usually issued to authorize the company to register the prospectus and to proceed with the listing in principle, sometimes subject to certain conditions, typically around three weeks prior to listing.

A number of documents also need to be submitted to the regulator or exchange in addition to the prospectus, including various confirmations, statements, undertakings, and consents by the issuer and its directors, the auditors and the sponsor banks, the company's accounts, application forms, and copies of corporate documents. Often, a precise timetable is set out for the submission of such documents. For example, the Stock Exchange of Hong Kong previously set out the documents to be submitted precisely 25, 20, 15, 10, and 4 business days prior to the date of the listing hearing, although that timetable has been amended, and also considerably simplified, since the first edition of this book.

A green light by the regulator or exchange may sometimes be given to proceed, but with some conditions for the public offering or listing. For example, in the US$2.2 billion IPO of United Company Rusal, a leading Jersey-incorporated producer of aluminium from Russia, on the Stock Exchange of Hong Kong in 2010, one of the local regulators (the SFC, the other one being HKEx itself) decided to set up a high minimum board lot for the stock by ruling that the shares could not be offered to investors placing orders below HK$1 million in this particular case, thereby effectively restricting the marketing of the IPO pretty much exclusively to professional investors—high net-worth individuals and institutions.[43] Orders from no fewer than 260 institutional investors were said to have been received in the book of demand, with the offering allegedly fully subscribed after only three days of roadshows. The board lot was subsequently lowered twice within a period of 12 months after listing.[44]

Disclosure regimes vary greatly between jurisdictions. In the US, a line-by-line analysis of a company's accounts in a management discussion and analysis of financial condition and results of operations (MD&A) is required to be included in the prospectus. This is not always true for offerings made outside the US, or only targeting offshore US institutions, although regulations in the EU now provide for a similar exercise to be undertaken, as they do in Hong Kong, and indeed nowadays across all major financial jurisdictions.

It is often necessary to draft more than one version of the prospectus. For example, in Spain, the format of the local version of the prospectus, as prescribed by the local regulator, the Comisión Nacional del Mercado de Valores (CNMV), used to be quite different from that most commonly used for international ECM transactions. Most of the information therefore needed to be "re-packaged" and expanded into a format that international institutions were familiar with, and obviously also had to be written in English rather than Spanish. Much has now changed with the introduction of the European prospectus directive, which is explained in more detail in Section 2.7.1.

2.3.3   The marketing phase

If no pre-IPO investor round is conducted, in most markets the marketing phase of an IPO is itself rather compressed—about four weeks in total, of which usually only two weeks or so account for actual order-taking from investors. This enables the lead banks to create a sense of urgency with investors, and to minimize the exposure to what can be volatile market conditions at times. This is not universal. IPOs in Australia are notorious for their long lead-times, perhaps as a result of their heavy retail investor bias, although some forms of equity offerings there, such as rights issues, can now be conducted on accelerated timetables.

In those jurisdictions allowing pre-deal research—most of the world excluding the US, Canada, and Japan—once the prospectus is near its final stage, a presentation will be made by the senior management of the issuer to the research analysts of the banks included in the syndicate. The research analysts are then typically given up to two (or at best three) weeks to publish their rather extensive initial reports, after which some of them will embark on a pre-marketing or pre-deal investor education (PDIE) tour of various jurisdictions around the world for a further two weeks. During this tour they will meet with institutional investors, convey the details of the investment case, obtain their feedback, address any concerns, and, most importantly, assess the perceived valuation of the business by such institutions.

While no research is published in the US, the research analysts there are able to conduct pre-marketing on the back of the registration statement (on Form F-1, for foreign private issuers, or on the more general form of registration statement, Form S-1, for US companies).

The main objective of PDIE is the setting of a price range, on the basis of which the offering will formally be marketed to investors. Once a price range has been determined, the offer itself is launched and orders gathered from both institutional and retail investors. Such institutional and public offers can be simultaneous or sequential, in which case the retail offering follows the institutional offering. They typically take about two weeks in total, after which time the books are closed and the offer price determined on the basis of the investor demand that has been generated.

A recent trend, particularly in Europe, has been for "de-coupled transactions", whereby the roadshow starts without the price range having been decided. This enables the price range to be set backing response to feedback gathered from actual meetings between management and investors, in addition to investor meetings with research analysts. In this case, the bookbuilding is shortened and usually takes place simultaneously with the second week of roadshows. This mirrors to some extent the practice in the US, where price ranges often change throughout the marketing phase of a deal (either up or down) in response to investor demand, perhaps because the lack of published pre-deal research there means that clear valuations for businesses to be listed may not always be available (and comprehensively tested with potential investors) at an early stage.

Allocations to individual institutional investors and, through balloting, to retail investors are then made, often overnight or over a weekend, followed by listing, settlement (also called "closing"), and the start of trading, generally after a period of a few days. Such a deadline is often necessary so that settlement details and confirmations can be gathered from investors, although trading starts pretty much immediately following pricing and allocations in markets such as the US or the UK. In some markets, however, that deadline can be much longer. It can total up to 10 days in Malaysia, perhaps because it takes time to gather retail demand from bank branches in Eastern Malaysia, and to send to and reconcile the information at the head offices of the receiving banks in peninsular Malaysia, although the general trend globally is for settlement timetables to generally become shorter.

2.3.4   Aftermarket activities

The last leg of an IPO consists of aftermarket activities. Once an IPO has started trading, the share price can generally be stabilized by one of the lead banks for a period of up to a month after the date of the final prospectus: the mechanisms for this will be discussed in detail in Chapter 4, Section 4.1. A cooling-off or blackout period, during which no research is conducted on the stock on the part of those banks that have participated in the IPO, is also enforced for a roughly similar period, typically 40 days from listing. Lastly, the issuer, the selling shareholders, pre-IPO, and—in some markets only—cornerstone investors, if any, are often subject to a lock-up during which they cannot sell shares on the market, usually for a period of 6 to 12 months from the date of listing. The reason for the lock-up is to reassure investors that, at least for an initial period of time after the IPO, no further large blocks of shares, whether primary nor secondary, will come to market and depress the share price.

2.3.5   Other considerations on the timetable

During the marketing leg of the timetable, care should be taken to avoid pricing taking place on or around the announcement of important economic statistics or other events that might affect global financial markets, for example the dates for the Federal Open Market Committee (FOMC) meetings, when key decisions are made about interest rates and the growth of the money supply in the US. It is also wise to avoid—to the extent practicable—marketing, during the last week of roadshows, at the time of major competing ECM offerings, that is, transactions in the same geographical market or industry sector. It is especially important to try to avoid being in the market at the same time as very large or "must own" transactions that may result in institutions, particularly those with index funds, overlooking or spending less time assessing the IPO in favour of a more visible offering. Equity syndicate desks will often discuss and check with each other to avoid two or more transactions hitting the market at exactly the same time although on occasion there can be very busy weeks in the primary markets with many offerings clashing with each other.

In addition, certain periods of the year have traditionally been closed to issuance, such as the months of August and December, largely because many institutional investors are away on holidays during the summer and because they often close their books early at the end of the year to prepare their annual accounts—and also to go on Christmas holidays. Chinese New Year in Asia (usually around January or February) or the Holy Month of Ramadan across the Middle East are obviously not conducive to primary ECM activity there for the same reasons. However, market practice has changed, particularly in Asia, and it is now not uncommon to see billion-dollar offerings coming to market in mid-August or IPOs and other ECM offerings marketed until at least a week before Christmas. Requests for proposal sent by issuers in South Korea after 20 December actually appear to be a recurring feature of ECM activity in Asia (and as an investment banker I was at the receiving end of a number of these)!

Conversely, there is often a great deal of issuance activity from September to the end of November, as well as from March to June, as companies' interim and annual accounts become available for publication, and as corporates rush to come to market after a period of lull, before the issuance window closes again. The start of the calendar year prior to Chinese New Year is also frequently a busy time for new issues in Asia. Again, the general rule is that the availability of financial information usually dictates the timetable for an IPO, as already discussed in Section 2.3.1.

2.3.6   Go and no-go decisions

Throughout a transaction, a series of go and no-go decisions can be made at important milestones, with each of these milestones resulting in an increasingly third-party visibility and public profile for the IPO.

A decision not to proceed with an offering can be made at any time during the preparation or drafting work, and prior to the submission of the draft prospectus to the regulator or stock exchange. The next milestone is typically the presentation to research analysts, when the transaction group widens, and when leaks about the transaction may therefore occur in the media. In addition to the research analysts themselves, research assistants and editors for the research reports also become aware of the offering at this stage, hence potentially increasing the risk that confidentiality may be breached.

The key next step is the publication of pre-deal research, when the transaction effectively becomes public knowledge, with details of the deal often relayed in the financial and general media. Pulling a deal after this stage invariably becomes a decision that enters the public domain.

Thereafter, the key milestone decisions are the setting of the price range and the determination of the offer price. It is nearly impossible not to go ahead with an IPO once the offer price has been set (and the deal underwritten) and allocations sent to investors unless a *force majeure* event has occurred. An issuer or its shareholders can, however, relatively easily decide not to proceed with an IPO if they do not like the price range or, indeed, the final offer price. In this case, a statement, generally about weak or unsuitable market conditions, needs to be communicated to the market, since the offering will at that stage already have been extensively pre-marketed, or indeed marketed, to institutions by the research analysts and salespeople. Obviously, cancelling a transaction at such a late stage can result in major sunken costs.

Assuming the price range has not changed during the bookbuilding stage (except, as already mentioned, in the US), and that enough, decent-quality investor demand has been gathered to more than cover an offering at the bottom end of the range, it would be rather unusual to pull a deal on the basis of the final offer price if the price range has previously been accepted by the issuer and if the offer price is determined within that range. It may, however, perhaps become necessary to re-size the offering to a smaller transaction if the deal is only barely covered, or if the quality of the demand gathered in the institutional book is lacking, in which case investors must first be informed of the new parameters for the offer.

Investment banks will generally insist on keeping full momentum during the course of a transaction on the premise that "time kills deals". Once the execution of an offering has been interrupted, for whatever reason, it is often difficult to put an IPO back on track on the same basis. Other investment banks may be appointed alongside or instead of the incumbent bookrunners, while selling shareholders may also start looking for other ways to exit, such as, for example, an outright sale to another corporate or to a private equity firm. Deals are often relaunched as smaller transactions, on lower valuations, and with smaller syndicates of underwriters, to achieve greater focus and accountability. Investment banks know this and will generally push their clients hard to quickly reach the stage when a deal is effectively marketed to investors.

2.3.7   Dual-track processes

In some cases, particularly when significant secondary offerings are part of the offer structure, dual-track IPO processes may be carried out, whereby the major selling shareholders will often look at mergers and acquisitions (M&A) options to dispose of their stakes, in tandem with conducting an IPO process. This can help maximize proceeds and, ultimately, choose the option most likely to generate the best value for shareholders.

A recent (if perhaps extreme) example is the sale of the AIA insurance business in Asia by its parent AIG in 2010. Banks were initially appointed to conduct an IPO. But the process was subsequently put on hold to sell the business in an

M&A transaction to Prudential of the UK. As financial markets tumbled, and
as investors failed to support Prudential at the price it had initially agreed with
AIG for the acquisition, AIG then decided to revert to an IPO solution for AIA,
announcing in July 2010 that Deutsche Bank, Goldman Sachs, and Morgan Stanley
had been appointed as joint global coordinators. Citi was added as a fourth global
coordinator a few weeks later. The flotation, the value of which represented US$20.4
billion equivalent, after exercise of a 20% option to upsize the offering and exercise
in full of the over-allotment option, was launched and priced in October 2010, with
a further seven joint bookrunners (Bank of America Merrill Lynch, Barclays Capital,
Credit Suisse, JPMorgan, UBS, ICBC International, and Malaysian investment bank
CIMB) having also been added to the deal in addition to the global coordinators.[45]
Another example of a dual track process is AS Watson, the retailing division of
Hong Kong's Hutchison Whampoa—known for its chains of beauty and health
stores—which was reportedly well on its way to listing in both Hong Kong and
London in a multi-billion dollar IPO in the first quarter of 2014. In March that same
year, Hutchison decided to sell a 24.95% stake in the business to Temasek Holdings,
a sovereign wealth fund from Singapore, in a deal arranged by Bank of America
Merrill Lynch, DBS, Goldman Sachs, and HSBC, thereby delaying an IPO.[46] As a
last example, in July 2019 US brewer Anheuser Busch InBev had planned to raise as
much as US$9.8 billion through a spin-off IPO of its Asia-Pacific operations in Hong
Kong, to reduce its debt that, at the time, totalled many billion US dollars. When
the company and its shareholder could not realize the price they wanted through a
flotation, they decided to pull the deal and, shortly thereafter, sold the company's
Australian operations in an M&A deal to Japan's Asahi Group for US$11 billion.
The IPO of Budweiser Brewing Co. APACc was later successfully relaunched (in
October 2019, and at a lower valuation), raising about US$5 billion in what was, at
the time, the second largest IPO that year.

In general, the milestones for deciding whether or not to proceed with an
outright sale in a dual-track process are either the date of the presentation to
research analysts, when a larger number of parties become involved in, or at least
engaged in a dialogue about, the transaction; or the publication of pre-deal research;
or, when no research is allowed, when the PDIE starts. After these milestones, the
public profile of the IPO is considerably increased, and it therefore becomes more
difficult, although certainly not impossible, to backtrack and pull the transaction
from the market.

When a dual-track process is involved, and in order to better manage conflicts
of interest, different banks—although not systematically (the banks involved in the

sale of AS Watson, for example, were also said to be those working on the IPO)—can be engaged to manage each avenue separately for the sale of the business.

On rare occasions, a triple-track process may also be initiated, for example when a leveraged buy-out (LBO) or a private equity solution is also contemplated, in addition to an IPO or a trade sale or M&A transaction involving one or more corporates.

2.4   The IPO execution process

The execution of any IPO starts with a kick-off meeting, in which the principal parties involved in the transaction, generally the issuer, an independent adviser (if any), the lead banks, the legal advisers, and, often, the auditors, are introduced to each other, and also briefed by the lead banks on the objectives and initial timetable for the transaction. The kick-off meeting is generally immediately followed by initial due diligence sessions with management. At the kick-off meeting—or perhaps immediately before—a project name is normally decided between the parties so that the transaction can be referred to in a confidential way in the future. As we have already seen, it is preferable that the IPO remains confidential until much closer to launch of the transaction. Publicity guidelines (see Section 2.4.5) are often also communicated to all parties at that time.

2.4.1   Working groups and steering committee

Execution work is most commonly articulated around three modules, or working groups, each comprising members of the corporate IPO team, investment bankers, and, as appropriate, other third-party advisers. These modules focus on documentation, valuation, and marketing. When several banks are involved in a lead role and on an equal footing, a practical way to split the work is to assign primary responsibilities among the banks for each of these working groups (although each of them will in any event be involved in the other working groups as well). Each module will have its own list of tasks and issues.

These modules are usually coordinated by a steering committee, comprising senior representatives of the issuer (and perhaps its shareholders), together with senior bankers from all of the lead banks. The steering committee should meet regularly, perhaps fortnightly, and more frequently as the transaction nears completion, to review the work of each of the working groups. Its functions are to ensure that the timetable for the offering is being adhered to, to address critical steps in the process when decisions by senior management are needed, and to resolve

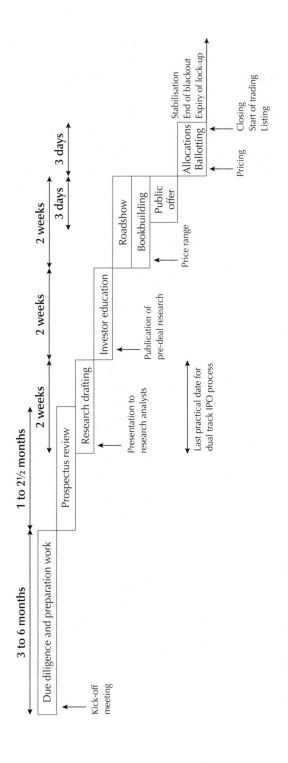

Figure 2

The building blocks of an IPO timetable

any practical difficulties that may arise. Issues related to the composition of the board are also probably best discussed in this smaller (and more senior) forum. It helps if an agenda is drawn up in advance for, and minutes taken of, each meeting of the steering committee, to keep this focused and for future reference, and to keep all key parties abreast of developments. A junior banker is generally assigned to this task, which makes for a good learning experience. When an independent adviser is appointed, and in cases where such appointment is disclosed to the lead banks, it should also participate in the meetings of the steering committee (and will perhaps also take a lead role in such proceedings).

2.4.2   Documentation

Broadly speaking, the documentation working group is primarily concerned with the drafting of the prospectus. While the initial draft of the prospectus is, most of the time, first produced and maintained by the legal advisers to the issuer, all parties (and especially the sponsor bank or banks) are expected to contribute to reviewing and commenting on it. Many sections can often more or less be recycled (with a few changes) or updated from prospectuses for previous, recent, and similar transactions, but a number of these, such as the description of the business, strengths, strategies, and risks, or sections pertaining to financial information, must be drafted from scratch and are clearly unique to a particular issuer.

In addition to dealing with the drafting of the prospectus, the documentation working group is concerned with, and works on, the publicity guidelines (although these are primarily the responsibility of legal advisers), the research guidelines, the form evidencing application to listing, the legal opinions, due diligence reports, and disclosure letters (if any) to be provided by the legal advisers, the presentation of the financials (which may vary, for example if any segment disclosure or an MD&A (see Section 2.6.3) are to be included), and the auditors' comfort letters. This also covers engagement letters for the various advisers and the agreements to be entered into between the banks and the issuer, as well as between the banks themselves and between banks and investors, for example in a pre-IPO or cornerstone investor round, or in the case of placing letters. This may also include arranging and coordinating early visits to the stock exchange and local regulatory body. Finally, to the extent there are third party experts (such as property valuers or geological experts), there will also be engagement letters and forms of reports to be negotiated among the working group.

2.4.3   Valuation

In turn, the valuation working group's main responsibility is the review of the company's corporate business plan and financials, and of the company's capital structure; the identification of comparable companies; and the computation of a discounted cash-flow analysis (if applicable) and comparable company multiples. In some markets, a profit forecast is sometimes included in the prospectus; if so, this will also be the responsibility of this module. In addition, this working group is often tasked with drawing up a computerized financial model that accurately reflects the prospects of the company, to check that the market's expectations are broadly aligned with the reality of the business. This is also a good way to conduct financial due diligence on the issuer.

2.4.4   Marketing

Lastly, the marketing working group is entrusted with a wide variety of tasks, including determining the most appropriate offer structure for the IPO, and with managing, as the name suggests, all the marketing aspects of the deal. This includes:

- the decision on how to access the US market, which needs to be made at an early stage;
- the design of the broad offer structure, which may perhaps involve the use of qualitative and quantitative market research for complex, privatization retail offerings;
- the split of the global offering between various tranches;
- the appointment of more junior banks in the syndicate;
- the research guidelines and selling restrictions, to ensure compliance with local and other regulations;
- the drafting of a presentation to research analysts and of the roadshow video, slides, script, and sample questions and answers for management, themselves in accordance with the contents of the prospectus;
- the management of a pre-IPO or cornerstone investor round (if any);
- financial PR issues and briefings to the media;
- the drafting of "rules of engagement" and of a presentation to syndicate banks;
- the early identification of likely major institutional investors;
- the coordination of pre-marketing, bookbuilding, and of the roadshow (including any internet roadshow), and presentations and briefings to sales teams; and
- managing the decisions on the price range and offer price, as well as allocations of stock to investors, balloting, and stabilization.

To summarize, equity corporate finance and country teams within investment banks will tend to focus more on documentation, industry sector teams on valuation, and ECM teams and equity syndicate desks on marketing issues. Working groups and their principal responsibilities are also summarized in the chart provided as Figure 3.

2.4.5   Publicity guidelines

Importantly, all the parties working on an IPO, including the company, the investment banks, and all external advisers should be briefed by the legal advisers (generally the legal advisers to the issuer) at the outset of the transaction on publicity guidelines. These stress confidentiality, and also explain what may and, more generally, what may not be disclosed about the offering to the public and to the media. In addition, these guidelines typically set out procedures for issuers and shareholders to follow, such as identifying a small number of people at the company in charge of clearing any such communications, as well as for vetting these with the legal advisers and the investment banks, as appropriate. Such guidelines also cover all publications and communications made by the company in the ordinary course of its business, including appearances at conferences, trade shows, and other events, the company's website, and also press releases and other means of communication, such as internal and external newsletters.

It should be noted that not adhering to such publicity guidelines can have unfortunate legal consequences. For example, in the US, this can lead to the SEC imposing a delay on the transaction or to request the inclusion of additional information in the registration statement. To the extent the release of information is found to have been authorized by the issuer, additional disclosure-based liability may apply to the extent there are any material misstatements or omissions with respect to this information. This can, in turn, make it difficult for legal counsel to deliver a legal opinion, for example if certain forecasts have been released by the issuer, or for some investors to participate in the transaction if some contacts with market participants have been initiated during the "quiet" execution phase of the transaction. A good example of this is the US$2.9 billion NYSE IPO of ADSs in PetroChina, China's largest oil producer, in 2000. Ahead of that transaction, Goldman Sachs mistakenly sent an email to 77 hedge funds and institutional investors in the US that included information on the company and reasons to buy the stock. In order to correct the error, it then had to publish the entire email in the risk factors section of the offering circular for the IPO. It was subsequently revealed that the individuals responsible had been involved in similar practices in other equity offerings, including those of China Mobile (Hong Kong) and Taiwan's

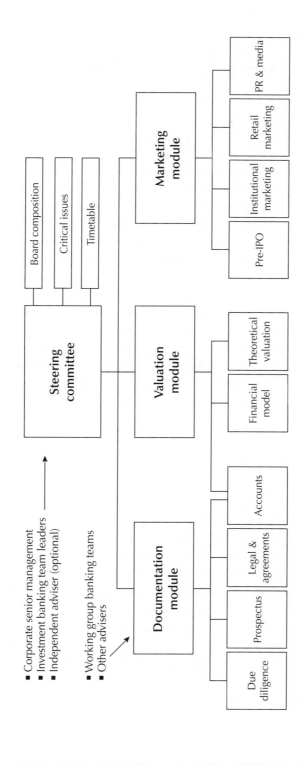

Figure 3

How working parties are best organized to execute an IPO

Gigamedia. Goldman Sachs reportedly paid US$2 million to settle allegations on the part of the US regulators that it had improperly tried to spur interest in these share sales, ahead of the official launch of these IPOs.[47]

2.4.6   Conference facilities

Given the multiple calls that take place throughout the execution of an IPO, and to ensure ease of communication, it is useful to set up at the outset a dedicated dial-in number for conference calls for the core transaction team. This can then be changed a few times during the course of the deal for security reasons and to retain confidentiality. The dial-in number may also be used in the event of an emergency, when members of a particular working group, or indeed of the steering committee, must be convened at short notice to make an important decision and react to events that have occurred. All the major investment banks have "branded" dedicated conference call facilities. Alternatively, these facilities can also be set up directly through telecoms operators. Nowadays, working parties may also make use of online video conference facilities, such as Skype, Zoom, Cisco Webex Meetings, Microsoft Teams, or Adobe Connect, all of which in my experience offer broadly similar functionalities. It should be noted, however, that some issuers, investment banks, and their legal advisers, will likely favour some of these over others, depending in particular on the location of their computer servers, among other factors.

2.5   Due diligence

Due diligence is the process through which the parties involved in the execution of an IPO investigate the affairs of the company, so as to satisfy themselves of the adequacy of the business and the financial and legal aspects of the issuer. Due diligence also helps ensure that all the necessary material information required by a reasonable investor to invest in the IPO has not only been accurately included in the prospectus, but also has not been omitted. Conducting appropriate due diligence provides the basis for any due diligence defence against prospectus liability.

There are three aspects to due diligence in an IPO.

The first is business due diligence, through which the parties involved familiarize themselves with the activities of the company to ensure that these are properly described in the prospectus. Then comes financial due diligence, where the capital structure, budgets, business plans, and financials, both historic and forecast, of the issuer are thoroughly investigated through discussions with management, the reporting accountants, and other procedures. And finally, there is legal or documentary due diligence, which consists of one or more reviews of contracts, certificates, and other legal documents by the legal advisers to check their enforceability and compliance with relevant laws, rules, and regulations, as well as the consistency of the disclosure.

Both the business and financial due diligence generally consist of a series of interviews of, presentations by, or question-and-answer sessions with senior and operational management from relevant divisions of the issuer. Sponsors are also usually asked to ascertain that the directors and management teams are suitably qualified and have the requisite experience to run the business.

Stock exchanges and regulators typically do not provide much guidance or specify the extent of or areas that due diligence should cover. When they do, this is usually by way of example only (the listing rules in Hong Kong specify in a document known as Practice Note 21 (or PN21) some aspects of due diligence to be conducted by sponsors in connection with an IPO, but these are by no means exhaustive; PN21 is, in any event, a fairly short document). In other words, it is for the sponsor(s) and, as applicable, other lead banks of an IPO to determine, on a case-by-case basis, what they will investigate, so as to provide investors with all the material information they need and not omit any information that may be relevant. This is in a way perhaps slightly unfair since a number of sponsors have been handed down fines and other penalties for failing to conduct adequate due diligence in connection with IPOs, even though precise guidelines to that effect were in practice not available or, at best, limited. Accordingly, due diligence very much depends on judgement calls on the part of sponsor banks (and, to some extent, their third-party advisers, although ultimately final responsibility in this regard rests with the IPO sponsors themselves).

2.5.1   Questionnaires, verification notes, and responsibility

Typically, detailed questionnaires are circulated in advance to the issuer by the investment banks and the legal advisers. These form the basis for meetings with management, during which the business of the company is examined in detail. This enables all the parties involved to have a good understanding of the business and of the financials of the company, so that they can be appropriately reflected in the offering document.

This also enables the identification of potential issues, problems, or risks associated with the IPO so that they can be resolved before the company comes to market. For example, it may become apparent that certain key assets, or contractual or intellectual property rights, are actually owned by a parent or third-party company. It may also be the case that certain covenants under existing loans granted to the company may prevent the company from becoming public or require prior consent.

During the course of these discussions, management can be challenged on certain issues. This is also good preparation for their meetings with investors at a later stage. In certain jurisdictions, for example the UK, the US, and Hong Kong, every narrative in the prospectus is subject to a formal check in the form of a "verification note" by the legal advisers, so that it can be confirmed, sourced, and ultimately signed off by an appropriate party involved in the offering (typically this will be the issuer itself).

Traditionally, information included in the prospectus and specifically provided by the underwriters to the issuer is very limited and either mentioned in the underwriting agreement or in a separate document known as a "blood letter".[48] Investment banks (other than the sponsor banks, who have a particular responsibility with respect to due diligence and disclosure of information on the issuer to the stock exchange, regulator, and investors) will only generally formally sign off on information pertaining to, or statements related to, themselves, since the prospectus is ultimately the responsibility of the issuer and in some cases in part of the selling shareholders (if any). Comfort on the financials, as we have seen earlier, is also provided through the auditors' comfort letters. Recently, there have been some attempts on the part of regulators to make senior underwriters (other than sponsors) take responsibility for the disclosure of information by issuers although, as of the first quarter of 2021, this has been (understandably) strongly resisted by investment banks and has not come into effect.

2.5.2   Business and financial due diligence and site visits

Business due diligence is usually spread out over many sessions, held over a number of days, to enable a review of all the aspects of the business. This review ranges from the origins of the company, to its strategy, strengths, weaknesses, threats, opportunities and prospects, shareholder and capital structure, directors and management team, principal lines of business activities, competitors, suppliers, clients, management information systems, insurance arrangements, and possible risks of, or existing, litigation. Third parties may also be contacted, for example lending banks, insurers, major suppliers, or clients, to cross-check information. Physical due diligence also takes place through visits to offices, factories, plants, or other production facilities to ascertain that the company possesses the assets, equipment, and inventory necessary to the conduct of its business. For example, I have visited facilities as diverse as rice processing and packing plants, steel mills, and a textile retailer's production and storage units in Spain; computer centres in Germany; factories for handheld electronic devices and stainless steel goods in mainland China; shipping, logistics facilities, and business parks in Singapore; bank branches in South Korea; concessions for tropical hardwood harvesting in Borneo in Eastern Malaysia; shopping malls in Thailand; and pisciculture basins for the breeding of shrimps in Indonesia.

It should be noted that, increasingly, regulators expect sponsor banks to, among other things, fully interact with third parties when conducting due diligence. Notes must be kept of meetings with such representatives (including full details of their identities) and detailed questions asked about their relationship with the issuer (which should also be documented). One can no longer rely on simple written confirmations, and original documents, rather than copies, must also be sighted. The information gathered must be cross-checked through other means, and any discrepancies fully investigated. To the extent that an issuer has, for example, obtained certain licences, these must be verified *in situ* at the licensing office, rather than taking what management says at face value, or rely on photocopied documents. The same is true of degrees, diplomas, or education certificates, which should ideally be verified directly with the issuing bodies. Nowadays failure to follow such procedures (although this was typically not the case only a few years ago) can result in heavy disciplinary consequences (including fines, naming and shaming, or even licence holidays) for the sponsor banks.

Consultants or experts may also be appointed to assist in the due diligence process and to "expertise" the disclosure. These may include specialist consultants or experts, depending on the nature of the company's activities, as well as private investigators such as Kroll Associates, FTI-International Risk, Control Risks, or PICA Corporation and, in Asia more specifically, Hill & Associates, Lyriant Advisory (formerly known as Spectrum Asia Partners), or ChinaWhys, to establish the existence, legality, or legitimacy of the business, especially in emerging markets.

The same is applied to the financials, much as an audit team would review the accounts in pre-identified cycles. This will also generally include a discussion with the company's current auditors and, often, past auditors, ideally without the presence of the issuer itself, although this is not always possible. Again, increasingly, IPO sponsors cannot fully rely on the information provided by such experts, must approach it with a "questioning mind", and be able to demonstrate that they have taken steps to cross check it and investigate any potential issues that could reasonably have been identified by them. While IPO sponsors are not expected to conduct forensic investigations into the business of an issuer, what is expected of them nowadays can be very demanding indeed. On occasion, even the results of a financial audit cannot always be taken at face value if it can be shown that the sponsors ought to have identified certain issues while discharging their duties.

It may sometimes be necessary to update prior due diligence because of new developments. "Bring-down" due diligence, in addition to bring-down comfort letters delivered by the auditors, is also performed to re-confirm the absence of new issues prior to pricing, closing, and often the exercise of an over-allotment option, so as to satisfy all parties. In some cases it may not be possible for the auditors to deliver a bring-down comfort letter upon exercise of the over-allotment option since, by then, 135 days will already have expired since the date of the latest set of financials included as part of the disclosure for the IPO. In such cases, conducting bring-down due diligence becomes even more important.

Detailed notes are usually kept of due diligence meetings. Indeed, it is sometimes a requirement by stock exchanges or regulators to keep minutes of the meetings of a dedicated due diligence or declarations committee formed to investigate the affairs of the issuer. The reason for this is that such notes or minutes are often the only way through which IPO sponsors can demonstrate to a regulator that (and how) they have focused on certain aspects, and investigated some issues that may later become litigious. Another school of thought opposes this to minimize liability in the event of litigation and potential discrepancies with statements included in the prospectus, although this is likely more applicable to firms that are not acting in a sponsor capacity. A reasonably comprehensive, although by no means exhaustive, generic business and financial due diligence checklist is included in Appendix 2.

2.5.3   Documentary due diligence

The format for documentary due diligence varies. Usually, a list of documents requested from the company is compiled by all the legal advisers working on the transaction so that documents can be made available for consultation in a data room, much as would be the case for M&A transactions, although generally over a much longer period of time and of a more comprehensive nature. The requested information typically ranges from, for example, certificates of incorporation of the issuer and of its material subsidiaries to minutes of the board of directors and of board committees (both for the issuer and for its subsidiaries); major employment contracts; documents covering related-party or connected-party issues; internal documents on company procedures; insurance policies, material supplier contracts; contracts with the company's main clients; certificates of title for properties and for the company's main assets; major loan and other finance agreements; and tax records and certificates. Usually, the legal advisers, investment banks and the issuer agree on a threshold to determine materiality at the outset of the process. For example, this may perhaps be defined as 5% of assets, sales, or, more rarely, profits. The documents are then primarily reviewed by the legal advisers, as well as other parties working on the transaction.

Documentary due diligence is also used to substantiate or corroborate statements made by the issuer during business or commercial due diligence. For example, the banks and their advisers may want to verify the issuer's claims to have a number one or leading position in a particular field or business activity, or to have a particularly collaborative relationship with certain customers or suppliers (typically through physical interviews, which must be documented, and increasingly in detail). Again, it may be necessary to add new documents as the transaction progresses.

Nowadays, a shared, virtual data room (VDR) is generally used rather than a physical data room for the upload, storage, and review of documents for due diligence purposes. These password-protected websites (often run by VDR providers owned by financial printing companies or by the legal firms working on the transaction themselves) also enable several advisers to peruse documents simultaneously and remotely, thereby saving time and making the process more efficient.

2.5.4   Syndicate and other due diligence

A call or meeting with management to offer an opportunity to the junior members of a syndicate of underwriters (co-lead and co-managers) to conduct limited due diligence is sometimes convened by the lead banks. In addition, a limited number of documents may also be made available to junior members of the syndicate. In practice, however, junior underwriters rely heavily on due diligence conducted by the sponsor banks, global coordinators, bookrunners, and legal advisers, and, in any event, do not have the liability risk of houses acting in more senior roles, and especially that of the sponsor banks.

Finally, it is also usual to conduct one or more due diligence sessions with the shareholders of a company, especially when a sell-down is conducted by such shareholders, either in connection with an IPO or once the company has become listed for a follow-on transaction. Such due diligence can serve to corroborate information gathered from the issuer and to further ascertain that no unforeseen events or announcements will take place shortly after the sell-down has been conducted. Obviously, in the event of a spin-off IPO (see Chapter 1, Section 1.1.3), due diligence with the parent company will for obvious reasons be considerably expanded, as opposed to that conducted in connection with a more simple sell-down by one or more shareholders.

2.6   Financial information

Financial information is one of the most important components of the prospectus registered with the regulator or stock exchange and sent to investors in connection with an IPO. Indeed, as noted earlier, the availability of financial information is often one of the key factors driving the timetable for a new listing, particularly when a company has undergone significant changes in the years preceding the offering.

When sizeable acquisitions or disposals have been completed during the current or prior financial year, it is usually necessary to draw up pro forma accounts, so as to show the financial position of the company as if the company structure immediately following completion of such transaction had been in existence at the beginning of the preceding years. These obviously take time to compile. Under EU rules for pro forma accounts, only the latest financial year and any applicable interim period of pro forma information is actually required to be included, with a materiality test representing 25% of assets, revenue, and net profit or loss. Under US rules (governed principally by "Regulation S-X"), disclosure for similar periods is also required, though the materiality thresholds and tests differ in various respects. Alternatively, historical "combined" financial information may be included in the disclosure if no pro forma adjustments are required and, as is often required, the same auditor has been responsible for the audit of all the financial information. In such a case, the "combined" financial information may go beyond one year, as this information is historical, and a "high level" of comfort, often "audit-level comfort", can be given by the auditors. Some exchanges, however, insist that pro forma accounts are shown for the entire period under review (that is, generally, at least three full financial years). In addition, although most regulators require only pro forma profit and loss statements and balance sheets, some (such as in Malaysia) additionally require pro forma cash-flow statements. In either case, the working group may need to work to limit the amount of such information provided and increase the level of comfort, so as to reduce the liability inherent in providing pro forma information for such a long period.

In the case of a newly acquired company, stand-alone financial information may be required alongside the pro forma financial information. This may also be required when meeting materiality thresholds under the relevant disclosure rules or for marketing purposes. Conversely, when issuers have spun off or sold a subsidiary or company during the period under review, creating accounts carving out the financials for such a subsidiary or company can also take a considerable amount of time, especially when conducted over several financial reporting periods.

Requirements for the inclusion of financials vary according to the regulator or stock exchange on which the company lists. Most of the time, except for minerals or project companies, three years of historic, consolidated financials are required. The rules also specify the accounting standard under which the accounts may be presented. Sometimes, several accounting standards are accepted by the regulator or the exchange, and the company is given the option to choose one or another. For example, the Stock Exchange of Hong Kong accepts both Hong Kong Financial Reporting Standards (HKFRS) as well as International Financial Reporting Standards (IFRS) and, in certain circumstances, US GAAP. In addition, it also accepts and recognizes China Accounting Standards for Business Enterprises (CASBE) for PRC companies. Increasingly, however, IFRS is now pretty much the norm globally. Details of the accounting standards accepted by major stock exchanges around the world are set out in Appendix 8.

Three types of financial information are generally included in a prospectus.

2.6.1   The F pages

First are the accounts themselves, generally found at the back of the document, in the so-called F pages, which are typically numbered F-1, F-2, and so on, hence their name. These will include the auditors' reports for each financial year, including the auditors' opinion on the financial statements, as well as the consolidated profit and loss accounts, balance sheets, cash-flow statements, and notes to the accounts for the same periods. In some cases, when the end date for the latest audited accounts is older than a specified period of time (usually four to six months), then interim accounts should also be included, together with interim accounts for the comparable, stub period in the previous year. Interim accounts are generally not audited, but are instead subject to review by the accountants. Another reason for including interim accounts may be when more than 135 days have elapsed since the latest published accounts. This is because audit firms will then resist providing comfort letters that include negative assurance language. This will be further discussed in Section 2.8.

2.6.2   Other financial information

In addition to the accounts themselves, financial information always appears elsewhere in the prospectus. This will often take the form of a summary of the financials, which is generally included in the first few pages of the prospectus, a section on the company's capitalization and indebtedness, and details of the company's dividend policy. Financial information may also be included within narratives throughout the document, for example when describing the business of the company, or in the management discussion and analysis, which I discuss in the next section.

2.6.3   The management discussion and analysis (MD&A)

When the IPO is marketed in the US, for example, pursuant to a Rule 144A private placement, as well as to comply with disclosure requirements by certain stock exchanges (e.g., in Hong Kong, Malaysia, Singapore, or, more generally, throughout Europe), it is market practice also to include a management discussion and analysis of financial condition and results of operations (MD&A). This consists of a narrative discussion and explanation of the key factors affecting financial results and the changes in the principal line items in the company's consolidated profit and loss account and cash-flow statements for the periods under review for the full financial years and interim accounts, when included. A similar analysis is also conducted on the company's capitalization and indebtedness. MD&As typically include a summary of the company's critical accounting policies, to enable readers to gain a better understanding of which significant accounting policies may be impacted by judgements made by management. Other information commonly found in an MD&A includes: material commitments and contractual obligations; off-balance sheet arrangements and contingent liabilities; quantitative and qualitative disclosure about risk (credit, liquidity, market risk—foreign exchange, interest rate risk, or equity price risk—and the fair value of financial instruments); key financial ratios; government, economic, fiscal and monetary policies (if relevant); prospects; tax issues; seasonality impacts; and disclosure of any material adverse change in the financial or trading position of the company since the end of the period reported on in the accounts.

SEC-registered offerings (by companies listing in the US) always include an MD&A, so the aim in a Rule 144A private placement is generally to mirror what is required for US offerings. Conversely, while it was not previously necessary to include an MD&A in a prospectus for Reg. S offerings, many investment banks will still nevertheless insist that issuers do so, and this is, in any event, becoming the norm for all IPOs. It is also usually a requirement for offerings of DRs.

In addition, in Europe, and particularly in the UK, there has now for some time been a requirement for issuers to include an operating and financial review (OFR), which is similar to an MD&A.

Where included in a prospectus, MD&As are often placed before the description of the company's business. This is in my view not entirely logical but nevertheless reflects market practice.

2.6.4 Segmentation of accounts

It is often helpful, and it is normally a requirement when listing in the US, to assist in the analysis and comprehension of the consolidated accounts, if segment information is included as part of the profit and loss account for revenues and operating profit, for example, on a divisional or geographical basis, or to help the analysis of a company's assets. Obviously, this may not be necessary for a company that has a simple or straightforward and/or purely domestic business. Companies are sometimes reluctant to disclose such information as they feel it may give away too much to competitors. This matter should be discussed with the lead banks early in the transaction since including such information may also generate significant additional work on the part of the reporting accountants. For companies reporting under International Financial Reporting Standards (IFRS), IFRS 8 deals with the segmentation of accounts; such segments are normally required to be included when they represent more than 10% of the revenue, profit or loss, or assets of the company. As previously mentioned, in Malaysia, when more than 50% of a company's net profit is generated within Malaysia, a dedicated tranche targeted at *Bumiputera* investors must be included as part of the IPO. Companies not subject to this requirement may obviously also choose to do so on a voluntary basis, perhaps for political reasons (e.g., if they are a government-linked company, otherwise known as a GLC).

2.6.5 Profit forecasts

In some jurisdictions, for example in Hong Kong, a profit forecast for the coming financial year end may be included in the prospectus, although this is not a requirement under the listing rules. This takes the form of a "not less than" figure and is generally only included in the domestic version of the listing document. It is rare for such profit forecasts to be included in offering circulars that are distributed in the US. When a profit forecast is included, it is essential that the forecast is not only met by the issuer later on, but also, ideally, comfortably exceeded. In March 2014, night club operator Magnum Entertainment announced a profit warning barely two months after its blow out, US$16.3 million IPO in Hong Kong, which saw its retail tranche almost 3,600 times subscribed by members of the public and its share price double on the first day of trading. This triggered a sharp fall in the stock to well below the IPO offer price. Rather curiously, the profit warning was blamed on "non-recurring listing expenses", obviously something that listing candidates should clearly try to avoid and ideally should have been able to identify at a relatively early stage.[49]

In Hong Kong, profit forecasts are typically included in a prospectus when a company comes to market at a time that is close to its financial year end. In such cases, the issuer and its advisers will in normal circumstances have good visibility on the company's future financials, and should be able to disclose a profit forecast with reasonable accuracy.

As mentioned above, all (or at least the vast majority of) the financial information included in the prospectus, whether in the F pages, summary of financial information, section on capitalization, narratives, or in the MD&A, is typically the subject of comfort letters delivered by the accountants. Comfort letters are addressed in detail in Section 2.8.

2.6.6   Financial disclosure in the US

For international (i.e. non-US) companies listing in the US, which are also referred to as "foreign private issuers", it is usually necessary to include, in the registration statement, financial information either in conformity with US GAAP or under the local GAAP, with a reconciliation of material differences between local GAAP and US GAAP, together with an explanation of the material differences between such local GAAP and US GAAP. The reconciliation to US GAAP is normally required for shareholders' equity and net profit.

However, since November 2007 (and effective since 4 March 2008), private foreign issuers listing in the US do not have to reconcile their accounts to US GAAP if they report under International Accounting Standards Board (IASB) IFRS. The rules are applicable to the financial years ending after 15 November 2007. It should be noted that, while most companies reporting under local variations of IFRS in the EU should be able to state that they are effectively reporting under IASB IFRS for the purpose of filing with the SEC, some may not. In particular, hedge accounting under IAS 39 (subsequently replaced by IFRS 9, which was published in November 2013, and which deals with the recognition and measurement of financial instruments) may be different under IFRS as adopted by the EU and IASB IFRS, and accordingly may not qualify for disclosure in the US under SEC rules without a reconciliation to US GAAP.[50] In 2013, the IASB tentatively decided to require an entity to apply IFRS 9 for annual periods beginning on or after 1 January 2018.

As an example, while accounts were published in conformity with US GAAP for the Nasdaq IPO of Shanda Games in 2009,[51] in the case of Banco Santander Brasil's

IPO on the NYSE in 2010, reporting was under IFRS as well as under Brazilian GAAP.[52] Case studies for both offerings are included in Appendix 1. In any event, US GAAP and IFRS are converging, and in 2013 more than 120 countries allowed or required the use of IFRS.[53] According to the IFRS website, this had increased to 166 countries in 2019 (that is, two-thirds of all the countries recognized by the United Nations and almost 85% of the countries recognized by the US).

In the US, audited income and cash-flow statements for the last three years and audited balance sheets and changes in shareholders' equity for the last two or three years, depending on market practice in the issuer's country of incorporation, are required to be presented on a consistent basis. In addition, where the company has been in existence for more than three years, condensed or selected financial information is required for up to five years.

For foreign private issuers, interim reporting in the US can be on the basis of home country and stock exchange practice rather than in the form of quarterly reports, although in practice non-US companies listed in the US generally publish quarterly interim reports. In addition, while federal securities laws require clear, concise, and understandable disclosure about compensation paid to CEOs, CFOs, and certain other high-ranking executive officers of public companies, disclosure of executive compensation may be conducted on an aggregate basis rather than through individual disclosure, if permitted in the issuer's home country.

It should be noted that many jurisdictions now require quarterly reporting on the part of companies listed on their main board, one notable exception being companies listed on the Main Board in Hong Kong (even though companies listed in Mainland China are required to issue quarterly accounts). Companies listed on GEM, the Second Board of HKEx, must report on a quarterly basis, however.

Lastly, as outlined above, segmentation of financial information, on a geographical basis or according to the issuer's principal activities on a divisional basis, is normally required for revenue, operating profit, and assets in the US.

2.7   The prospectus

The prospectus is, legally, the only publication that investors should use in order to make an investment decision to buy shares (or certificates evidencing shares) in an IPO. This generally takes the form of a physical and often rather bulky document, although recent technological developments mean that, more often than not, soft copies are now made available to investors in Adobe Acrobat .pdf format, subject to local rules and regulations. As I discovered working on an IPO in Malaysia, there are physical limitations as to how many pages (approximately 1000 or so) can actually be included in a single printed and bound prospectus. However, printing more than one volume, although probably unwieldy and cumbersome, is always—in theory at least—an option.

Following a recent consultation, companies seeking to list shares in Hong Kong through public offers are now able to distribute paper application forms as long as the prospectus is available over the internet and on the stock exchange's and the issuer's websites, subject to certain conditions.[54] In addition, the first IPO there (in practice a secondary listing) for which prospectuses were exclusively published as soft copies was that of Alibaba (for US$11.2 billion) in 2019.

Prospectuses generally follow a prescribed format, which varies from country to country and depends on the regulator or the stock exchange on which a company chooses to list. As mentioned earlier, they can sometimes appear in more than one version or language, in which case the prospectus will be drafted in one language, usually English, and certified translations will be used for the other version. English is commonly used for prospectuses distributed internationally. Prospectuses are used for both retail and institutional investors, although different versions (one of which will be slightly redacted) are often drafted for each tranche. They are meant to include all the information deemed relevant to potential investors.

Often, the term "offering circular" is also used to describe a prospectus, although technically an offering circular only forms part of a prospectus and only includes information necessary for institutional, rather than for retail investors. In the US, a prospectus is part of the wider registration statement that is filed with the SEC for an SEC-registered offering. Here, I use the terms "prospectus", "offering circular", "registration statement", and "listing document" indifferently to keep things simple and to avoid unnecessary confusion, since they all ultimately refer to the main document, even if produced in slightly different versions, that is published by an issuer in connection with, and used to market, an IPO.

Irrespective of the format and country, prospectuses will generally have similar contents. Indeed, more than 115 jurisdictions, regulating more than 95% of the world's financial markets, have adopted common guidelines on disclosure standards through the International Organization of Securities Commissions (IOSCO), an association created in 1983 and based in Madrid comprising organizations that regulate the world's financial markets.[55] In the EU, the European prospectus directive has also harmonized disclosure requirements within member states.

2.7.1   The European prospectus directive

The European prospectus directive was introduced at the end of 2003 (for implementation by member states by mid-2005) to simplify and harmonize the disclosure requirements for issuers of securities in the EU by establishing a "single passport regime" for prospectuses. Broadly speaking, issuers in the EU are now only required to use a single prospectus once approval by the competent listing authority of one of the EU countries has been obtained. For issuers incorporated in the EU, the authority that may grant the authorization to list equity securities is that of the member state in which the issuer is incorporated.

The directive has also eliminated the need to publish additional prospectuses in the case of multiple listings within the EU. It has also contributed to generalizing the use of English as a language "customary in the sphere of international finance" for the drafting of prospectuses, although translation of a summary in a local language can still be required in certain circumstances.[56] As of the first quarter of 2021, it was not exactly clear whether there would be any changes to disclosure in the UK as a result of Brexit, although I suspect that, if any, these would be minimal.

Most importantly, the prospectus directive has introduced detailed requirements for the form and content of prospectuses, largely based on standards set out by IOSCO. These are, in fact, also fairly similar to US disclosure standards. In particular, the directive has introduced:

- the split of a prospectus into three distinct components: a registration document, in effect a detailed document similar to an annual report, but covering the entire period under review, typically three years; a securities note, detailing the terms of the securities on offer; and a summary, thereby facilitating the regular issue of securities by frequent issuers, effectively through a "shelf" registration mechanism similar to that existing in the US for well-known seasoned issuers (WKSIs) or for fixed-income medium-term note programmes;
- rules for listed companies on the disclosure and publication on an annual basis of information issued in connection with securities laws; and
- the generalization of International Accounting Standards (IAS), and subsequently International Financial Reporting Standards (IFRS), or equivalent accounting standards, for the publication of accounts for companies listed in the EU.

2.7.2   Additional disclosure for US investors

When an IPO is marketed in the US, additional disclosure is included for the benefit of US investors. In such a case, the prospectus will also include standard language warning US investors about limitations on the enforceability of civil liabilities since, usually, most of the assets of a non-US issuer will be located outside the US. This includes statements to the effect that it may not be possible to: effect service of process; enforce court judgments obtained against the company, its directors, or executive officers in the US; or enforce through legal action abroad liabilities predicated upon US securities laws.

For companies that are listed in the US, Regulation S-K of the Securities Act of 1933 (as amended) itemizes what must be disclosed in the registration statement to be filed with the SEC, with a focus on non-financial information, whereas financial information to be included in such registration statement is covered under Regulation S-X. Note that disclosure requirements for US companies are somewhat different from those for foreign private issuers in the US.

2.7.3   House formats or styles

Each investment bank usually has a recognizable (but only to people working in the financial services industry!) "house" format or style for the cover and (less visibly) inside pages of prospectuses. However, a "neutral" format and typeface is generally negotiated and agreed upon when more than one lead bank is working on the same transaction. The names of the lead banks are also often stated in alphabetical order on prospectus covers to avoid petty politics about appearance (for more information on appearance, see Chapter 1, Section 1.8.8). Since appointing more than one lead bank is now pretty much the norm, except for small or very small IPOs, the use of such neutral prospectus covers has become commonplace. Some exchanges also favour a certain format—the IPO prospectuses for deals in Hong Kong all tend to look pretty much the same nowadays.

2.7.4   Detailed contents

A prospectus includes general and statutory information, such as the company's name, registered address, a summary of the company's memorandum of association and selected by-laws, and other contact details, for example details of any corporate website. A summary of the prospectus itself, including a few paragraphs on the company and its business as well as selected financial information and operating data over four or five pages, is often included at the outset, although this should be read in conjunction with the entire document. The prospectus also usually includes a glossary of defined terms and abbreviations.

Risk factors generally figure in a prominent place at the start of the offering circular. These are factors that have been identified during due diligence and which, if they were to occur, would affect the financial condition and results of operations of the company and, ultimately, the value of the shares. While some are rather general or boilerplate, others point to specific factors unique to the company, which may present a risk for investors buying the shares. For example, the business of the company may be extremely dependent on a small number of senior individuals, or it may rely on a small number of suppliers or clients, the loss of any of which may materially affect the financial condition and results of operations of the company. Although they are ultimately included for the protection of the company, and to fend off claims on the part of investors in case of dramatic developments, the inclusion of risk factors is often a contentious issue with management teams when drafting the prospectus. This is because it can be felt that they portray the company in a negative light (which they undoubtedly do to some extent) and might therefore hinder the success of the offering, or at least the valuation of the shares in the IPO. Investors are, however, familiar with their inclusion and they do constitute an essential part the offer document. It is also relatively common (although less so in recent times) to include specific risk factors for the benefit of US investors when the IPO is marketed in the US. These will generally point to differences in market practice, disclosure, or use of currency in the country of listing, compared with those prevailing in the US. All risk factors include a heading, followed by a more detailed narrative. Risk factors are generally included in a logical order, starting with the most important ones. Examples of risk factors are included in Appendix 5.

Should the IPO include a primary offering, that is the raising of new money, information on the intended use of the proceeds should be given. The reason for the listing and effect of such capital raising, including any dilution, should also be shown in the summary of the company's capitalization and indebtedness and in the sections dealing with share capital and the company's ownership, both pre- and post-IPO as well as pre- and post-exercise of the over-allotment option, if any, and generally including all shareholders owning more than 5% of the share capital of the company. Particular attention should be paid to how the use of proceeds are described. These should be reasonably detailed (i.e., avoiding descriptors such as funds raised for working capital or general corporate purposes) and, generally, a specific statement should be included for 10% or more of the amount to be raised under the flotation. Typically, these are also listed starting from the larger percentage to which proceeds have been allocated, and then in descending order. As many internet companies discovered after the dot com boom, investors are wary of vague descriptions and will focus a great deal on the uses ascribed by issuers to new money raised in an IPO when building their valuation models. Ideally, amounts set aside for large and clearly identified purposes should be disclosed, although, at the same time, the company may also want to retain the flexibility to create a war chest or to constitute reserves, perhaps with a view to conducting acquisitions in the near future. Some examples of the use of proceeds from primary offerings are included in the case studies shown in Appendix 1.

Information on the capitalization of the company should be recent, generally not more than 60 days old (and typically a shorter period than this). A description of the company's shares and of its dividend policy is also required information.

In the event of a transaction marketed in the US, either by way of a private placement or of a local listing, or as required under the listing rules in other countries, an MD&A should also be included. As we have seen, the MD&A is in effect a discussion of the reasons behind the changes in selected main-line items for the accounts. The MD&A is actually required to be filed on a continuing basis with the SEC for companies listed in the US, and is generally in the form of an OFR in the EU. Alongside the MD&A, a summary of the principal differences between the accounting standards under which the accounts of the company are reported in the offering circular and IFRS or US GAAP is also included for Rule 144A private placements. This, however, has now become less usual for two reasons. First, many firms of auditors have now become reluctant to provide comfort on such summaries of principal differences between GAAPs. And secondly, many exchanges now require companies to disclose their accounts either under IFRS or under US GAAP anyway, so investors have gradually become familiar with these accounting standards in any event. Accordingly, such summaries have now been omitted from many IPO prospectuses, particularly in Europe, except perhaps in the event of a special case or particularly unusual line item requiring an explanation as a result of differences between GAAPs.

For those companies that choose instead to issue equity and list in the US, the accounts must generally be drawn up under US GAAP or include a reconciliation to US GAAP, both of which can be time-consuming and costly (especially the first time round). More recently, however, foreign private issuers listing in the US have been able to report under IFRS (see Section 2.6.6).

The main section in the prospectus is the one describing the business of the company. This includes a review of the industry it operates in, as well as of its major competitors, the origins and corporate structure of the group, and an in-depth review of all aspects of the business itself, as well as of its regulatory environment. Information on any material litigation to which the company may be party is also included. In addition, reports by property valuers or other experts may sometimes be found to assist in the understanding and valuation of the company, as well as of the market in which it operates (see Sections 2.1.3 and 2.1.4).

Details of senior management and of the board of directors are included in the form of curricula vitae, together with details of any board committees and other corporate governance considerations.

One also often finds disclosure of interested-, connected-, or related-persons transactions, such as details of transactions between the company and its principal shareholders, directors, or senior management that may give rise to conflicts of interest, if waivers have been sought and obtained from the regulator or stock exchange for such transactions. Specific waivers may be given, for example, if such transactions were made for a bona fide reason, on a continuing basis, on normal commercial terms (e.g., where an issuer rents its head office from its controlling shareholder at market rates) and/or are generally not material in the context of the company's business. Typically, continuing connected transactions are only permitted for a limited amount of time, generally up to three years.

More general sections describe the taxation regime in the country in which the country is incorporated (and US federal tax considerations may also be included for the benefit of US investors, if applicable). Information on transfer restrictions, clearance, and settlement for the shares or DSs, as well as information on recent exchange rates between the currency of the listing and major currencies (generally the US dollar), may also be found. A description of the local stock exchange is sometimes included, particularly in the case of listings in emerging markets.

A prospectus invariably includes details of the underwriting of, or a plan of distribution for, the shares, listing the names of the various banks involved in the offering; and a description of the various tranches in the IPO, application procedures for retail investors as well as the principal terms of the underwriting arrangements (chiefly, fees, expenses, and termination arrangements). Importantly, this will also mention selling restrictions, that is, information on, and disclaimers targeted at, investors to which the shares may be sold in a variety of jurisdictions, most commonly to institutional investors by way of private placements. For example, it is common in international equity offerings to limit the sale of shares to a maximum of 49 institutional investors in Japan to avoid making extensive filings and conducting a public offer locally. Similar practices will be observed and followed for other major or relevant financial jurisdictions.

Local market practice or rules, or listing requirements, also often specify additional disclosure, for example, a profit forecast, which may be included in the prospectus (see Section 2.6.5).

The back section of the prospectus, or F pages, is devoted to the audit reports and to the company's financials (including notes) and can run over several hundred pages for large and complex companies, or when pro forma financials have also been included. This is also typically where other information, such as logos and trademarks owned by the company, or details of intellectual or real property or other assets it may possess, can be found.

Traditionally, the back cover lists all the major parties involved in the IPO in a "football team" display, although this may not be observed in all markets (and is actually more common for debt, rather than equity, issues nowadays).

In the UK, the accountants' long-form report on the company's financial statements traditionally forms the core of the prospectus, while in the US, the SEC prescribes in detail what should be included and filed in the registration statement (see Section 2.7.2).

2.7.5   Domestic and international prospectuses

There are usually at least two versions of the offering circular—a version prepared for listing on the local stock exchange where an offering is conducted to institutional as well as to retail investors, and a separate version that includes additional information for international (and invariably institutional) investors, usually in the form of a US or international "wrap" (also known as the "W" pages), supplemented by the local version of the document, which is included as a "sandwich". Some information included in the "domestic" version may, however, sometimes be omitted from the international prospectus, for example, any profit forecast. In general, however, most of the contents of both the local and international versions of the document are fairly consistent and similar. It is sometimes also the case that the international version of the offering circular may itself be split between a Rule 144A and a Reg. S sub-versions, most particularly when the auditors provide a different form of comfort on the financials for each of these two tranches (because of liability issues). In such a case, the IPO will include at least three versions of the listing document. Other versions may also be produced, for example in the case of a public offering without listing (POWL) in Japan, when a securities registration statement (SRS) and prospectus in Japanese must also be drafted and filed with the Kanto Local Finance Bureau (KLFB), a subdivision of the Japanese Ministry of Finance (see Section 2.14.5).

2.7.6   Preliminary and final prospectuses

Traditionally, two distinct sets of the international version (only) of an institutional offering circular are published in sequence in an IPO. First the preliminary offering circular, which does not include an offer price (or, more rarely, includes a price range) and which is distributed to institutional investors after the price range has been set at the end of pre-marketing or PDIE; and, subsequently, the final offering circular, which is published after pricing and includes the final offer price. In the rather rare fixed-price IPOs, only one version of the prospectus is published.

The preliminary offering circular (also called "pathfinder" in the UK) is subject to completion and amendment, and a statement to that effect is traditionally included vertically on the side of the cover page in a bold red ink statement, hence the term "red herring" or "red" that is often used to describe the preliminary prospectus. The preliminary offering circular is in effect a marketing document that is given a wide distribution to institutional investors, whereas the final offering circular is generally published in smaller quantities since it is primarily destined for those institutional investors that have been allocated shares in the IPO. There is, however, usually only one version of the domestic prospectus since public offers are normally underwritten at the outset and either conducted on the basis of a maximum or fixed price, rather than using a price range, as is the case for institutional tranches. More recently, starting in Europe, there has been a trend only to publish a preliminary institutional offering circular when the price range is set, with a short supplement including pricing information published after pricing.

In Singapore, the public offer prospectus is put on display on the website of the regulator (the Monetary Authority of Singapore, or MAS), where the prospectus is lodged on a system called Offers and Prospectuses Electronic Repository and Access or MAS OPERA Public Portal for usually a couple of weeks, to allow for any comments from the general public before formal registration takes place and the retail offering can start. Malaysia has a similar practice with a public display of the draft prospectus on the website of the Securities Commission, the securities regulator there, although at an earlier stage. Hong Kong has more recently adopted under its new IPO regime (introduced in October 2013, and which entered its second phase on 1 April 2014) a similar process, with the publication of both the listing application (i.e., the draft prospectus sent to the listing division of the exchange for review and comments) and, following the hearing of the listing application by the listing committee of the exchange, of a post-hearing information pack (PHIP), in effect a near final prospectus (but redacted, to exclude certain information pertaining to the offer structure and underwriting terms), on the website of the parent company of the Stock Exchange of Hong Kong (Hong Kong Exchanges & Clearing Limited, also known as HKEx), so as to provide retail investors with information about the IPO at an early stage. Australia has a broadly similar process, with an "exposure period" with the local regulator, the Australian Securities and Investments Commission (ASIC).

2.7.7   Plain English and prospectus covers

There has been a trend in recent years (and it is actually now a requirement in the US) to make prospectuses more "user-friendly", to banish overly technical or legal terms, and to use "plain" English. The style in which offering circulars are written has therefore evolved to reflect the fact that this is a document published by the company itself. Where one would find "Company business" as a section title a few years ago, "Our business" would now be more common, as would the use of "we" as the main subject throughout the narratives. Prospectuses now also commonly include pictures of the issuer's offices or production facilities on the cover, often replicating the themes used in the issuer's annual report or advertising campaigns to promote its business and corporate identity.

A sample list of the contents for an international IPO prospectus is set out in Appendix 4.

2.8   Comfort letters

Auditors' comfort letters are required to provide comfort to both the issuer and the underwriters on financial information included in the offering circular. They constitute an essential part of the due diligence defence to verify the accuracy of the financial information. The international standard for comfort letters is the SAS 72 letter, whose name is derived from the American Institute of Certified Public Accountants' (AICPA's) statement on Accounting Standards 72.[57]

2.8.1   Versions of the SAS 72 letter

In the late 1990s, following the collapse of Enron and the consequent fall of Arthur Andersen, reporting accountants became very cautious about delivering comfort letters, particularly for capital markets transactions involving distribution in the US (given the litigious environment there). This led to jurisdiction clauses being introduced to limit their liability and reliance by recipients in certain countries (chiefly, the US). Typically, several versions of the comfort letter are now delivered, one for the public offer (where applicable) and/or one for the Reg. S tranche of the offering, and one for the Rule 144A tranche of the offering (should this form part of the offer structure). All such letters are pretty much identical, save for jurisdiction clauses that provide geographical limitations on reliance. The first two forms of the comfort letter require the underwriters and the issuer to sign lengthy engagement letters with the auditors, whereas the delivery of a Rule 144A comfort letter is simply subject to representation by the underwriters that they have conducted due diligence in a manner substantially consistent with that for an SEC-registered offering. The comfort letters generally cover all (or substantially all) of the financial information included in the offering circular, including summaries of accounts, the MD&A, the accounts and notes themselves (both for audited and reviewed financials), as well as financial information included in the narratives. In addition to the form of local jurisdiction comfort letter(s) (e.g., the HKSIR 100 and HKSRS 4400 formats in Hong Kong), other formats such as International Capital Markets Association (ICMA) comfort letters may sometimes alternatively be issued, depending on the nature of the comfort to be provided by the auditors, and on what has been negotiated by the lead banks

In practice, the comfort letters include details of the procedures that have been carried out by the auditors, as well as a list of symbols for each of these and a copy of the relevant pages of the offering circular or prospectus as an attachment. In the listing document, each individual financial information on which comfort is being provided is "ticked", "ticked and tied", or "circled" with one or more symbols or letters included to indicate the manner in which it has been verified and where the information has been sourced.

2.8.2   Timing of delivery and negative assurance

Comfort letters are delivered at the time of publication of the prospectus and preliminary/final offering circular, and again at the time of closing (when the shares start trading on the exchange and are delivered to investors). They may also be delivered at the time of the exercise of the over-allotment option, if any. Comfort letters that are delivered after initial comfort letters are commonly called "bring down" comfort letters, as they are meant to restate the comfort initially provided as of a more recent date when they are subsequently delivered. Despite their name, "bring down" comfort letters do not always simply restate the prior comfort letters but may also cover additional matters, such as interim financial statements or management accounts that have been finalized since the date of the prior comfort letter(s). Importantly, comfort letters generally include a "negative assurance" clause, whereby the auditors state that:

- "nothing has come to their attention that would cause them to believe that any modifications should be made to the unaudited interim financial information [if any] for them to be in conformity to generally accepted accounting principles (GAAP) and that they comply as to form in all material respects with the applicable GAAP"; and that

- "nothing has come to their attention that would cause them to believe that there have been material changes in certain financial statement line items since the date of the latest financial statements included in the offering circular".

The "Big Four" auditors typically resist providing this negative assurance if 135 days or more have elapsed since the date of the latest audited or reviewed accounts. They may also require the reporting accountants to perform what is called a "SAS 100 review" of interim, unaudited accounts. So the 134th day after the publication of the accounts is effectively the latest day on which an SAS 72 negative assurance can be delivered without an interim review being required.

A recent trend has been for auditors only to deliver their "international" version(s) of the comfort letter on, and at the time of publication of, the final offering circular although, in this case, issuers and investment banks are normally comfortable with the auditors delivering a letter or email at the time of the preliminary offering circular stating that the draft comfort letter is in agreed and final form with no further changes to be made or introduced until delivery. As already mentioned, prospectuses for domestic, local tranches are usually only published once, unlike offering circulars for institutional/international tranches.

2.8.3   Agreed-upon procedures and agreement on comfort letters

Typically, the legal advisers to the underwriters will take the lead on reviewing and commenting on the various sets of comfort letters, though legal advisers to the issuer will commonly review these as well. When the underwriters are unable to represent that they have carried out due diligence substantially consistent with US standards (such as in the case of a Reg. S offering with diligence procedures perhaps more limited than those usually conducted in connection with a Rule 144A private placement), or when 135 days or more have elapsed since the latest audited or reviewed accounts, the reporting accountants may deliver a lower standard of comfort letter called an "agreed-upon procedures letter".

Since the availability of financial information for publication in the offering circular is often what primarily drives the timetable for an IPO, so as to avoid any unfortunate misunderstandings down the line, the nature, contents, and timing of issue for all the comfort letters to be provided by the auditors should ideally be discussed and agreed (at least in principle) between the latter, the company, and the lead banks as soon as possible after the kick-off meeting. Such discussions will usually be coordinated by a US counsel (in the case of an IPO with a Rule 144A private placement) employed by the international legal advisers to the underwriters.

2.9 Legal opinions, due diligence reports, and disclosure letters

A number of legal opinions are sought in connection with any IPO, the delivery of which takes place at, and is usually a condition precedent to, underwriting or closing.

2.9.1 Legal opinions and due diligence reports according to jurisdictions

Generally speaking, one or more legal opinions are required to be delivered, as conditions precedent to underwriting/closing—and as stated in the underwriting and sale and purchase agreements—by each of the legal firms working on the transaction and for each of the jurisdictions for which they have been providing legal advice. This will usually cover, among other things, the due incorporation of the issuer, its power to conduct the IPO, the due execution and delivery of the IPO documents, and other relevant matters. For example, in the case of a mainland Chinese company listing in Hong Kong and conducting a Rule 144A private placement, either through H shares (shares of a company incorporated in the mainland of China) or as a "red chip" (after a re-organization and transfer of its assets and liabilities to an offshore entity, usually a Cayman Islands company), legal opinions will be sought:

- from the legal advisers to the issuer on Hong Kong law;
- from the legal advisers to the issuer on US federal and (usually) New York State law (often the same firm as for Hong Kong law);
- from the legal advisers to the issuer on laws of the PRC (often one law firm only is appointed in an IPO to advise on PRC law);
- from the legal advisers to the underwriters on Hong Kong law;
- from the legal advisers to the underwriters on US federal and New York State law (often the same firm as for Hong Kong law); and
- also from other law firms advising on the laws of other jurisdictions, where relevant, such as a firm advising on Cayman Islands law (in the case of a red chip) and perhaps, for example, say, a Canadian law firm advising on selling restrictions into certain provinces in Canada.

In addition, it is common for the lead underwriters to request from the legal advisers (and, again, usually for the major applicable jurisdictions), due diligence reports covering a variety of issues pertaining to the issuer, such as shareholding arrangements; litigation; licences; banking facilities; insurance policies; intellectual property; sale and purchase agreements; subsidiaries and affiliated companies; joint ventures; corporate information; restructurings; and other relevant matters.

These will typically largely be finalized at an earlier stage and prior to the banks entering into an underwriting and sale and purchase agreement with the company and its controlling/major shareholder(s).

2.9.2   US legal opinions and disclosure letters

US legal opinions and disclosure letters are generally sought if the offering is marketed into the US pursuant to a private placement. These will generally be delivered pursuant to federal laws rather than to State (also called "Blue Sky") laws. These may include:

- a "no-registration" opinion, stating that the offering need not be registered with the SEC in the US; and
- a 10b-5 letter in the case of a Rule 144A private placement.

A 10b-5 letter is a fairly standard (although onerous) negative assurance statement by US counsel that "upon reviewing the offering circular, and having conducted business and documentary due diligence, nothing has come to their attention to suggest that the offering circular contains any untrue statement of material fact or fails to state a material fact necessary in order to make the statements made, or in light of the circumstances under which they were made, not misleading".

In short, a 10b-5 letter is a negative confirmation by a firm of US lawyers that, based on their diligence procedures, the prospectus does not omit any material information. It establishes a basis for due diligence defence against litigation in the US. Banks have differing internal policies for the delivery of the 10b-5 letters, which can also be rather costly. This is not systematically required in the case of Reg. S offerings, when an offering is distributed to US offshore institutions only, or perhaps only one 10b-5 letter by the legal advisers to the underwriters may be requested. Given the litigious environment in the US, however, usually 10b-5 letters from both the legal advisers to the issuer and to the underwriters are required when Rule 144A private placements (or indeed full US listings) are made.

Increasingly, and in addition to 10b-5 letters, "local" versions of a disclosure letter are also requested by the lead underwriters. These are provided by the other (i.e. non-US) principal legal advisers advising on an international IPO. Like the legal opinions, the 10b-5 letters and these "10b-5 lookalike" letters are delivered upon, and as conditions precedent to, the underwriting/closing (i.e., settlement) of the transaction.

On occasion, a "1940 Act" US legal opinion may also be sought, stating that the issuer does not constitute an investment company required to be registered in the

US under the Investment Company Act of 1940. Investment companies are distinct from operating companies and may include conglomerates or holding companies whose main businesses consist of investments in other entities. In addition, investment companies (under the 1940 Act) may also include so-called "inadvertent investment companies", which are entities that do not hold themselves out to be investment companies, but nevertheless fall within the definition of an Investment Company under the 1940 Act. Compliance with the provisions of the 1940 Act places severe limitations on companies, including restrictions on the granting of stock options, additional requirements for the appointment of independent directors, and limitations applying to their capital structure. Complex tests (in particular, whether the company owns investment securities representing more than 40% of its total assets on an unconsolidated basis under a specific formula) are required to ascertain whether an issuer is an investment company under the 1940 Act.[58] A 1940 Act opinion is only required for IPOs that are marketed in the US (e.g., pursuant to a Rule 144A private placement or through an SEC-registered offering) and when there are doubts that the company might be construed as an investment company. This should not be an issue in the context of Reg. S-only offerings.

Separately, issuers and investment banks may be required to ascertain through their legal advisers whether a non-US company constitutes a passive foreign investment company (PFIC) for US tax purposes. PFIC tax rules, which are subject to interpretation by the internal revenue service (IRS) in the US, impose additional tax liability on US investors on gains or dividends derived from investment in a PFIC. Holding companies, companies with significant cash holdings, or start-up companies may sometimes be classified as PFICs, although the latter two categories are most probably unlikely in any event to qualify for listing following an IPO.[59]

2.10   The question of underwriting

Underwriting (and hard underwriting in particular) is often a contentious issue that comes up when investment banks pitch for ECM transactions. The question is not so much whether an offering is underwritten, since all deals will be at some stage—indeed it is sometimes a requirement by the regulator or stock exchange that an offering be fully underwritten (e.g., retail tranches in a number of countries are usually hard underwritten; other types of equity offerings such as rights issues are also typically underwritten pursuant to the relevant listing rules)—but at what point in the transaction a deal becomes underwritten.

2.10.1 What is underwriting?

Underwriting is evidenced by the signing of an underwriting or sale and purchase agreement whereby the shares on offer are effectively bought at a fixed price by one or more investment banks from the issuer and/or the selling shareholders. Underwriting decisions therefore commit the banks, in terms of both risk and capital, and are made in underwriting committees comprising senior personnel, usually from the banking and markets sides of the business, together with risk and compliance professionals.

Because of the generally large amounts involved, and because markets can be volatile, investment banks always try at all costs to avoid underwriting shares other than for a short period of time, after which the risk of owning the shares can be passed on to other parties. Such other parties can be either other banks taking sub-underwriting positions (for a fee) or institutional or retail investors. Except on rare occasions, early commitments made on underwriting for IPOs are, more often than not, subject to many conditions and, in effect, rather useless other than to provide some degree of comfort that the valuation can, in the end, be achieved.

2.10.2 Hard underwriting

In secondary market transactions, such as block trades, there is a trading history for the stock and senior traders will generally have a good feel about the level of pricing at which an offering can clear. Such transactions can therefore sometimes be "hard" underwritten at the outset in what is commonly called a "bought deal" to enable the bank to win the mandate. This is not generally the case for IPOs.

2.10.3 Soft or settlement underwriting

While issuers and selling shareholders would clearly like to have an unreserved commitment well in advance with regard to the price they will receive upon closing for their shares, institutional tranches in IPOs (with rare exceptions, such as in Indonesia or, until the mid-1990s, in Spain) are actually underwritten after the final offer price has been determined, which implies that sufficient demand has been gathered from investors to cover (and ideally more than cover) the book of demand. What is then effectively underwritten is the risk of institutional investors defaulting in the settlement process, which actually occurs very rarely. One then talks of "soft" or settlement underwriting. Soft underwriting is sometimes also called "best efforts" underwriting. In Hong Kong, I am aware of one instance, in 2019, when a cornerstone investor defaulted on its (rather substantial) commitment to buy shares under an IPO, which created all sorts of issues in the latter stages of the deal.

Specifically, China Saite, a construction company, failed to pay as agreed almost US$30 million worth of shares in the US$1.16 billion IPO of Chinese brokerage Shenwan Hongyuan. This is, however, an extremely unlikely occurrence.

2.10.4 Retail tranches

By contrast, retail tranches are often underwritten prior to the shares being offered to the public. However, since initial retail tranches are generally small and retail investors normally pay in advance to apply for shares and get reimbursed at a later stage for any differences between the price paid and the actual offer price, as well as between the amount of shares applied for and their final allocations, the actual underwriting risk for the banks is effectively low.

It would not be completely inconceivable for an institutional (also called placement) tranche, or even for an entire IPO, to be fully hard underwritten at an early stage and, indeed, this still happens in some countries. But, because the issuer's shares obviously have no prior trading history, the deep discount and significant fees that would be required would render this a pretty unattractive proposition in most cases. In addition, any bank hard underwriting an IPO would most probably be tempted to get rid of its exposure as quickly as possible, perhaps regardless of the quality of investors in the book of demand. Lastly, in the case of an IPO that would have been hard underwritten but where only low or limited demand would have been gathered from investors it is doubtful that a listing could be conducted in any event since requirements relating to the spread of shareholders (e.g., 300 in Hong Kong) and free float (usually 25% for an IPO) would in such a case most probably not be satisfied.

Accordingly, all that can generally be provided at the outset of an IPO is nothing but an indication of what the final offer price might be, based on a theoretical valuation (often involving comparable companies) and market conditions prevailing at the time. Such indication gets refined as due diligence progresses, as research analysts provide valuation indications in their pre-deal reports, as feedback from investors is gathered during pre-marketing, and, ultimately, as investor demand is collected in the bookbuilding process.

Sometimes the investment banks can get it completely wrong. High valuation indications may get provided during the pitching process, only for the banks (and a rather disgruntled issuer) to realize down the line that the market is not prepared to pay up to invest in the business. In such cases, it may sometimes be necessary to lower the price range, or even the proposed offer size, during the latter phases of bookbuilding to ensure a relatively healthy aftermarket performance. On occasion, when insufficient investor demand has been gathered, IPOs can be pulled or postponed. Insufficient investor demand can be for a variety of reasons, ranging from an unattractive investment case to an unreasonably high valuation or large offering, to simply a sharp deterioration in market conditions or events beyond the control of the issuer and the lead investment banks.

The IPO of Essar Energy on the LSE in 2010, a case study of which is included in Appendix 1, is an example of an offering that was ultimately priced below its initial indicative bookbuilding price range.

On occasion, however, the market sometimes expresses such an enthusiasm at an early stage for an offering that the price range is increased or more shares are offered to investors, perhaps through a previously disclosed upsize option, to satisfy pent-up demand. It is actually fairly common for the price ranges of IPOs in the US to be increased in the light of investor demand, although this is conversely rarely seen in Europe or Asia. Such a decision should, however, be carefully assessed before it is made by the lead banks. Also included as a case study in Appendix 1, the IPO of Shanda Games on Nasdaq in 2009 is an example of a deal that was increased in size at an early stage in the marketing process.

One thing is certain, irrespective of the outcome of an IPO, how much a company is worth is ultimately always determined by market forces—and nothing else.

2.11   Valuation

Valuation is clearly an important consideration for all issuers since this is what will, ultimately, drive most of the demand and the IPO offer price paid by investors. There are many ways to value a business. Valuation will depend on the industry sector in which the company operates, the size of the IPO—generally a fairly simple methodology will be used for smaller transactions—and market practice prevailing at the time of the offering.

Sometimes, several valuation methodologies are used, either because the issuer is involved in distinct businesses to which separate valuation techniques need to be applied. Or just one primary methodology may be used, and then cross-checked against other valuation techniques to refine an initial range or to confirm assumptions that may have been made.

For example, MTR Corporation, which operates Hong Kong's mass transit railway system, was generally valued at the time of its US$1.4 billion equivalent privatization IPO in 2000 by research analysts through a sum-of-the-parts valuation, using a variety of methodologies. A discounted cash-flow (DCF) analysis was used to assess the value of its railway operations. A price-to-net-asset-value valuation was then separately used for its real estate business, which largely consists of office, commercial, and residential property assets located above urban railway stations, based on the open-market valuation report published by the property valuers in the offering circular. In addition, a variety of other techniques were used to value peripheral assets—for example, the company's majority ownership of a business operating the Octopus smart cards widely used by residents of Hong Kong to travel on trains and buses, as well as revenue derived from sharing arrangements with operators for mobile telecommunications made in the metro system.

In 2012, valuation for the US$2.1 billion equivalent IPO of hospital owner and operator IHH Healthcare, in both Malaysia and Singapore, was primarily conducted on the basis of its forward enterprise value, divided by prospective earnings before interest, tax, depreciation, and amortization (EV/EBITDA), and looking at a group of regional primary peers (Apollo Hospitals and Fortis Healthcare in India, as well as Raffles Medical Group in Singapore) and other comparable companies in Southeast Asia (Bangkok Dusit Medical Services, Bumrungrad International, and Bangkok Chain in Thailand, as well as KPJ Healthcare in Malaysia). To this were added the valuations for a new hospital in Singapore that had yet to become operational, Mount Elizabeth Novena, and that was accordingly generally valued on a DCF basis, as well as for two listed companies in which IHH Healthcare was a shareholder, Parkway Life REIT in Singapore and Apollo Hospitals in India (as mentioned above, also used a peer for the valuation of the company's core business). In addition, prior to the IPO, IHH Healthcare had secured a controlling stake in Acibadem, a hospital business listed in Turkey, which was also taken into account when compiling the sum-of-the-parts valuation.

Valuation can be made on a stand-alone basis or involve a comparative analysis, effectively benchmarking the business against companies that are already listed and for which there are obviously already prices ascribed by the market. When multiples of comparable companies are used, these are most of the time compiled on a prospective basis—that is, only multiples using forecasts of sales, cash-flow, earnings, or dividends are used, rather than historic (or "trailing") multiples. The market always looks forward.

When undertaking a valuation exercise in connection with an IPO, it is important to distinguish between a pre-money valuation, that is, without taking into account primary proceeds raised by the issuer as part of the flotation, and a post-new money valuation, which includes such an amount. As the free float typically initially represents around 25% of a listed company, there could be a considerable difference depending on whether or not new money is taken into account. Accordingly, this should be made clear to potential institutional investors in pre-deal research reports and/or when conducting PDIE.

2.11.1 Earnings multiples

The most commonly used valuation technique is the simple price-to-earnings (P/E or PER) multiple, defined as the price per share divided by earnings per share (EPS) or, alternatively, as the expected market capitalization divided by forecast earnings. It is simple to compute, does not necessitate in-depth analysis, and is widely understood by the financial community. Generally, one would consider the P/E for the following financial year (rather than the trailing P/E that uses earnings for the last 12 months), or perhaps a blend of the P/Es for the next two financial years, assuming forecasts by either the company or more often research analysts are available. The higher the P/E, the higher the value of a company. There are, however, clear limitations to the use of P/E multiples. For example, when one is comparing P/Es of various companies listed across several jurisdictions, this does not account for differences in taxation, which can be significant. It may also be the case that the companies being compared have widely different accounting policies or different asset or capital structure profiles, hence differences in net interest, depreciation, and amortization (including amortization of goodwill), which may also distort P/E comparisons. Such a methodology is also often not appropriate for valuing companies that generate significant recurring cash-flow but are also highly geared. In such cases, EBITDA multiples are perhaps best used as an alternative.

2.11.2 Sales and cash-flow multiples

Depending on the nature of the business, other multiples can be used, such as price-to-cash-flow; EV/sales, which gives investors an idea of how much it costs to buy a company's sales; EV/EBITDA, which is used especially to value highly cash-generative businesses; or, more rarely, EV/EBIT, to (arguably) compare companies on a more level footing.

A price-to-cash-flow multiple is defined as the price per share divided by cash-flow per share. EV stands for enterprise value, and includes both the equity value of the company and its net debt. Where net cash would be present on the balance sheet instead, this would be deducted from the equity value. It is then divided either by the turnover of the business or by earnings before net interest, tax, depreciation, and amortization (effectively cash-flow), or by earnings before interest and tax, as appropriate. For example, companies in particularly cyclical industries—a producer of commodities, for example—can be valued on an EV/sales basis, which ignores periods when profitability may be most affected. Mobile telecommunication companies are often valued on an EV/EBITDA basis, to assess their cash earnings generation, ignoring what can be widely differing capital investments and a lack of net profitability in the early stages of the business. As for the P/E, the higher the ratio, the higher the valuation of the company.

Internet or e-commerce companies specifically, which are often not yet profitable upon IPO, are often valued on the basis of a multiple of their revenue. Such a multiple will depend on a number of parameters, for example, the number of monthly unique visitors for the business, the customer conversion rate, the bounce rate, the average order value (AOV), the number of monthly active users (MAU), the average revenue per user (ARPU), the monthly recurring revenue (MRR), the revenue run rate, the margin per customer (both per order and after marketing costs), the customer acquisition cost, the churn and burn rates, and other factors.

2.11.3 Growth multiples

Among other multiples frequently used is the price-to-growth (PEG) multiple, which is calculated as PER/increase in EPS, and is useful also for looking at the growth in earnings rather than simply at the earnings themselves.

2.11.4 Normalized multiples

When an investment bank is carrying out a theoretical valuation at an early stage in an IPO (or for an IPO pitch) or when the market is particularly depressed but expected to improve soon, "normalized" multiples, using average multiples over a longer period of time, can be chosen to provide a more relevant indicator for the valuation that might be achieved by the company in a more stable market environment.

2.11.5 Price-to-book or price-to-net-asset-value (NAV) ratios

The price-to-book ratio, defined as the share price divided by the equity of the company, or total assets excluding intangible assets and liabilities, is also a basic ratio commonly used to value many companies. It is generally used to value issuers in the financial sector, especially banks. This ratio is also commonly used for property assets or the valuation of properties in the real estate sector. In this industry, the independent valuation provided by the property valuers in the offering circular generally provides a good indication of the net asset value of the property assets, and the ratio of price-to-book value or price-to-net-asset-value (NAV) enables useful comparisons across listed comparable companies of the same asset class.

In times of particularly volatile markets—for example, following the recent credit crunch—when it becomes more difficult to value companies on the basis of their earnings, investors tend to focus more on price-to-book ratios, even for industrial companies or businesses not in the financial or property sector.

Again, as with most financial ratios, the higher the price-to-book, the higher the valuation.

2.11.6 Per pop valuations

For companies in specific industry sectors, unique valuation methodologies are sometimes devised. For example, a "per pop" valuation, that is, putting a price on each individual customer or user for the market under licence, is often also used to value internet or mobile telecommunication companies. This valuation methodology acts as a proxy for a discounted cash-flow valuation of the business upon reaching maturity. It takes into account market penetration, the revenue per subscriber, the profit margin of the business, a cash-flow multiple, and a discount rate.

2.11.7 Dividend and distribution yields

For real estate investment trusts (REITs), business trusts, or companies in the real estate or property and infrastructure sectors, the dividend or distribution yield, defined as the dividend per share or per unit, divided by the price per share or per unit and expressed as a percentage, is also a popular valuation technique. The distribution yield spread over a risk-free rate, generally the yield on a benchmark government bond, is commonly used too.

2.11.8 Discounted cash-flow valuations and embedded value

For companies that offer good long-term visibility with predictable cash-flows, a discounted cash-flow (DCF) valuation may be used; examples include companies in the mining, transport, or infrastructure sectors, most of which would also generally benefit from the inclusion of a report by an expert in the offering circular. Such a methodology is also appropriate for valuing businesses that are still at an early stage of development but for which growth and maturity are clearly perceptible. Typically, such a valuation methodology would also be used to value biotechnology businesses, many of which are not yet profitable at the time of their IPOs.

The value of a company calculated using a DCF varies greatly depending on the assumptions that have been used, so it is also important to have reliable financial forecasts for the business. This method determines the value of the business using future expected cash-flows, discounted at a rate that reflects the riskiness of the cash-flows. It involves discounting the cash-flows at a weighted average cost of capital (WACC), taking into account the company's capital structure, that is, the proportion between debt and equity capital, where such equity and debt are currently priced, how much of the company's debt is currently outstanding, as well as the company's tax rate.

A somewhat related methodology is used to value life insurance companies. In such cases, an "embedded value" for the business will be calculated as the sum of the company's NAV (using current market prices for investments made) and of the present value of future cash-flows derived from life insurance policies currently in force (i.e., only insurance policies already sold and written by the company). A life insurer will generally be worth a multiple of its embedded value since this methodology does not take into account additional policies to be sold in coming years.

2.11.9 Share price and number of shares

Once the approximate valuation of a business has been determined, it is important to decide on the total number of shares in the company by effecting stock splits or reverse stock splits, if required, so that one can arrive at a share price that is broadly consistent with those of companies already listed on the same stock exchange. For example, companies listed on the same stock exchange might generally have their share prices within a range of, say, US$10 to US$20 equivalent on that particular market. Institutional investors are not particularly concerned with the absolute denomination at which the share price might be set, but such a consideration can be important when a retail offering is included in the offer structure, so that the general public's perceptions of the "value" of the company are in line with those for other local stocks that they already trade, and with which they are familiar. A related consideration is to avoid the share price (and initially the price range) being set at too low a level, so that the stock is not perceived as a "penny share", that is, a stock with little value and prospects, given its low denomination. Conversely, a share price that would be set too high might perhaps deter more modest individual investors from buying the securities.

To summarize, a variety of techniques may be used to value businesses. Research analysts sometimes churn out new methodologies, each claiming to be fairer or more accurate than the rest. In theory, none is necessarily better than the others, and the right methodology at any given time for a given business is really the one most widely accepted and used by market participants. It is also essential to bear in mind that, irrespective of the methodology used, investors will ultimately pay no more than what they believe a business to be worth.

2.12   Institutional investors

Institutional investors come in multiple guises and many investor types are targeted in an IPO. They can be generalists or have a dedicated regional, country, industry sector, company type (e.g., small- or mid-cap), or theme focus (e.g., increasingly, an ESG bias). They can manage sovereign money, insurance companies' assets, funds owned by other institutions, pension money, charity donations, high net-worth individuals' investments, or, indeed, their own proprietary portfolios. They can be subject to strict procedures and criteria for their investment decisions, or have a large degree of freedom to invest and react to market developments, as is the case for many hedge funds or family offices. Some can invest across the whole spectrum of financial assets and products, while others are more particularly dedicated to shares or cash equities. Some are "long only" funds, while others adopt "long/ short" strategies. They can manage total return funds, whose objectives are to maximize "alpha" (a component of the capital asset pricing model (CAPM) and a risk-adjusted measure—through skill—of the active return on an investment) or they can be benchmarked to particular indices, the performance of which they try to replicate. Some like growth while others prefer yield; some like to participate in IPOs, or can commit to pre-IPO or cornerstone investments, even accepting lock-ups to achieve sizeable allocations, whereas others have a bias towards investments made in the secondary market; some have smaller portfolios with large positions, while others prefer to widely diversify their holdings.

Every IPO book of demand is different, and it is the role of ECM teams to help the issuer navigate the maze of investor types and to identify those regions and those investors most likely to participate in the offering.

In established markets, such as the US, the UK, and Australia, many pension or superannuation funds are tasked with the financing of pension plan benefits. Although they often have a fixed-income bias, they are generally also a significant source of demand for equity offerings.

Mutual funds or collective investment schemes, as well as close-ended investment trusts, are also a major source of institutional investor money. Hedge funds are a more recent phenomenon, having appeared in the last 20 years or so; they have, in a short space of time, become major participants in IPOs and can on occasion account for 50% or more of total institutional demand.

2.12.1 Sovereign wealth funds

Sovereign wealth funds (SWFs) have, by contrast, been in existence for a long time (since 1953 in Kuwait) but have of late become a rather topical issue, in particular following their investments in US and European investment banks at the time of the credit crunch between 2007 and 2009: among these were a US$3 billion investment in Citi and US$2 billion in Merrill Lynch by the Kuwait Investment Authority (KIA); a US$7.5 billion investment by the Abu Dhabi Investment Authority (ADIA) in Citi; and a US$9.75 billion investment in UBS by Singapore's Government of Singapore Investment Corporation (GIC). Similar investments were also made at or around that time in Barclays, Credit Suisse, Deutsche Bank, HSBC, Morgan Stanley, and Standard Chartered.

SWFs include revenue stabilization funds (such as the Reserve Fund run by the US$600 billion-plus KIA) that are designed to temper the impact of volatile revenues (e.g., oil or gas revenues); holding funds (such as Temasek Holdings in Singapore, with assets under management of more than US$300 billion, or Khazanah Nasional Berhad in Malaysia) that manage government participations or direct investments in state-owned or private sector companies; and savings funds, typically devoted to the funding of future pension liabilities (such as the Government Pension Fund in Norway or the Fonds de Réserve pour les Retraites in France). Other SWFs are set up to manage excess foreign reserves: among these are China Investment Corporation (CIC), with US$940-plus billion in assets under management; Korea Investment Corporation (KIC); Abu Dhabi's US$600 billion ADIA; and the US$335 billion Qatar Investment Authority (QIA).[60] A variety of investment styles, depending on the purposes of such funds, can be found among SWFs, but a number of names are well known as significant, high-quality investors in ECM offerings. Examples of SWFs (or *de facto* SWFs) across Europe, the Middle East, and Asia are set out in Table 6.

Aside from their geographical location, institutional investors for the purposes of ECM transactions are often classified according to their investment style or their perceived quality.

2.12.2 Income and value investors

Looking at investment styles first, "income" or "income value" investors typically look for stocks that have a high payout ratio and therefore a significant dividend yield. This is one of the most conservative investment styles among the universe of institutional investors. Similarly, "yield" investors will focus on investments that offer a pick-up in yield, such as REITs, infrastructure funds, or utility stocks.

European sovereign wealth funds	Middle East sovereign wealth funds	Asian sovereign wealth funds
Caisse des Dépôts et Consignations (France)	Abu Dhabi Investment Authority—ADIA (UAE)	Brunei Investment Agency—BIA—(Brunei)
Fonds de Réserve pour les Retraites (France)	Abu Dhabi Investment Council—ADIC (UAE)	China Investment Corporation—CIC (China)
Fonds Stratégique d'Investissements (France)	Dubai International Capital (UAE)	National Social Security Fund (China)
	Dubai World (UAE)	SAFE Investment Company (China)
Government Pension Fund (Norway)	Emirates Investment Authority—EIA (UAE)	
	Investment Corporation of Dubai (UAE)	Hong Kong Exchange Fund (Hong Kong)
	Istithmar World (UAE)	
	Mubadala Development Company (UAE)	Korea Investment Corporation—KIC (South Korea)
	RAK Investment Authority (UAE)	
	Mumtalakat Holding Company (Bahrain)	Khazanah Nasional Berhad (Malaysia)
	Kuwait Investment Authority—KIA (Kuwait)	Fullerton (Singapore)
		Government of Singapore Investment Corporation—GIC (Singapore)
	Libyan Investment Authority (Libya)	Pavilion (Singapore)
		Seatown (Singapore)
	State General Reserve Fund (Oman)	Temasek Holdings (Singapore)
	Qatar Investment Authority—QIA (Qatar)	
	Kingdom Holding Company (Saudi Arabia)	National Stabilisation Fund (Taiwan)
	Public Investment Fund (Saudi Arabia)	
	Saudi Arabia Monetary Authority—SAMA (Saudi Arabia)	

Table 6

Sovereign wealth funds in Europe, the Middle East, and Asia

By contrast, "deep value" investors use a strategy whereby they invest in stocks with very low prices, typically with a price-to-book ratio below one or with a single digit P/E. They use a variety of valuation methods to identify such investments, and fundamentally believe that these stocks are under-valued and that their value will increase over time. These stocks also often trade at above-market average dividend yields.

"Core value" or "value" investors typically invest in companies with a large market capitalization, with below average P/Es, price-to-book, or price-to-cash-flow multiples, but typically higher-than-average dividend yields. Such investors will generally conduct significant, in-house fundamental analysis on the stocks they buy.

Overall, value investors tend to hold investments for a considerable period of time (perhaps over three to five years) and their investment decisions are usually relatively unaffected by macro events. Instead, they tend to focus more on specific corporate issues and on the company's ability to deliver value over industry cycles. Examples of value investors include Capital Research & Management, INVESCO, Prudential, UBS Asset Management, and Wellington.

2.12.3 Index investors

"Index" investors (such as Vanguard, State Street, Barclays Global Investors, BlackRock Institutional Trust, TD Asset Management, and TIAA-CREF Asset Management) try to replicate the performance of commonly used stock indices and will accordingly be significant, but rather passive, buyers of stocks included in such indices. This category has enjoyed considerable growth in recent years with the development of exchange traded funds (ETFs). ETFs also typically exhibit low entry fees, which make them particularly popular with retail investors, while at the same time providing exposure to a wide and ever-expanding range of investment themes.

2.12.4 GARP and growth investors

"Growth at a reasonable price" or "GARP" investors (e.g., Fidelity Management & Research, T. Rowe Price, and Legg Mason) look at both value and growth characteristics when selecting stocks. They focus on consistent growth in companies, but will perhaps avoid those exhibiting either very high value or very high growth characteristics.

"Core growth" investors invest in stocks that have good growth earnings potential, whereas "growth investors" use an investment strategy focused on companies that exhibit above-average growth. Growth investors often use a variety of valuation methodologies, including a bottom-up analysis of the key factors that might affect the growth of a company. These may include macro, industry-, or company specific factors. Internet, e-commerce, and biotechnology companies are typical of such investments. This is the opposite of value investing and, indeed, some growth investors even believe that the payment of dividends can hinder the potential growth of a company. Examples of growth investors include funds managed by Baillie Gifford, DBS Asset Management of Singapore, Goldman Sachs Asset Management, JPMorgan Asset Management, Putnam, RCM Capital Management, Schroder Investment Management, and TCW (formerly known as Trust Company of the West).

"Aggressive growth" or "momentum" investors (e.g., Driehaus Capital Management and Oberweis Asset Management) are focused on stocks that exhibit fast and increasing growth, perhaps because companies have manufactured a revolutionary product or are in a "hot" or extremely rapidly growing sector.

2.12.5 Specialty, quantitative investors, and hedge funds

Specialty funds focus on particular investment themes (e.g., cyclical stocks, commodities, or IPOs) and effectively bridge a gap between diversified and sector investors. For example, Templeton Asset Management, managed by Mark Mobius, and Mirae Asset from South Korea are well known for their focus on emerging markets. Black River Asset Management, a subsidiary of Cargill, is more particularly focused on natural resources sectors, including agriculture, food, clean energy, and metals and mining.

By contrast, quantitative investors focus on trading statistics, stock performance trends, and numbers, almost irrespective of the business of a company. By definition, quantitative investors (or "quants") are not major buyers of IPOs since at that stage there is no trading history for these companies in the public markets.

Lastly, hedge funds (including Brevan Howard, Bridgewater, Citadel, D.E. Shaw, Farallon (formerly known as Noonday), GLG Partners, Jabre Capital Partners, Man Group, Marshall Wace, Och-Ziff, Polygon, Susquehanna, and TPG-Axon) typically manage money owned by high net-worth individuals, with assets under management of at least US$1 million equivalent, or accredited investors, with assets under management of over US$5 million equivalent (among other types of investors), and often subject their investment in the fund to a lock-up, which can be up to several years. Some larger institutions and even other hedge funds are also commonly found as hedge fund investors. They generally focus on liquid investments and can adopt a variety of investment strategies, often (but not always) hedging their investments using short selling or derivatives. Hedge funds have been significant buyers of IPOs the world over in recent years, frequently buying large amounts in an aggressive fashion and making quick investment decisions. Some, such as Chris Hohn's TCI, Steel Partners, or Elliott are also well known as particularly "activist" shareholders, and for being vocal in criticizing management teams that do not deliver value. Hedge funds are often also called "alternative investment funds". Hedge funds probably constitute the fastest-growing category among institutional investors, with many portfolio managers (PMs) leaving established asset management platforms to raise money and set up their own funds. As an example, some of the new funds established in Hong Kong and Singapore in or around 2013 included Hillhouse (with about US$8 billion of assets under management), Dymon Asia (with US$3.2 billion), Janchor Partners (with at least US$2 billion), Myriad Asset management (with US$2.3 billion), and Azentus (with US$1.1 billion under management). Other smaller hedge funds, including 9 Masts, Tybourne, PureHeart, Summit View, and Karst Peak were also set up in Hong Kong around that time,[61] as was Admiral, a fund that focuses on investments in REITs and real estate assets. More recently, according to Financial News in June 2020, the following hedge funds, each with assets under management of at least US$1 billion, had been launched between October 2019 and March 2020: Crake Asset Management, Aslan House, Helikon Investments, Maniyar Capital Advisors, and MAN GLG Japan Alternative Fund, among others. Some 480 new hedge funds were reportedly launched in 2019 (compared with 1,040 in 2014), according to the consultancy HFR, this lower number being another casualty of the COVID-19 pandemic.

2.12.6 Contrarian investors

Contrarian investors go against established trends and believe that most other investors are wrong in their assessment of the market. On occasion, this strategy can yield them handsome results. Famous contrarian investors include Anthony Bolton and his Special Situations Fund, which he launched in 1979 at Fidelity; David Dreman's Dreman Value Management; Eduardo Elsztain, an early investor in the property market in Argentina; Marc Faber (also known as "Doctor Doom"), who reportedly predicted "Black Monday" in the US in 1987 and the bursting of the bubble in Japan in the early 1990s; John Neff's Windsor Fund at Vanguard; John Paulson, who made US$20 billion in 2007 and 2008 by betting against sub-prime mortgages and financial companies in the US; "investment biker" Jim Rogers in Singapore; and, last but not least, George Soros and his Quantum Fund, which made a fortune betting against the British pound in the 1990s.

2.12.7 Cornerstone and anchor investors

In an IPO, the best allocations in a book of demand often go to cornerstone investors, that is, to accounts that have committed to investing at a particularly early stage in the IPO. This is a very common feature in Asian IPOs in particular. Cornerstone investors are generally prestigious SWFs such as GIC or Temasek Holdings in Singapore, CIC in China, ADIA in the United Arab Emirates, Kuwait's KIA, or Qatar's QIA; well-known and large asset managers such as Fidelity, Capital, Prudential, or Schroders; or large hedge funds such as Och-Ziff. These can also include local tycoons, particularly in Hong Kong, such as Li Ka-shing, the richest man in Hong Kong and third richest man in Asia in 2010 according to Forbes,[62] and a controlling shareholder of Cheung Kong (Holdings) Limited and of its subsidiary Hutchison Whampoa; Dr Lee Shau-kee, the second richest man in Hong Kong and fourth richest in Asia in 2010 on Forbes' list and majority owner of Henderson Land Development, a property conglomerate; Joseph Lau, who runs Chinese Estates Holdings Limited; or the Kwok brothers, who control Sun Hung Kai Properties Limited, one of the territory's largest property developers and ranking fifth on Forbes' list of Asian billionaires. SWFs from the Middle East in particular often target individual investments of at least several hundred million US dollar equivalent, or more, in new listings. At the time of writing, the largest number of cornerstone investors ever assembled in a single Asian IPO was still thought to be 22, in the US$2.1 billion equivalent new listing of IHH Healthcare in Malaysia and Singapore in 2012.

In most cases, their involvement greatly raises the profile of a transaction, and provides leadership and momentum by sending a clear signal to other investors that significant household names "are behind" the deal. Such investors generally commit, prior to the start of bookbuilding, to participating for a fixed monetary amount, and at any price within the price range, thereby signalling to the broader market that the pricing of the transaction will be set at an attractive level. While cornerstone investors receive large, pre-agreed allocations in dollar terms, they do not have the benefit of any discount (or, indeed, of any other advantages), and their holdings can also (but not always) be subject to a lock-up, so as to provide for an orderly aftermarket once the IPO starts trading and beyond. In Hong Kong, cornerstone investors have to abide by a strict six-month lock-up, whereas there is no such requirement in Singapore. In Malaysia, there was a time when structured lock-ups were introduced, pursuant to which cornerstone investors were only locked-up above a certain amount of shares that they owned, but lock-ups were subsequently lifted altogether. Also in Hong Kong, pre-agreed allocations to cornerstone investors, if expressed as a percentage of the placement tranche (part of an IPO targeted at institutional investors), are also protected against the possible re-allocation of shares from the placement tranche to the retail tranche of the IPO. Conversely, cornerstone investors in Hong Kong are not permitted to undertake "double dipping", that is, to place orders in the institutional book of demand above and beyond their pre-agreed allocations. But they can, and indeed should generally be encouraged to, buy more shares in the aftermarket, once trading in the shares has started.

Potential cornerstone investors are initially contacted ideally several months before the start of the management roadshow for the IPO, agree to become "insiders", and are subsequently asked to sign confidentiality agreements in exchange for draft advanced copies of the preliminary offering circular. They are generally given the opportunity to meet or talk with management, following which their potential interest is ascertained and their commitment (if any) evidenced by the signing of a subscription agreement to which the company and the bookrunners are parties. Importantly, cornerstone investors should not be given additional information above and beyond that provided later to other investors in the IPO, so as to ensure a level playing field. Because of their generally high profile, and so as to comply with stock exchange regulations on disclosure, their name and the details of their commitment, as well as a short narrative covering the nature of their business, and details of any lock-up for their shares, are then included in the prospectus for all to see. On occasion, some investors approach the issuer or its advisers directly ahead of the proposed IPO, expressing interest in taking a substantial stake at an early stage in what is called a "reverse roadshow". A trend in Southeast Asia has been to disclose aggregate commitments by cornerstone investors rather than individual allocations, as is conversely done in Hong Kong. In addition, cornerstone investors are generally not entitled to any direct or indirect benefits (e.g., board representation, waiver of brokerage commission, buy-back arrangements, or sharing of underwriting fees) beyond their pre-agreed allocations. If this were to be the case, they would instead be treated as pre-IPO rather than cornerstone investors, and subject to different rules and additional restrictions.

Typically, several cornerstone investors commit to investing in an IPO, and their combined holdings can represent perhaps up to 20% or 25% of the placement (institutional) tranche, although this can sometimes be substantially more for smaller transactions or for transactions carried out in a difficult environment. For example, Khazanah Nasional Berhad, the Malaysian SWF, took a 30% participation in the US$90 million IPO of Chaowei Power Holdings, a Chinese manufacturer of batteries in Hong Kong in June 2010.[63] The cornerstone tranche in the US$12 billion

H share IPO of Agricultural Bank of China at the same time represented almost 50% of the offering,[64] and was at the time one of the largest cornerstone tranche in the history of IPOs in Hong Kong, no doubt a reflection of the tough market conditions and a form of insurance to ensure the success of the deal. The cornerstone tranche in the IPO of IHH Healthcare, which I have already mentioned, represented almost 58% of the shares offered in the IPO (after exercise of the over-allotment option).

A very large holding on the part of a single cornerstone investor (or indeed on the part of a pre-IPO strategic investor), however, may, in extreme circumstances, trigger a threshold for a mandatory takeover, so care should be taken to balance the positive psychological effect of the inclusion of pre-IPO investors with the negative implications that can also be associated with their participation. Indeed, where commitments by cornerstones are subject to a lock-up for a period of time, the market will often anticipate a possible disposal of shares by cornerstone investors, particularly nearer to the expiry of the lock-up. This may create an "overhang" effect on the share price, and prevent it from rising until such a block of shares has been sold, unless clear statements on the long-term nature of the holding are released.

It is market practice that full fees be paid to the bookrunners on shares allocated to cornerstone investors. However, in 2013, Chinese commercial real estate developer Hydoo International disclosed in the underwriting section of the prospectus for its US$212 million equivalent IPO in Hong Kong that the gross fees of 2% due to the underwriters under the IPO would not be payable on shares subscribed by cornerstone and other selected investors, perhaps an indication that these had in truth been procured by the company itself or by its legacy shareholders. In that transaction, the cornerstone orders, all placed by individuals and corporates, represented more than 61% of the shares on offer under the offering.[65] As noted in Chapter 1, Section 1.8, the same thing happened with the IPO of Agricultural Bank of China (ABC) in 2010.

By way of illustration, Table 7 sets out details of the allocations made to cornerstone investors in the two of the largest H share IPOs in the Hong Kong market.[65] In addition, mainland Chinese cornerstone investors would also have been allocated under the A share tranches of the global offerings for these IPOs. Many of these are well-known and often frequent investors in large IPOs in that market.

As another example, in October 2010, it was announced that KIA would invest US$1 billion as part of a US$1.92 billion cornerstone tranche (with a six-month lock-up) in AIA's US$20.4 billion equivalent IPO in Hong Kong, while Peter Woo Kwong-ching's Wharf Holdings would commit to buying US$200 million of shares

IPO date	Issuer	H share IPO size (US$ billion equivalent) (1)	Cornerstone investors	Approximate value of IPO shares allocated (US$ million equivalent)
July 2010	Agricultural Bank of China	12	Qatar Investment Authority	2,800
			Kuwait Investment Authority	800
			Standard Chartered Bank	500
			Rabobank Groep	250
			Seven Group Holdings (2)	250
			Temasek Holdings	200
			China Resources	200
			China Travel Services (3)	150
			Archer Daniels Midland (4)	100
			Cheung Kong (Holdings)	100
			United Overseas Bank (5)	100
October 2006	Industrial and Commercial Bank of China	16	Kuwait Investment Authority	720
			China Life Insurance (Group)	565
			Gov. of Singapore Invest. Corp.	360
			China Life Insurance (Hong Kong)	255
			Dato Dr Cheng Yu-tung (6)	205
			Dr Lee Shau-kee	205
			Qatar Investment Authority	205
			Sun Hung Kai Properties	205
			United Overseas Bank	205
			Mr Peter Woo Kwong-ching (7)	205
			Mr Kuok Hock-nien (8)	205
			Mr Chen Din Hwa (9)	185
			Cheung Kong (Holdings)	100
			Hutchison Whampoa	100
			CITIC Pacific	100
			Mr Yung Chi-kin (10)	100
			Ms Chen Wai-wai (11)	20

(1) After exercise of the over-allotment option
(2) A significant, diversified group controlled by Australian tycoon Kerry Stokes
(3) The tourism and travel agency of the government of the PRC
(4) A leading American company in agricultural processing and producing
(5) From Singapore
(6) Owner of Chow Tai Fook Enterprises and controls New World group
(7) Chairman of Wheelock and Company Limited and The Wharf (Holdings) Limited
(8) Related to Ms Chen Wai-wai and controls Nan Fung Group Limited
(9) Chairman of Nan Fung Textiles Consolidated and Nan Fung Development Limited
(10) Chairman of CITIC Pacific
(11) Related to Mr Kuok Hock-nien and controls Nan Fung Group Limited

Table 7

Examples of cornerstone investor tranches in two major H share IPOs in Hong Kong

Source: IPO prospectuses.

in the same offering. They both joined other cornerstone investors, including New World and Chow Tai Fook (both then controlled by the late Cheng Yu-tung), who committed for US$50 million each; as well as, from Malaysia, Guoco Group, who reportedly committed for US$420 million and Kumpulan Wang Persaraan (Diperbadankan), better known as KWAP, a pension fund, said to be investing US$200 million.[66]

A trend in the mid- to late 2010s in Hong Kong was for Chinese corporates and state-owned enterprises to increasingly participate as cornerstones in IPOs by issuers from the Chinese mainland, in sharp contrast to the institutional investors or tycoons that bought stock in that capacity in prior years. One of the reasons for this is probably the requirement to abide by a lock-up, which many market participants are often reluctant to commit to, against a background of volatile market conditions. By way of illustration, there were no cornerstone investors in the multi-billion-dollar IPO of pork producer W.H. Group in 2014.

In addition to cornerstone investors, Asian (and other) IPOs also often include anchor investors. In Asia, these are often institutions that were approached by the bookrunners to subscribe for shares as cornerstones, but that were reluctant to see their names disclosed or to agree to a lock-up. Instead, they choose to place an early order in the institutional book of demand and will generally be well treated in the allocation process, although without the guarantee that a cornerstone subscription brings. Together with cornerstone investors, they enable the bookrunners to announce to the market on the first day or days of bookbuilding that the book is already covered, normally triggering considerable additional demand by a wider contingent of investors and enabling the IPO to be priced at a higher valuation within the price range. This practice, which seeks to target "leadership" institutional accounts to anchor a transaction, is also known as "pilot fishing" in the UK and Europe.

For more information on cornerstone and pre-IPO investors more generally, readers may wish to refer to my book *Cornerstone Investors: A Practice Guide for Asian IPOs*, also published by Hong Kong University Press.

2.12.8 Grading institutional investors according to quality

Next in the ranking, still with high allocations, are high-quality institutional investors and hedge funds that place orders in the book of demand during bookbuilding. Such Tier 1 investors often (but not always) invest with a long-term horizon and in large amounts. Individual orders in the region of US$30 to US$60 million, or even more in sizeable IPOs, are not uncommon. They are also usually the investors that meet with management in one-on-one meetings during the roadshow. They are known for carrying out significant in-house research and fundamental analysis in addition to talking to research analysts. Invariably, they are among the most active institutions in the secondary market and are therefore the highest payers of commissions to investment banks and serviced by senior members of the equity sales teams.

Tier 2 accounts include smaller asset management firms and hedge funds, typically with fewer assets under management, and a more active profile, that is, a shorter investment horizon. They may not necessarily meet with management in one-on-one meetings, but perhaps during smaller meetings or group presentations, together with other investors. Their allocations as a percentage of demand will be lower as a result of their more active profile. Such investors also often have a more "general" bias to their investments and may not have the detailed buy-side in-house research capabilities of the larger institutions. They are also serviced by broader, generalist salespeople and their typical order size most of the time does not exceed US$10 million equivalent.

Tier 3 accounts (and beyond) include even smaller asset managers, brokers, as well as private banks and trading or proprietary accounts of investment banks. Their investment horizon is relatively short term and they are more momentum-driven than focused on growth or value. Their allocations as a percentage of demand are accordingly generally low, although their inclusion may sometimes be useful to generate aftermarket liquidity. In a much-oversubscribed transaction, many of these investors will receive no allocations at all. Their typical order size will be in low single-digit millions in US dollars (or below), or, conversely, can sometimes be considerably inflated (for example, in relation to their assets under management), and their orders may also change throughout bookbuilding, as positive news about the level of over-subscription is released, particularly in the case of private banks and high net-worth individuals.

When actually allocating a book of demand, a bookrunner may also choose to grade investors in perhaps four or five tiers rather than three, although more than that becomes impractical.

2.12.9 Bottom-up and top-down demand estimates

Attempting to predict or assess institutional investor demand in an IPO can be done in a number of ways, most commonly by using "bottom-up" or "top-down" demand estimates. A bottom-up analysis involves compiling a list of those institutions most likely to invest in an offering and estimating for each of them the extent of their demand in monetary terms, generally based on demand gathered for comparable prior offerings. This is then added up to provide an overall demand estimate. Ranges for potential, individual orders are often used for such a purpose.

By contrast, a top-down approach is more theoretical and often involves the use of market indices. If a company and an IPO are large enough, then it is likely that the issuer will be included in one of the most commonly followed stock indices (see, for example, the case study for Essar Energy's IPO on the LSE in Appendix 1, or the example of Russian telecoms company MegaFon, already mentioned in Chapter 1, Section 1.3.5). By estimating the company's weight in a country or other index based on its likely valuation and free float, as well as taking into account the weight of the country of listing or industry in a global portfolio—for example by using the Morgan Stanley Capital International (MSCI) global indices, probably the most widely used global equity benchmarks by institutional investors—one can in turn estimate the amount of passive, index-based demand for the stock. A combination of a bottom-up and top-down analysis can therefore give a reasonable, though still only approximate, indication of the likely demand from investors for the IPO. Much obviously also depends on market conditions prevailing at the time of launch.

2.13   Retail investors

Retail investors, or the general public, can represent a sizeable proportion of market participants not only in new equity issues, but also in the secondary market for stocks that are already listed and traded. This is for example the case in Hong Kong, South Korea, Taiwan, Japan, and in Australia in particular.

2.13.1   Fixed price offerings and advance payment

In IPOs, given the number of people involved, it is generally not practical to build a book of demand from retail investors, with orders placed at various prices within a price range. Rare exceptions to this include India, which has a system of auction in place for offerings to the public, and France, where the *offre à prix ouvert* (OPO) system enables orders to be placed at various prices within a range, as is the case in a bookbuilding process. For this reason, public offerings are usually conducted on a fixed-price basis.

In IPOs where deals are marketed to institutions on the basis of a price range, retail investors generally pay the maximum price in advance and are subsequently reimbursed, without interest, a few days or weeks later if the offer price is set at a lower level. They are also reimbursed for the difference between the number of shares they apply for and their actual allocation (if any). In theory, payment in advance prevents order inflation in the hope of receiving better allocations, and other techniques have been developed over time to prevent additional speculation in the form of multiple applications by the same individuals.

The reality, however, in markets where retail investment in IPOs is popular, is that many investors borrow on margin from banks and brokers to place sizeable orders in the hope of receiving large allocations. This can prove a risky strategy since no interest is usually paid on monies paid to receiving banks at the time of the application, so there needs to be an immediate significant capital gain in the aftermarket to make this an attractive proposition.

Most of the time, several bands are created, depending on the size of the retail orders, and a balloting process is generally set into motion by the share registrar to determine actual allocations. An example is shown in the case study for the CapitaMalls IPO in Singapore in Appendix 1.

As we have seen earlier, in larger offerings or in privatizations, retail investors sometimes benefit from incentives, for example discounts (over the price paid by institutions) or bonus shares, to encourage their participation, although such features are now rarely included in public offerings.

2.13.2 Methods of application

There are various ways for retail investors to apply for shares in an IPO. Traditionally, application forms had to be filled and deposited with receiving banks together with application monies. This practice still exists: in Hong Kong, for example, long queues of applicants outside bank branches were until fairly recently generally a sign of healthy demand, that an IPO would be "hot", and the share price would spike immediately after the start of trading. In South Korea, applications by domestic investors were placed in a rather formal fashion in sealed envelopes and opened at the end of the offering upon pricing; this could be a cumbersome and rather uncertain process, so retail brokers there were often asked to underwrite public offerings to avoid last-minute surprises with demand at a late stage in the IPO. Since the early 2000s, however, and where allowed, most banks acting in a receiving bank capacity have put in place internet platforms for the public to participate in new issues, and this has now become the preferred method used by retail investors to apply for shares in an IPO. These generally include disclaimers and ask for an acknowledgement that the applicant has read the offering circular and understands the risks associated with capital markets investments. In Hong Kong, the US$11.2 billion equivalent secondary listing by Alibaba (in 2019) was the first-ever IPO in the city in which applications by retail investors were made solely electronically.

The most innovative system, however, is in Singapore, where participants in retail offerings for IPO, or indeed other ECM transactions with a public offering, can readily apply for shares through automated teller machines (ATMs). This is one of the most common ways for the public to participate in offerings there and retail tranches are, in many cases, fully covered within less than an hour. Applicants using ATMs even have the option of investing part of their retirement money held in Central Provident Funds (CPF) to participate in new issues. Such technological advances can probably be explained by the relatively small size of Singapore, and also because public offerings there, unlike in other markets, are generally of a modest size (in the order of 5% to 10% of an IPO), the market being principally driven for primary equity offerings by institutional investors. Internet applications are of course also popular, as elsewhere.

2.14   Deciding on an offer structure

The offer structure for an IPO generally depends both on market practice in the country of listing as well as on the size of the transaction.

2.14.1   Institutional and retail tranches

Broadly speaking, the offer structure for an IPO incorporates both an offering to institutional investors, domestically as well as internationally, often known as a "placement tranche", as well as an offering to members of the public in the country of listing.

Rather confusingly, these tranches can differ from those used to actually underwrite an offering, or from tranches defined to provide comfort on disclosure by way of legal opinions or comfort letters. As we have seen earlier, for underwriting or "comfort" purposes, market practice is usually for placement tranches to be divided between offerings made in the US (e.g., where a Rule 144A private placement is part of the offer structure) and offerings made outside the US (including to offshore US investors under Reg. S). This applies even to non-US companies or to international offerings not placed in the US at all (in which case they will be described Reg. S-only transactions). This is probably for historical reasons, since much of the early international practice for capital markets transactions derived from that in the US and, at least initially, to a significant extent also involved US investment banks as well as US firms of legal advisers. In addition, many large IPOs were in the past listed in the US as it was thought that other markets did not have the depth of demand (perhaps with the exception of Japan and, to some extent, the UK) to cater to offerings of a billion US dollars equivalent or more. Much of this is, of course, no longer true, but the way investment banks and law firms look at IPOs to this day still conforms to US practice. In addition, and for comfort purposes only, domestic offerings to institutional investors and to retail investors are sometimes considered as one tranche, for example for the delivery of SAS 72 comfort letters.

Domestic offerings are easy to understand and set up and obviously do not involve the marketing of shares outside the country of listing. Offering shares (or related instruments) internationally as well as domestically considerably broadens the spread of investors who may buy into the investment story but, at the same time, increases disclosure and the logistics involved to reach out to many more segments of the global investor community.

In the past, placement tranches for international offerings were often divided into a number of distinct, ring-fenced sub-offerings across various regions: for example, a local institutional tranche, a UK tranche, a continental European tranche, a US tranche, and a tranche for the rest of the world (see Chapter 1, Section 1.8.2, for an example of an offering with a regional syndicate set-up). Most institutional offerings, except perhaps when dual or multiple listings are conducted, now only comprise a single, global tranche with syndicate members generally free to access investors around the world, subject only to the licences they may possess. Examples of global syndicates can be found in the detailed case studies set out in Appendix 1.

2.14.2 Allocating and re-allocating between tranches and upsize options

Allocating shares between tranches is usually at the discretion of the bookrunner banks on behalf of the issuer and its shareholders. However, as explained earlier, in certain cases (and chiefly in Hong Kong, most likely because of the historic weight and influence of smaller brokerage firms there), mechanisms exist to automatically re-allocate shares between the placement and retail (or public) offers, through claw-back triggers. In very large transactions, waivers can be granted so that the public offering in dollar terms does not become too large, and therefore does not negatively impact the volatility of trading in the aftermarket, as public investors are often not considered to be long-term shareholders. For example, large IPOs in Hong Kong usually involve less than 10% initially allocated to retail investors, with the claw-back triggers also lowered from the usual requirements (see Appendix 8), which may see up to 50% of the allocations made to retail investors if the public offer is more than 100 times subscribed by them. For the same reasons, and also because shares in these issuers will likely be actively traded just because of the latter's size,

IPOs there by companies with a market capitalization of more than HK$10 billion (approximately US$1.3 billion) may represent between 15% and 25% of the share capital of a listing applicant, rather than the prescribed minimum free float of 25% for other companies.

Claw-forward mechanisms are also generally included in addition to claw-back provisions in an inter-syndicate agreement: in the event that a public offering is under-subscribed, shares can then be re-allocated to the placement tranche, assuming of course enough demand there has been generated, and enough shareholders overall have bought the shares to satisfy the listing requirements laid out by the stock exchange. Claw-back and claw-forward arrangements apply to firm shares only and not to shares that are the subject of an over-allotment option. This is because the over-allotment option used to stabilize the share price in the first days or weeks of trading, and which applies to the institutional offering, or placement, only, is exercised well after closing and after any re-allocation between the tranches of a global offering has been made. The over-allotment option may also be exercised only partially, or even not at all, depending on the circumstances of a particular transaction (see Chapter 4, Section 4.1, for more information). While many institutions take a long-term view when investing, the general public is often (although not always) more interested in quick monetary gain—in many jurisdictions, retail investors tend to sell their holdings soon after the share price pops up in the first few days of trading (one notable exception being Japan). In some countries, the split between both tranches is left for the banks to decide, although past transactions generally provide a good benchmark for what both the institutional and retail markets can absorb.

IPOs may also sometimes include an upsize option, whereby the issuer can opt to increase the size of the offering by a fixed, previously disclosed percentage, subject to investor demand. For example, this was the case in the IPO of AIA in October 2010 in Hong Kong, where the size of the IPO was increased by 20% to reach the equivalent of US$17.8 billion (prior to exercise of the over-allotment option), making it at the time both the largest-ever IPO in Hong Kong as well as the largest-ever IPO by an insurance company. In this particular case, the upsize option applied to the institutional tranche only and the 10% public offer tranche, which was approximately ten times subscribed, did not trigger a claw-back. Following the exercise in full of the over-allotment option, on the first day of trading, the IPO of AIA increased in size to US$20.4 billion equivalent, becoming the third-largest ever world-wide at the time.

2.14.3 Accessing the US market

As explained earlier, a key decision, and one that is often (but not always) influenced by the size of the company and IPO, is how the US market and US investors are accessed, since selling shares to US investors entails additional costs with respect to disclosure and the level of comfort that will be sought from third-party advisers, particularly legal firms and accountants. In addition, listing in the US, rather than merely selling shares there, also often entails, except perhaps in the case of extremely large offerings, paying much higher IPO fees than is the case elsewhere, with gross fees of up to 6.50% or 7.00% in some cases, as compared with around 2.00% to 3.50% in many other markets. Examples of gross fees paid by issuers to underwriters in IPOs across various jurisdictions can be found in the case studies included in Appendix 1.

For most smaller international IPOs, say, up to US$150 million or US$200 million equivalent in size, a Reg. S offering is generally appropriate, that is, an issue that will only target offshore US institutional investors, in addition to institutions domestically and internationally and retail investors in the country of listing. This is because, for an IPO of this size, the incremental demand that may be derived from investors in the US in many cases does not justify the additional expense, disclosure work, and potential liability risk. It also means that research analysts will not be visiting the US on their PDIE tour—in any event, no research reports can be distributed in the US—and that the roadshow will also not be visiting American cities.

Back in the 1990s, however, it would have been pretty much inconceivable to conduct the IPO of a company much above the US$1 billion or US$1.5 billion mark without registering the offering with the SEC and listing in the US. The US$3 billion private sector IPO of Swedish truck manufacturer Scania in 1996 is a case in point. The company was listed both in Stockholm and on the NYSE in an offering led by SBC Warburg (as it was known at the time), Morgan Stanley, and Sweden's Enskilda Securities. The same also applied to many privatizations in Europe, in France, Italy, Spain, and other countries. Deutsche Telekom, from Germany, listed in Frankfurt, on the NYSE, and on the Tokyo Stock Exchange (TSE) in a massive US$13.2 billion IPO that same year, although it later de-listed from both the NYSE and the TSE in 2010. However, in the case of some European (and, in particular, UK) privatizations, mass local retail offerings conducted with much fanfare and advertising were able to absorb significant amounts of stock, encouraged by generous retail incentives. Indeed, many of the early privatizations in the UK in the late 1980s and early 1990s were multi-billion-pound offerings with significant retail tranches, including the

£2.5 billion IPO of British Steel in 1988, the £5.2 billion IPO of the water authorities in the UK in 1989, and, twice, a £5.4 billion secondary offering for British Telecom (BTII in 1991 and BT3 in 1993).[67]

Listing a company in the US implied conforming to the stringent disclosure and reporting requirements of the SEC, NYSE, or other US exchanges, a costly and demanding process, both initially and on a continuing basis. Accordingly, in early 1991, Rule 144A of the Securities Act of 1933 was enacted to enable foreign issuers to offer securities in the US by way of an institutional private placement to QIBs, without the need to register with the SEC. This was on the premise that large US institutions were mature enough and, in any event, already active around the world so as to be generally satisfied with the disclosure and reporting standards used by issuers in their local markets, subject only to a limited amount of additional information being included in new issue offering circulars for the benefit of US buyers. I worked at S.G.Warburg in New York when Rule 144A came into force and saw first-hand how this became an immediate success, with a variety of issuers around the world taking this new opportunity to access US institutional demand.

Nowadays, many multi-billion US dollar offerings (including all the mega IPOs by Chinese banks in recent years) have featured Rule 144A private placements, and US listings of foreign issuers are no longer the norm, even for very large IPOs, although perhaps with the exception of internet and new economy companies. While some US investors can still only buy SEC-registered securities, a Rule 144A private placement enables an issuer to access most US institutional investors with discretionary assets under management above US$100 million, alongside smaller banks and savings and loan associations with an audited net worth of at least US$25 million and registered brokers or dealers managing on a discretionary basis assets of at least US$10 million. This readily covers the vast majority of accounts (several thousand), which can, in theory, be interested in an international equity offering. In this case, disclosure will be somewhat more demanding. For example, an MD&A will then be required to be included in the offering circular—although OFR disclosure under the EU directives now pretty much achieves the same, and some exchanges, such as that in Hong Kong, now also require MD&As to be included in prospectuses anyway—and the legal advisers to deliver 10b-5 letters; research analysts will need to conduct investor education in the US; and the roadshow will, at the very least, tour New York and Boston, perhaps with the addition of other cities in the US.

A wider exemption from registration requirements than Rule 144A also exists in the US through what is called an "offering under Regulation D of the Securities Act of 1933 (as amended)". This enables access to "accredited investors", a

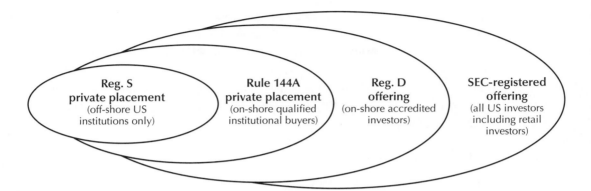

Figure 4

Accessing US investors

somewhat wider universe of investors than QIBs, provided that they are deemed to be sophisticated enough. This exemption is normally used for follow-on and block trade transactions only. The diagram in Figure 4 shows the various levels of access to US investors that can be used in ECM offerings.

2.14.4 Accessing European investors and focus markets

Any mid-size or larger international IPO will see demand from investors in England, and often from Scotland, where many pension funds are managed, and all new issues in Asia will see demand from investors from Hong Kong and Singapore. However, demand among continental European institutional investors tends to vary greatly, depending on the profile of the issuer and the investment story.

For example, significant amounts of money placed with French institutions were, prior to Brexit at least, actually managed from London. Participation by Swiss or German investors will often by heavily influenced by the industry sector of the issuer. For example, there is frequently good interest from Swiss investors for international IPOs in the healthcare sector, because of the presence of a strong local pharmaceutical sector with significant on-shore following. Things may perhaps change to some extent, now that Brexit has been implemented, as some investment firms relocate some of their portfolio managers (PMs) from the City of London to the continent.

Investors in Australia, where placing the bulk of IPOs with retail or high net-worth investors in the norm, have until fairly recently been focused on domestic issues, but are now starting to open their portfolios to overseas investments, with the local institutional investor Platinum Asset Management taking the lead for international equities. They are also particularly receptive to issuers from the natural resources, infrastructure, and property sectors. And investors in the Middle East (in Kuwait, Qatar, Abu Dhabi, and, to a lesser extent, in Saudi Arabia, Dubai, Jordan, and Oman) are now increasingly being targeted by ECM teams, especially in the case of larger IPOs.

2.14.5 Selling to Japanese investors

Japanese IPOs are traditionally almost exclusively placed with individual and high net-worth investors. While there can be strong interest for international new issues, this is usually only the case for large, well-known, and prestigious companies (typically privatizations), rather than for smaller deals. Without listing in Japan, private placements to institutions there are in any event limited by law to up to 49 institutions. In my experience, institutional demand on the part of Japanese institutions also tends to be fairly limited in the case of a "normal" and conventionally structured IPO. For large international IPOs, however, there exists a mechanism called public offering without listing (POWL), which enables the sale of securities to the Japanese public without the need to conduct a formal listing in Japan by filing a securities registration statement (SRS) with the Kanto Local Finance Bureau (KLFB), a subdivision of the Japanese Ministry of Finance. The process cannot be stopped after filing of the SRS. Such a POWL, however, entails additional due diligence and the drafting of a prospectus in Japanese, as well as ongoing disclosure in Japanese, including work on the company's accounts to be performed by Japanese accountants. While some of the execution work for a POWL can take place simultaneously with that for the rest of the IPO, incorporating such an offering in a global offer structure can add up to a few weeks to the overall timetable. In addition, in a POWL formal demand is actually gathered from investors on a fixed-price basis once the offer price for the global offering has been determined. So, while the subscription itself will have been underwritten by the Japanese broker(s) prior to the offer taking place, and some early indications of demand (rather than actual demand) can be obtained at an earlier stage, the momentum that can be generated by a POWL to "boost" global demand in an IPO globally is debatable. The main advantage of including a POWL in an IPO (which is only really applicable and relevant to very large, visible, and sizeable offerings) is to diversify investor demand (and allocations).

Still, actual demand from Japan can, for the right deal, represent very large amounts. In the US$12 billion H share IPO of Agricultural Bank of China in July

2010, the POWL, which was led by Nomura and Daiwa, reportedly generated more than 40% of demand under the placement tranche, compared with lower individual amounts raised from international hedge funds, long-only accounts, corporate investors, and private wealth investors. In the end, however, Japanese investors only received a total allocation in the order of a much lower, single-digit percentage.[68] Similarly, in the US$20.4 billion IPO (including the over-allotment option) of insurer AIA in Hong Kong in October 2010, POWL demand was said to have represented US$5.5 billion, for a dedicated Japanese tranche of US$300 to US$400 million.[69] Increasingly, there has been a trend whereby two arrangers rather than a single one are appointed to manage a POWL: for example, both Daiwa and Nomura were appointed in that capacity in the multi-billion-dollar IPO of Chinese pork producer W.H. Group in 2014, as was the case for AIA. It is questionable whether this actually adds more value than mandating one broker only.

2.14.6 American depositary receipt and global depositary receipt tranches

For foreign issuers listing in the US, as well as for some issuers internationally, particularly from emerging markets, depositary receipts (DRs) evidencing shares in the form of US dollar-denominated certificates are sometimes issued instead of or in addition to shares. DRs are discussed in greater detail in the following section.

These have traditionally taken the form of American depositary receipts (ADRs), of which there are several levels with increasing disclosure requirements, and which may or may not be listed on one of the US, or more recently, other, stock exchanges; and of global depositary receipts (GDRs), generally listed in London, Luxembourg, or Singapore (although other markets, such as Frankfurt, Hong Kong, and Japan, now also allow the listing of DRs).

When DRs are offered alongside ordinary shares, and when the currency in which such shares are denominated is easily traded, investors will often opt to buy the shares, which will exhibit greater liquidity, rather than the DRs. In some extreme cases, no certificates at all may be issued under the DR tranche if all the participating institutional investors opt to receive shares rather than DRs upon closing of the deal. In some countries, however, DRs are the only instruments that can be offered internationally. This has historically been the only way international institutional investors could get access to companies through primary equity offerings in India, Taiwan, or South Korea, although this is now largely no longer the case, provided that they can obtain foreign investor IDs. Investors, however, always have the possibility of redeeming such DRs into ordinary shares. In fact, there is usually a "flow-back" of DRs to ordinary shares over a relatively short period of time, particularly for companies in the mid-cap segment, as the liquidity in the shares is often much greater.

It is now rare for companies listed on major international stock exchanges to issue DRs, with the notable exception of international companies listed in the US. While an offering of ordinary shares may sometimes have a separate ADR tranche, GDRs are typically always offered as a stand-alone offering.

Outstanding DRs under a programme are traded, either as listed entities or over the counter; their value, relative to the ordinary shares and taking into account the prevailing exchange rate, can be expressed as a premium or discount to the ordinary shares. DRs traded at a premium are an indication that such instruments are in demand by investors, which can be for a variety of reasons, but generally because they are easier or less burdensome to trade than ordinary shares. Conversely, DRs traded at a discount point to a lack of interest on the part of the market for such instruments relative to a company's ordinary shares. DRs are discussed in more detail in the next chapter.

Figure 5 illustrates the various components of an offer structure, incorporating a Rule 144A private placement in the US, across classes of investors. Cornerstone investors would be included either under the Reg. S or the Rule 144A tranches or perhaps under high net-worth investors. A DR tranche (if any) would, in this example, form part of the Rule 144A offering in the form of Rule 144A ADRs.

2.15   Depositary receipts and depositary shares

Depositary receipts (DRs) are securities representing the ownership and economic interest in underlying equity shares. DRs represent a set number of shares in a company. For example, each DR may represent two ordinary shares. Such shares are issued or can be acquired on the stock exchange on which they are traded, and held by a custodian in that country on behalf of a depositary bank. The depositary then issues DR certificates representing the shares it holds. In turn, holders of DRs can request the depositary to exchange the DRs they hold for the shares they represent.

DRs enable companies to issue equity, perhaps on better terms than could be achieved in their domestic market, which is often, but not always, an emerging market, as well as to diversify their shareholder base. In turn, they provide investors with the opportunity to gain exposure to a company's shares that may otherwise be unavailable. DRs are normally (but not always) denominated in US dollars and settled on internationally recognized settlement systems in Europe or the US. Broadly speaking, there are two types of depositary receipts:

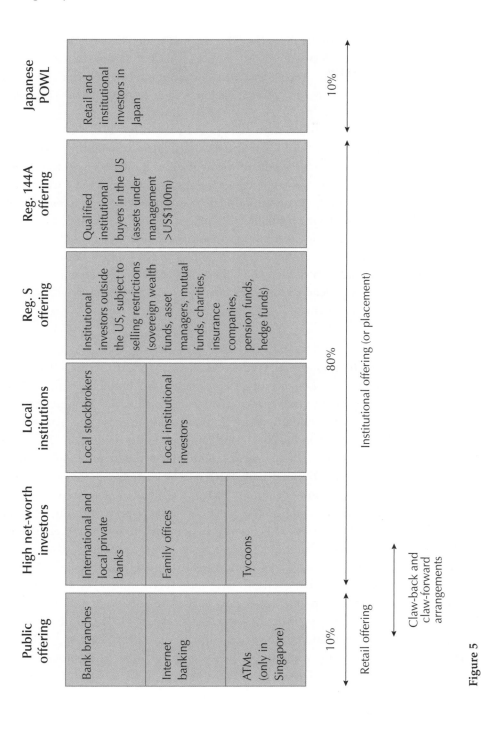

Figure 5

The various components of an offer structure

GDRs, which are usually in registered form, and traded between international investors and US QIBs, generally using the Euroclear and Clearstream settlement systems in Europe, and the Depositary Trust Company (DTC) in the US; and

ADRs, which are traded by international and US investors via the DTC in the US.

ADRs and GDRs themselves are evidenced by instruments called "American depositary shares" (ADSs) and "global depositary shares" (GDSs), respectively. Depositary shares are actually the instruments that are traded by investors, while the depositary receipts themselves remain in the clearing system. Even if technically wrong, it is common in the financial industry to informally refer to issues of DRs rather than DSs when talking about such placements of certificates. However, offering circulars and underwriting documentation will of course accurately mention DSs. On the issuer's share register, holders of DRs appear in one large lot as the depositary bank, which then takes charges of shareholder action items, such as the payment of dividends. How such shareholder action items are handled is covered in a deposit agreement.

2.15.1 Listing DRs

Issuing ADSs can be done on a stand-alone basis or as part of any other ECM transaction involving the issuance of ordinary shares. As noted in Section 2.14.6, GDSs, however, are usually issued in stand-alone transactions. DR programmes can also be established independently of any capital-raising exercise and, sometimes, without any involvement on the part of the company at the request of a broker in response to investor demand. In such cases, liquidity in the programme will generally be low. GDSs and often ADSs are usually listed on a stock exchange, generally in the UK or in Luxembourg or other countries (such as Germany or Singapore) for GDSs (or their local equivalents), and on the NYSE, Nasdaq, or on NYSE American for ADSs. Some ADSs are also separately traded in London, Frankfurt, and Singapore. However, ADSs can also be unlisted. In some cases, an issuer can have the choice to list on the main board or on another market created by the exchange. In the recent past, stock exchanges in other countries have introduced similar DR programmes, sometimes denominated in local currencies, such as in Hong Kong (HDRs), where they have, however, not been much of a success, Singapore (SDRs), India (IDRs, for example, as issued by Standard Chartered Bank in May 2010),[70] Taiwan (TDRs, for example, as issued by the mainland Chinese company Yangzijiang Shipbuilding, also in 2010),[71] or Japan (JDRs). Further information on these DR instruments is provided in the glossary.

2.15.2 Global depositary receipts (GDRs)

In order to establish a GDR programme, additional parties above and beyond those in a normal IPO team need to be appointed, namely a depositary and a custodian. The depositary coordinates with the lead investment banks appointed by the company, as well as with its legal advisers, to implement the various steps in the programme. It is also tasked with preparing and issuing GDR certificates to investors. The custodian receives the underlying shares, which it then holds in custody for the account of the depositary, and also transmits dividend payments. It is therefore necessary for the issuer to prepare and sign a deposit agreement, which constitutes the principal legal instrument underlying the issue of DRs, and to include a summary of the same in the offering circular. Separately, a custodian agreement is entered into directly between the depositary and the custodian. Other documents and procedures for the issue of GDRs are roughly similar to those for any other IPO. Depositaries generally do not charge much (if anything) in terms of fees to issuers, but are paid by investors for the issuance and redemption of DRs, the payment of dividends, and any corporate actions that they undertake on behalf of issuers. They will often subsidize (or in some cases even cover in full) the legal costs and the costs of documentation related to such programmes to win business from issuers (see Section 2.1.8). As mentioned above, when a company has issued DRs/DSs, the depositary (rather than the end-holders of the DRs) will appear as the shareholder on the register. There are various methods pursuant to which the DRs can be voted on behalf of holders, usually through the depositary.

2.15.3 American depositary receipts (ADRs)

ADRs are fairly similar to GDRs, but with a focus on the US market. It is thought that there are around 2000 ADR programmes for a variety of companies from about 70 countries, according to website thebalance.com. Like (most) GDRs, they are US dollar-denominated instruments and represent the ownership and economic interest in underlying shares. They therefore enable US (and also European, Asian and other) investors to acquire and trade non-US securities without the settlement difficulties associated with certain markets, in particular emerging markets. They also help non-US companies increase their visibility in the US and provide them with another means of access to the US equity markets. The custody and other arrangements are roughly similar to those for GDRs, except that clearing and settlement for ADRs is in the US through the DTC. In addition to the US, some ADRs can also be traded in Europe on Deutsche Börse®, on the LSE, or in Singapore, in the latter case to enhance investor access to ADRs issued by Asian companies during trading hours in Asia.

There are four types of ADRs: unsponsored, level 1, level 2, and level 3, the last three being partially sponsored or sponsored ADRs. In addition, ADRs may also be issued when a Rule 144A private placement is conducted in the US.

2.15.3.1 Unsponsored ADRs

Unsponsored ADR programmes are not initiated (or controlled) by the issuer, but are instead created at the initiative of a broker working with a depositary bank in response to US investor demand. They involve the filing by the depositary of a simple registration statement called Form F-6 with the SEC. Such programmes, many of which are illiquid, trade on the over-the-counter (OTC) market on what is called the "pink sheets", which is literally a list of all unsponsored DR programmes, originally printed on pink paper. Because the company has no control over an unsponsored ADR, the programme can sometimes be duplicated by more than one depositary bank, without the company's consent. Converting to a sponsored ADR can therefore provide a company with a greater degree of control. This, however, entails the payment of cancellation fees for outstanding unsponsored DRs, which can in some cases represent a relatively large amount of money.

2.15.3.2 Sponsored ADRs

A level 1 (or partially sponsored) ADR programme is, by contrast, initiated by a company. It also involves the filing of Form F-6 with the SEC, but exempts the company from providing each individual US holder with information filed in its home market. Instead, such information is simply sent to the SEC pursuant to an exemption from full registration requirements under Rule 12g3-2(b). A level 1 ADR programme requires the signing of a deposit agreement with a depositary bank. It cannot, however, be listed on a US stock exchange, and therefore also trades in the pink sheets on the OTC market. The main advantage is that the company only has to deal with one depositary, which also maintains an accurate record of outstanding ADRs and of the holders of such ADRs/ADSs. Capital-raising activity on a US stock exchange is also not permitted under a level 1 programme. Here, no cancellation fees are needed to upgrade to level 2. The majority of ADRs in the US are issued through a Level 1 programme.

By contrast, a level 2 ADR programme involves full registration with the SEC. In addition to the filing of Form F-6, this requires a company to file an initial registration statement—in effect a full US standard annual report—with accounts prepared under US GAAP or with a reconciliation of the accounts to US GAAP, except where the issuer already reports under IFRS, on Form 20-F with the SEC. This entitles the company to have its ADSs listed on the NYSE, NYSE American, or on Nasdaq, and to take advantage of US investor demand for its shares.

The only major difference between a level 2 and level 3 sponsored ADR is that the level 3 ADR programme enables a public offering of equity. This, in turn, requires the filing of a full US standard offering circular, in effect an expanded version of the Form 20-F annual report, again with a reconciliation of the company's accounts to US GAAP or with the accounts computed in conformity with US GAAP, except where the issuer reports under IFRS, on Form F-1 with the SEC. For example, in 2002, Chunghwa Telecom, the incumbent telecom operator in Taiwan, listed on the NYSE in a US$2 billion offering of ADSs. While technically not an IPO—the company had already previously listed in Taipei—the ADS offering was effectively marketed as a quasi-IPO with a price range given the low (single-digit) free float and illiquid market in its shares as a result of its prior, small public flotation and domestic listing. The listing of Banco Santander Brasil on the NYSE in 2009, a case study for which is included in Appendix 1, is another example of such a level 3 ADR programme.

2.15.3.3 Rule 144A ADRs (RADRs)

When a company chooses to access the US market by way of a Rule 144A private placement, typically in conjunction with a domestic public offering in another country and with a Reg. S private placement to institutions outside the US, it may elect to issue Rule 144A ADRs (or RADRs) alongside its ordinary shares. As for other ADRs, this also involves the appointment of a depositary bank and the signing of a deposit agreement but, in this case, no registration with the SEC. Instead, a copy of the prospectus is simply sent to the SEC but without any review of the document on its part. The work is similar to that for any other IPO with a Rule 144A tranche, except that a section on the ADRs needs to be included in the offering circular and that ADRs will be offered, alongside shares, to investors (including QIBs) in the IPO.

As mentioned earlier, except for issuers from emerging markets, in many cases, investors will often place orders for the most liquid securities and generally elect to buy shares rather than the ADRs. RADRs therefore are now becoming less common. RADRs are traded by market makers and QIBs. Initially, RADRs required eligibility under a platform called PORTAL (Private Offerings, Resale and Trading through Automated Linkages), established by the National Association of Securities Dealers (NASD, now known as FINRA) in 1990, to ensure that they met the requirements of

Rule 144A, although this is no longer the case. Nowadays, PORTAL is no longer the only way through which RADRs can be traded (in any event, PORTAL never really took off as a bona fide trading facility and many RADRs were, and still are, traded privately between QIBs). RADRs clear through the DTC, as do other ADRs.

2.16   Real estate investment trusts (REITs)

Real estate investment trusts (REITs) are popular instruments used to monetize real estate assets in IPOs and follow-on capital raisings. Through a REIT, an owner of property assets, also called a "sponsor" (which is distinct from the sponsor bank working on an IPO), can transfer ownership of such real estate assets to institutional and public investors through the listing of a new vehicle, of which it retains partial ownership.

The sponsor can then set up a REIT manager, which is paid management fees as a percentage of the value of the deposited properties owned by the REIT, as well as performance fees, either based on net property income or on the unit price performance of the REIT (REITs are quoted as units rather than shares). Acquisition fees on the value of new property acquired, as well as divestment fees on the value of divested property, are also charged.

Although it has generally been negatively affected by the credit crunch and subsequently by fears over rising interest rates over the last few years,[72] the REIT market has experienced significant growth over the last decade: in Asia alone, the growth in market capitalization (which in 2010 stood at well over US$70 billion) was over 80% from 2002 to 2007. EY estimates that the global REIT market capitalization grew from US$300 billion in 2003 to over US$1 trillion in September 2013.[73] According to Real Capital Analytics (RCA), REITs globally accounted for 20% of real estate transaction volumes in the first half of 2013.[74] The technique originated in the US and, in the Asia Pacific region, in Australia and Japan, but quickly spread out to other countries, particularly Singapore (where they are known as S-REITs). In 2007, REITs in Japan accounted for about 45% and in Singapore for about 20% of the value of the listed real estate market.[75] In Asia, listed REITs are also found in Hong Kong (H-REITs) and Malaysia (M-REITs) in particular. In Europe, REITs were first introduced in France in 2003 through the SIIC structure (*sociétés d'investissements immobiliers cotées*), but have also spread to the UK, Germany, Italy, and, in 2007, to the Netherlands.[76] In 2014, a REIT listed in Dubai in a US$175 million IPO in 2009, as the emirate's first new listing since the financial crisis,[77] while mainland China was also about to see the listing of its first domestic REIT.[78] REITs can also be found in Belgium, Canada, Mexico, New Zealand, South Africa, and Turkey. REITs can be set up with almost any kind of property asset, including office towers, mixed-use property, industrial assets, hotels, hospitals, and retail and residential property.

According to Nareit, a Washington, DC-based association representing a large and diverse industry that includes equity REITs, mortgage REITs, REITs traded on major stock exchanges, public non-listed REITs, and private REITs, as of the first quarter of 2021, 39 countries had adopted REIT legislation and the total market capitalisation of the FTSE EPRA/Nareit Developed Real Estate Index totalled US$1.7 trillion. There were also 477 listed real estate companies included in the FTSE EPRA/Nareit Global Real Estate Index, and 52% of the latter by market capitalisation were by non-US constituents. In other words, REITs are now very much a widely available and household investment product that can be found across most of the major financial markets, and even in countries such as Kenya, Pakistan, Saudi Arabia, and Cambodia, among many others.

2.16.1 The basic structure

Listed REITs can generally be established using a corporate or trust structure. As with any listed company, they have to comply with the rules laid out by the regulator or stock exchange on which they choose to list. Their investments in real estate assets can be made by way of direct ownership or through a shareholding in a special purpose vehicle (SPV). REITs are run by a management company, with a trustee holding assets on trust on behalf of the investors and a property manager providing the more routine property management services. The trustee must be independent from the manager.

REITs are generally subject to restrictions. For example, in both Singapore and Malaysia, a minimum proportion of their total assets (at least 70%) must comprise real estate or related assets, often with a cap (or in the case of Malaysia a prohibition) on property development assets, except if these are held for the purpose of holding a property due for completion. As of the first quarter of 2021, the regulatory authorities in Hong Kong were still capping to 10% the ability of REITs there to invest in property development and related activities. REITs are also usually prevented from owning vacant land and mortgages, with additional limits ascribed to the proportion of assets that can be invested in individual securities. Asset valuations must be done at least annually. REITs are tax-efficient vehicles but are required to distribute the vast majority (often at least 90%) of their pre-tax income as dividends. They are also limited as to the level of gearing they can take on; sometimes the limit is subject to credit ratings they may obtain.

2.16.2 Focused and diversified funds

REITs can be focused instruments, say, focused on owning shopping centres, which achieves savings in operation and transaction costs, translating into higher dividend distributions. Such REITs also make for easier investment stories to be conveyed to investors, particularly in the more mature markets. However, focused REITs only allow exposure to certain defined classes of property assets. By contrast, more diversified REITs achieve better risk diversification and a more stable portfolio yield, as different property sectors rather than a single asset class may post a better performance through an economic cycle. They are, however, more costly from an operational standpoint and more difficult to value and understand, and to market to investors given the dynamics of several property asset classes. There are also few precedents of diversified REITs outside emerging markets.

In the case of "volatile" assets that may be more particularly affected by an economic downturn (e.g., hotels, which were particularly affected during the COVID-19 pandemic), it is possible to structure a REIT whereby such assets are leased to a lessee under a lease agreement, with the lessee paying the REIT a ground rent, perhaps with an additional performance "kicker" linked to the profitability of the operations of the assets, in return for the right to operate the assets. This insulates the REIT somewhat from direct exposure to the operations of the property assets. In this case, the lessee is primarily responsible for the routine maintenance of the assets, and may also engage a separate manager to run the assets themselves, for example, a hotel management company.

2.16.3 Managing the fund

When setting up a REIT, it is important to engage a credible manager for the fund, so as to provide a rubber stamp of quality to investors. Well-known surveyors, property valuers, or experts should also be appointed to check the physical and structural condition of the assets, to ensure compliance with building or other regulations, and to issue authoritative valuation reports. The sponsor of the REIT (i.e., the entity injecting the assets into the vehicle) generally retains, on a continuing basis, a significant level of ownership, typically in the order of 35%, so as to not only keep its interests aligned with those of public unit-holders, but also retain a degree of management control. This percentage can, on occasion, be significantly lower.

For investors, the main attraction of owning a REIT is in the level of distribution yield it pays, both relative to other funds managing similar assets and over the relevant risk-free rate of a government bond. In this sense, they can be viewed more as fixed-income instruments, although they also offer characteristics of listed companies in that they have growth potential through asset enhancement and (for property assets) rental reversions, as well as through the further acquisition of yield accretive assets.

2.16.4 Financial engineering and growing the fund

In some cases, particularly in Hong Kong, REIT managers have used considerable financial engineering to devise yield-enhancement mechanisms with the objective of increasing the dividend per unit (DPU). These have included interest swaps to hedge the interest rate risk on debt owned by the REIT, convertible bonds, waiving the DPU on units owned by the sponsor to provide a higher dividend yield, fee waivers and rental guarantees over certain periods of time, and one-off special distributions. Such enhancement mechanisms above and beyond the "naked yield" of the fund have generally been negatively perceived by the market, as aggressive financial engineering is seen as having a negative impact on yield quality and the long-term stability for the instrument. In addition, in Hong Kong specifically, REITs have often been used to monetize assets, some of average quality, rather than to create a separately listed vehicle that could be further grown over time.

Indeed, it is important to remember that these funds are listed equity instruments that are expected to develop, and not just another way of selling property. Achieving a stable growth in the DPU, long-term growth in capital value, and rental reversions or higher occupancy rates are key considerations. So too are the management of the capital structure through gearing and the maintenance of effective cost control. Growth via acquisitions is also important for yield accretion and to add more diversified and value-added assets, whether the fund is focused or diversified. Figure 6 illustrates the various parties to, and the basic structure of, a REIT.

2.17 Business trusts and infrastructure funds

Business trusts and infrastructure funds follow broadly the same format as REITs, but are not limited to the real estate sector. Typically, they involve investments in infrastructure assets, such as toll roads, ships, aircraft, telecoms assets, airports, tank farms (dedicated sites with large tanks for the bulk storage of oil), bridges, turnpikes, or wind farms in lieu of (or in addition to) property. This can also extend to "social" infrastructure, such as retirement homes, student accommodation, and even prisons.

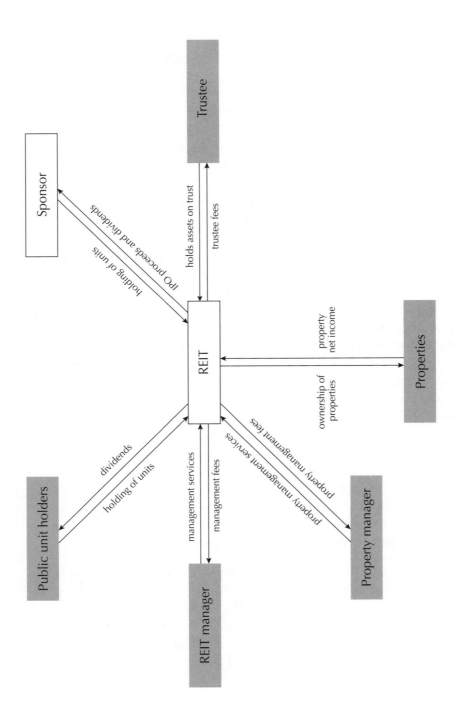

Figure 6

Basic structure for a real estate investment trust

While infrastructure funds have been in existence for a long time in Australia, in particular in response to requirements for yield investments by local superannuation and pension funds, business trusts were first introduced in 2004 in Singapore. In August 2013, more than 15 had been listed in the city-state, including hospitality trusts (comprised of hotel assets); ports, shipping, and infrastructure trusts; property trusts (but distinct from S-REITs); retail sector trusts; a healthcare trust; and a telecoms, media, and technology trust.[79] Business trusts were subsequently introduced in Hong Kong in 2011 (including one in the real estate sector), although, as of the first quarter of 2021, just like REITs, they had not spread as widely there as in Singapore, perhaps because Hong Kong is primarily a financial market that is focused on growth, rather than yield stocks.

2.17.1 The basic structure: Singapore versus Hong Kong business trusts

As with REITs, investors in a business trust own units in a vehicle that is publicly listed and traded on a stock exchange. A trustee-manager holds, manages, and operates the assets in which the trust invests for the benefit of all unit holders. A key difference is that business trusts enable the distribution (typically of 90% and up to 100%) of free cash-flow, rather than limiting distributions to accounting profits. In addition, business trusts have greater flexibility to acquire and own assets as compared to other trusts, for example REITs.[79]

There are several important differences between the business trust regimes in Singapore and Hong Kong: In Hong Kong, business trusts use share stapled units in a company as well as units in the business trust itself, whereas the structure only includes business trust units in Singapore. In addition, the trustee-manager in Singapore plays a more active management role whereas this is more of an administrative function in Hong Kong, where key business decisions are generally made at the holding company level; accordingly the trustee-manager in Hong Kong does not receive management fees or other incentives and is only entitled to the reimbursement of its costs and expenses. The trustee manager may also be removed upon a decision by 50% of share staple unit holders in Hong Kong, whereas this requires a majority threshold of 75% of unit holders in Singapore. Lastly, in Hong Kong, the trust is not permitted to incur debt (although there are no such restrictions on the company or its subsidiaries), while in Singapore, there are no restrictions on the level of gearing that may be incurred by a business trust or its operating companies.

The diagrams set out in Figure 7 set out the typical structures of business trusts in both Singapore and Hong Kong. In addition to business trusts, infrastructure funds are sometimes structured as listed companies incorporated in the Cayman

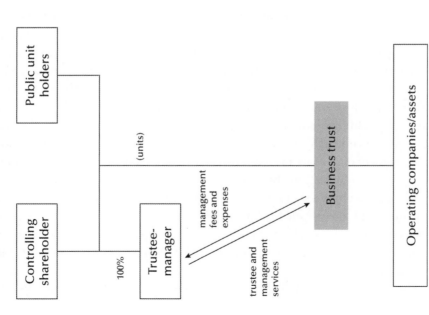

Figure 7

Singapore and Hong Kong business trust structures

Islands or as Bermuda mutual fund companies (as was the case with the Macquarie International Infrastructure Fund, which listed in a US$480 million equivalent IPO in Singapore, subsequently conducting a US$255 million equivalent secondary offering that same year).

As with REITs, it is important that business trusts be actively managed, both through internal and external growth, in order to secure long-term capital value. Bundling initial assets in a trust is one thing, but subsequent sales, acquisitions, cost control measures, and changes in the vehicle's capital structure must also feature, so as to ensure unit growth over time for both legacy and public investors.

3
Marketing the deal

3.1   The importance of sell-side research

All the major investment banks have active and sizeable sell-side research departments. These research departments support their sales and trading efforts in the secondary market across a variety of securities. In many countries, research is also important to assist in the marketing of IPOs to investors.

3.1.1   Types of research analysts

On a macro level, banks have economists who advise their institutional investor clients on major market events, as well as strategists who make recommendations on asset allocation, based on trends and high-level market developments. Investment banks also often have research analysts covering currencies, commodities, fixed income, and equity securities. On the equities side, in particular, research analysts generally have a regional or country focus, or an industry sector specialty. For example, a research analyst might specialize in telecoms companies across Europe; another might cover Spanish stocks only; while a third analyst might be responsible for the coverage of mining stocks in the Asia-Pacific region.

An individual research analyst is therefore on average responsible for the coverage of up to a dozen companies, reporting continually on results announcements and corporate events for each of these companies, and making calls on when to buy, sell, or remain neutral on individual stocks. Stand-alone corporate notes, from a few paragraphs to sometimes up to 100 pages or more, are published on a regular (and for the shorter ones often almost daily) basis, as are industry sector, country, or regional reports. Institutional investors now also often have electronic access to such research.

3.1.2   Analyst rankings

The accuracy of research analysts' predictions and calls, as well as their popularity with institutional investors, are regularly appraised in investor surveys, such as the well-known Extel survey in the UK or the regional surveys or polls compiled by *Institutional Investor* magazine or *Asiamoney*, or awards such as the StarMine analyst awards handed out by Thomson Reuters. These identify "stars" among the research analyst community. Highly ranked research analysts are much in demand and can be remunerated handsomely.

3.1.3   Pre-deal research in IPOs

Research is also used for IPOs, although in a very strict and tightly regulated way. This is because the prospectus and offering circular (in its various versions) are legally the only documents that investors, both retail and institutional, can use to form an investment decision in a primary equity offering. Research guidelines drafted by legal advisers (normally, the legal advisers to the underwriters) are always distributed to research analysts working on a particular IPO. These outline restrictions derived from local legislation and market practice. A pre-deal research report can be distributed only to institutional investors, not to the general public, which is deemed not sophisticated enough in matters of finance (although public investors are increasingly given access online to early—although slightly redacted— drafts of prospectuses posted on the websites of stock exchanges or regulators), and also cannot materially deviate as to its contents from what is included in the offering circular. In addition, it cannot, like those reports published in the secondary market to cover listed stocks on a continuing basis, include recommendations to make calls on the shares of the issuer (a "buy", "accumulate", "neutral", or "sell" recommendation, for example). Pre-deal research reports are also subject to restrictions as to the profit and loss account forecasts made by the research analysts that can be included; these will often be for a limited number of years only, except perhaps when valuation is conducted by way of a discounted cash-flow analysis (DCF). Sometimes no forecasts at all will be allowed. In many cases, research guidelines now also specify that several valuation methodologies must be used and that only a wide valuation range (but not individual valuations under each methodology) can be provided in such research reports. Pre-deal reports also always include significant disclaimers, generally on the cover and/or inside cover as well as on each page of the report, and cannot be distributed in the US, Canada, and Japan, where local rules and regulations prohibit their publication. One of the tasks of junior equity capital markets (ECM) bankers or, more commonly now, of compliance professionals, is to check the research distribution lists for a particular IPO to ensure this is the case. Obviously, while investors in such jurisdictions must be excluded from the list, salespeople who cater to them, as internal recipients of research reports within an investment bank, should not.

Pre-deal research reports are checked for factual accuracy against the contents of the prospectus by legal advisers working on the transaction (again, generally, by the legal advisers to the underwriters), as well as by the banks' compliance departments working in research "control rooms". In the past, it was not uncommon for the corporate finance or ECM bankers working on an IPO, and indeed for the issuer themselves, to help draft, review, or comment on pre-deal research reports to make them more "punchy" and akin to a "sales" document. This is recounted with much humour by my former colleague at S.G.Warburg, David Freud (now Lord Freud), in his memoirs from the mid-1980s to 2003. In his book, he recalls in particular a few memorable "eureka moments" as an investment banker on how some major IPOs, such as those of Eurotunnel, Euro Disney, and Railtrack, should be "packaged" and presented through research to best appeal to the investor community.[80] In the post-dot com era, however, this is now strictly prohibited, and research analysts are required to work on, and to publish, their reports completely independently and without interference from colleagues working in other areas of the bank—at least in theory.

3.1.4   Why bother with pre-deal research?

If pre-deal research reports need to conform to the prospectus as to their contents, and if some major jurisdictions, such as the US, actually ban their publication in connection with IPOs, why bother with them at all? The reason is simple: offering circulars are above all legal and disclosure documents and include many statements that are useful in limiting the liability of the issuer, but they do not necessarily offer a condensed and easy-to-read summary of the investment case. Institutional investors are by nature busy people, and they need to be able to screen through many potential investment opportunities within a short space of time. Pre-deal research reports are written in a format they recognize and understand (since they are readily published for stocks that are already listed), and therefore enable potential investors to find quickly and easily the information they require for their investment committees. By contrast, prospectuses can run to several hundred pages, much of them taken up by discussions of risk factors and accounting reports.

However, in making investment decisions, institutions should rely only on the offering circular. A letter stating this often accompanies a pre-deal research report to stress the point, and investors are sometimes also asked to further acknowledge this by returning a signed statement to that effect. Lastly, pre-deal research reports are generally all numbered, and a record is kept of the hundreds (or even thousands) of accounts that have been sent a copy by each bank. This can be useful for tracking down leaks.

Indeed, because pre-deal research reports are circulated to many investors around the world ahead of an IPO, it is not uncommon for their contents to be leaked to the financial press. Therefore, once pre-deal research is published, a transaction very much comes into the public domain and may, to some degree, lead to further speculation both by the market and by the media if the deal does not proceed at a later stage.

Once pre-deal research has been published, a blackout for further publication of research on the issuer by all the members of the syndicate comes into force, although it obviously does not apply to investment banks not involved in the IPO who are free to publish what they want. Whether they can have access to the right information is obviously another matter.

3.2   Presenting to research analysts

A key step in any IPO, where pre-deal, sell-side research is allowed, is the presentation to research analysts. This happens once the preliminary offering circular is in a nearly final shape, and takes the form of a meeting between the senior management of the issuer—often the chairman, CEO, CFO, and other key personnel—and the research analysts from participating banks from the syndicate. Generally, this includes a fairly small number of participants, but in some very large IPOs, particularly when the business of the company is complex or diversified, and when more than one research analyst may be appointed by some houses, this can become a sizeable gathering, totalling perhaps 25 or more attendees.

3.2.1   Research guidelines and the presentation to research analysts

The presentation to research analysts generally starts with short explanations by ECM bankers of the proposed timetable for the review by legal advisers and for the publication of pre-deal research reports. They also outline restrictions adhering to the publication of research reports in the context of the proposed IPO. Other than introducing management and explaining the timetable for the publication of research, ECM and investment bankers within the Chinese wall, if present at the presentation to research analysts, will usually remain silent throughout the rest of the meeting. Research guidelines are generally distributed at that time, or they can alternatively be relayed to the research analysts at a later stage through ECM desks or compliance departments. Copies of the draft offering circular are also often made available to the research analysts, as are copies of the 75 to 100 (or so) slides used by management in their presentation: the contents of these slides are entirely consistent with the prospectus, summarizing key features of the business, and addressing the history, competitive environment, strategy, key markets, clients, suppliers, and financials of the issuer. More recently, market practice has been, on occasion, for the slides to be made available to the research analysts during the meeting but to be returned at the end, so that only the draft offering circular can be left with them. This often leads to some frantic note-taking on the part of the attendees!

The research analysts are given the opportunity to ask many questions and to challenge management on how they run their business. This acts as a useful preparation for the roadshow since management needs, for the first time, to convince participants from the "markets" side of the banks of the merits of the investment case, and because the research analysts themselves will need to persuade investors about the equity story during pre-marketing. The presentation to research analysts does not involve any investors, and therefore takes place in a somewhat friendly and closed environment, where tips and suggestions can be provided or exchanged. However, the management of the issuer still needs to convey to the research analysts that this is an attractive opportunity, which the markets side of the investment bank can offer to its investor clients. Management will obviously previously have been well rehearsed by ECM and banking teams, including through the use of suggested questions and answers provided by the latter. Much, if not all ,of the presentation is also actually scripted.

3.2.2 Drafting pre-deal research

Research analysts are then, most of the time, given about two or up to three weeks to write their draft research reports, often with the opportunity to catch up again with management over another meeting or a conference call, so that any outstanding issues can be clarified. ECM teams can also relay further questions arising after the meeting to management, which can be addressed in writing or by way of another meeting or call. Sometimes, not ideally, the timetable for the offering is such that interim results may be published after the presentation to research analysts has taken place. In such a case, a follow-on call with management is generally arranged so that details of such financials can be included in the research reports in time for publication, and any related matters discussed. These interim accounts will then obviously also be included in the offering circular. Draft research reports are then sent to legal advisers and compliance departments for factual checking and also to make certain that the required disclaimers have been included so as to ensure compliance with the research guidelines. Then the green light is given for publication.

Research analysts are by nature creative people and, on occasion, video CDs or DVDs have also been sent to investors as part of their pre-deal research, after they have been vetted and authorized by the legal advisers, so as to stand out from the research reports published by other banks. This in turn helps salespeople to secure orders from investors during the marketing phase of the transaction, as they will seek to reward those houses that have stood out above others as part of the process.

3.2.3   The blackout period

Once pre-deal research has been published, a blackout or cooling off period is in place, generally for a period of 40 days after the date of listing. No pre-deal research by any syndicate member can be published after the start of the blackout period, and no further research on the company can be issued by them until the end of the blackout period. This, obviously, does not apply to banks not involved in the IPO, but it is unlikely that these would have access to management, at least prior to listing, to prepare any reports they may choose to draft, because the Chairman, CEO, CFO, and their teams will be increasingly busy as the IPO nears completion, and also on the road for the roadshow.

3.3   Briefing the syndicate

At some point following the presentation to research analysts, or sometimes before it takes place, a presentation is generally held by the bookrunner banks for the benefit of all the banks in the syndicate appointed for the IPO. In the past, these could be large gatherings, but, more often than not nowadays no physical presentation actually takes place. Several dozen slides are sent by email to the ECM or equity syndicate desks of the junior banks involved, which are then free to call the lead banks if there are any issues that need clarification. This also may take the form of a long email rather than of a slide presentation.

3.3.1   The rules of engagement

This effectively serves to brief the more junior banks in the syndicate (below bookrunner level) on the rules of engagement for the offering, since these houses will not have been involved in discussions about the transaction—at least prior to the invitation to the research analysts presentation. These generally include:

- a summary of the IPO's offer structure, identifying the issuer and any selling shareholders; the various lead banks involved in the offering and their respective roles; details of the proposed listing; the number of shares outstanding upon IPO as well as the number of shares offered, distinguishing between primary and secondary shares; and the size of the over-allotment option, if any;
- a summary of the offer structure, including the various underwriting tranches; the board lot in which the shares will be traded; details of any lock-ups, claw-back/claw-forward and reallocation provisions; the use of proceeds (in the event of a primary offering); the various codes and tickers for the stock (if already known); and details of the various advisers involved in the IPO;
- details of the overall syndicate structure;
- a preliminary offering timetable, generally from the start of the research analyst presentation to closing;
- a documentation timetable and, in particular, deadlines for powers of attorney to be returned to the lead banks;
- details of the economics for the transaction (gross spread, management and underwriting commissions, and selling concession, brokerage, *praecipium*, details of fees for any over-allotment option, details of any pot system, designations and split order rules, and a timetable for the payment of fees);
- details of research and publicity restrictions;
- the timetable, responsibilities, and feedback forms to be used for pre-marketing;
- details of the institutional roadshow, including a tentative schedule, contact details to attend presentations, rules for inviting institutions, and details of any internet roadshow;
- demand and allocation arrangements, including the timetable for bookbuilding and input of investor demand; details on how demand can be indicated—currency, shares, depository receipts (if any);
- details of portfolio managers to be provided; procedures for private client orders, allocation procedures and allocation criteria;
- selling and trading restrictions, such as the selling restrictions for the main jurisdictions—for example, the list of 49 Japanese institutions to which sales may be made; prohibition on grey market trading, use of derivative products;
- contact details for the lead banks across corporate finance, ECM, equity syndicate, settlement and roadshow coordination teams; and
- forms to be used to order prospectuses for each of the tranches in the global offering, as well as for each type of application form for clients (if relevant), and where the forms should be delivered.

3.3.2   Advertising and legal names

The banks will also often be asked how their advertising and legal names should appear in the prospectus. The advertising name is the short form name as it should appear on the cover of the prospectus, for example "Deutsche Bank", or, more likely—since it is now rare for the names of junior houses to appear on the covers of offering circular—in any advertising made in connection with the offering. The legal name is the full name as used in the various agreements evidencing the underwriting of the IPO, as well as within the offering circular in the "underwriting" or "plan of distribution" section, for example, "J.P.Morgan Securities (Asia Pacific) Limited". Generally, advertising a transaction in a tombstone advertisement (i.e., a factual advertisement listing the "bare bone" facts of a past equity offering, as a matter of record only) is under the control of the issuer and of the lead banks. As already mentioned, the names of the banks will, usually (but not always) appear in alphabetical order.

3.3.3   Invitation telexes

The syndicate presentation now sometimes replaces the invitation telex that was previously sent to banks to invite them to participate in a transaction. However, in some cases, a telex is still also sent (although nowadays it is an email) in addition to the presentation, but at a later stage, generally prior to, and sometimes even following, launch.

3.4   Pre-deal investor education (PDIE) and setting the price range

Pre-deal investor education (PDIE), previously—until the mid-2000s or so—called pre-marketing, was probably first introduced in the UK at the end of the 1980s. Its objective is for research analysts to physically meet with institutional investors to convey the merits of the investment case. Where allowed, such investors will already have received copies of pre-deal research reports. PDIE is usually on a non-exclusive basis and, invariably, several of the investment banks involved in an IPO send their reports to the same portfolio managers since no real investor targeting takes place at this stage, other than in the case of a cornerstone investor tranche. Indeed, many portfolio managers are interested in discussing the features of the company with more than one research analyst (although clearly not a dozen!), to gain complementary perspectives on the business. Such investor education meetings can be set up by all syndicate members once notification has been received from the lead banks.

3.4.1   How PDIE is performed

Subject to legal restrictions, the lead banks each send one or more research analysts around the world to meet with investors, talk through short presentations, summarize their individual pre-deal research reports, stress the key points of the investment proposition, and answer questions that may be raised. This can be a very intensive exercise, as it is common for research analysts to meet with perhaps 8 to 12 investors in any given day throughout a period of approximately two weeks, covering multiple cities across a number of time zones. There will be individual meetings with the larger accounts, as well as small group meetings, perhaps over breakfast, lunch, or dinner. When more than one research analyst per house, and more than one lead bank, are involved, this can cover a very wide range of potential accounts: it can therefore provide an accurate view of the market's take on both the investment case, and the likely valuation for the business in the proposed IPO.

Importantly, the research analysts liaise on a regular (often at least daily) basis with their ECM and equity syndicate desks to convey the feedback gathered in their meetings with investors. This includes both feedback on individual portfolio managers' views on valuation and the identification of recurring themes or issues that may need to be addressed by management during the roadshow.

As an example, at the end of 2009, Macquarie and Citi pre-marketed a US$443 million equivalent offering for South Gobi Energy Resources, one of the largest coal mining companies in Mongolia, which involved both a listing in Hong Kong and a concurrent secondary offering in Canada. Two sovereign wealth funds (SWFs), China Investment Corporation (CIC) and Singapore's Temasek Holdings, had already each committed to invest US$50 million in the company. In connection with the transaction, one of the bookrunners reportedly conducted a pre-marketing programme involving three research analysts visiting a total of some 60 investors over Christmas and the New Year, including more than 10 investor meetings in the US, a dozen meetings in London, more than 25 meetings in Hong Kong, and about 15 meetings in Singapore. Given the size of the offering, and also having regard to the number of research analysts involved by this bookrunner, this represented overall a relatively small quantum of investors, although the successful result of the cornerstone process, as well as the timing of the transaction no doubt affected the scale of coverage. In this case, the total number of institutions visited during PDIE for the deal was also probably significantly higher in light of additional investor education, in particular as performed by the other bookrunner. In the US$2.1 billion equivalent IPO of hospital owner and operator IHH Healthcare in Malaysia and Singapore in 2012, 10 research analysts from six investment banks engaged more than 240 institutional investors through a PDIE process across Malaysia (involving 40 investors), Singapore (54 accounts), Hong Kong (52 accounts), the UK and continental Europe (47 accounts, in London, Scotland, Paris, and Frankfurt) and the US (47 investors in New York, Boston, Chicago, and the West Coast).

In more difficult or challenging market conditions, it can pay to reach out to as wide a universe of investors as possible, to leave no stone unturned, and to maximize exposure to generate interest for the deal, even though some banks may in such times advocate conducting a "club deal" among a small number of select institutions instead, given the difficulties they face in trying to bring the transaction to market.

In US-listed deals, where no publication of pre-deal research is allowed, the research analysts perform investor education on the back of the registration statement (Form F-1 or Form S-1, as applicable). This often leads to a shorter timetable for PDIE there, or to one overlapping with roadshows and bookbuilding. The results on valuation are also typically less accurate, and it is not unusual in the US for a marketing price range for an IPO to change (often by being increased) in response to actual investor demand.

3.4.2   PDIE other than by research analysts

Obviously, not all the potential investors in an IPO can be visited by the research analysts themselves. Accordingly, the equity sales forces, which will have made initial calls to the main accounts to arrange the PDIE schedule, also call other investors on a global basis (depending on the offer structure for the IPO) to educate them on the company and gather their views on the story conveyed in the pre-deal research reports. Prior to this, upon publication, the research analysts will usually have briefed the various sales teams within their respective investment banks by way of one or more teach-ins through meetings and conference or video calls to stress the key points that need to be conveyed to the market. ECM teams will also have prepared crib sheets, typically laid out as two overlapping laminated sheets in small print, summarizing the key issues and financials, to enable them to efficiently pre-market the deal and answer questions. On the telephone, salespeople often have only a few minutes to pitch the deal to an institution, so it is important in briefing them to have distilled the key selling points and attractions of what can at times be a particularly complex investment case.

3.4.3   Feedback forms

The more junior members of the syndicate are generally not expected to fly their research analysts around the world to meet with investors, especially as their own expenses are not reimbursed, but are nevertheless asked to gather feedback from a minimum number of investors, perhaps 20 for co-lead managers and 10 for co-managers, so as to increase the overall level of feedback gathered from the market. However, they still most likely conduct physical one-on-one meetings with investors in the city where they are based. For example, a co-lead manager based in London would meet with a handful of institutions there. The feedback is generally provided electronically on a spreadsheet or form, and individually for each institution that has been contacted. It may include the investor's views on:

- regional and local equities;
- the issuer's industry sector;
- companies deemed most comparable to the issuer;
- the most likely valuation parameters for the issuer;
- specific views on the company with respect to its valuation (also called "price talk"), growth or value potential, and management team;
- likes and dislikes about the company as well as the identification of key issues or concerns;
- the investor's willingness to participate in meetings with management (either through one-on-one or group meetings); and
- details of any potential order, including the order size and any price limit, to be placed during bookbuilding.

A sample pre-marketing feedback form is included in Appendix 6.

At the end of the customary two-week PDIE period, all such feedback will have been collected in an agreed, consistent format and presented to the senior management of the issuer. This feedback is also useful for amending, if necessary, the roadshow presentation to take into account issues not previously identified that may have been conveyed by investors.

By that time, clear views on valuation will also have emerged, enabling the setting of a price range to formally market the IPO in a bookbuilding exercise.

3.4.4   Setting the price range

The price range must be narrow enough to provide clear guidance to investors, but should also allow for some upside for the deal to be priced at a higher level in the event of significant over-subscription and quality demand. Typically, the width of the range is therefore set at around 15% to 20%. A range of more than 20% would generally be considered rather wide, and significantly above that percentage guidance would be pretty vague. The bottom end of the range is often set at an attractive level so as to act as an anchor pricing for investors, while the top end is often on the aggressive side.

In more volatile or difficult market conditions, price ranges tend to be wider to add a degree of flexibility, and also because there may be less of a clear view on the valuation for the company. This may also be the case when limited or vague feedback only has been provided to the lead banks by investors. In May 2012, high-end diamond retailer Graff Diamonds had set a price range of HK$25 to HK$37 (equivalent to 18 to 24 times forecast earnings for 2012) for its IPO in Hong Kong, representing a width of 48% based on the bottom end of the range and of more than 32% on the top end, perhaps an indication that the banks involved did not have an accurate perspective on the valuation at which the shares should be marketed.[81] In the event, the IPO was pulled as sufficient investor demand failed to materialize for a flotation that was meant to raise approximately US$1 billion for the company and its shareholders.

The aim of bookbuilding is usually to price in the upper half of the range, typically in the upper quartile. Pricing at the top end is not necessarily an objective in itself, as it may tactically be better to be seen to leave "something on the table", although this may for some shareholders be difficult to justify if levels of over-subscription and the quality of investor demand are so high as to leave no other alternative. The case studies for the IPOs of CapitaMalls Asia in Singapore and IHH Healthcare in Malaysia and Singapore, both set out in Appendix 1, provide examples of issuers and their selling shareholders that perhaps felt it prudent to leave some upside for investors by not pricing their offerings at the very top end of their respective ranges, despite healthy over-subscription levels and strong books of demand.

Once the price range has been determined, the preliminary offering circular—which may or may not include the range (sometimes the offer price is just left blank)—is printed and distributed to potential investors. I have already mentioned earlier de-coupled transactions, whereby the price range is not determined until some institutional investors have held meetings with management during the roadshow, which is actually fairly similar to common market practice in the US.

3.4.5   Fixed price IPOs

In rather rare cases nowadays, international IPOs can be conducted at a fixed price, rather than as a two-step process with a price range followed by the determination of an offer price. This can, for example, be the case when the company being floated is a mutual fund company or a fund of funds. The US$480 million IPO of the Macquarie International Infrastructure Fund (MIIF), a Bermuda-incorporated mutual fund company that listed in Singapore in 2005, is an example of such a transaction. The deal was marketed at a fixed offer price of S$1.00 to institutions and retail investors alike. In that particular case, the business of the issuer comprised a number of investments in both listed and unlisted funds and corporates across a variety of jurisdictions, and made pursuant to a ten-year, total-return swap.

A fixed-price IPO may also sometimes be appropriate when the investment case or valuation is particularly complex, when a particularly innovative type of IPO comes to market, or when an offering is marketed more on the unique characteristics of a company rather than on the basis of valuation considerations, perhaps because the issuer is the only company of its kind to provide the type of goods or services that it sells.

In fixed-price IPOs, PDIE is still conducted, although not so much with the objective of determining a price range, but more to prepare the ground for the marketing of the deal. It is still important in these transactions to assess at an early stage the market's appetite for the deal, and to identify the investors who may have interest in participating in the IPO, as well as those that may meet with management in one-on-one meetings.

It may also happen that, following PDIE, the market is not felt to be receptive to the offering being marketed on a fixed-price basis. This was the case with the very first real estate investment trust (REIT) ever to be marketed in Singapore in 2001. In such instances, as in the case of the latter, the offering may need to be re-structured before it can successfully be re-launched.

3.5   The management roadshow

The management (or investor) roadshow is the process through which the senior management of the issuer, rather than the research analysts, travel around the world to present the investment case to investors. Often, potential issuers ask for the roadshow itinerary at the pitching stage. In reality, though, it is difficult for investment banks to decide on this, except for the major financial centres, prior to at least part of the PDIE having been completed. For example, there is not much point in visiting Germany on a roadshow if the response from German institutions has been negative (or very subdued) at the investor education stage; it would be a better use of management's time to focus on another, more promising market, where significant orders may be gathered.

Sometimes, for very large transactions or companies with large management teams, two (or perhaps even three) teams can simultaneously embark on a roadshow, doubling or trebling the number of locations where investors can be met. In such a case, care should be taken so that the most senior officers can be equally split between the teams. To better manage egos (and investors' sensitivity) , teams are often labelled with a particular colour (i.e., the green and blue teams) rather than the A or B teams or Team 1 and Team 2. No one wants to meet with the junior team if it can be avoided!

Four types of meetings can take place during an IPO roadshow.

3.5.1   Large-scale presentations

First are the "iconic", large-scale, theatre- or town hall-style presentations that take place in the main financial centres. These generally include the city where the stock will eventually be listed, as well as, typically, London, Edinburgh, New York, and Boston (for companies to be listed in the US or marketed there pursuant to a private placement under Rule 144A). For companies in Asia, in addition to the local market, large-scale presentations will often be made in Hong Kong and Singapore, and perhaps Tokyo for non-Japanese companies, if a public offering without listing (POWL) or, more rarely, if a private placement to 49 investors is included in the offer structure.

These presentations are highly rehearsed events often held in the ballrooms of major hotels, where management is generally introduced by a senior investment banker from one of the lead banks. When more than one lead bank has been appointed, the banks usually decide in advance how opening and closing remarks are allocated between themselves across the various venues. At the outset of the presentation, a short three-minute video is often shown to introduce the issuer and its business in a more visual format. Following this, two or three members of the issuer's senior management will talk for 25 minutes on perhaps 20 or 25 slides, usually drafted by the lead investment banks, to summarize the key features of the business. The format of such presentations is quite generic, starting with a slide on the number of shares on offer and on the structure and timing for the IPO, followed by pages on how the company began, its strategy, main business activities, financials, and future prospects, and, to conclude, a short, sharp summary of the key points in the presentation. The Chairman or CEO typically starts the presentation, until and including the section on the strategy for the business, while the CFO usually covers, at the very least, the section on financials. The presentation invariably concludes with the Chairman or CEO repeating the key takeaways, prior to opening up for questions. Often, many questions from investors can be anticipated, and investment banks will have prepared a set of slides (perhaps 25, although this can be up to 100, as was the case with Repsol from Spain for its IPO) to illustrate certain topics that may come up in the Q&A session.

Management are generally scripted when talking on the slides, with the script, again, having been drafted by the lead investment banks and often vetted by the legal advisers as well: they will have been well rehearsed in the previous weeks. By the end of the roadshow, management definitely no longer need to look at their notes to deliver the presentation, having gone through it many, many times over! After presenting and taking questions, the members of management are generally able to mingle with investors over a quick lunch at one of the tables in the venue for the conference. There is often much jostling between the investment banks to have "their" key investors seated next to the senior presenters, with a view to securing subsequent orders from them in the bookbuilding process. When preparing a roadshow presentation and script, the flow is generally better if the script is written first, with the slides then drafted to illustrate the major points. Most of the time, however, the slides are drafted first, sometimes giving a dry and mechanical feel to the presentation.

In some cases, simultaneous translation is used when management teams are not fluent in English for the international portion of the roadshow. Often, one or more dry-run presentations will also have been held for the presenters to brief the combined (or individual) sales forces of the lead banks in a physical location, perhaps with a video link to address trading floors in other time zones.

Often a sit-down lunch is served to attendees, as an incentive to attend. In London, such presentations can be held in livery halls in the City (where many investors are still based, although some of the larger hedge funds prefer real estate in Mayfair), rather than in hotels.

Invitations in the joint names of all the lead banks are generally sent not earlier than a week in advance, and the bookrunners will coordinate among themselves to gather RSVPs. As previously mentioned, logistics are sometimes managed by specialist consultants.

Major key and optional roadshow destinations for an international IPO across the Americas, Europe, the Middle East, and the Asia-Pacific region are summarized in Table 8.

3.5.2   Small group presentations

In addition to the large presentations in major cities, small group presentations are sometimes also held. Similar to those arranged during pre-marketing, these are usually conveyed over breakfast, lunch (although more rarely), or dinner, and may

Key cities in the Americas	Key cities in the EMEA* region	Major cities in the Asia-Pacific region
New York	London	Hong Kong
Boston	Edinburgh	Singapore
	Frankfurt	Tokyo
	Paris	
	Zürich	
Optional cities in the Americas	**Optional cities in the EMEA region**	**Optional cities in the Asia-Pacific region**
Atlanta	Amsterdam	Beijing
Baltimore	The Hague	Shanghai
Chicago	Rotterdam	
Dallas		Kuala Lumpur
Denver	Brussels	
Houston	Dublin	Seoul
Kansas City	Glasgow	Taipei
Los Angeles	Geneva	
Miami	Luxembourg	Melbourne
Milwaukee	Madrid	Sydney
Minneapolis–Saint Paul	Milan	
Philadelphia	Moscow	
San Diego	Munich	
San Francisco	Stockholm	
Toronto	Abu Dhabi	
	Dubai	
	Doha (Qatar)	
	Kuwait City	
	Manama (Bahrain)	
	Muscat (Oman)	

* EMEA = Europe, Middle East, and Africa

Table 8
Key and optional cities to be visited on a management roadshow for an international IPO

involve a small (single-digit) number of investors, probably not more than four or five at any given time. These will be more informal gatherings, without a video screening (or perhaps only on a laptop computer), although management may sometimes refer to large A3 format slides that all can easily see while sitting around a table to illustrate particular points. More likely, management will spend most of the time answering questions rather than delivering a full-length speech, as is the case in the larger presentations and venues.

3.5.3   One-on-one meetings

The major institutional investors, however, do not attend group presentations and expect to meet with management during one-on-one meetings, generally held at their own offices. In other words, they are "given face" because they will, invariably, place the largest orders in the book of demand. One-on-one meetings are usually only arranged by the bookrunners. Forty-five minutes to not more than an hour are then allocated to each one-on-one meeting, with management shuttling from one meeting to another in chauffeured cars. The format for one-on-one meetings can vary greatly. Some investors will ask management to deliver a full presentation (without the short video, or, again, this could perhaps in some cases be shown on a laptop computer with a wide enough screen), to be followed by questions. Others will prefer to spend most of their allocated time asking a list of previously compiled questions. Some investors are also notorious for insisting on seeing management without any of the accompanying investment bankers and salespeople being in attendance, and will send any to wait in the corridor or at the reception of their offices. Each institution has its own peculiarities, and management will have been briefed by senior salespeople or by ECM bankers on what to expect, as well as on the profile and investment style of each of them.

Because one-on-one meetings are only held with the largest and most prestigious investors, and because such investors are also those likely to place the most sizeable orders, the split of one-on-one meetings among investment banks is often made after considerable negotiation. Each bookrunner will compile its own list of candidates, and the banks will either draw or take turns to pick names, until the number of one-on-one meetings in the schedule is exhausted. In addition, from a logistical standpoint, one-on-ones need to be grouped, so as to minimize the travel time between meetings. For example, a typical roadshow day in London could see a small group breakfast and three individual meetings in the West End in the morning, followed by a large group presentation in one of the livery halls in the City, and a further three or four individual meetings in the City, perhaps to be concluded by a small group dinner there or at another location. This avoids having to shuttle back and forth amid what can be heavy traffic between sometimes distant areas of a major metropolis.

Most important for the lead banks is to achieve a high conversion rate (or hit rate) in percentage terms by generating actual orders in the book of demand from those investors for which they have arranged one-on-one meetings. High hit rates, compared with those achieved by banks appointed in a similar position, feature prominently in case studies that are included in subsequent ECM pitches.

When no physical meeting is possible, some of the larger accounts can be accommodated by way of individual or group conference calls or video conferences (perhaps through platforms such as Zoom, Microsoft Teams, Skype, Cisco Webex Meetings, or Adobe Connect). For example, this can be arranged for investors in the Middle East or in Australia if it is not planned for the roadshow to visit these regions. In the case of the Middle East, however, it is often possible to schedule a presentation on a Sunday, which is a working day there, as opposed to other parts of the world.

In a famous example, in the US$460 million privatization IPO of Singapore Post in 2003, the roadshow had to be conducted entirely by conference calls and video conferences since the outbreak of avian flu in Asia prevented management from travelling around the world to meet with investors.[82] This will also have been the case for many deals during the COVID-19 pandemic, with Zoom being one of the most popular platforms for such presentations. Irrespective of the technology used, however, it is important that the presentation be rehearsed and seamless, to avoid any technical glitches spoiling the proceedings.

As an example of how a particularly wide universe of investors can be covered in a short space of time, the roadshow for the US$12 billion H share IPO of Agricultural Bank of China in 2010 in Hong Kong reportedly involved two management teams each visiting ten cities over ten days, holding more than 90 one-on-one meetings, as well as meetings with more than 400 other investors through group or small group presentations. The roadshow for the institutional offering (in addition to a POWL in Japan) was said to have visited Abu Dhabi, Boston, Dubai, Edinburgh, Frankfurt, Hong Kong, London, New York, San Francisco, and Singapore.

In the US$2.2 billion IPO of United Company Rusal from Russia earlier that year, in January 2010, and also in Hong Kong, two management teams were said to have visited, over a period of nine days, a total of 640 investors through just below 90 one-on-one meetings as well as group or small group presentations involving a total of more than 550 other investors. The roadshow visited more than ten cities, including Boston, Edinburgh, Frankfurt, Geneva, Hong Kong, London, Moscow, New York, Paris, Singapore, and Zurich.

Looking at a smaller transaction (already mentioned earlier) by way of comparison, the management of South Gobi Energy Resources reportedly met, on the roadshow for its US$443 million offering, a smaller number of 45 investors through one-on-one meetings and a further 160 investors through other presentations across North America, Europe, and Asia, over eight days.

3.5.4   Internet roadshows

In addition to management physically meeting with investors, most IPOs now also include a virtual or internet roadshow. This enables investors to view (but not to download) the roadshow slides used by management and to simultaneously hear the script by logging onto a password-protected website. Such websites do carry disclaimers and conform to restrictions in place for the marketing of IPOs in countries such as the US. In practice, such websites and platforms (e.g., netroadshow.com) have generally been vetted by the Securities and Exchange Commission (SEC).

Roadshows can take their toll on management teams. They are very intense and a large number of investor meetings are packed in a very short space of time. At the same time, a mad scramble generally takes place simultaneously to finalize the offering circular for the public offer, as well as the legal agreements for underwriting. Frequently, controversial issues are left to the end to be negotiated and the CEO and CFO of the issuer can often find themselves on conference calls late at night after a whole day of meetings to help resolve critical issues. And they also obviously have a business to run on top of all this!

3.6   Bookbuilding

Bookbuilding, also known as an "open price offer" or as a "price discovery process" (except when fixed-price IPOs are conducted), takes place simultaneously with, or in the case of de-coupled transactions shortly after the start of, the roadshow, typically for a duration of two weeks. It is followed by the determination of the final offer price. In simple terms, this is the process through which orders are gathered from institutional investors within a price range and compiled in a common ledger for further analysis and allocations by the lead banks.

The main advantages of conducting the now widely accepted method of bookbuilding over a fixed price offer are that a better price can generally be achieved and price tension can be created among investors. The process is more transparent and offers more flexibility to both the issuer and the bookrunner banks. Bookbuilding is also preferable to tender offers, where prices are often inflated and where allocations can be made in full to investors who bid above the strike price. Most importantly, it also enables the bookrunner and the issuer to assess the quality of investors prior to making allocations.

Physically, institutional orders in a bookbuilt IPO are taken and compiled directly by the bookrunners, with the more junior banks in the syndicate reflecting their own orders to the bookrunners. It is, however, now rare for junior syndicate members to gather any orders at all, and the system deliberately encourages investors to place orders directly with the bookrunners, since they (and, most of the time, they alone) will determine allocations. As explained earlier, junior syndicate members are these days more often expected to contribute, if anything, only through pre-deal research and investor education, and are being paid a fixed flat fee for doing so.

Bookbuilding can only start at a time agreed between the bookrunners and, for other syndicate members, once notification has been provided by the bookrunners. In some cases, some syndicate members try to "jump the gun" in order to have early access to some institutions. Nowadays, all the banks in a syndicate are generally free to contact investors on a global basis, with no exempt list of investors—that is, certain investors, perhaps located in a particular region, that only certain banks may contact.

3.6.1   Types of orders and bookkeeping

An electronic system created by Dealogic called DealManager (previously called Bookbuilder and DealManager ECM) with dedicated, online linked terminals is now almost universally used by bookrunners around the world to compile orders from institutions. Orders can be submitted at a particular price within the price range, in which case they are called "limit orders"; (more rarely) in various amounts expressed at various limits, as staggered orders or stepped bids; or without price limits, where investors then pay at the offer price that will ultimately be determined for the IPO—these are called "strike orders". Cornerstone investors, as we saw earlier, place orders (ahead of other investors) at the strike price, that is, they are prepared to pay any price within, and up to, the top end of the range.

The book of demand records the date and time of each order (which is important to identify opportunistic late-comers), the amount in shares or depositary shares (DSs) (if any) or in any currency, typically the currency of quotation and US dollars—but other currencies could feature in the case of dual or multiple listings, or investors based in other regions who may prefer to express orders in the currency they most commonly use; the price limit at which the order is placed (if any); and the name, nationality, and type of investor, and details of the salesperson who has taken the order. Once individual allocations to investors have been determined, the system will send back to those salespeople who have taken the orders details of the allocations for each of their clients, for them to convey in turn to the investors they serve.

Orders by private banks or, more precisely, their high net-worth individual clients can sometimes be in a relatively small size, so it is common in this case to aggregate all such orders and to only provide a total amount at each price limit for any individual private bank. In all other cases, "transparency" is generally required for all submitted orders, although disclosure of individual orders is typically only made above a certain monetary amount, usually US$250,000. An example of part of a book of demand is set out in Figure 8.

Each bookrunner will compile its own book of demand. Usually, these individual books will be electronically "swapped" between the bookrunners, and aggregated and shared in a common book at an agreed time at the end of each working day throughout the bookbuilding process.

3.6.2   Manual demand forms

Orders from co-lead or co-managers, if any, can be sent through the Dealogic system or by fax or email, on a form included in the presentation sent by the bookrunner banks to syndicate members, and then manually included by one of the bookrunner banks into the system. This is now rare as most banks include orders electronically (and junior banks hardly generate any orders these days anyway), but the "manual" demand form faxed or emailed by co-lead and co-managers generally includes:

- the contact details for each syndicate member;
- the date of the order;
- the name of the investor, together with, generally, the name of the fund (or portfolio manager) placing the order;
- the investor type, which can be either a bank, broker, corporate, insurance company, investment manager, pension fund, retail investor, hedge fund, or another type of investor to be specified;
- the nationality of the investor;
- the type of order, for example, whether this is an order placed by a new investor in the IPO or, conversely, an increase, decrease, amendment, or cancellation of a prior order;
- whether such order is provided in the form of shares or local currency, US dollars, or other currency, or indeed DSs;

Date	Time	Investor	Nationality	Type	Shares	ADRs	Local currency (m)	US$ m	Price limit	Sales person
03-Feb	11:15	Schroder AM	UK	Asset manager	–	0	0	25	100	AC
03-Feb	11:22	DWS	GER	Asset manager	–	0	20	–	Strike	TM
04-Feb	09:30	Citadel	US	Hedge fund	400,000	0				
04-Feb	09:35	HSBC								

Figure 8

Example of part of an institutional book of demand

- the price limit of the order, if any, in local currency, or for (most) DSs in US dollars; and
- any other comments that the syndicate member may wish to add.

An example of such a demand form is included in Appendix 7.

3.6.3   Designations and split orders

Note is also made of designations of the selling concession, that is, of the percentage of the selling concession that has been designated by an investor placing an order with a particular bank, for payment to one or more other banks, which the investor would nevertheless like to reward, for example as a result of a high quality pre-deal research report. As previously explained, this is also how a pot system works in the US. In some cases, the rules of engagement specify a period of 48 hours following the close of the book to enable the more junior banks to "chase" designations from investors. Split orders (i.e., orders placed by institutions with more than one bank) may or may not be allowed in the offering, depending on what has been decided at the outset (see Chapter 1, Section 1.11.3).

3.6.4   Demand curve

Over time, a pattern emerges for the level of subscription of the institutional tranche, as well as of the level of price sensitivity in the book of demand. Often, the level of over-subscription will sharply drop at a certain level within the price range, making it easier to gauge the level around which the offer price may be set (although it is still important to price an IPO at a level where there is a healthy level of oversubscription, rather than at the level where the deal is only subscribed once: this is because investors' orders should be scaled back to encourage these institutions to top up their allocations in the aftermarket, and lead to an increase in share price upon start of trading). In addition, not all orders warrant an allocation— let alone a full one!—and much ultimately also depends on the quality of the investors brought about by the underwriters. A graphical illustration of a book of demand is set out in Figure 9.

3.6.5   Managing the book

The daily level of over-subscription (if any) is usually not made available to the general public and only restricted members of the ECM and equity syndicate teams are privy to the contents of the book of demand (such information is generally not released to the sales teams for them to act upon, or perhaps only to one senior salesperson who is also a permanent insider for compliance purposes). However,

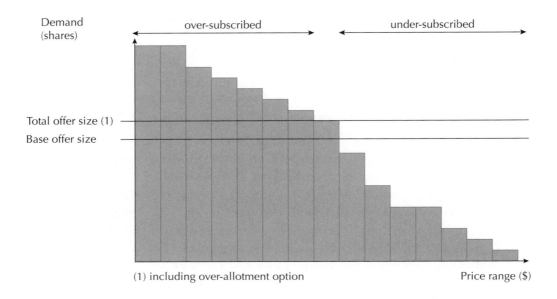

Demand (shares) · over-subscribed · under-subscribed · Total offer size (1) · Base offer size · (1) including over-allotment option · Price range ($)

Figure 9

A typical book of demand. In this case, the offering (including the over-allotment option) is no longer covered beyond the middle of the price range.

messages are sometimes released by the lead banks to the market about how the deal is progressing. For example, if the offering has been substantially covered very quickly at the bottom end of (or, indeed at any other level within) the price range, the lead banks may want to release this information to indicate to investors that they may want to increase the price limits for their orders if they want to receive any allocations, since it is likely that the offering will, over the remainder of the bookbuilding process, become substantially covered at a higher level. As an example, in late January 2021, the up to US$1.8 billion London IPO of bootmaker Dr Martens was fully covered by the book of demand, and this was communicated (or, more likely, leaked by syndicate members) to the financial and other media. Similarly, communicating a level of over-subscription at another stage during the bookbuilding process will send a clear message to the market about where accounts need to pitch their orders if they are to receive any shares.

In some cases, however, issuers are legally required by the local rules to make public the level of interest received in the bookbuilding process. For example, this is the case in Hong Kong, although typically only fairly vague indications (such as the offering having been "moderately oversubscribed") will be provided in the case of institutional tranches, as opposed to public offer tranches, for which precise levels of subscription will be disclosed.

3.6.6   Adjusting the price range or the deal size

As mentioned earlier, although fairly rare (except in the US) and subject to local regulations, price ranges can sometimes be adjusted either downwards or upwards to react to investor response or unexpected market developments. The deal size can also, on occasion, be adjusted in a similar way, in particular where the deal incorporates an upsize option. The IPOs of Shanda Games and Essar Energy, included as case studies in Appendix 1, provide examples of such adjustments. In addition, the lead banks may decide to close the book early in the event that investor demand becomes overwhelming, so as to enable an orderly and fair allocation process. For example, this was the case in the US$20.4 billion IPO of AIA in Hong Kong in 2010, where the book of demand was closed two days ahead of schedule. This is usually the case for particularly "hot" deals, for which investor demand grows very quickly, exceeding expectations.

Generally, the book closes at the same time in different regions (say, 5:00 p.m. respectively in Asia, Europe, and the US), so that the closing is phased over several hours to enable the banks to input the latest orders into the system and tidy up the overall book of demand by cross-checking investors' orders with each other. For IPOs, books often (but not always) close on a Friday, so that management can travel back from the roadshow and be physically present at pricing, underwriting, and allocation meetings over the weekend in the time zone where the company will be listed. This also gives ample time for the syndicate desks to decide how to make allocations. Conversely, pricing (although not necessarily allocation) meetings now also often take place in the city where the roadshow has ended, often in New York, given how time zones are set up and for those IPOs that are marketed in the US pursuant to a private placement. To maximize the time available for marketing, roadshows generally follow the sun, and start in Asia (or Europe, for companies that are not being listed in the Far East), and end in an American city (when a Rule 144A private placement is part of the offer structure for the deal).

Where banks are concerned about market risk and where major moves may have an impact on the transaction, banks may close the books on, say, a Thursday, to allow allocations to investors to be sent out and confirmed before the weekend on the Friday.

3.7   Public offerings

Most IPOs include an offering to the public or to retail investors in addition to one or more institutional tranches, although this is not necessarily the case in all countries. Retail or public offerings normally run over a much shorter period than institutional bookbuilt offerings, often not more than two or three days and usually for a specified minimum period of time, in accordance with the listing rules. The main exception is probably Australia, where offers can run over several (typically four) weeks. Retail offerings are usually made at a fixed price, although some countries, such as France and India, have auction or bookbuilding systems for retail investors too. They can be conducted on a concurrent or sequential basis (see Figure 10). Indeed, some jurisdictions, such as Singapore, even allow both. In many markets, advertisements for, or notices of, the IPO are published at the time of the retail offering in the media. When this is the case, such advertisements must carry statutory disclaimers.

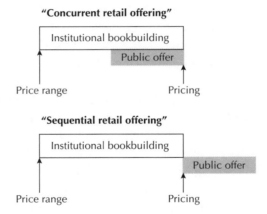

Figure 10

Differences between concurrent and sequential retail offerings

3.7.1   Concurrent offerings

Concurrent public offerings are held in the last few days of the institutional bookbuilding, when news about the success (or failure) of the institutional offer enable retail investors to have a good idea about the potential aftermarket performance of the deal. In such a case, because the offering has not been priced at that stage, investors are asked to pay (in advance) at the top of the indicative price range, and will be reimbursed subsequently (without interest) should the IPO be priced at a lower level. In a concurrent offering, except where specific regulations apply, the bookrunners generally retain the flexibility to decide the split between the placement and the public offer tranche right up to the end of the order solicitation process. A concurrent offering also allows for a faster settlement process for institutions, as opposed to a sequential offering, and is generally preferred by institutions as it enables them to finalize their demand indications after observing the retail investor response to the offering (although this will typically only be done by smaller and more speculative investors, who will not generally receive high allocations in any event). In a concurrent offering, as in a sequential offering, retail investors are also reimbursed for the difference between the amount they apply for and the number of shares they ultimately receive as an allocation (which can be very different in the case of a hot deal in particular, where allocations are significantly trimmed).

3.7.2   Sequential offerings

In sequential retail offerings, the offer to the public takes place after the institutional offer has been priced, that is, retail investors effectively subscribe for the offering during the settlement period for institutional investors. For example, this is normally the way public offerings are conducted in Poland, although offer structures including a "maximum" subscription price for retail investors also work there. As for the concurrent offering, there is still a fixed price and advance payment by retail investors, although, in this case, the IPO price is known at the outset so the only reimbursement is to account for the difference between demand and allocations. As mentioned above, Japanese POWLs are another form of sequential public offering.

3.7.3   Retail investor pools

In some markets, the rules distinguish between several categories of retail investors for balloting purposes. For example, in Hong Kong, public offers include two pools of investors. Pool A includes retail investors applying for shares representing HK$5 million or less in total, while Pool B includes retail investors applying for more than HK$5 million and up to the value of that pool. Shares are allocated on an equal basis between retail investors in each pool, and re-allocation arrangements exist between Pool A and Pool B should one of the pools be under-subscribed. In addition, multiple applications are prohibited within or between pools, and no retail investor can apply for more than the shares originally allocated to each pool within the public offer.

As mentioned above, claw-back and claw-forward mechanisms also allow for the re-allocation of shares between the institutional and retail offerings in the event of either over- or under-subscription. This can either be left at the discretion of the bookrunners or governed by the IPO regulations, such as in Hong Kong (see Appendix 8 for more information on applicable claw-back triggers for that jurisdiction).

3.7.4   Other types of retail offer

In Australia retail offers often have several components. These may include a general offer to the public and an offering to employees, both of which are common in most other markets; a priority offer, for example to existing shareholders of one or more related companies; and a broker firm offer. A broker firm offer is a type of retail offering frequently used in Australia, and open to Australian as well as, usually, New Zealand resident retail investors who have received firm allocations from their broker. IPO offers in Australia run over several weeks following an initial "exposure period" for the disclosure document (prospectus) with the regulator, the Australian Securities and Investments Commission (ASIC), when the market and ASIC can consider information included in it, before the issuer can accept applications under the IPO.

In the US, offerings to "friends and family", either prior to the IPO or by way of directed or reserved shares in the offering, are common but subject to a lock-up of, generally, at least six months.

3.7.5   Retail incentives

It was common in the 1980s and 1990s, and up to the turn of the last century, especially in privatization offerings, to introduce incentives to encourage domestic retail investors to participate in IPOs and other offerings. Most commonly, such incentives were in the form of bonus shares and retail discounts, sometimes used concurrently.

With bonus shares, investors receive one or more free shares for a certain number of shares held after a period of time after the IPO, typically, one free share for ten held over 18 months, in order to prevent them from selling their shares immediately after receiving their allocations. Bonus shares were probably first introduced more than 25 years ago in the £4 billion privatization IPO of British Telecom (the largest-ever IPO world-wide at that time), which was led by Kleinwort Benson in 1984 in the UK. They were subsequently used in many other privatization offerings around the world in Europe, Asia, and beyond.

Retail discounts are generally expressed as a percentage deducted from the institutional offer price. They have also been used extensively, including in combination with other discounts. For example, the US$1.4 billion privatization IPO of MTR Corporation in Hong Kong in 2000 included both a price discount and bonus shares for retail investors and was probably one of the last few major government sell-downs to do so. The discount can either (and usually) take effect at closing or, like bonus shares, involve a minimum holding period. Retail discounts, where used, are normally in the order of lower single-digit percentages.

Governments have also used in the past partly paid shares for retail investors, allowing them to pay for shares over a period of time, and generally in two stages, with no interest. Partly paid shares are traded separately on the secondary market. Again partly paid shares were introduced probably for the first time in the mid-1980s, as were bonus shares and retail discounts.

There are other, rarer, forms of retail incentives. In the past these have included electricity or gas vouchers for utility stocks and (partial) money-back guarantees for a certain period of time in the event of a fall of the share price below the retail offer price. Retail investors could also sometimes receive better allocations as a result of registering their interest early. The £770 million IPO of Eurotunnel in 1987 even included free trips as an incentive for retail shareholders.

The use of retail incentives now appears to have pretty much disappeared, and multi-billion-dollar offerings are now commonly brought to market without any preferential treatment for public investors who, in the internet age, are increasingly familiar with equity capital markets.

3.8   Employee share ownership programmes (ESOPs)

Companies going public in an IPO often set up an employee share ownership programme (ESOP) either prior to, or at the time of listing. Often an employee offer takes place at the same time as the public offering. Although the broad principles of an ESOP are generally fairly simple, this can become a complex matter, particularly for companies that operate across a variety of jurisdictions and tax regimes.

3.8.1   Objectives and scale

The objectives of an ESOP are generally to incentivize, retain, and attract staff, and can apply either to a selected group of employees or to staff across the whole company. Such offerings are common and have been in existence for a long time. For example, the IPO of Abbey National, a building society that was transformed into a bank in a demutualization and floated in a £1.6 billion flotation in the UK in 1989 (before being acquired by Banco Santander of Spain in more recent times), included an allocation of free stock to each of its 5.6 million customers at the time.[83] Often, several schemes are introduced at the same time, depending on the level of seniority of the beneficiaries, for example, top management, staff above a certain pay scale or rank, and other employees more generally. ESOPs generally account for about 5% to 15% of share ownership in a company,[84] and can be structured in a number of ways. Employees may be able to buy stock (often on preferential terms) or may also be entitled to receive shares or stock options as part of a bonus or incentive payment.

3.8.2   Human resource (HR) and performance consultants

It is important to decide at the outset how much the company is prepared to spend on the scheme (or schemes) and to structure the programme, taking into account local regulations and tax incentives. Accordingly, a specialist HR and performance or remuneration consultant can add much value and provide examples of schemes devised for other comparable businesses with a similar profile and spread of activities. The consultant can also advise on tax and national insurance contributions that may be payable by the company or employees in connection with such schemes. Unlike profit-sharing schemes, share schemes involve the payment of shares, or securities convertible into, exchangeable for, or giving the right to buy shares, over a period of time, and the benefit that can accrue to employees is forward-looking rather than linked to past performance.

3.8.3   Key considerations

Key considerations in designing an ESOP include the following:[85]

- the size of the company and market practice in the industry;
- identifying the beneficiaries, or groups of beneficiaries, and whether a minimum qualifying length of service is required;
- identifying the origin of the shares (whether from an existing holding (such as treasury stock) or new shares);
- voting, dividend, and other rights (such as participation in rights issues) applying to the shares;
- allocation and grant rules;
- lock-ups and deferred instalment arrangements;

- potential matching by the company of share purchases by employees;
- rules applying to employees voluntarily leaving or retiring from the company, as well as for employees made redundant (except for cause) by the company;
- setting up a trust structure to run the scheme and hold shares on behalf of the employees; and
- dilution considerations.

Most countries have a variety of both revenue-approved and taxed schemes for consideration. These include, for example, Share Incentive Plans (SIPs), Save As You Earn (SAYE), Company Share Option Plans (CSOPs), and Enterprise Management Incentives (EMIs) in the UK.[86]

3.8.4   A typical three-tier ESOP

As an illustrative example, a typical three-tier ESOP could include:

- stock options, granted to top employees at a discount to the IPO price, or stock acquisition rights granted (perhaps at nominal value), and exercisable for a period of time (generally up to ten years) after listing, subject to a minimum no-exercise period;
- shares available for purchase at a discount by "mid-level" employees; and
- free shares granted to other, more junior employees in connection with the IPO.

Certain restrictions may also attach to options or shares granted to employees. These may be forfeited if the employee voluntarily leaves the company before a certain amount of time has lapsed or joins a competitor. Other instruments related to shares may also be used, such as bonds or preference shares that may convert into shares in the future. In addition, ESOPs that are introduced after a company has been listed should generally conform to rules of the relevant stock exchange.

An example of a successful employee offer in connection with an IPO is provided in Appendix 1 in the case study of the CapitaMalls IPO in Singapore.

3.9   Pricing

Once the overall book of demand has closed, the first task is to agree on an offer price with management. The institutional portion of the offering is then underwritten by all the banks in the relevant tranche of the syndicate at the offer price (less fees). Most of the time, only the global coordinators and bookrunners—together with, perhaps, some of the other bookrunners—will be present to sign the underwriting and other agreements; the more junior banks in the syndicate will have signed and sent powers of attorney to one or more of the lead banks (coordinating this on behalf of the others) to sign on their behalf.

Pricing and allocating an IPO is really more of an art than a science. It needs to take into account the priorities of the issuer, of the selling shareholders (if any), and of the investors so as to encourage aftermarket buying and a steady increase in the share price—ideally relatively modest at first, rather than a sharp spike at the start of trading. In 2013, the shares in Royal Mail in the UK increased 38% on their first day or trading after the company's US$3.3 billion equivalent privatization IPO. This, coupled with an increase of more than 70% after only five months, triggered a parliamentary enquiry and criticism by the UK's National Audit Office (the NAO) on suspicion that the new listing had been under-priced by the banks and advisers involved, and that the British government could have achieved a better deal for the taxpayer.[87]

3.9.1   Deciphering the book of demand

The issuer and its shareholders will often seek to maximize the offer price and argue for pricing at the top end of the range, even if the IPO has only been just covered at that level. This ignores order inflation on the part of some investors and considerations pertaining to the quality of the book, and the bookrunners can bring much value in "decoding" or deciphering the book, so as to determine the true levels of over-subscription throughout the price range. In addition, as noted, the quality of the book should be taken into account, to ensure that a sizeable proportion of anchor orders by large, well-known, generally long-only accounts with a long-term investment horizon can be allocated. Assuming the deal is over-subscribed, if most of the orders at strike are from poor-quality investors, and if the deal were to be priced at the top of the range, then there is a higher likelihood that trading will have a poor start, with the share price even falling below the offer price, and that many of these new shareholders will exit at the earliest opportunity. Much discussion can therefore take place to agree on pricing, particularly when the IPO involves management and shareholder teams that have not gone through this process previously and are accordingly unfamiliar with it.

3.9.2   Pitching the right price

Assuming sufficient demand has been generated through the bookbuilding process to cover the deal ideally a number of times and to build a good-quality order book, a successful IPO should ideally be priced in the upper quartile of the price range. Pricing at the top end of the range is not necessarily an objective itself, and it may perhaps be desirable to "leave something on the table", although in some cases a very high level of over-subscription may render this difficult to justify. "Hot" IPOs are often known for a sharp spike when the share price pops up as trading starts, prompting some academics (particularly in the US) to point to the systematic under-pricing of IPOs.[88] However, in some cases large offerings that have been subscribed multiple times can have a disappointing start of trading, or indeed quickly fall to below the IPO offer price after a strong debut, as was the case with the US$16 billion IPO of Facebook in 2012, which was increased in size by 25% on the back of investor demand, and also saw the price range increased from US$28–US$35 to US$34–US$38 per share. The IPO, priced at US$38 per share, initially saw an increase in share price to US$45, before the shares closed at US$34.03 at the end of the second day of trading. The deal was most certainly overpriced on account of the hype and momentum generated by such a high-profile IPO.

This can be because the book of demand is not sufficiently strong or of a high enough quality to sustain the level of pricing. Or it can be because market conditions have suddenly deteriorated as a result of factors beyond the control of the company or of the lead banks. Appendix 1 gives examples of the start of trading for IPOs across a variety of countries, from the US to the UK, continental Europe, and Asia.

3.9.3   What happens after pricing

Once the lead banks and the issuer have agreed on the offer price, the institutional allocation process can begin. At that stage, both the number of shares in the book at the offer price (which has just been determined) and the number of shares on offer, that is both firm shares and shares subject to an over-allotment option, which I will discuss in Chapter 4, Section 4.1, are known. Therefore, the bookrunners are now able to decide which investors will be allocated shares and by how much to reduce their respective orders.

Upon pricing and prior to signing the underwriting and sale and purchase agreements (and often prior to the pricing discussions themselves), a (usually relatively) short discussion with management will also take place to conduct "bring-down" due diligence. In effect, the lead banks and the legal advisers then ask the management team of the issuer if there have been any new developments affecting the standing of the company over the last few days that should be reflected in the final offering circular and disclosed to the market. A similar process is also conducted just prior to closing, as well as prior to the exercise of the over-allotment option, if any.

At that point, the sale and purchase agreement for the institutional tranche is signed by the lead banks (the underwriting agreement for any retail tranche will, in turn, typically be signed prior to the start of that offer, as it will with any subsequent POWL offer in Japan), also on behalf of the rest of the syndicate, using powers of attorney, and the shares become formally owned by the banks until the closing of the deal. The final offering circular—including the offer price, statistics based on the offer price, the gross and net proceeds expected from the offering, as well as any changes or developments that have occurred and need to be disclosed since the publication of the red herring—is also prepared at that time, usually overnight for publication on the following business day. More often than not, these days, however, a simple pricing schedule is published instead of a full, final offering circular, as previously explained.

3.10   Underwriting and other agreements

A number of agreements are signed between various parties upon the pricing of an IPO. First, the banks formally purchase the shares in the placing tranche at the offer price, net of commissions, from the issuer and from any selling shareholders, through the signing of a sale and purchase agreement. This agreement is distinct from the "domestic" underwriting agreement for the public offer or retail tranche, which is underwritten at the start of the public offer, although both agreements are generally conditional upon each other.

3.10.1 Major clauses in a sale and purchase agreement

In practice, the sale and purchase agreement evidences the underwriting of institutional settlement between the pricing and the closing of the transaction. Accordingly, the banks commit to paying the issuer come what may, should one or more investors default on their payment obligations. The sale and purchase agreement applies to the Rule 144A and/or Reg. S international institutional offering and therefore typically includes US-specific representations and warranties. Broadly speaking, the sale and purchase agreement generally includes a number of conditions precedent, such as the registration of the prospectus, agreement on the offer price for the IPO, admission of the stock to listing, signing of the underwriting agreement for the domestic tranche, and delivery of a number of specified documents on particular dates (e.g., legal opinions and the auditors' comfort letters) to the lead banks. It also includes representations and warranties on the part of the issuer and of the selling shareholders, concerning their ownership of the shares—for example, representations that these have not been pledged to a third party, information disclosed in the offering circular, maintenance of listing, and their ability to enter into the various agreements. They also warrant that they will abide by the terms of their respective lock-ups.

The sale and purchase agreement includes details of the commissions to be paid to the underwriting syndicate, as well as arrangements for the reimbursement of expenses. The issuer and the selling shareholders provide the syndicate with an indemnity against misstatements in, or omissions from, the offering circular, as well as against breaches of laws and of the terms of the agreement, although in reality, if something goes wrong with an IPO all the parties who worked on it typically end up suing each other, in addition to likely being investigated by a securities regulator!

3.10.2 *Force majeure* clauses

Importantly, the sale and purchase agreement also includes a *force majeure* clause, pursuant to which the underwriting of settlement by the banks may be terminated on the occurrence of certain extraordinary events. Such events generally include war, terrorism, epidemics, earthquakes, fire, tsunamis, or other acts of God affecting financial markets and the trading of securities, or the business of the company more generally. In some countries, the practicalities of enforcing such *force majeure* provisions can be hindered by local market practice. For example, in the past in Spain, once allocations had been inputted into the system used by the stock exchange, it was nearly impossible for the shares not to go through to investors, irrespective of whether *force majeure* was invoked or not. Local market practice and underwriting agreements for Spanish offerings consequently evolved to take this into account. *Force majeure* clauses have only rarely been invoked in the past, most famously in recent times at the start of the first Gulf war in 1990, and, more recently, in relation to the oil spill in the Gulf of Mexico in 2010.

In recent years in Asia, underwriters have insisted that settlement default by a cornerstone investor (i.e., the inability of a cornerstone investor to pay for the shares that it has subscribed for in the IPO prior to the start of bookbuilding) should rescind the banks' underwriting obligations under the sale and purchase agreement. This is because, they argue, cornerstone investors are increasingly important to the success of IPOs, and if one were not to ultimately participate in the deal, it would be unreasonable to request the banks to underwrite the offering. Where more than one cornerstone investor participates in an IPO, issuers and their shareholders may, however, perhaps prefer to agree instead on a set number of shares defaulting under the cornerstone subscriptions as the trigger, rather than on a single cornerstone investor default. Each case is different, and much also depends on the nature of such a cornerstone investor and on the amount agreed to be subscribed by it that, in turn, may (or may not) put a deal at risk. However unlikely, a high-profile SWF such as ADIA defaulting on obligations totalling several hundred million US dollars clearly should not have the same consequences on an IPO as a small Chinese corporate ultimately not paying for US$2 million worth of shares.

3.10.3 Public offer underwriting

The underwriting agreement for the public offer, whether concurrent with the institutional offering or sequential, is in most jurisdictions signed at the start rather than after the close of the retail offering. In both cases, retail investors (unlike institutions) pay at the time of their application rather than upon closing. The obligations of the underwriters under both international sale and purchase agreements and domestic underwriting agreements for IPOs are several (rather than joint and several), with each member of the syndicate undertaking to take up a proportion of the shares on offer but not shares underwritten by a defaulting underwriter (although some element of additional "pick up" by the underwriters sometimes features). The clauses in the underwriting agreement for the public offer are broadly similar to those for the sale and purchase agreement, except that this is obviously a purely domestic offering, so US-specific clauses need not be included.

Sometimes, the pricing of the offering itself is the subject of a simple, separate price determination agreement, although such information can also be included directly in the agreement itself.

3.10.4 Inter-syndicate agreement

In addition to the agreements for the placement and public tranches of a global offering, an inter-syndicate agreement is also sometimes signed at the time of pricing. The parties to this agreement are the banks underwriting each tranche. The main purpose of the inter-syndicate agreement is to govern the possible re-allocation of shares between such tranches, and how commissions will then be apportioned in the event of re-allocation. For example, should an automatic claw-back provision be triggered in Hong Kong, the size of the retail offering could increase from, say, an initial 10% of the global offering to 50%, should the public offering become more than 100 times over-subscribed (see Appendix 8 for details of the claw-back triggers normally applicable to IPOs in Hong Kong). The inter-syndicate agreement will then stipulate this; it will also perhaps mention that the management and underwriting fees will remain with the banks on the basis of the institutional and retail tranches as they were at the outset, but that the selling commission will "move across" tranches and be paid on the basis of the revised size of the tranches, after the claw-back provision has been triggered. The reverse may apply with the application of a claw-forward provision, should the retail offering remain under-subscribed at the end of the public offer. In such a case, the unsubscribed shares will be re-allocated to the institutional offering (and the relevant commissions transferred accordingly), assuming of course that there is sufficient demand and the required minimum number of shareholders for listing on the exchange has been achieved. In some cases, when there is not enough demand on the part of institutions to absorb such shares, the agreements might specify (although rarely) whether the banks are required to underwrite a certain set amount of additional stock in proportion to their original underwriting commitments. More likely, however, the offering will be cut as to its size, or re-priced, or pulled altogether, given the likely poor aftermarket performance of a barely or under-subscribed transaction.

3.10.5 Agreements among managers

In addition to the inter-syndicate agreement, the underwriters of the placing tranche will often sign a separate agreement among managers, governing the relationship between themselves—for example, their respective titles and which bank will act as stabilizing manager, and how fees and the reimbursement of expenses are to be allocated. Traditionally, a bank's management and underwriting commissions are available to absorb unreimbursed expenses and losses arising from the stabilization of an offering. Since most junior banks are, however, now paid on a fixed-fee basis, this no longer applies much in practice. Fixed-fee arrangements for junior syndicate members generally remain confidential.

3.10.6 Receiving bank agreements

Upon signing of the domestic underwriting agreement, a separate agreement is signed between the issuer, the lead banks, and the receiving banks. This covers the distribution of prospectuses and application forms for the public offering and also specifies how the receiving bank will be paid, often including interest on money collected from retail investors to apply under the IPO.[89]

3.10.7 Delivery of legal opinions, comfort letters, and other documents

With the pricing of the IPO and the publication of the final version of the offering circular, the comfort letters from the accountants are also delivered, with subsequent "bring-down" letters delivered at closing and perhaps also upon the exercise of the over-allotment option. The delivery of the comfort letters, as well as of other documents such as legal opinions, disclosure letters, and certificates required from other advisers, generally constitutes conditions precedent to the subsequent closing of the offering—although such documents should obviously be either signed (for the comfort letter) or be substantially in agreed form by the time the IPO is priced and the final offering circular published. This is the case for the legal opinions, any disclosure letters and deposit agreements, which are actually delivered at closing. The contents of legal opinions (including disclosure letters) and comfort letters were discussed in Chapter 2, Sections 2.8 and 2.9, respectively.

3.11 Allocating a deal

A sensible allocation strategy must ensure that institutional investors do not receive full allocations, so as to encourage them to top up their holdings in the aftermarket, which in turn ideally leads to an increase in the share price.

3.11.1 Allocation criteria

In general, allocation criteria take into account:

- the perceived quality of an institutional investor;
- the size of its order relative to its normal order size in comparable transactions (and, perhaps, assets under management);
- the investor's participation in marketing activities such as the roadshow, one-on-one meetings, research calls, and investor education;
- the investor's expected trading behaviour in the secondary market;
- the timing of the investor's order relative to the marketing schedule (e.g., an investor having a one-on-one meeting with management on the last day of the roadshow would not be penalized for placing a late order);
- the type of investor; and
- consistency with PDIE feedback (e.g., an investor providing lukewarm feedback about the offering at the PDIE stage, but placing a sizeable order on the last day of bookbuilding, would generally be considered as being driven by momentum and therefore would be unlikely to receive a sizeable allocation).

Investors who are known for short-term speculative buying and selling, as well as "late" investors, will often be penalized with low allocations or, indeed, no allocations at all.

Allocations are made in practice by the bookrunner(s) although in some cases, the issuer can have a major role in directing how allocations are made. For example, in the case of French privatizations, the French Treasury has compiled over the years an extensive database of institutional accounts and is known to be very hands-on in deciding how shares should be allocated among them. Legally, the allocations are done at the discretion of the issuer, and investment banks nowadays also generally send letters to issuers to inform them that allocations are their responsibility. Regulators expect issuers to be in control of this process to avoid conflicts of interest. While technically still done by the banks, allocations therefore usually take the form of "recommendations made to the issuer". I have worked on a number of IPOs where issuers, including private sector issuers, were very hands-on and also had strong views on how the book of demand should be allocated. This is not always the case and it usually reflects the degree of sophistication of the company. The more experienced management are, the more they will seek to allocate a book as they see fit, sometimes to the dismay of their underwriters!

3.11.2 Allocating a book of demand

In an IPO (and, indeed, in any equity offering) all allocations are made in shares (or other securities, depending on the offer structure), rather than in currency. The process seeks to ensure first and foremost that a core group of large and stable anchor investors, generally with a long-term outlook, are allocated a significant portion of the institutional offering, perhaps between 30% and 40% of the offering, or even a higher percentage in particularly challenging market conditions. The allocation process therefore focuses initially on the larger orders. Smaller investors, however, as well as those with a more speculative investment style, are also allocated shares so as to ensure liquidity in the aftermarket, although in lower amounts as a proportion of their demand. In the case of a very over-subscribed book of demand, most smaller and lower quality investors and those investors at the lower end of the price range will be "zeroed".

Accordingly, investors will usually have been graded by the syndicate desks of the bookrunners throughout the bookbuilding process. That is to say, they will each have been assigned a rating, say from one to four or five, depending on their perceived quality, with one meaning a high-quality investor and five a highly speculative one. Generally, there is broad consensus on most of the accounts if the names are well known. The largest and most prestigious money managers (e.g., Capital or Fidelity) will generally be awarded a top mark, and therefore receive the largest allocations in the book. When the syndicate desks disagree on a particular name, this is then discussed at some length, and some element of negotiation or horse trading takes place, with each house attempting to justify the grade to be assigned to their individual orders. Every bank has its "home accounts", those that trade with them frequently in the secondary market, and hence will be keen to "look after" those names. In most cases, however, it is pretty clear which accounts are high quality and which are not.

Institutional allocations should be made in a fair and consistent manner, and not on the basis of commissions paid to a particular bank. This is obviously a fairly grey area, since the largest accounts, which also generally happen to be the most active aftermarket participants by virtue of their size, will often also be the major clients dealing in cash equities for most investment banks.

Algorithms are then used with the system, and tentative "allocation runs" are made at the offer price. For example, 45% of demand can be allocated to orders graded 1; 25% to orders graded 2; 15% to orders graded 3; 3% to orders graded 4; and no allocations at all to orders graded 5. Once the result is relatively close to the number of shares on offer in the global offering, manual adjustments are made on a line-by-line basis to ensure that each investor is allocated a round number of shares, also reflecting a multiple of the board lot, that is, the round number of shares in which they are traded; for example, for stocks traded in multiples of 1000 shares, so as to ensure that no investor is allocated an odd lot, say 1789 shares. The process continues until the number of shares on offer is exhausted and all the bookrunners are happy with all the final allocations, a process than can, and often does, take all night.

3.11.3 Split orders

When an institutional investor has placed a split order, that is, more than one order with more than one bookrunner, then such orders (where allowed) should be treated in exactly the same way and allocated the same percentage of shares relative to demand, which is only logical.

3.11.4 Free retention

In some cases, where one of the banks has a sizeable number of small orders that would be difficult to allocate individually by the bookrunners, such bank can be given a "free retention" amount of stock to allocate as it sees fit. It should, however, generally revert to the bookrunners with disclosure of its final allocations, since in some markets details of allocations (or some of the allocations) need to be filed with the regulator or stock exchange. Bookrunners sometimes also keep an amount of free retention to be able to later top up allocations for some of their own accounts (but in such a case excluding split orders).

3.11.5 Other considerations for institutional allocations

Once the allocations have been finalized, they are generally presented to the issuer for confirmation. In some cases, management may ask for a few adjustments if there are investors they believe should be favoured more than others, perhaps as a result of a particularly productive one-on-one meeting held during the roadshow. Alternatively, and even though it remains legally their responsibility, management teams (particularly in the case of smaller companies) often have few or no comments on the allocations made by the banks. The allocations then need to be conveyed to the individual salespeople who have taken the orders, so that they can in turn be reflected back to the institutions. This can be done either by e-mail or, more commonly nowadays, directly through the bookbuilding system. Inevitably at this stage there is often much complaining on the trading floor, particularly if the issue has been a "hot deal", as salespeople obviously want to be seen by their clients to have been pushing their case very hard to receive a good allocation. Some shares might have been set aside by the syndicate desk in a "dummy" order, perhaps in the name of the bookrunner itself, to allow for last-minute adjustments: this is not really ethical and is now less frequent. Free retention amounts agreed among all bookrunners are more commonly used for this purpose nowadays.

3.11.6 Placing letters

The allocations to institutions are then often formally reflected in placing letters, which they are asked to sign and return to the banks' settlement or operations departments. The placing letters include an acknowledgement of the selling restrictions—for example, that shares bought in a Rule 144A placement by US qualified institutional buyers (QIB) investors can only be re-sold (in the US) to QIB investors. Such placing letters will also include details of the brokerage commission (if any) that may be charged to investors for participating in the IPO (typically up to 1% of the allocation at the offer price). In Hong Kong, the brokerage for securities transactions has been freely negotiable between brokers and their clients since April 2003. Investors should then return the signed placing letters with details of their brokerage accounts for delivery of the shares upon closing.

3.11.7 Retail allocations

Retail offerings are usually allocated by way of a balloting mechanism by the registrar, whereby different allocation ratios are applied to various bands of number shares validly applied for. This may also differ between retail investor pools, if any (see Section 3.7.3). In some cases, for the smaller applications, no balloting may be applied, resulting in such applicants being allocated in full (indeed, the issuer may perhaps decide, demand permitting, that every retail applicant will receive some shares in the IPO). Through the balloting mechanism, a set number of shares then become allocated to each successful applicant under each band. As with institutional allocations, care should be taken to ensure that successful applicants are each allocated a board lot (or a multiple of the board lot). An example of the balloting bands used in a recent offering can be found in the case study for the IPO of CapitaMalls Asia in Singapore in 2009, which is set out in Appendix 1.

3.11.8 Brokerage, transaction fees, and levies

In addition to brokerage (generally but not always set at around 1% in the case of IPOs), investors may also be required to pay trading fees or transaction levies to stock exchanges and regulators. For example, the Stock Exchange of Hong Kong charges investors a trading fee of 0.005% (per side of transaction) and a transaction levy of 0.0027% (per side of transaction) is also charged by the local regulator, the Securities and Futures Commission (SFC). A prior investor compensation levy of 0.002% per side of transaction was suspended by the SFC in 2005. This applies to both institutional and retail investors. In addition, although not applicable to IPOs (as the above duties are), brokers in Hong Kong are required to pay to the stock exchange a trading tariff of HK$0.50 on every purchase (or sale) transaction; and all securities listed on the exchange are subject to a stamp duty at the rate of 0.1% on the value of each transaction (this was increased to 0.13% in the first quarter of 2021). The government in Hong Kong also levies a transfer deed stamp duty of HK$5.00 payable by the registered holder of a share certificate and, independently of the quantity of shares traded, the registrar of each listed company also levies a transfer fee of HK$2.50 per share certificate from the registered holder. In addition, additional Italian and French financial transaction taxes are charged and collected by brokers on securities from these countries and their derivatives that are listed in Hong Kong (although this remains marginal as they are only a handful of them).

In general, all sales to institutions are deemed final, and no reallocations by institutions of the numbers of shares allocated to them are allowed to take place.

Then begins a frantic chase, usually over a few days at most, by operations and back-office departments for settlement details to be gathered and for payment and delivery instructions to be finalized.

3.12   Closing and listing

Closing pretty much constitutes the end of the IPO process. This is when investors pay for, and receive in their brokerage accounts, the shares issued by the company and, possibly, sold by the selling shareholders. In most markets, settlement is on a delivery versus payment (DVP) basis and in local currency, with the exception of DRs/DSs for which settlement is usually (but not always) in US dollars.

3.12.1 The settlement flow

Often, to simplify the settlement process, the global coordinator/bookrunner will settle all orders from institutions: it will deliver all securities to institutions against payment, passing on the proceeds to the issuer and to the selling shareholders (if any) after deducting the gross fees. The fees are then paid to other syndicate members after a period of time. The selling concession is often paid relatively quickly after closing, with a delay of often up to 90 days after closing for the payment of the management and underwriting commissions, to allow for the deduction of unreimbursed expenses, calculation of stabilization profits and losses, and the allocation of fees among all syndicate members.

When more than one global coordinator/bookrunner has been appointed, these will either share the settlement process, with one settling on behalf of certain members of the syndicate and another for others, or, more likely, it may be the case that one of them, perhaps with a more senior role in the transaction, will settle on behalf of all the banks in the syndicate. In the case of designations and split orders, that bank will also "bill and deliver" the securities on behalf of the institutions.

Depending on the type of equity security issued and the jurisdiction, the settlement process may involve further twists. For example, in the case of American depositary shares (ADSs) or global depositary shares (GDSs) issued by issuers in South Korea, where an issue of new shares is involved, the gross proceeds must be received by the receiving bank first, following which commissions get paid to the lead banks. This is because the share registrar must record the amount of gross proceeds paid in order to "create shares" even though, in practice, both steps are pretty much simultaneous.

3.12.2 Bring-down due diligence

Upon closing, a short due diligence call will generally take place (as will have been the case for pricing), and the legal advisers will verify that all the conditions precedent to closing included in the underwriting and sale and purchase agreements have been satisfied. Bring-down due diligence is more than a mere formality. In

2004, the US$3.8 billion-equivalent privatization IPO of what was then the world's largest REIT, The Link REIT in Hong Kong, had to be postponed as a result of judicial proceedings with the local Court of Final Appeal initiated at the eleventh hour by a public housing tenant. The IPO, which was led by Goldman Sachs, HSBC, and UBS, was, however, subsequently re-launched and successfully closed in 2005 once the issue had been cleared. In late 2020, the US$34.5 billion-equivalent IPO of fintech giant Ant Financial (owned by subsidiaries of Alibaba), in both Hong Kong and Shanghai, was pulled at a very late stage as a result of regulatory concerns in the PRC about the business of the company. It is thought that the amount of money flowing through the company's platforms unnerved the authorities in China, which ultimately led management and its shareholders to have no other choice but to pull the plug on the deal. The IPO of Ant Financial could have been the largest-ever globally, had it proceeded to closing. As the saying goes, nothing is over until the fat lady sings! As of April 2021 there was however speculation that the IPO of Ant Financial might be revived at some point in the future and/or that it might dispose of some of its assets under one or more M&A transactions.

Following bring-down due diligence, proceeds monies can then be released from escrow and paid to the issuer and other beneficiaries.

There is not always grey market trading (i.e., trading among market participants prior to the start of official dealing in the shares; also called conditional trading in the UK) for international IPOs, although the levels of over-subscription generally provide a good indication on what trend might be expected at the opening. Indeed, this is usually the object of much commentary by the media and research analysts of brokers not involved in the IPO, and accordingly not restricted by blackout on research during the quiet period. However, in the UK or in the US, for example, it is possible to see the "grey price" movement, including any shorting of the shares (where allowed) , between allocation and settlement. In other countries, such as in Poland, for example, no grey market trading takes place. In Hong Kong, only one broker (Phillip Securities) provides grey market trading ahead of the official dealings in IPOs, although volumes are often low. Such information is often mentioned in the financial media ahead of a company's debut on the stock exchange.

3.12.3 The start of trading

Shortly thereafter, the shares start trading on the stock exchange (or exchanges) on which the issuer has chosen to list. Often there is a slight delay at the opening of the market to allow for the pricing of the shares in what will generally constitute unusually high volumes for at least a few days. The price can either be set by auction (as is the case on the New York Stock Exchange or NYSE American) or, more commonly, through a matched bargain or order-driven basis. Trading volumes usually fall to more normal levels after a few sessions.

Many academic studies have been devoted to the deliberate under-pricing of IPOs. The reality is that any flotation must reconcile widely differing objectives. Issuers generally always seek to maximize the offer price, while investors obviously try to pay as little as possible for new issues, often asking for better terms than those for comparable listed stocks (the famous "IPO discount", usually thought to be in the order of 10% to 15%). Investment banks are involved on both sides of the equation but are paid as a percentage of gross proceeds, and so in theory are incentivized to maximize value for the issuer and its shareholders, even though they are also obviously keen to look after their institutional clients. The advent of bookbuilding in the early 1990s has done much to lessen the first day "pop" in IPO share prices, compared with fixed-price or auction-based IPOs, by setting out a dynamic offering process aimed at finding an equilibrium in the market between supply and demand. Appointing an independent adviser, or two or more houses as bookrunners, where possible, can also help in "keeping the banks honest" and in ensuring that the offer price reflects the maximum amount that the market as a whole is prepared to pay at that point for the IPO, while at the same time ensuring a stable and positive aftermarket performance. However, every now and then spectacular failures do happen, with IPOs either vastly over- or, indeed, under-priced. First day "pops", rather than more modest single-digit percentage price increases, also remain fairly common in emerging markets in particular, where significant institutional investor pools can be scarce or unsophisticated in their approach to new listings, or where retail investors account for a significant pool of stock trading. Rather strangely, they are also not uncommon in the US, perhaps because of the sometimes sub-optimal system to set pricing ranges there, as already discussed.

3.12.4 The closing ceremony

In most cases, a formal ceremony is held at the stock exchange itself with the issuer and the lead banks to officiate at the start of trading, "ring the bell" (or, in Hong Kong, a gong), take photographs, and grant interviews to the financial press and other media.

It is customary for the closing of IPOs to be followed by a "closing" dinner or ceremony hosted by the issuer, to which many of the parties who have worked on the transaction are invited. On large and complex transactions, this can mean hosting a very large ceremony indeed. In addition, it is traditional for the investment banks to present the issuer, as well as perhaps senior representatives of the principal third-party advisers, with a memento of the transaction. This generally takes the form of a lucite or acrylic paperweight in which the tombstone for the transaction has been embedded. Sometimes, the banks may wait until the end of the stabilization period to finalize this "deal toy" so that the final number of shares sold or issued can be included, after the over-allotment option has been exercised. It is generally the responsibility of junior ECM bankers to design and prepare this, and it is an opportunity for them to show their humour and creativity. Over the years, as an ECM banker I collected many such tombstones, of varying sizes, design (and weight, with some weighing up to several kilogrammes!), which all ended up gathering dust in a cardboard box somewhere, as they inevitably take a lot of space by the end of one's investment banking career.

4
After the IPO

4.1 Price stabilization

In every IPO and primary equity offering there is the possibility of immediate instability in the aftermarket, when the stock is traded between short-term buyers and sellers. This may, on occasion, affect the share price, which may temporarily fall below the offer price (when there are more sellers than buyers at a given point in time). It is therefore common for the issuer to appoint, generally from within the global coordinators and bookrunners, a stabilizing agent (also sometimes called a stabilizing manager) to go into the market and buy (or offer to buy) the securities to stabilize or maintain their price during the initial period after listing.

4.1.1 The stabilizing agent and safe-harbour exemptions

There can only be one stabilizing agent in an IPO, and its name is normally disclosed in the offering circular, usually at least on the front cover of the document and/ or in the underwriting (or plan of distribution) section. Generally, the stabilizing agent is also the bank in charge of settlement (as one needs money to be able to stabilize an equity offering). Recent market practice in Europe has been to involve two banks—one stabilizing agent and one settlement bank—both of which liaise at the end of each trading day throughout the stabilizing period. Such stabilizing activity is generally covered by detailed market rules, which offer a "safe harbour" from allegations of market manipulation. For example, the US, the UK, France, Spain, Hong Kong, Singapore, Malaysia, South Korea, and Japan all have explicit "safe-harbour" exemptions from market manipulation when stabilization is carried out. By contrast, there are no specific exemptions in some other countries, usually in emerging markets. Stabilization rules broadly cover the manner, timing, record-keeping requirements, and price limitations associated with such activities. The rules also generally call for the disclosure of possible stabilizing activity to be made in various documents (chiefly the offering circular), and often for actual stabilization activity to be disclosed to the public from time to time, as and when it occurs.

4.1.2   Over-allotment options

In most markets, stabilization can be conducted through the use of an over-allotment option. This is also called a Greenshoe, derived from the name of the first issuer for which the technique was devised in the US, Green Shoe Manufacturing (now Collective Brands, formerly known as the Stride Rite Corporation, and which includes, among other brands of footwear, Saucony and Sperry Top-Sider). Greenshoes most of the time represent approximately 15% of the base offer size. Much more would send the signal to the market that the bookrunners expect a particular volatile start of trading. Much less than 10% probably would not reassure investors that the stabilizing agent has enough shares or "ammunition" at its disposal to ensure orderly trading in the first weeks after the IPO. In some markets, such as Singapore, a maximum of 15% is actually a legal requirement.

In most markets where it is allowed, stabilization can generally be conducted through buying stock at or below the offer price, and for a maximum of up to 30 calendar days after start of trading. In Taiwan, since 2005, stabilization can only be conducted for up to five days in light of a 7% daily limit on increases or decreases in share prices in that market. In addition, price stabilization activities must be properly separated, through the use of a dedicated stabilization account, from other trading activities, for example, proprietary trading activities.

4.1.3   How a Greenshoe works in practice

The way an allotment option works in practice is as follows. Upon allotment of the book of demand, an additional amount of stock is allocated, demand permitting, at the same time and at the same offer price to institutional investors, above and over the "base", "firm", or initial amount of stock in the offering. As noted, the amount of additional stock is typically around 15% of the base offer size. In order to be allocated without just shorting the stock, these additional shares are typically borrowed, usually at no cost, from one or more of the major existing shareholders in the company, although such "covered" sales are not always allowed for stabilization purposes in some markets. For example, in the US, there is effectively a "failed settlement" for the shares making up the Greenshoe. The borrowing is generally for a period of up to 30 days, which is also typically the length of time during which stabilization can be conducted. The borrowing agreement (where permitted) is conducted at no cost to the banks since issuers and major shareholders are at that point locked-up following the signing of the underwriting and sale and purchase agreements. Accordingly, they are prevented from monetizing their holdings in any event, in addition to benefiting from the stabilization process, which is conducted on their behalf by the stabilizing agent.

The Greenshoe, for practical reasons, generally takes the form of existing shares (rather than of new shares to be issued), although it is also possible to structure a Greenshoe in connection with a primary offering. This, however, can have a diluting effect in terms of earnings or dividend per share, which needs to be taken into account, especially when marketing an IPO with a significant dividend yield, for example, a real estate investment trust (REIT), or a business trust.

Once allocations to investors (including the Greenshoe) have been made and trading has started, the stabilizing agent will monitor the share price in the aftermarket. If the share price trades at, or above the offer price, then no stabilization is necessary. An over-allotment option will then be exercised at the stabilizing agent's discretion, and the net effect is that a further 15% additional shares will have been sold (or, more rarely, issued) at the offer price.

If the share price dips below the offer price, then the stabilizing agent will post one or more stabilization bids in the market in order to stabilize the share price by buying shares, effectively "eating" into and reducing the additional amount of stock that has been allocated to investors every time shares are bought back in this manner. Such stabilization bids typically increase in size at staggered levels at, and below the offer price—for example, assuming an offer price of US$1, perhaps one million shares at US$1, two million shares at US$0.99, and three million shares at US$0.98. If the share price goes back up, then the over-allotment option will be exercised at any time up to the end of the 30-day period, albeit only partially. If all of the Greenshoe amount has been used up to stabilize the share price, then the over-allotment option will not be exercised at all, and all the borrowed shares that have been bought back are returned to the lending shareholder.

Generally, amounts of stock bought back from the Greenshoe cannot be re-sold, although in rare instances, local regulations allow the stabilizing agent to "refresh the shoe".

Typically, Greenshoes are exercised either within a week or a few days from the start of trading or at the end of the stabilization period—more rarely in between. By way of example, as already mentioned, the Greenshoe for the US$20.4 billion IPO of AIA in Hong Kong was exercised on the first day of trading, as the share price closed more than 17% above the offer price. In rare instances, some large IPOs are structured without a Greenshoe. This was, for example, the case with the US$530 million IPO of conglomerate SM Investments in the Philippines in 2005.

4.1.4   Penalty bids

In the US, in addition to the Greenshoe, the bookrunners may impose a penalty bid on an underwriter if shares are bought back by the stabilizing agent from an investor brought about by that underwriter during the stabilization period. This penalty bid takes the form of reduced commissions, whereby the selling concession payable on the allocation for that particular investor is reclaimed by the bookrunners. In effect, penalty bids are a way to discourage flipping of the shares by investors in the first days or weeks of trading.

4.1.5   Naked shorts

In some jurisdictions, including the US, it is also possible to allocate an additional amount on top of the Greenshoe, so as to provide further "ammunition" to stabilize the offering. This is then done through the use of a naked short (in addition to the Greenshoe shares themselves, which, as already mentioned, are also allocated in the US through the use of a naked, rather than a covered, short), whereby the shares are not borrowed and the stabilizing agent simply goes short by a further amount of shares, using its own balance sheet if it anticipates a particularly volatile aftermarket. This is rare outside the US; indeed, in many markets the use of naked shorts to stabilize IPOs or equity offerings is actually prohibited and only a limited number of stocks can legally be shorted in some jurisdictions (for example, this is the case in Hong Kong). On occasion, some investment banks have lost substantial amounts of money by shorting shares with a view to stabilizing offerings when that did not prove to be necessary, therefore resulting in a stabilization loss.

An illustration of how a Greenshoe and a naked short work is shown in Figure 11.

4.1.6   Some controversial issues associated with stabilization

Rather perversely, stabilizing an offering that has started to trade down usually generates additional revenue for the lead banks, since Greenshoe shares are sold to investors at a price higher than those at which they are bought back (i.e., they are sold at the offer price and bought at prices below and up to that offer price). This results in a stabilization profit, which is then retained by, and distributed to, the banks in accordance with the terms of the agreement among managers. Accordingly, in recent years, issuers and selling shareholders have sought to share stabilization profits, if any, earned by the banks. For example, the issuer had agreed to share stabilization profits with the underwriters on a 50/50 basis in the IPOs of Samsonite in Hong Kong in 2011 and of IHH Healthcare in Malaysia and Singapore

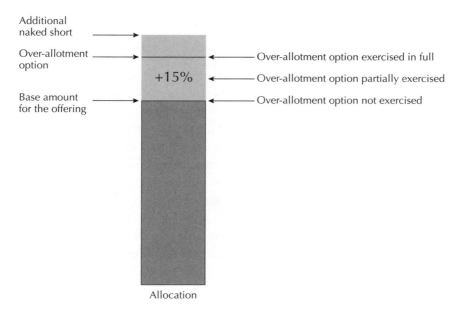

Figure 11

A graphic representation of an over-allotment option and naked short

in 2012. Conversely, such a 50/50 split was between the underwriters and the selling shareholder in the IPO of Chow Tai Fook Jewellery, also in Hong Kong in 2011.[90] Such arrangements are rare, however, and I am personally not aware of other examples.

Since Greenshoes are not really technically underwritten by investment banks, but allocated to investors usually on the basis of a borrowing agreement, itself generally at no cost to the banks, the practice of paying management and underwriting commissions on over-allotment options has sometimes been criticized, particularly in the case of privatizations. Market practice, however, continues to dictate that full fees be paid on Greenshoes.

4.1.7 Other stabilization issues

Greenshoes are generally allocated to placement tranches only, and not to retail or public offerings. In most jurisdictions, announcements must be made at the outset of the intention to stabilize an offering, as well as upon exercise (whether in full, in part, or not at all) of the Greenshoe. An interim announcement may also be required to update investors on the progress of stabilization activities. Records must also be kept of all stabilization carried out on equity capital markets transactions, details of which may be requested by regulators.

Over-allotment options do not always work, though. In some cases, the selling pressure may become so extreme that the stabilizing agent may need to let the share price fall and find a natural level before it can try to buy in the market again. An example of this is the US$5.8 billion business trust IPO of Hutchison Port Holdings Trust in Singapore in 2011. In that transaction, all the units comprising the Greenshoe were bought back by Deutsche Bank, acting as stabilizing manager on behalf of the syndicate of underwriters. Accordingly, the over-allotment option could not be exercised as repeated market purchases were unable to stop the slide in the unit price.[91]

Other examples of IPOs where Greenshoes have been exercised, whether in full or partially, and of others where over-allotment options could not be exercised at all, are included in Appendix 1.

In some relatively rare cases, the lead banks may prevent syndicate members from marketing, selling, buying, or entering into contracts to sell or buy derivative, hybrid, or synthetic products related to the shares of the issuer for a period of time, so as to further assist in the establishment of a smooth start of trading for the securities of the company. This can sometimes be an issue for banks that have sizeable wealth management or derivatives operations, which often issue warrants on shares of newly traded companies given the volatility and high trading volumes (at least initially) of IPO stocks.

4.2   Other types of IPOs

As of the first quarter of 2021, a new type of IPO known as a direct listing or sometimes as a disintermediated IPO had gradually appeared over the last couple of years. In short, with such a deal structure, there is no traditional price-discovery process, no bookbuilding, no investor meetings arranged by financial advisers, and also no underwriting. Similarly, there is also often no fixed or determined number of shares for sale and often no shareholder lock-up (although some direct listings can be structured with a capital raising). All of this can obviously save quite a bit of money and is also seen as convenient, particularly by the founding shareholders of new economy companies since, as we have seen earlier, IPOs can be a costly exercise, especially in the US, where gross fees paid to investment banks can be in the 6% to 7% mark. The legacy shareholders of unicorns are also probably likely to be attracted by the novelty aspect of an offer structure that effectively bypasses investment banks.

With a direct listing, which is one way to list on the NYSE or on Nasdaq in New York, the initial pricing is established through an auction. A designated market maker (DMM) sets a reference price, but the rest is basically purely down to investor demand and all investors can participate, if they so wish, in the setting of the price. As with a normal IPO, however, companies going down the direct listing route are required to file a prospectus with the US SEC and, subsequent to the listing, to comply with ongoing disclosure, such as the filing and publication of annual reports, as well as proxy filings.

The main advantage of a direct listing is a lower overall cost for the transaction. There are, however, a number of potential disadvantages. For a start, through a direct listing there is no traditional allocation process that takes into account feedback and demand from investors met by management and, in particular, the one-on-one meetings held with the highest-quality investors, that is, those major accounts that are generally long-term holders of the shares and form a solid institutional shareholder base for the counter. In a direct listing, the quality of the investors who receive shares is simply not a consideration, which can clearly be an important issue. Trading in the shares can also exhibit considerable volatility as a result.

One example of a direct listing is that by (the rather unfortunately named) Slack Technologies, a San Francisco-based software company that designs and develops real-time messaging for businesses. Slack listed on the NYSE in the summer of 2019, in a transaction that valued it at a rather eye-popping US$24 billion. For Slack's listing, a DMM set a reference price at US$26 per share and trading next opened well above that level, at US$38.50, and closed at US$38.62 on the same day, creating another tech billionaire in the process. After the initial "pop" the trading volume in the shares gradually subsided but, perhaps because of the size of the company, continued to maintain a reasonably healthy level after listing. As of mid-April 2021, Slack's shares were trading just below US$42.4 (although they had been hovering around the US$30 mark until early 2021).

It is probably too early to say if direct listings will evolve as a bona fide alternative to traditional IPOs—there are simply not enough examples of these transactions around to come to such a conclusion. They probably work best for very large companies and are, accordingly, not exactly for everyone.

4.3   Investor relations (IR)

A number of restrictions continue to apply after an issuer has started to trade for the first time following an IPO.

4.3.1   The research blackout or "quiet" period

A research blackout or "quiet" period remains in force for those investment banks that have participated in the IPO as underwriters. This generally lasts for a period of 40 days from the date of listing or closing. At the end of the blackout, the underwriting banks are free to formally re-initiate coverage, with reports including both share price targets and recommendations on whether to buy, hold, or sell the shares (or similar recommendations, as per their usual market practice). Needless to say, it would be bad form for a bookrunner to re-initiate coverage shortly after an IPO with a sell recommendation on the stock, unless the share price has skyrocketed to such an extent that it would be impossible to do otherwise. The other restrictions applying to pre-deal research reports are also lifted. Investment banks not involved in the syndicate for the IPO are, of course, not subject to blackout, although writing a detailed report on the company generally entails holding extensive discussions with management, which the latter may or may not want to entertain in the immediate aftermath of the IPO and while the blackout remains in force for other houses.

It is important for any newly listed company to have a core group of houses active in researching the stock, effectively promoting the investment story to investors on a continuing basis. This is one of the main reasons for the inclusion of co-lead managers in the syndicate for an IPO, although it is likely that a number of houses will pick up research coverage of most large market capitalization companies, since these are likely to generate significant trading business for their brokerage operations in any event. Obviously, recommendations will change and, on occasion, research analysts will recommend selling the stock if the share price has risen significantly or if the company's business faces difficulties. Nevertheless, research coverage remains an essential tool for investors to continue to remain interested in, and to follow, the issuer and, ultimately, in no small measure, to contribute to active trading in its securities.

4.3.2   Issuer and shareholder lock-ups

Lock-ups on the sale of shares by the major existing shareholders, perhaps also including pre-IPO and cornerstone investors, as well as on the issue of new shares by the company, also remain in place for a considerable period of time after an

IPO. Restrictions vary depending on the regulator or stock exchange on which the shares are listed, as well as what has been negotiated with the bookrunners in the subscription and sale and purchase agreements. Generally, however, the company will be prevented from raising new equity and material shareholders from offloading all or part of their holdings for a period of six months to a year after the publication of the final prospectus. Sometimes, such as in India, lock-ups are staggered, whereby material or existing shareholders are freed from selling part of their holdings, with the rest of their stakes remaining subject to a lock-up for a further period of time. As noted earlier in Chapter 2, Section 2.12, such lock ups also apply to cornerstone investors in Hong Kong (although this is not the case in Malaysia and Singapore).

In the weeks preceding the expiry of lock-ups, the share price is often negatively affected given the "overhang" such sizeable holdings sometimes create. Selling by some of the existing shareholders after a lock-up has expired often constitutes a good source of further primary equity business for investment banks, and the timing of the lock-up expiry is often carefully monitored to drum up new ECM business and execute placements or block trades (see Section 4.4). The bookrunners on a deal can often have a good marketing advantage to win this aftermarket business, since they can rightfully claim to know which institutions have bought shares initially in an IPO, and which accounts in particular may therefore have an appetite for further stock.

Underwriting agreements generally provide the bookrunners, in their sole discretion, with the ability to waive the lock-up for existing shareholders. This is rarely exercised, but in a notorious case in 2007 UBS waived the lock-up for Baring Private Equity Asia, a cornerstone investor in the US$525 million IPO of Hidili, a coal producer from mainland China, less than a month after listing to allow a US$40 million sell-down. This sale attracted much controversy at the time (also because allegedly no prior notice was given to the company), but was perhaps justified on that occasion by the strong increase in the share price since the IPO (+120%), as well as on the grounds of increasing liquidity in the stock.[92]

4.3.3   Ongoing disclosure and listing requirements

Once listed, a company must comply with the ongoing disclosure and listing requirements laid out by the regulator or stock exchange. This generally entails the filing of an annual report within a few months following the year end. In the US, a filing on Form 20-F for international companies or on Form 10-K for US companies must be made to both the stock exchange and the SEC.

In addition, interim (six-monthly) reports must be filed periodically and within prescribed deadlines. In some cases, quarterly reports are also required, for example, for companies listing under the Prime Standard on Deutsche Börse® in Frankfurt or, normally, for companies listed in the US (rather curiously, this is not the case for companies listed on the Main Board in Hong Kong, although companies that are also listed in mainland China as well as in Hong Kong will disclose such information, as do companies that are listed on the Hong Kong exchange's Second Board, GEM).

Lastly, most regulators or exchanges require listed companies to file ad hoc reports disclosing material events, for example, for non-US companies on Form 6-K with the SEC and the stock exchange in the US. In Hong Kong, listed companies are required to disclose: material events and developments; results announcements; financial statements; securities buy-backs; trading arrangements; changes in directorships; notices of general meetings; proxy forms; results of general meetings; as well as to publish various other circulars. There are generally tight deadlines for the disclosure of such material information. In some cases, listed companies are also required to publish a financial calendar or even to hold regular analyst conferences, for example in Taiwan (sometimes research can be subsidized by the exchange or the securities regulator, such as in Singapore) as part of the ongoing listing requirements.

4.3.4   Communicating with investors

Once a company becomes listed, it is important for management to continue communicating on recent developments, both with the sell-side (i.e., brokers) and the buy-side (i.e., investors) financial communities. Crucially, communication should take place in good as well as in bad times, so that research analysts and investors alike are kept abreast of issues that may affect the share price. This obviously includes results announcements, which are the subject of regular stock exchange filings in any event, but also extends to the signing of major contracts, the winning or losing of significant customers, senior personnel hires or dismissals, mergers, acquisitions and disposals, further debt and equity capital raisings, as well as other material events.

In some markets, it is also a requirement that newly listed companies must appoint a compliance adviser for a period of time after the IPO (usually for one year). In Hong Kong, a compliance adviser must be a licensed corporate finance advisory firm that is also eligible to act as an IPO sponsor. Newly listed issuers must consult and seek advice from their compliance adviser prior to the publication of any regulatory announcement, circular, or financial report, as well as in respect of any notifiable or connected transactions. Compliance advisers are also involved in cases of any inquiries into companies on the part of the exchange or regulator, for example, where there have been unusual movements in the share price or trading volume or a change in the use of the proceeds raised under the IPO. In addition, in the case of mainland Chinese companies listed in Hong Kong, the compliance adviser often also serves the role of local representative on behalf of the issuer, liaising with the exchange to answer questions and attend to requests.

4.3.5   IR departments and their roles

A newly listed company may want to appoint one or more dedicated individuals to look after investor relations (IR). These individuals may perhaps be drawn from the corporate management team previously assembled for the execution of the IPO and are part (for the senior member or members) of the necessarily limited list of people authorized to talk to third parties (perhaps including the financial media) on behalf of the company. It generally makes sense for these professionals to be appointed in such a role during the IPO itself rather than after the company has become listed, and for them to participate in the roadshow to meet investors that may ultimately become shareholders in the company, and be able to start a dynamic interaction with investors immediately after the offering. IR entails monitoring the share register and promoting the equity story to market participants in general, including seeking to widen research coverage, responding to requests for information and answering queries, assisting in the preparation of general meetings of the company, and regularly embarking on roadshows around the world to meet with analysts and (mainly) institutional investors.

While major investors will generally expect to see the Chairman, CEO, CFO, or COO of a company regularly, the IR department should remain the primary port of call for accounts that own, or are interested in owning, shares in the company. The IR department will often work hand in hand with both the CFO and the media or corporate communications department of the company to ensure that consistent messages are communicated about the business.

Depending on the size of the company, management may also sometimes find it useful to appoint specialist consultants or dedicated departments of investment banks (often under the name of "corporate access") to help with IR. Appointing one or more dedicated brokers is actually a stock exchange requirement in the UK. Corporate broking (or corporate access) departments of investment banks often host company roadshows to enhance their secondary market equities business. This can also include inviting companies to some of the thematic investor conferences they regularly arrange around the world. Examples of such conferences are the annual UBS transport conference in London, the Credit Suisse investor conference in Hong Kong (which is held every year around the same time as the Rugby Sevens tournament there, so as to entice international participants to attend!), and the annual Nomura Asia Equity Forum, which is held in the US, UK, and Singapore. As outlined earlier, financial communications agencies can also assist IR departments in the performance of their duties, in particular with respect to the organization of non-deal roadshows, the widening of research coverage, and the formulation and communication of key messages to the buy- and sell-side communities.

IR departments are also usually tasked with liaising regularly with investment banks and maintaining a watching brief on developments in capital markets. In addition, they are generally involved in setting up and managing employee share option programmes alongside HR departments and, perhaps in tandem with the treasury team, when the company raises further debt, equity, or hybrid capital to finance growth or optimize its capital structure.

4.4   Further capital raising and aftermarket transactions

Understanding how research analysts think and becoming familiar with investors are key to enabling a company to successfully tap the market after an IPO, through the offer of either primary or secondary shares—for example, through the sale of treasury stock owned by the issuer or by one of its subsidiaries. This can entail additional sell-downs by controlling investors, marketed primary or secondary equity offerings, rights issues, block trades, accelerated bookbuildings, convertible bond or exchangeable bond issues, monetizing property assets through REITs or other assets through the listing of business trusts, dedicated funds, or wholesale private placements. Aftermarket transactions may also include equity capital markets offers that do not involve fund raising or the sale of securities, such as scrip issues or share buy-backs. There are many possibilities.

In the US and in Europe, since the European prospectus directive, issuing further equity is facilitated by the concept of shelf registration (formally known in the US as SEC Rule 415), whereby a company can file with the regulator or stock exchange to conduct a follow-on equity offering up to three years in advance, subject only to normal ongoing disclosure.

The main changes from selling shares in an IPO with follow-on equity capital markets transactions are that, in most cases, price ranges are usually no longer used—or at least not price ranges as wide as those for IPOs—and that a company's live share price as well as the trading volume in the shares have to be taken into consideration. In follow-on transactions, the level of pricing is necessarily done by reference to the prevailing share price, as well as to trading volume. Generally, it is done at a discount.

4.4.1 Marketed offerings

Follow-on transactions can be conducted in a similar fashion to IPOs, with a prospectus and a management roadshow to convey the merits of the issuer and capital raising to the market, and also to attempt to minimize the selling pressure that generally accompanies the announcement of a sell-down or a dilution. In 2007, HDFC Bank, one of India's foremost lenders already also listed in New York, came to market to raise US$607 million in new proceeds in a follow-on capital raising by way of an American depositary shares marketed offering. This involved the publication of a US-style prospectus, as well as a full roadshow around the world by the senior management team led by Chairman Deepak Parekh, one of India's best-known businessmen. In the event, the timing of the transaction was perfect, having regard to the global credit crunch that ensued, and the deal was extremely well received by investors, enabling the bookrunners to price the offering at the volume-weighted average price (VWAP) on the day of pricing, equivalent to only a minute discount to the closing price.

4.4.2 Rights issues

Traditionally, companies listed in the UK, Hong Kong, Singapore, and certain other jurisdictions raise further capital by way of rights issues. Rights issues are fixed-price offerings that are generally fully underwritten at the outset by a syndicate of banks and provide certainty of proceeds for issuers. In a rights issue (or rights offering), existing shareholders are entitled (but not required) to exercise their right to buy shares in the company in proportion to their respective holdings at the time—for example, the right to buy one new share for five old shares held. This effectively gives them a right of first refusal to protect themselves from dilution.

Shareholders can either exercise their pre-emption rights and take up their rights to subscribe pro rata in the new issue or, alternatively, decide to sell their rights, or part of the rights they own, to other investors on the stock exchange. While shareholders selling their rights face dilution, they effectively incur no loss in value as a result of the sale. Rights sold by shareholders not willing to participate in the rights offering are separately traded "nil paid" during the subscription period. Rights not taken up by shareholders (thereby renouncing their rights) lapse and are automatically sold in a controlled manner by way of a "rump" placement on the last day of the rights issue, thereby diversifying the shareholder base of the company and further improving liquidity. Shareholders can also engage in a practice known as "tail swallowing", whereby they sell enough rights to buy new shares to allow them to take up as many shares as they can without having to pay under the rights issue.

Typically, companies can raise a proportion of new capital (around 5%) without first offering shares to existing shareholders in a rights issue. But authorization can also be sought, typically on an ongoing basis, in a shareholders' meeting to waive pre-emption rights under a "general mandate" to enable the company to raise equity capital through other means. Shares in a rights issue are typically offered at a significant discount (around 20% or more) to the prevailing share price, so as to entice shareholders to take up their rights. Timetables for rights issue are also generally longer than for other follow-on transactions. For example, in the UK and in Hong Kong, rights issues last 21 days in total. Australia, however, has in recent years shortened the timetable for such transactions in what are known as "accelerated rights issues". A long timetable can sometimes depress the share price, which can, on occasion, fall below the rights issue price.

The price at which the shares trade after the announcement of the rights issue but before its launch is called the "cum" price, whereas the theoretical price at which the shares should trade after launch is called the "theoretical ex-rights price" (TERP), when both shares and rights trade separately in the market. The TERP is calculated as the market value of the issuer before the rights issue plus the proceeds to be raised from the rights issues (ignoring fees and expenses), together divided by the number of shares after the rights issue. In effect, the TERP is an objective measure of the value of a company's shares after a rights issue. The TERP is "theoretical" in the sense that the percentage of shares that will be taken up under the rights issue by existing shareholders remains unknown until the close of the offer period. The calculation of the TERP therefore assumes that all the newly issued shares are taken up by existing shareholders.

The subscription price and discount are selected at the start of the rights offering process. Setting the price for the rights issue at a high discount to the TERP encourages participation and minimizes speculative behaviour, as well as the likelihood that the share price will fall below the rights issue price. Conversely, setting the rights issue price at a low discount to the TERP may encourage shorting of the stock.

There are added complications when a rights issue is conducted internationally in that the issue may have to exclude retail investors to prevent public offerings being registered and conducted across a number of jurisdictions. In such a case, the rights owned by retail investors are often simply sold at the end of the offer period. Indeed, trying to align rights issue periods across different markets is an extremely complex exercise. Rights issues have commonly been adopted in many jurisdictions around the world, and in recent times, particularly in 2008 and 2009, to help recapitalize a variety of financial institutions and other companies affected by the credit crunch. Many such rights issues were conducted at a deep discount to encourage participation. However, rights issues remain very rare in certain markets, such as the US.

One obvious advantage of rights issues, other than preventing dilution for existing shareholders, is that they are generally fully underwritten, so they provide certainty of proceeds for issuers. In May 2018, the Stock Exchange of Hong Kong removed the obligation to fully underwrite rights issues, although this remains a commercial decision between issuers and their underwriters. As a form of marketed offering, rights issues require the publication of a prospectus.

As an illustration, in September 2007, Genting International, a Singapore-listed member of a major Malaysian gaming, leisure, and real estate group, raised approximately US$1.42 billion in a three-for-five renounceable underwritten rights issue on the Singapore Exchange to repay borrowings and for general project financing amid particularly volatile markets. The rights issue was conducted at a discount of 31.8% to the previous day's close and at a 22.6% discount to the TERP. The rights offering was a success, receiving 90% of acceptances from existing investors as well as 30.5% in excess applications from the placement of the rump. The company (since renamed Genting Singapore PLC) subsequently announced and executed a further one-for-five renounceable underwritten US$1.14 billion rights issue in September 2009 to take advantage of the strong performance in the share price, with 60% of net proceeds earmarked for future strategic opportunities and the remainder set aside for working capital purposes. The second rights issue was conducted at a slightly wider discount of 32.8% to the previous day's close and at a 28.9% discount to the TERP. In that offering, acceptances were received from 98.8% of existing investors, with 36.3% in excess applications from the placement of the rump.[93]

4.4.3   Accelerated bookbuildings and block trades

In some cases, a shorter bookbuilding exercise or accelerated bookbuilding (also known as ABB) may be conducted over not longer than a few days to create momentum and a sense of urgency with investors, and to minimize market exposure, but at the same time benefit from limited marketing on the part of management. Depending on the size of the transaction, it is not always necessary to publish a full prospectus, and these transactions are usually only marketed to institutional investors.

Alternatively, as is often the case nowadays to reduce the exposure time to volatile markets, sell-downs or primary offerings can be marketed very quickly, often over a few hours or overnight, by way of a block trade, with no offering documentation other than a terms sheet, a simple letter agreement, and placing letters. This can also sometimes enable the company to conduct such transactions on a hard underwritten basis. In both cases, a key factor is the liquidity of the shares, and how much the market is able to absorb in one go and at short notice. The higher the multiple of the average daily trading volume (calculated over 20 days or one month) the block represents, the more difficult the transaction and the greater the discount.

An example of an accelerated bookbuilding is the US$491 million equivalent placement in South Korea's Hynix Semiconductor, conducted in July 2010 on behalf of creditor shareholders in the company arranged by Credit Suisse and Nomura and two Korean investment banks, Shinhan Investment Corp and Woori Investment & Securities. The placement followed a successful earlier transaction in March 2010 by the same selling shareholders and the same investment banks, and represented about 4.1% of outstanding shares, enabling the selling shareholders to reduce their holdings to 16.5%. The offering, which was conducted over just a couple of hours after the close of market, was marketed at a tight price range of KRW23,200 to KRW23,950. The bottom end of the range was equivalent to a discount of 3.1% to the closing price on that day, with the top end of the range equivalent to the closing price. In the event, strong investor demand, with reportedly some 50 investors participating in the placement, enabled the deal to be priced at market. The selling shareholders were subject to a three-month lock-up, although further sales by way of an M&A transaction were reportedly carved out.[94]

4.4.4   Top-up placements

A technique very commonly used in Hong Kong consists of the combined placing to independent investors of existing shares by one or more shareholders of a company and in the issue of new shares to that (or those) existing shareholder(s) by the company in a simultaneous top-up placement to replenish its/their holding(s). The issue of new shares must be made at a price not lower than that for the placement to investors and for a number of shares not exceeding that of the placement. The issue of new shares is usually made pursuant to a general mandate. This enables issuers to raise funds faster than they would otherwise in a primary offering only, and is also a way to get around shareholder approvals and pre-emption rights for the issue of new shares. For example, in July 2010, Brightoil Petroleum, an oil bunkering company from mainland China listed in Hong Kong, raised the equivalent of US$135 million through Bank of China International in a top-up placement with some 25 investors at a 9% discount to the closing share price.[95]

4.4.5   Convertible and exchangeable bonds (CBs and EBs)

Convertible and exchangeable bonds (CBs and EBs) are interesting alternatives that can enable a company to borrow debt at a relatively attractive rate of interest and to issue, or, in the case of an EB, to sell, equity at a premium rather than at a discount to the prevailing share price. CBs ultimately enable companies to issue their own equity, whereas through an EB they are able to dispose of a stake held in another company or to sell treasury shares (see Section 4.4.8). Accordingly, execution and disclosure are normally more complex for an EB than for a CB in that an EB usually involves disclosure on two companies rather than one.

In effect, a CB is a debt instrument with an embedded equity call option. However, the conversion of the bond into equity very much depends on the performance of the share price and there may also be in some cases re-adjustments in favour of investor holders, also called re-sets or re-fixes, which are particularly popular in convertible bonds issued in Asia—for example, re-adjustments to the conversion price if the share price fails to perform as expected.

In a CB or EB, the issuer often has a call option whereby, at any time after a set date, it can force bondholders to convert or exchange their bonds into equity prior to maturity or to sell the underlying shares it owns in the case of an exchangeable bond. Typically the "hard no call period" is for a period of two or three years after the issue of the CB. Thereafter, the forced conversion is generally only possible if the share price of the company exceeds a pre-agreed threshold, usually 120% or 130% of par, or of the redemption price for the bond. Conversely, and more rarely, investors sometimes benefit from a put option whereby they can, at pre-agreed dates, obtain buy-back or reimbursement by the issuer of the value of the bond at par, or at the redemption price for the bond.

While issuing further equity strengthens the balance sheet, it brings with it dilution concerns, which can become an issue in the long run, for example for firms controlled by families. Over the years, investment banks have therefore attempted to devise complex, hybrid structures that try to bring together the best features of debt and equity capital to allay dilution concerns, while achieving equity balance-sheet treatment by credit rating agencies and research analysts. However, such products often have a relatively narrow distribution base and are not for every issuer. They also often require a considerable leap of faith on the part of investors, and there can be strings attached if things do not proceed as expected.

For example, in 2007, Tata Motors, a member of the Tata Group listed in India and on the NYSE, raised US$450 million in an issue of Convertible Alternative Reference Securities (CARS), through Citi as bookrunner and JPMorgan as joint bookrunner. The CARS took the form of a zero-coupon bond convertible after 4½ years, and at a 40% premium to the issuer's closing share price, into a security as yet unlisted (but expected to be listed prior to, or upon, maturity), with different voting rights. While this innovative offering was well received at launch, in the long run its success for Tata Motors very much depended on its ability to successfully list the underlying securities as described in the terms sheet and prospectus at the time of the offering. In the event, conversion did not, or could not, take place, and the issuer was required to redeem any outstanding bonds at maturity at a 31.8% premium of the principal amount, in addition to accrued interest.[96] In the event, part of the debt incurred through the issue of CARS by Tata Motors was repaid in 2010 through a debt facility provided by 13 banks to also refinance loans incurred for the acquisition of Corus, while the balance of the CARS was redeemed upon maturity in 2012.[97]

4.4.6   Private investments in public equity (PIPEs)

Private investments in public equity (PIPEs) involve selling publicly traded equity to private investors, either in the form of ordinary shares, usually at a significant discount to the market price; preferred shares; or, more commonly, convertible bonds. PIPEs are relatively common in the US and Japan, and are particularly targeted at companies that would otherwise be unable to tap the public markets for financing. Accordingly, their terms are often biased in favour of investors and may involve downside protection against falls in the market price in the form of multiple resets or the issuance of additional equity. This can result in significant dilution and what has often been termed a "death spiral".

PIPES also commonly include a variety of other advantages for investors beyond price adjustments, for example: put or exit options; director nomination rights; veto rights; anti-dilution rights; profit guarantees; negative pledges; prior consent for certain corporate actions or changes in articles; exclusivity rights; information rights; representation and attendance rights; rights of first refusal; or tag-along rights, although not all such arrangements are always possible for publicly listed companies in all markets.

4.4.7 Preferred shares

Preferred shares, sometimes also called preference shares, are hybrid, usually perpetual, instruments that have both debt and equity characteristics. They rank ahead of shares in the event of liquidation, but below bonds, borrowings, and other creditors. Preferred shares are normally non-voting and usually pay a fixed rate, although on occasion they pay a floating rate dividend, prior to any dividends being paid to holders of ordinary shares. Such dividends may also be cumulative, should payment not take place in any given year, or non-cumulative. Preferred shares are often listed and may be rated by rating agencies. They can also sometimes be convertible or exchangeable into ordinary shares, for example, in the event of a change of control of the issuer. Sometimes a company will have several series of preferred shares with different characteristics. Preferred shares are very common in the US and Canada and are also found, for example, in Brazil, Germany, South Africa, Taiwan, and the UK. As of the first quarter of 2021, legislation had just been introduced for preferred shares to be issued in mainland China.

4.4.8 Share buy-backs

Share buy-backs are the opposite of a capital raising exercise. They became quite common in recent years, especially in combination with the simultaneous raising of new money, for example through the issue of a convertible bond to effect such a buy-back, and were a popular mechanism prior to the credit crunch and liquidity crisis. Quite simply, a share buy-back is the process through which a company buys or re-purchases, pursuant to a mandate given by its shareholders, its own shares, either to be kept as treasury stock (also known by the French term *autocontrôle*), and therefore available for sale at a later stage, or, more commonly, to be cancelled.

The main advantage of a share buy-back programme is that, because of the reduction in the number of outstanding shares, it increases earnings per share (EPS). Share buy-backs are generally well liked by management teams as executive compensation is often linked to EPS targets. They also conveniently put excess cash, which can negatively affect for example an EV/EBITDA valuation, to use. Share buy-backs have also been used as a currency to acquire assets.

There are a number of ways through which share buy-backs can be carried out. Usually, this is done by way of simple open market purchases, subject to pre-agreed or regulatory limits, over a period of time. Alternatively, a share buy-back may be carried out more formally by way of a fixed price or Dutch auction tender. Selective share buy-backs targeted at certain shareholders or through the purchase of put rights may also be carried out. In addition, share buy-backs can to some extent be used as a form of protection against a hostile takeover since they involve the repurchase of stock in the market.

The main disadvantage of share buy-backs is that spare cash for a repurchase tends to be available mainly in boom times, when company valuations are generally higher; therefore, they may not always represent the best use of capital for shareholders. Paying a special dividend, perhaps with an option to re-invest in the company's stock, may sometimes offer a better alternative. Share buy-backs have also more recently shown their inefficiencies when companies (including a number of financial institutions) with very substantial share buy-back programmes became forced to issue new shares at a lower price per share than those at which they had repurchased stock.

Usually, most regulators impose on companies that request the authorization to embark on a share buy-back programme to disclose the future use of such shares. This can, for example, include cancellation, currency for the acquisition of assets, and stock option attribution. Regulators can also ask those companies to report explicitly afterwards the effective use of such buy-backs and stringent regulations have come into force to prevent abuses from taking place. Most regulators now limit the amount available as *autocontrôle* to not more than 10% of outstanding share capital, and such shares also cannot be voted in a general meeting of the company.

As an example of a share buy-back, Swiss bank UBS announced in late January 2021 that it planned to execute a US$4.5 billion share buy-back after its income for the fourth quarter of 2020 had jumped 137%.

4.5   Conclusion: What makes a successful IPO?

Only once a deal has come to market and closed, and only after stabilization has ended, is it possible to reflect on the success or failure of an IPO. The most successful and high-profile deals are often much talked about in the general and financial press, and even qualify for awards handed out by trade magazines, as do the investment banks and other advisers associated with them. But what really makes a blow-out deal?

4.5.1   It starts with a story

Invariably, behind every successful IPO is an attractive story. While businesses with "borderline" or average investment cases can be brought to market, truly great deals can only be conducted for companies with particularly strong businesses. These issuers capture the imagination of both the sell-side and buy-side communities, as well as of the general public. A unique business model or a "pure play" on a particular industry segment of which the company is the uncontested leader is easier to understand, to assess, and to value, and can become the darling of investment committees and portfolio managers.

4.5.2   A strong management team

Behind every great story is a management team with a clear vision of where the business is heading. Often, the company will be led by an entrepreneur or a well-known businessman with a strong personality, as well as an ability to communicate in a clear, concise, and authoritative manner. Investors are deluged with opportunities and need to make hard choices as to where they put to work the funds they manage. Shares of an issuer that stands out of the crowd because its management team does are much in demand. The roadshow is a great opportunity to make a strong initial impression. Embarking regularly on investor tours and visits around the world after the IPO also helps support the share price and sustain market interest.

4.5.3   Size and liquidity

Size matters. Not all the best-loved companies are large, however. Telepizza, a small pizza delivery business led by a charismatic Cuban exile, which floated in Madrid in a US$79 million IPO in 1996, became a phenomenon with the media and fund managers after a strong rally in its shares made it one of the most successful flotations of that era in Spain. Nevertheless, sizeable offerings are more noticeable, generate more "buzz" and liquidity, and, ultimately, more following among research analysts and investors. A business that is coming to market for the first time should balance the need for funds to finance its growth and development with the overall impact it may be able to make on the markets. Small-caps and micro-caps, IPOs of which have been greatly facilitated in recent years in the US through the enactment of the Jumpstart Our Business Startups Act (or JOBS Act), are more particularly followed by specialist research analysts and investors and, overall, remain more marginal investments. Not everyone agrees, though: in January 2021, Hong Kong market activist David Webb (who made a fortune trading small cap stocks) criticized on his website (www.webb-site.com) the stock exchange there for proposing to increase the minimum profit listing requirement (having already more than doubled the minimum market capitalization requirement in 2018), as it would considerably reduce the possibility of new listings by small companies.

4.5.4   Picking the right time

Markets are volatile, and floating at the right time can make a world of difference. Successful IPOs are often launched when the market is on the up, when investors are making money, and when sentiment is positive—not in the middle of a market downturn. Clashing head on with a much larger transaction that may soak up liquidity from primary market investors is also not a good idea. Coming to market when the market offers (or appears to offer) good visibility is often also what makes a deal stand out from other offerings.

4.5.5   Offering good value

An IPO has to be seen to represent good value. This does not mean that the deal should be under-priced, but there has to be a logical line of argument to justify the price asked from investors who will often also look for that elusive "IPO discount". Is the company growing faster than its peers? Are its margins consistently higher? Does it gain market share year after year? In such a case, parity with or even a premium over comparable businesses may well be justified. Above all, things have to be kept simple. Many investors unfortunately do not read much of the offering circular and rely heavily on the short calls made to them by salespeople to pitch the deal, as well as on brief encounters with management during the roadshow. There has to be clear, convincing logic as to why the price to be paid makes the investment a good one. In addition, above and beyond the price paid for investors in the IPO, the shares have to offer good growth potential and an ability to create, over time, substantial capital appreciation. This is also what enables companies to return to market and tap investors through further equity financing transactions. Squeezing every single cent from investors at the time of IPO only to see the share price in continuous free fall after the deal is not a good strategy.

4.5.6   Investor distribution

Successful IPOs are well distributed among investors. Many, good-quality names will have placed orders in the book, the offering will have been significantly over-subscribed, and the allocation process will have been conducted in a way such that accounts are left with enough unsatisfied, pent-up demand to top up their orders in the aftermarket. At the same time, a core group of orders from leadership investors will have been allocated to anchor the deal and create a stable public shareholding for the future. Such anchor investors will obviously sell some shares over time as their price objectives are met. But they are usually there for the long run rather than to take a short punt on the share price. Often, some of these orders will have come as a result of a cornerstone and/or anchor investor process. Speculators and "stags" will have been "zeroed" in the book as a result of the allocation process. Where the IPO is distributed internationally, a relatively even distribution has been achieved across markets, reflecting the broad appeal of the business around the world.

4.5.7 A successful aftermarket

Winning transactions obviously trade well in the aftermarket. The over-allotment option is usually exercised in full, the offer price goes up steadily, although not necessarily dramatically at first, which is a sign that the deal may have been under-priced and public investors are sitting on healthy profits over a period of time. Trading volumes for the shares are high, even months after the IPO, indicating that the market remains interested in the company, story, and management well beyond bookbuilding and its immediate aftermath. Research reports are consistently produced on the business, most of them with a positive outlook, and new research analysts, beyond those included in the IPO syndicate, have started to pick up coverage.

Regardless of how successful an IPO has been and how a company evolves as a publicly listed business, though, it is important to retain a sense of perspective. In the long run, systematically beating the market is not always an option.

Appendices

Appendix 1: Case studies

I have set out here seven case studies of international IPOs conducted across different major markets around the world. These include:

- the US$1.0 billion IPO of Shanda Games, a Chinese developer and operator of online games, listed on Nasdaq;
- the US$8.0 billion IPO of Banco Santander Brasil, the Brazilian subsidiary of the Spanish banking group Santander Group, which was spun off as a stand-alone company, on the New York Stock Exchange (NYSE);
- the US$1.9 billion equivalent IPO of Essar Energy, an Indian energy group, on the London Stock Exchange (LSE);
- the US$1.4 billion equivalent IPO of CFAO, a French non-food distribution company, on NYSE Euronext (now known as Euronext);
- the US$787 million equivalent IPO of L'Occitane, a Luxembourg-incorporated cosmetics company with its origins in France, in Hong Kong;
- the US$2.05 billion equivalent IPO of CapitaMalls Asia, a Singapore shopping mall development and management company, on the Singapore Exchange (SGX); and
- the US$2.1 billion equivalent IPO of IHH Healthcare, a Malaysian healthcare company, on Bursa Malaysia and the SGX.

These transactions were some of the largest IPOs that came to market in their respective regions between 2009 and 2012 and are, I believe, typical of some of the international transactions that now dominate the headlines. Many of the practices highlighted earlier in this book were readily used or applied in these offerings.

By their nature, case studies provide a necessarily partial and incomplete view of a transaction. The case studies here are meant to illustrate some of the key features of these IPOs, but in no way do they purport to include exhaustive information or to offer any view, opinion, or investment advice by the author whatsoever, whether on the issuers discussed here or on the offerings undertaken by each of them.

A Nasdaq IPO: Shanda Games

Background

Shanda Games Limited ("Shanda Games") is a leading online game developer, operator, and publisher in China, which was incorporated in the Cayman Islands following a re-organization. Shanda Games is a spin-off from Shanda Interactive Entertainment Limited ("Shanda Interactive"), which also listed on Nasdaq. At the time of listing, it offered a diversified game portfolio, including some of the most popular massively multi-player online role-playing games (or MMORPGs) in China, targeting a large and diverse community of users. Shanda Games had revenue in the financial year ended 31 December 2009 of about US$704 million, with a net income of over US$213 million.

The company was listed on Nasdaq's Global Select Market in a US$1 billion IPO in September 2009, with the ticker "GAME". The CUSIP for the securities was 81941U105 and the ISIN US81941U1051. Upon listing, Shanda Games was valued at US$3.6 billion, making its IPO the third largest on Nasdaq in 2009.

Syndicate structure

The IPO was led by Goldman Sachs and JPMorgan, acting as joint bookrunners and joint lead managers. Goldman Sachs was the lead bookrunner for the transaction, underwriting 48% of the global offering, with JPMorgan underwriting a total of 28%. Nomura, Susquehanna Financial Group, and Oppenheimer acted as co-managers of the IPO, underwriting 15%, 6% and 3% respectively of the global offering. In addition to its co-manager role, Nomura also acted as sole bookrunner of a POWL in Japan.

Legal and other advisers

The issuer was advised by Davis Polk & Wardwell as to US federal and New York State law and by Conyers Dill & Pearman as to Cayman Islands law. Jade & Fountain acted as PRC lawyers to the issuer. The underwriters were advised by Simpson Thacher & Bartlett as to US federal and New York State law and by Commerce & Finance Law Office as to PRC law. Shanda Games' auditors were PricewaterhouseCoopers Zhong Tian. JPMorgan Chase was the depositary bank.

Offer structure

The global offering was conducted by way of an SEC-registered offering of 83.5 million ADSs. Each ADS represented two Class A ordinary shares in Shanda Games. It included a US offering, targeted at US institutional and retail investors for approximately 58% of the global offering, and an offering targeted at international institutional investors for about

42%, including a POWL, targeted at institutional and retail investors in Japan that was said to be about US$75 million in size. In addition, the offering included an over-allotment option representing 15% of the firm shares.

The offering mainly took the form of a secondary offering of existing shares in Shanda Games by Shanda Interactive (for about 84%), with the balance (16%) issued in a primary offering by Shanda Games for general corporate purposes, including capital expenditures and the funding of possible future investments, joint ventures, and acquisitions. Up to approximately 1.8% of the offering was reserved for Shanda Games' directors, officers, employees, business associates, and related persons through a directed share programme.

Fees and expenses

The gross spread for the offering was 6.25%, split 20/20/60 between management and underwriting commissions and a selling concession, respectively. Accordingly, the total gross fees payable to the underwriters represented just over US$65 million. The total expenses for the global offering were estimated in the IPO prospectus to be approximately US$4.7 million, including SEC registration fees of about US$67,000, FINRA filing fees of US$75,500, a Nasdaq Global Select Market listing fee of US$150,000, printing expenses of approximately US$500,000, legal fees and expenses of approximately US$2.6 million, accounting fees and expenses of approximately US$1.2 million, roadshow costs of approximately US$100,000, and travel and other out-of-pocket expenses of approximately US$50,000. The underwriters had also agreed to reimburse Shanda Games for up to an estimated US$6 million in connection with the expenses for the offering.

Notable features of the transaction

Shanda Games had initially filed and planned for a smaller IPO of just over 63 million ADSs (excluding the over-allotment option). The offering was upsized from a base amount of up to US$788 million to US$1.04 billion after the first week of investor education, reportedly in response to investor interest. The price range, initially determined to be US$10.50 to US$12.50 per ADS, was, however, left unchanged. The range was said to value Shanda Games at a multiple of forecast earnings in the low teens.

The book of demand was reported to have been covered many times over and, in the end, the IPO was priced at the top end of the bookbuilding range.

At the start of trading, however, the ADS price fell 14% on the first day, hinting that the size of the transaction should perhaps not have been increased, or that the offering might perhaps have been better priced below the top end of the range.[98] Shanda Interactive's share price, which had rallied strongly during bookbuilding, fell 11.9% on the same day. Shanda Games' price continued to fall after the IPO and was down more than 47% after six months. Consequently, the over-allotment option could not be exercised.

Shanda Group founder Tianqiao Chen subsequently sold his stake in Shanda Games in 2014. In 2017, the Shanda Games brand was acquired by Zhejiang Century Huatong Group. In March 2019, following the buyout, Shanda Games changed its name to Shengqu Games.

Source: IPO prospectus, SEC filings, and financial and other media.

An NYSE IPO: Banco Santander Brasil

Background

Banco Santander (Brasil) S.A. ("Santander Brasil") is a leading full-service bank in Brazil. Santander Brasil's operations are located across Brazil but are concentrated in the South and Southeast, an area that accounts for almost three-quarters of Brazil's GDP, and where the bank has one of the largest branch networks of any Brazilian bank. Santander Brasil, which is incorporated in Brazil, was just below 85% owned (post-IPO) by the Santander Group (itself listed on the NYSE), the largest financial group in Spain and one of the largest financial groups in the world as measured by market capitalization. Santander Brasil had total income in the financial year ended 31 December 2008 of about R$15,971 million, with shareholder's equity of R$49,318 million. The company was listed on the NYSE in a US$8.0 billion IPO, including a simultaneous offering in Brazil, in October 2009, with the ticker "BSBR". The ISIN is BRSANBCDAM13. Upon listing, Santander Brasil was valued at around US$50.4 billion, making its IPO the largest on the NYSE in 2009 and also the largest-ever IPO in Brazil. Santander Brasil is also one of the largest companies as ranked by market capitalization on the BM&FBOVESPA in Brazil.

Syndicate structure

The IPO was led by the Santander Group's own investment banking arm ("Santander Investment") and Credit Suisse, acting as joint global coordinators. Together with Bank of America Merrill Lynch ("Merrill Lynch") and UBS, they acted as joint bookrunners and joint lead managers of the US tranche, while Merrill Lynch and Banco Pactual acted as joint lead managers of the Brazilian tranche. Santander Investment was the lead bookrunner on the transaction, underwriting about 31% of the global offering, with Credit Suisse underwriting just above 30%. Merrill Lynch underwrote about 26% of the global offering, UBS about 6%, and Banco Pactual just under 5%. In addition to the bookrunners, Banco Bradesco, Barclays Capital, Calyon, and Deutsche Bank were co-managers of the US tranche, underwriting just under 0.3% of the offering each. They, together with Banco de Investimento, BES Investimento do Brazil, Banco Itau, and Morgan Stanley were also included as selling group members (but not underwriters) for the Brazilian tranche.

Legal and other advisers

The issuer was advised by Davis Polk & Wardwell as to US federal and New York State law and by Pinheiro Neto Advogados as to Brazilian law. The underwriters were advised by Shearman & Sterling as to US federal and New York State law and by Machado, Meyer, Sendazc e Opice Advogados as to Brazilian law. Santander Brasil's auditors were Deloitte Touche Tohmatsu. JPMorgan Chase was the depositary bank.

Offer structure

The global offering was conducted by way of an SEC-registered offering in the form of ADSs and a concurrent Brazilian offering in the form of units, together totalling 525 million units. This was split approximately 57% for the offering of ADSs and approximately 43% for the offering of units in Brazil. Each unit represented 55 common shares and 50 preferred shares in Santander Brasil, with each ADS representing one unit. Up to 15% of the units in the global offering were reserved for the issuer's employees, directors and officers, and its customers in Brazil at the public offering price for the Brazilian offering. In addition, the offering included an over-allotment option representing slightly more than 14% of the firm ADSs and units, split 57% for the ADS offering and 43% for the offering of units in Brazil.

The global offering took the form of a primary offering by Santander Brasil to expand its business in Brazil by growing its physical presence and increasing its capital base.

Fees and expenses

The gross spread for the offering was 1.75%, split between management and underwriting commissions and a selling concession. Accordingly, the total gross fees payable to the underwriters of the global offering represented around US$140 million. The total expenses for the global offering were estimated in the prospectus to be just over US$10 million, including SEC registration fees of about US$418,800, an NYSE listing fee of US$250,000, FINRA filing fees of US$75,500, Brazilian filing and listing fees of US$47,200, printing expenses of approximately US$1.7 million, legal fees and expenses of approximately US$2.5 million, accounting fees and expenses of more than US$4.6 million, and other costs and expenses of approximately US$570,000.

Notable features of the transaction

Although the transaction was described as an IPO, 1.98% of Santander Brasil was already held by minority shareholders before the offering. The price range was determined at R$22.00 to R$25.00 and the offering was priced at the middle of the range at R$23.50, equivalent to US$13.40. This represented about three times the bank's tangible book value and was generally said to be fully priced, even though Santander Brasil was deemed better capitalized than its competitors.

Little was disclosed about the level of over-subscription or geographical split of demand for the transaction, although it was reported that Aabar, an investment company owned by the Abu Dhabi government, had invested some US$328 million in ADSs of Santander Brasil. Aabar reportedly subsequently sold its stake in November 2010.[99]

At the start of trading, Santander Brasil's shares ended down 3.7% on the São Paulo Stock Exchange and the ADSs in New York fell 2.9%. The share price traded slightly upwards thereafter, enabling 96% of the over-allotment option to be exercised, before falling below the offer price again.

In the fourth quarter of 2009, Santander Brasil's ADSs were said to be among the most actively sought-after stocks by hedge funds according to a Thomson Reuters analysis of US regulatory filings by 30 top equity-oriented hedge funds.[100] By the end of 2009, two months after the IPO, the share price for Santander Brasil was up around 2%. Ten months after the IPO, the share price for Santander Brasil was down by just below 3%.

Source: IPO prospectus, SEC filings, and financial media.

An LSE IPO: Essar Energy

Background

Essar Energy plc ("Essar Energy") is an India-focused energy company incorporated in the UK, with assets across the power and oil and gas industries. Essar Energy was created after a re-organization by combining the existing energy portfolio of the Essar Group, a diversified conglomerate in India. At the time of the IPO, Essar Energy owned 86.7% of Essar Oil, a listed company in India with a relatively low free float of 10%. Essar Energy had revenue in the financial year ended 31 March 2009 of about US$8,453 million, posting a net loss of US$167 million. In the sixth month ended 30 June 2010, it had revenue of US$4,765 million and profit after tax of US$112 million. The company was listed on the Main Market of the London Stock Exchange in a £1,274 million (then equivalent to US$1.9 billion) IPO in May 2010, with the ticker "ESSR". The ISIN for the securities was GB00B5SXPF57. Upon listing, Essar Energy was valued at US$8.3 billion, making its IPO the largest on the LSE in 2010, and Essar Energy the largest ever India-focused company to list in London.

Syndicate structure

The IPO was led by JPMorgan Cazenove and Deutsche Bank, acting as joint global coordinators and joint bookrunners. JPMorgan Cazenove was sole sponsor and financial adviser. BNP Paribas, Nomura, and Standard Chartered acted as co-managers. JPMorgan Cazenove was also appointed as stabilizing manager.

Legal and other advisers

The issuer was advised by Freshfields Bruckhaus Deringer as to English and US law and by Amarchand & Mangaldas & Suresh A Shroff & Co as to Indian law. The underwriters were advised by Linklaters as to English and US law. Essar Energy's auditors were Deloitte. RPS Energy, Advance Resources International, and Netherland, Sewell & Associates provided expert reports as technical consultants on certain oil and gas assets, which were included in the prospectus. The registrars were Computershare Investor Services.

Offer structure

The global offering was conducted by way of an offering of new shares by Essar Energy to fund existing growth projects, including the completion of power plant projects, the acquisition of captive mines, the exploration and development of oil and natural gas blocks, and the expansion of a refinery's capacity, as well as for general corporate purposes, including working capital requirements for the company's oil and gas business. In addition, the offering included an over-allotment option representing 10% of the firm shares.

Following the IPO, around 24% of the company's share capital was held in public hands. The global offering included an offering under Reg. S to investors outside the US and a private placement to QIBs in the US pursuant to Rule 144A.

Fees and expenses

The gross spread for the offering was 2.25%, split between management and underwriting commissions and a selling concession. In addition, an incentive fee of 1% was payable at the discretion of the issuer to the joint global coordinators. Essar Energy estimated in its prospectus total fees and expenses for the IPO of £64 million.

Notable features of the transaction

Essar Energy reportedly decided to list in London, among other reasons, because of more flexible regulations for follow-on offerings, compared with India's requirement for a floor price.[101]

The offering was initially announced as a larger, US$2.5 billion IPO. The price range was determined at £4.50 to £5.50 per share, said to represent a multiple of forecast earnings in the low teens. Essar Energy was reportedly viewed as an attractive proposition on account of the growth of its business sectors in India, and also as a way to buy into Essar Oil, whose low free float makes it a difficult investment to consider for many foreign investors.

At the time of closing the book, the company announced that the offering was fully covered within the price range. However, perhaps because the level of subscription was not sufficiently high, and against the background of particularly difficult market conditions, it then decided to conduct on the day of pricing a fixed price offer at £4.20 per share. The offering was successfully closed at that level.[102]

Essar Energy had a difficult start of trading with its share price falling 7% on the first day, reportedly the worst debut performance by a newly listed company on the LSE for eight years. Nevertheless, the share price recovered, enabling a modest 1.3% of the over-allotment option to be exercised. Essar Energy shares were trading up 2.3% after one month and Essar Energy became a constituent of the FTSE 100 index in June 2010. In 2014, Essar Energy attracted controversy as Essar Global Fund Limited (its 78% shareholder controlled by brothers Shashi and Ravi Ruia) attempted to take the company private at what was said to be a particularly low valuation, in light of a very significant fall in the company's share price since its IPO. The company was eventually acquired by its majority shareholder.

Source: IPO prospectus and financial media.

A Euronext IPO: CFAO

Background

CFAO is a French company with a focus on the distribution of industrial products and services in Africa (excluding South Africa) and the French overseas territories. It is active in the automobile distribution sector and imports and trades pharmaceutical products. It is also involved in the distribution and integration of information and communication technologies and in the manufacture and distribution of other consumer products. At the time of listing, the company had operations in 31 African countries and in seven French overseas territories, as well as in Mauritius and Vietnam. CFAO is a spin-off from PPR, the leading French retail conglomerate, which is also listed on Euronext. CFAO had revenue in the financial year ended 31 December 2008 of about €2,864 million, and a net profit of around €128 million. The company was listed on NYSE Euronext in a €926 million IPO (equivalent to US$1.4 billion) in December 2009, with the ticker "CFAO". The ISIN for the securities is FR0000060501. Upon listing, CFAO was valued at about US$2.4 billion, making its IPO the second largest on NYSE Euronext (now known as Euronext) in Europe in 2009.

Syndicate structure

The IPO was led by BNP Paribas, Calyon, Goldman Sachs, and Société Générale Corporate & Investment Banking as joint global coordinators, joint bookrunners, and joint lead managers. Lazard-Natixis was senior co-lead manager while ABN AMRO, HSBC, and UBS were co-lead managers.

Legal and other advisers

Cleary Gottlieb, Steen & Hamilton advised CFAO and PPR as to French and US law, while Bredin Prat advised the issuer on certain aspects of French law. Sullivan & Cromwell advised the underwriters as to French and US law. CFAO's principal statutory auditors were Deloitte, with KPMG as second statutory auditors and BEAS as deputy statutory auditors.

Offer structure

The global offering was conducted by way of a sell-down by PPR for just over 50% of CFAO's share capital. In addition, the offering included an over-allotment option representing 15% of the firm shares, bringing the amount of share capital in public hands to just below 58%. The global offering included a public offering (on an open-price basis) in France, a placement under Reg. S to institutional investors outside the US, and a private placement to QIBs in the US pursuant to Rule 144A.

Fees and expenses

The gross spread for the offering was 2.25%, split between management and underwriting commissions and a selling concession, representing €20.85 million in fees for the underwriters at the offer price, including the over-allotment option. Expenses for the offering were not disclosed.

Notable features of the transaction

The price range was determined at €24.80 to €29.00 per share and the offering was priced at €26.00 per share, slightly below the mid-point of the bookbuilding range.

The roadshow reportedly visited Paris, London, Edinburgh, Stockholm, Frankfurt, Rotterdam, The Hague, Amsterdam, Geneva, Zurich, Brussels, Boston, and New York. Market sources indicated that CFAO's management attended a total of 63 one-on-one meetings; they also met with 224 institutions through large-scale presentations in Paris, London, and New York, and with a further 142 institutions in smaller group meetings in Paris, London, and other European cities.

The offering was said to have generated 240 orders from fund managers and insurers, with orders from the US and Europe representing the lion's share of institutional demand, said to have amounted to about 71 million shares, more than twice the number of shares on offer in that tranche. The retail offering in France generated orders from more than 15,700 applicants, all of whom were allocated in full. In the end, more than 93% of the global offering was allocated to institutional investors.

CFAO's shares rose 4% on the first day of trading and the over-allotment option was exercised in full. The shares continued to rise following the IPO before falling below the offer price in the second quarter of 2010.

Source: IPO registration document filed with the Autorité des Marchés Financiers, reference document, and financial media.

A Hong Kong IPO: L'Occitane

Background

L'Occitane International S.A. ("L'Occitane") is a global cosmetics company with its origins in Provence, France. At the time of listing, its products were sold in over 80 countries through over 1,500 retail locations, selling exclusively its own products and decorated in a standardized design. L'Occitane's three largest markets in terms of sales were Japan, the US, and France. The production facilities were located in Provence and Ardèche, France, and the group conducted its business from its headquarters in Switzerland, France, and Luxembourg, where the company is incorporated. In the year ended 31 March 2009, L'Occitane generated sales of approximately €537.3 million and profit attributable to equity holders of approximately €58.4 million. The company was listed on the Main Board of the Stock Exchange of Hong Kong in a HK$6.1 billion (equivalent to US$787 million) IPO in May 2010, with the stock code "973". The ISIN for the securities is LU0501835309. Upon listing, L'Occitane was valued at about US$2.8 billion. L'Occitane was the first-ever company from western Europe to list in Hong Kong, paving the way for several further listings by non-Asian (and non-Chinese in particular) issuers.

Syndicate structure

UBS was sole global coordinator for the IPO, acting as joint sponsor, joint bookrunner, and joint lead manager with CLSA and HSBC. No other houses were involved in a junior capacity in the placement tranche. The joint bookrunners, together with BOCOM International Securities, CAF Securities, Guotai Junan Securities, and Platinum Securities, underwrote the public offering.

Legal and other advisers

The issuer was advised by Freshfields Bruckhaus Deringer as to Hong Kong and US law, by Arendt & Medernach as to Luxembourg law, and by Zhong Lun as to PRC law. The underwriters were advised by Linklaters as to Hong Kong and US law. L'Occitane's auditors were PricewaterhouseCoopers. Jones Lang LaSalle Sallmans were property valuers. HSBC and Bank of China (Hong Kong) were receiving banks for the public offering in Hong Kong. The principal share registrars and transfer office were Banque Privée Edmond de Rothschild in Luxembourg, while the Hong Kong share registrars were Computershare Hong Kong Investor Services. In addition, Kingsway Capital in Hong Kong was appointed as compliance adviser starting on the listing date.

Offer structure

The global offering was conducted by way of an offering of new shares by L'Occcitane as to 50% to fund the opening of new stores globally, the extension and improvement of manufacturing plants, the development of research and development, the development of internet and e-commerce channels, and for working capital and general purposes. Fifty per cent of the global offering was by way of a sell-down by L'Occitane's holding company, sole shareholder of the company prior to its listing. In addition, the offering included an over-allotment option representing 15% of the firm shares. Following the IPO and the exercise of the over-allotment option, just over 27% of the company's share capital was held in public hands.

The global offering included a retail offering in Hong Kong, an offering under Reg. S to institutional investors outside the US, and a private placement to QIBs in the US pursuant to Rule 144A.

Fees and expenses

The gross spread for the offering was 2.5%, split between management and underwriting commissions and a selling concession. L'Occitane estimated in its prospectus total fees and expenses for the IPO of HK$196 million.

Notable features of the transaction

L'Occitane reportedly decided to list in Hong Kong to take advantage of the strong growth in the Asia-Pacific region, as well as on account of its significant presence in the Far East. L'Occitane had secured the appointment of CIC, China's sovereign wealth fund, as a US$50 million cornerstone investor in the IPO, ahead of launch. The price range was determined at HK$12.88 to HK$15.08 per share (eight being a lucky number for the Chinese), said to represent a multiple of forecast earnings in the high teens to the low twenties. The IPO was priced at the top end of the range. As is common with IPOs in Hong Kong, 90% of the shares at launch were offered to institutional investors, with 10% initially allocated to the retail offering. The placement tranche was said to have been many times subscribed, with the public offering receiving applications for about 160 times the number of shares on offer, triggering an automatic claw-back provision rebalancing the institutional and retail offerings to a 50/50 split.

In spite of the strong investor demand, L'Occitane's share price fell significantly at the opening, and was down by as much as 8.5% before closing just 0.9% below the offer price on the first day of trading, perhaps as a result of a sharp deterioration in market conditions between pricing and the start of trading and against the background of the financial crisis in Greece. The share price subsequently performed well and was up more than 20% after a month, enabling 75% of the over-allotment option to be exercised.

Source: IPO prospectus and financial media.

A Singapore IPO: CapitaMalls Asia

Background

CapitaMalls Asia Limited ("CapitaMalls Asia") is one of the largest listed shopping mall owners, developers and managers in Asia by total property value of assets and by geographic reach. CapitaMalls Asia, which is incorporated in Singapore, has an integrated shopping mall business model encompassing retail real estate investment, development, mall operations, and asset management and fund management capabilities. At the time of the IPO, it had interests in, and managed a pan-Asian portfolio of, 88 retail properties across 49 cities in the five countries of Singapore, China, Malaysia, Japan, and India, with a total property value of approximately S$21.8 billion and a total gross floor area of approximately 69.7 million square feet. CapitaMalls Asia's main shareholder is CapitaLand, one of Asia's largest real estate companies, headquartered and listed in Singapore. In the year ended 31 December 2009, Capital Malls Asia generated revenue under management of S$1,615 million, earnings before interest and tax (EBIT) of approximately S$521 million, and profit after tax and minority interests of approximately S$388 million. The company was listed on the Main Board of the Singapore Exchange in a S$2.8 billion IPO (equivalent to US$2.05 billion) in November 2009, with the ticker "JS8". The ISIN for the securities was SG1Z05950543. Upon listing, CapitaMalls Asia was valued at about S$5.9 billion, making its IPO the largest ever in Singapore.

Syndicate structure

JPMorgan was sole financial adviser for the IPO, acting as joint issue manager (i.e., sponsor bank) together with DBS Bank. JPMorgan, DBS Bank, Credit Suisse, and Deutsche Bank were joint bookrunners and joint underwriters. JPMorgan underwrote just below 33% of the global offering, DBS Bank just above 25%, and Credit Suisse and Deutsche Bank just below 21% each. Cazenove, CLSA, OCBC, and UOB were co-lead managers but did not underwrite the IPO. In addition, JPMorgan acted as stabilizing manager.

Legal and other advisers

The issuer was advised by WongPartnership as to Singapore law and by Allen & Overy as to US federal and New York State law. The underwriters were advised by Allen & Gledhill as to Singapore law and by Clifford Chance as to US federal and New York State law. CapitaMalls Asia's auditors were KPMG. DBS Bank was the receiving bank for the public offering in Singapore. The share registrar and share transfer office was Boardroom Corporate & Advisory Services in Singapore. In addition, several property valuers provided valuations for CapitaMalls Asia's assets.

Offer structure

The global offering was conducted by way of a sell-down by CapitaLand. In addition, the offering included an over-allotment option representing 15% of the firm shares. Following the IPO, 34.5% of the company's share capital was held in public hands.

The global offering included a retail offering in Singapore, an offering under Reg. S to institutional investors outside the US, and a private placement to QIBs in the US pursuant to Rule 144A.

Fees and expenses

The gross spread for the offering was 2.2%, split between management and underwriting commissions and a selling concession. The gross fees were equivalent to S$62.4 million. In addition, a discretionary incentive fee not exceeding 0.8% was payable to the joint bookrunners and underwriters at the vendor's sole discretion. CapitaMalls Asia estimated in its prospectus total fees and expenses for the IPO of S$77.5 million (nearly all of which was payable by the vendor), assuming exercise in full of the over-allotment option (but excluding the incentive fee). In addition to the gross fees, these included professional and accounting fees for S$8.2 million, printing and advertising costs of S$3 million, and other offering-related expenses of S$3.8 million.

Notable features of the transaction

The price range was determined at S$1.98 to S$2.39 per share.

The roadshow reportedly visited Singapore, Hong Kong, The Hague, Amsterdam, London, Boston, and New York. Market sources indicated that CapitaMalls Asia's management attended a total of 64 one-on-one meetings; met with a further 46 investors in small group meetings in both Singapore and Hong Kong, and with another 371 institutions through large-scale presentations held in Singapore and Hong Kong (together, including 285 investors), as well as in London, New York, and Boston.

As is usual in Singapore, more than 90% of the shares were earmarked for institutional investors, with the balance reserved for the public in a sequential offering conducted at a fixed price. The public offering was reported to be the largest-ever offering to retail investors in Singapore and was subscribed more than 4.9 times with 44,507 valid applications by retail investors (of which 36,073 were successfully balloted and allocated). The allocations for the public offer were made as follows:

Range of shares applied for ('000)	Balloting ratio	No of shares allocated by successful applicant ('000)	No of successful applicants
1	no balloting	1	7,593
2 to 9	39:50	2	17,148
10 to 19	38:50	3	7,400
20 to 49	38:50	6	2,356
50 to 99	38:50	9	939
100 to 499	37:50	12	593
500 to 999	37:50	26	28
1,000 and above	37:50	30	16

In addition, the IPO included an offering of shares reserved for directors, management, employees, and business associates of the issuer, CapitaLand, and their subsidiaries. Applications were received from a total of 1,285 applicants for the reserved shares in the IPO, with application moneys representing S$24.7 million.

The IPO was priced at S$2.12 per share, below the mid-point of the bookbuilding range.

Perhaps because of the prudent decision on pricing by the issuer, selling shareholder and bookrunners, the shares had a strong start of trading and were up 8.5% on the first day. The share price was up nearly 20% after a month, enabling the over-allotment option to be exercised in full. However, the share price fell below the IPO price in the second quarter of 2010.

At the time of the second edition of this book (2014), CapitaLand had offered S$3.06 billion (equivalent to a 23% premium to CapitaMalls Asia's closing share price on 11 April 2014) to take the company private, with a view to consolidating some businesses and boosting returns, and triggering a sharp increase in CapitaMalls Asia's share price. The offer was said to represent about 1.2 times CapitaMalls Asia's book value.[103] In July 2014, CapitaMalls Asia was eventually delisted by its parent, CapitaLand.

Source: IPO prospectus, filings with the SGX, and financial press.

A Bursa Malaysia and Singapore IPO: IHH Healthcare

Background

At the time of its listing, IHH Healthcare Berhad ("IHH") was the world's second largest listed private healthcare provider based on market capitalization. It focused on markets in Asia and the Central and Eastern Europe, Middle East, and North Africa (CEEMENA) region, which are highly attractive growth markets. It operated an integrated healthcare business and related services that had leading market positions in its home markets of Singapore, Malaysia, and Turkey. It also had healthcare operations and investments in the PRC, India, Hong Kong, Vietnam, Macedonia, and Brunei. At the time of its IPO, IHH operated 4,900 licensed beds in 30 hospitals, with one additional hospital in Turkey, the acquisition of which was pending completion. In the year ended 31 December 2011, IHH generated revenue of RM3,329 million and a profit for the year of RM394 million. IHH is incorporated in Malaysia. The company was listed on the Main Market of Bursa Malaysia in Kuala Lumpur (as primary market) and on the Main Board of the Singapore Exchange (SGX) in July 2012, with the tickers "5225" in Malaysia and "Q0F" in Singapore. The ISIN for the securities is MYL5225OO007. IHH was valued at about US$7.3 billion upon listing. Raising US$2.1 billion equivalent, its IPO was the first one to be simultaneously listed in Malaysia and in Singapore, as well as on two stock exchanges in the ASEAN region. It also ranked as the third largest IPO globally and as the second-largest in Asia in 2012.

Syndicate structure

Malaysian investment bank CIMB acted as principal adviser (i.e., as sponsor bank) in relation to the Malaysian listing and, together with DBS Bank, as joint issue manager for the Singapore listing. Bank of America Merrill Lynch, CIMB, and Deutsche Bank acted as joint global coordinators and, together with Credit Suisse, DBS Bank, and Goldman Sachs, as joint bookrunners of the global institutional offering, with Nomura, OCBC, RHB, and UBS acting as co-lead managers. CIMB and Maybank were underwriters and joint bookrunners of the Ministry of Trade and Industry (MITI) offering targeted at *Bumiputera* (ethnic Malay) investors. There were also 11 joint underwriters for the Malaysian public offering (which was led by CIMB and Maybank) and six underwriters for the retail tranche in Singapore (led by CIMB and DBS Bank).

Legal and other advisers

The issuer was advised as to Malaysian law by Kadir Andri & Partners; as to Singapore law by Allen & Gledhill; as to US and English law by Linklaters; as to Turkish law by Akol Avukatlik Burosu; as to PRC law by King & Wood Mallesons; and as to Indian law by Talwar

Thakore & Associates. The selling shareholder was advised as to English law by Freshfields Bruckhaus Deringer. The underwriters were advised as to Malaysia law by Albar & Partners; as to Singapore law by WongPartnership; as to US and English law by Allen & Overy; and as to PRC law by Jingtian & Gongcheng. IHH's auditors were KPMG. The share registrar in Malaysia was Symphony Share Registrars, while the share transfer agent in Singapore was Boardroom Corporate & Advisory Services. Frost & Sullivan acted as independent market researcher (IMR). Malaysia Issuing House acted as issuing house for the listing in Malaysia. WATATAWA was PR adviser. I acted as consultant to the issuer in connection with the IPO. IHH was approved as a Shariah-compliant stock by the Shariah Advisory Council of Malaysia's Securities Commission.

Offer structure

The global offering was conducted by way of an offering of new shares by IHH as to approximately 80.5% principally to repay bank borrowings, for working capital and general corporate purposes, and also to pay for listing expenses. The balance of the global offering was by way of a sell-down by Abraaj Capital. In addition, the offering included an over-allotment option representing 15% of the firm shares (including shares subscribed by cornerstone investors) provided by a subsidiary of Malaysian sovereign wealth fund Khazanah Nasional Berhad ("Khazanah"), the controlling shareholder of IHH at the time. Following the IPO and the exercise of the over-allotment option, 30.6% of the company's share capital was held in public hands.

The global offering included retail offerings in both Malaysia and Singapore, a voluntary MITI offering in Malaysia (since IHH Healthcare did not generate more than 50% of its net profit in Malaysia, this was technically not compulsory), an offering under Reg. S to institutional investors outside the US, and a private placement to QIBs in the US pursuant to Rule 144A. A significant portion of the global institutional offer was taken up by 22 cornerstone investors. In addition, eligible directors and employees of the group, as well as business associates who had contributed to the success of the group, were able to participate in the IPO as part of the Malaysian and Singapore public offerings.

Fees and expenses

The IPO fees totalled up to 2.50%, including a *praecipium* of 0.15%, payable to the joint global coordinators only, and a two-tier incentive structure, above the base fees of 1.60%. Brokerage, underwriting, and placement fees (including those pertaining to the over-allotment option) were estimated at RM176 million (about US$54.4 million). In addition, IHH had estimated in its prospectus additional expenses for the IPO of up to RM55 million (approximately US$17 million).

Notable features of the transaction

Part of IHH's business in Singapore, Parkway, had previously been listed there, hence some familiarity on the part of many local investors with the company. In addition, one of IHH's home markets is Malaysia and, at the time of listing, the company was controlled by Malaysian sovereign wealth fund Khazanah, hence the decision for a dual listing on these two trading platforms, a first in the ASEAN region. Prior to the launch of the global institutional offering, IHH had already secured commitments from 22 high quality cornerstone investors, representing almost 58% of the offer size (after exercise of the over-allotment option), as well as demand under the MITI offering representing 7.8 times the size of that tranche. The price range was determined at RM2.67 to RM2.85 per share in Malaysia (and the equivalent in Singapore dollars for investors placing orders for shares to be traded on the SGX). The IPO was priced just below the top end of the range, at RM2.80 in Malaysia and S$1.113 in. Seventy-one per cent of the shares were offered to institutional investors (including cornerstone investors), 15% under the MITI tranche, 7% under the Malaysia retail tranche, 4% under the Singapore public offering, and 4% under a reserved tranche for directors, employees, and other investors. The global institutional tranche (including the Greenshoe) was almost 60 times subscribed, with the public offerings also receiving high levels of applications. IHH's share price increased 10.4% and 10.1% on Bursa Malaysia and the SGX, respectively on its first day of trading. The share price subsequently performed well, enabling the over-allotment option to be exercised in full. IHH was subsequently included in the FTSE Bursa Malaysia KLCI, FTSE All-World, FTSE All-Emerging, FTSE Global Style, and MSCI Global Standard indices.

Source: IPO prospectus and financial media.

Appendix 2: Business and financial due diligence checklist

I have set out below a checklist (by no means exhaustive) for business and financial due diligence. This would be appropriate for a general industrial company. For businesses in other areas, for example in the minerals, resources, shipping, healthcare, or telecoms sectors, or for a financial institution, an additional, sector-specific list of questions should also be included in order to conduct a thorough investigation into the affairs of the company.

1. Share capital and dividends

- Authorized share capital of the company
- Classes of shares, including details of different voting rights, if any
- Current ownership of the company and anticipated changes, including as a result of the IPO
- Trust agreements and other documents regarding the shares and their voting rights
- Shareholder or other agreements regarding shares of the company or any of its subsidiaries, whether issued or unissued
- Charges or other encumbrances relating to the company's shares or their voting rights
- Outstanding contracts, warrants, options, conversion or exchange rights with respect to the shares
- Shareholdings by directors and employees
- Related- or connected-party transactions
- ESOPs or employee shareholder schemes
- Dividends declared by the company and its subsidiaries over the last three years
- Dividend policy
- Recent public, rights offer or bonus issues of share capital, convertible or exchangeable debentures or options, warrants or similar transactions resulting in dilution

2. Industry, business, competitors, and regulatory aspects

- History of the company
- Headquarters and divisional structure
- Key segments in which the company operates
- Major factors affecting the industry in which the company is active
- Market size, historical growth, and future growth prospects
- Trends in the industry
- Seasonality
- Key drivers of growth
- Major competitors
- Market positioning against competitors
- Regulatory aspects, policy, and regulations for the company

3. Strategy, objectives, opportunities, and risk factors

- Overview of the company's businesses
- Corporate structure of the group
- Business strategy
- Detailed business strategy by segment
- Outlook in the short, medium, and longer term
- Competitive advantages
- SWOT (strengths, weaknesses, opportunities, and threats) analysis
- Proposed alliances, mergers, acquisitions, or disposals
- Proposed changes in senior management
- Management of succession planning
- Long-term performance objectives
- Major risk factors
- Intended use of proceeds arising from the IPO (if any)

4. Markets, growth, suppliers, and clients

- Size of markets and growth rates over the last three years
- Projected growth rates
- Market shares, trends, and projections
- Key decision makers and buying factors
- Domestic and foreign operations
- Significant or anticipated developments
- Marketing, advertising, and promotional activities
- Principal suppliers by value and volume and procurement issues

- Largest clients by value and volume
- Changes in raw material prices, if applicable

5. Financial considerations

- Audited, consolidated income statements, balance sheets, cash-flow statements (with auditors' reports and notes), and operating data for the last [three] financial years
- Key financial ratios for the period under review
- Unaudited interim financials for the period under review
- Internal management reports for the last 12 months
- Reports prepared by outside consultants for the last three years
- Principal accounting policies and differences with GAAP and industry norms
- Depreciation policy for major assets
- Reserves taken and amortized
- Extraordinary charges and provisions
- Financing activity for the last three years
- Major capital expenditure for the last three years and in the future
- Future financing plans
- Budgeting and financial planning
- Details of performance versus budget for the last 12 months, and sensitivities
- Budget for the next 12 months
- Financial outlook for the next two years
- Review of capital structure and debt-to-equity and interest cover ratios
- Swap arrangements with counterparties
- Outstanding credit facilities and loans
- Debt repayment schedule
- Relationship with lenders
- Financial covenants, including existing or potential breaches of covenants
- Covenants requiring approval from lenders, in particular to proceed with the IPO
- Defaults on borrowings, past and present
- Summary of short- and long-term debt (credit ratings, holders, interest rates, maturities, amortization, and other key information)
- Copies of all material loan agreements
- Suppliers' credit obtained (or given)
- Guarantees or indemnities given (or obtained)
- Mortgages and security on assets of the company
- Investment grants, loans, subsidies, or financial assistance received from any supranational or government authority
- Material financing arrangements within the group

- Gearing and interest cover levels versus the industry
- Cash and treasury management
- Foreign currency exposure
- Hedging arrangements and derivatives
- Off-balance-sheet liabilities
- Material insurance policies
- Summary of tax charges for the last three years in any country
- Tax losses carried forward
- Tax audits
- Status of tax holidays, if any
- Existing and threatened tax disputes
- Receivables (recognition, treatment of bad and doubtful debt)
- Intangible assets (goodwill and others)
- Major subsidiaries
- Discussions with rating agencies
- Material agreements, including rating triggers
- Investments in other entities

6. Accounting policies and auditors

- Relationship with current auditors
- Details of the company's relationship with any previous auditors
- Qualifications under any recent auditors' reports and any disclaimers of audit reports
- Contingent liabilities discussed with auditors and not disclosed in the accounts
- Changes in accounting policies over the last three years and in the future
- Accounting and costing systems and management information systems (MIS), including any significant findings by auditors
- Off-balance-sheet items

7. Employee relations, human resources, and directors

- Schedule of employees broken down by main categories, country, and division
- Employee relations and unions, if any
- Health and safety issues
- Principal employee contracts
- Proposed changes to the remuneration of senior management or other important categories of personnel
- Incentives for management and employees
- Staff training and development

- Directors of the company and of material subsidiaries
- Terms of employment for directors
- Interests of directors in transactions with the company or subsidiaries
- Personal loans, guarantees, or indemnities furnished by or for the benefit of directors
- Directors or officers acting under powers of attorney
- Alternate directors
- Board committees (audit, remuneration, nomination, investment, risk, others)
- Pension arrangements and actuarial valuations
- D&O insurance arrangements

8. Environmental issues

- Significant environmental matters affecting, or potentially affecting the company
- Existing or proposed relevant environmental regulation
- Waste-disposal operations
- Environmental impact assessments and audits

9. Other matters, including ESG issues

- Other due diligence issues
- Other areas not covered above that might be relevant in the context of the IPO
- Major proposed public announcements prior to, or immediately after, the launch of the IPO
- Litigation, arbitration, administrative proceedings, governmental investigations, or enquiries (actual, pending, and threatened)
- Trade associations or similar bodies of which the company is a member
- Certifications or standards
- Copyrights, trademarks, and patents owned
- Websites maintained by, or on which information related to, the company or material subsidiaries appears

Appendix 3: Table of estimates for IPO fees and expenses

Category	Minimum	Maximum
Gross fees to underwriters:		
Incentive fees to underwriters:		
Out-of-pocket expenses of lead underwriters:		
Independent adviser/consultant:		
Legal advisers to the issuer (local law):		
Legal advisers to the issuer (US law):		
Legal advisers to the underwriters (local law):		
Legal advisers to the underwriters (US law):		
Other legal advisers:		
Auditors/accountants and tax advisers:		
Property valuers:		
Roadshow consultant:		
Financial public relations adviser:		
Depositary bank:		
Specialist consultants and experts:		
Financial printer, translator, and virtual data room (VDR):		

Category	Minimum	Maximum
Registrar(s):		
Remuneration consultant:		
Website consultant:		
Market research firm:		
Call centre:		
Advertising agency:		
Stock exchange initial listing fees:		
Other regulatory fees and levies:		

Appendix 4: Sample contents for an international IPO prospectus

The prospectus (in its various versions) for an international IPO will generally include all or most of the following categories. In its published version, plain English and writing in the first person would generally be used for the document (for example, "Our dividend policy" or "Our business" would nowadays commonly—and always in the US—be used as titles for the relevant sections).

- International and/or US wrap (W pages)
- Cover page
- Disclaimers (including on forward-looking statements)
- Summary and highlights, and selected financial information and operating data
- Offering timetable
- Glossary and defined terms
- Risk factors
- Future plans and use of proceeds (in the case of a primary offering, if applicable)
- Exchange rates
- Dividend policy
- Capitalization and indebtedness
- Dilution (in the case of a primary offering, if applicable)
- Management discussion and analysis of financial condition and results of operations
- Industry overview/independent market research (IMR) report
- Corporate structure
- Business
- Management and directors
- Share capital and principal shareholders
- Cornerstone investors
- Related-party/connected transactions and conflicts of interest
- Description of the local market

- Description of the shares
- Description of the depositary shares (in the case of an offering of DSs, if applicable)
- Information relating to the depositary bank (in the case of an offering of DSs, if applicable)
- Clearance and settlement
- Exchange controls (if applicable)
- Restrictions on foreign ownership (if applicable)
- Taxation
- Plan of distribution/underwriting
- Transfer restrictions
- Application procedures for local/retail investors
- Summary of significant differences between local GAAP, IFRS, and US GAAP (often optional)
- General and statutory information
- Index to consolidated financial statements
- Financial statements (F pages)
- Appendices (if any) (A pages) (details of material assets, material contracts, intellectual property)
- Parties to the transaction

Appendix 5: Sample risk factors for an international IPO

I have set out below, by way of example, risk factors that could be disclosed in the offering circular for the H share IPO and listing of a bank from the People's Republic of China (PRC) on the Stock Exchange of Hong Kong under a global offering. In this example, the global offering would also include a concurrent A share offering on the mainland, with a separate listing in Shanghai or in Shenzhen. Please note that only the headings have been listed here. In the published prospectus, each individual risk factor would be followed by a detailed narrative discussion, with the risk factors included in the printed version of the offering circular totalling perhaps up to 25 or 30 pages in aggregate.

Risks relating to our loan portfolio

- Our current results of operations and financial condition reflect certain extraordinary disposals of non-performing assets.
- If we are unable to effectively maintain the quality of our loan portfolio, our financial condition and results of operations may be materially and adversely affected.
- Our allowance for impairment losses may not be sufficient to cover the actual losses on our loan portfolio in the future.
- We have a concentration of loans to certain regions, industries, and customers, and if the economies of these regions or these industries or the financial condition of these customers deteriorate significantly, our asset quality, financial condition, and results of operations may be materially and adversely affected.
- The collateral or guarantees securing our loans may not be sufficient, and we may be unable to realize the full value of such collateral or guarantees in a timely manner or at all.
- Our loan classification and provisioning policies may be different in certain respects from those applicable to banks in certain other countries or regions.
- If we do not maintain the growth of our loan portfolio, our business operations and financial condition may be materially and adversely affected.

- Deterioration in the debt payment abilities of major customers to which we may extend loans may materially and adversely affect our asset quality, financial condition, and results of operations.

Risks relating to our business

- We face certain risks relating to our recently implemented operational reform initiatives.
- Our focus on certain counties or county-level cities under China's administrative division system and our related initiatives expose us to increased risks that may materially and adversely affect our business.
- If we are not effective in implementing enhanced risk management and internal control policies and procedures and in introducing certain information technology systems to assist with our risk management and internal controls, our business and prospects may be materially and adversely affected.
- Our expanding range of products, services, and business activities exposes us to new risks.
- We may face difficulties in meeting regulatory requirements relating to capital adequacy.
- We may not be able to detect and prevent fraud or other misconduct committed by our employees or third parties.
- We or our customers may engage in certain transactions in or with countries or persons that are the subject of US and other sanctions.
- If we fail to maintain our growth rate in customer deposits or if there is a significant decrease in customer deposits, our business operations and liquidity may be materially and adversely affected.
- Our business is highly dependent on the proper functioning and improvement of our information technology systems.
- We are subject to credit risk with respect to certain off-balance sheet commitments.
- We do not possess the relevant land use right certificates or building ownership certificates for some of our properties, and we may be required to seek alternative premises for some of our offices or business sites owing to our landlords' lack of relevant title certificates.
- We are subject to various PRC and overseas regulatory requirements, and our failure to fully comply with such requirements, if any, could materially and adversely affect our business, reputation, financial condition, and results of operations.
- We may not be able to detect money laundering and other illegal or improper activities fully or on a timely basis, which could expose us to additional liability and harm our business or reputation.

- The uncertainties in the global economy, the global financial markets, and, in particular, in China could materially and adversely affect our financial condition and results of operations.
- We may be involved in legal and other disputes from time to time arising out of our operations and may face potential liabilities as a result.
- We are subject to counterparty risks in our derivative transactions.
- We may not continue to enjoy certain favourable PRC governmental policies.
- Our major shareholders have the ability to exercise significant influence over us.
- We have expanded our business in jurisdictions other than the PRC, which has increased the complexity of the risks that we face.

Risks relating to the banking industry in China

- We face intense competition in China's banking industry as well as competition from alternative corporate financing and investment channels.
- Our business and operations are highly regulated, and our business, financial condition, results of operations, and future prospects may be materially and adversely affected by regulatory changes or other governmental policies, including their interpretation and application.
- We are subject to changes in interest rates and other market risks, and our ability to hedge market risk is limited.
- The growth rate of China's banking industry may not be sustainable.
- Future amendments to our accounting standards with respect to loans and investment assets for impairment and interpretative guidance on their application may require us to change our provisioning practice.
- The effectiveness of our credit risk management is affected by the quality and scope of information available in China.
- Certain PRC regulations limit our ability to diversify our investments and, as a result, a decrease in the value of a particular type of investment may have a material adverse effect on our financial condition and results of operations.
- We cannot assure you of the accuracy or comparability of facts, forecasts, and statistics contained in this document with respect to China, its national or regional economies, or its banking industry.
- Investments in commercial banks in China are subject to ownership restrictions that may adversely affect the value of your investments.

Risks related to China

- China's economic, political, and social conditions, as well as governmental policies, could affect our business, financial condition, and results of operations.
- Legal protections available to you under the PRC legal system may be limited.
- You may experience difficulties in effecting service of legal process and enforcing judgements against us and our management.
- You may be subject to PRC taxation.
- Payment of dividends is subject to restrictions under PRC laws.
- We are subject to the PRC government controls on currency conversion and risks relating to fluctuations in exchange rates.
- Any future occurrence of natural disasters or outbreaks of contagious diseases in China may have a material adverse effect on our business operations, financial condition, and results of operations.

Risks relating to the global offering

- An active trading market for our H shares may not develop, and their trading prices may fluctuate significantly.
- We are conducting a concurrent but separate A share offering, and the characteristics of the A share and H share markets are different.
- Future sales or perceived sales of a substantial number of our H shares in public markets or the conversion of our A shares to H shares could have a material adverse effect on the prevailing market price of our H shares and dilute our shareholders' H share holdings.
- You will incur immediate dilution because the offer price of the H shares is higher than the net tangible asset value per share.
- Dividends distributed in the past may not be indicative of our dividend policy in the future.
- We strongly caution you not to place any reliance on any information contained in any media regarding our A share offering and global offering or information released by us in connection with our A share offering.

Appendix 6: Example of feedback form for investor education

Initial Public Offering of [company]

Investor feedback form (for internal use only)

Bank: _____   Sales person: _____

Account _____   Fund manager _____ Date _____

Location _____   Visit ☐   Call ☐

| Type of Investor | Asian fund ○ | Global fund ○ | Hedge fund ○ | N/A ● |

Investor's views on

	Positive	Neutral	Negative	N/A		Positive	Neutral	Negative	N/A
Local equities	○	○	○	●	Sector	○	○	○	●
Regional equities	○	○	○	●	Peers	○	○	○	●

Key comparables

Which company do you consider the most comparable to [company]? _____

Valuation

Valuation parameters *Based on most applicable comparable, please indicate the level of importance*

	High	Neutral	Low
Yield	○	●	○
Dis/Prem to NAV	○	●	○
P/E (please state year)	○	●	○
EV/EBITDA	○	●	○

Company specific views

	Positive	Neutral	Negative	N/A		Positive	Neutral	Negative	N/A
1. Valuation	○	○	○	●	4. Stable income	○	○	○	●
2. Yield	○	○	○	●	5. ROE	○	○	○	●
3. Earnings growth potential	○	○	○	●	6. Management	○	○	○	●

Investor's key concerns / comments

Positive views: _____

Negative views: _____

Investor assessment

	Yes	Probably	No	Undecided
Likely participation in roadshow and/or one-on-one meeting?	○	○	○	●
(please specify) _____				
Likely participation in IPO?	○	○	○	●

Valuation: _____

Potential order size: _____ US$ million

Other comments

Appendix 7: Example of manual order form for bookbuilding

Syndicate member:
Contact name:
Contact telephone number:
Contact fax number:
E-mail address:
Date:

Date	Investor / Fund Name	Investor Type *	Nationality	Order Type ** N/I/D/A/C	Order		Price (US$)	Comments
					US$	Shares		

Notes:

TRANSPARENCY REQUIRED FOR ALL SUBMITTED ORDERS

* Investor type: BK=Bank, CO=Corporate, IC=Insurance Company, IM=Investment Manager, PF=Pension Fund, RT=Retail, HF=Hedge Fund, OT=Other (please specify)

** Order type: N=New, I=Increase, D=Decrease, A=Amendment, C=Cancellation

Price Limit: Limit in US$

Appendix 8: Initial listing requirements for major stock exchanges

Set out below are some of the principal initial listing requirements for the main boards of some of the largest stock exchanges in the US, the UK, continental Europe, the Middle East, and the Asia-Pacific region.

More specifically, I have included those for Nasdaq, the New York Stock Exchange (NYSE), the London Stock Exchange (LSE), Euronext, Deutsche Börse®, the SIX Swiss Exchange, Nasdaq Dubai, the Stock Exchange of Hong Kong (HKEx), the Singapore Exchange (SGX), Bursa Malaysia, the Tokyo Stock Exchange (TSE), and the Australian Securities Exchange (ASX).

I have focused on a) financial requirements relating to revenues, cash-flow, earnings, assets, shareholders' equity, or market capitalization, b) any required free float and minimum spread of shareholders, c) requirements on operating history and management, d) acceptable jurisdictions for foreign issuers, e) accounting standards, f) the type of companies that are suitable (or not) for listing, and g) other requirements and issues. In some cases, I have focused closely on those listing requirements for foreign companies seeking a listing on the relevant exchange.

In all cases, the following is only a summary of what the local rules require in order to secure a listing on each of the relevant stock exchanges. It does not in any way constitute legal, regulatory, or investment advice of any kind whatsoever. Maintaining a listing is also subject to additional, and often extensive, ongoing requirements. Such information is particularly subject to change and amendment. Therefore, any reader considering or working on the listing of a company on one of these stock exchanges should always consult a sponsor broker or bank, legal adviser, the stock exchange itself or the relevant regulator to ensure the completeness and validity of the listing requirements and the listing rules.

Listing in New York on Nasdaq

A summary of some of the principal initial listing requirements for the Nasdaq Global Select Market is given below. In order to list on Nasdaq, a listed company must register its securities with the SEC.

Requirements	Standard 1	Standard 2	Standard 3	Standard 4
Pre-tax earnings (income from continuing operations before income taxes)	Aggregate in prior three fiscal years ≥ US$11 million; and Each of the two most recent fiscal years ≥ US$2.2 million; and Each of the prior three fiscal years ≥ US$0	N/A	N/A	N/A
Cash-flows	N/A	Aggregate in prior three fiscal years ≥ US$27.5 million; and Each of the prior three fiscal years ≥ US$0	N/A	N/A
Minimum market capitalization	N/A	Average ≥ US$550 million over prior 12 months	Average ≥ US$850 million over prior 12 months	US$160 million
Revenue	N/A	Previous fiscal year ≥ US$110 million	Previous fiscal year ≥ US$90 million	N/A
Total assets	N/A	N/A	N/A	US$80 million in the most recently completed fiscal year
Shareholders' equity	N/A	N/A	N/A	US$55 million

Financial requirements

Companies seeking a listing must satisfy the criteria under at least one of the above standards (some of which apply to companies that are already listed elsewhere):

Public float and spread of shareholders

IPO and spin-off companies must have a minimum of 450 round lot holders (of 100 or more shares) or 2,200 shareholders. There must be at least 1,250,000 publicly held shares, with a market value for such publicly held shares of at least US$45 million.

Seasoned companies with currently trading common stock and affiliated companies are subject to additional requirements.

Operating history and management

Companies must comply with all the corporate governance requirements laid out by the exchange. In particular, setting up an audit committee is compulsory.

Acceptable jurisdictions

There are no stated restrictions on jurisdictions, but listing is at the discretion of the exchange.

Accounting standards

The accounts must be audited. Accounts must be prepared in accordance with US GAAP or reconciled to US GAAP, but Nasdaq also accepts financials prepared in accordance with IFRS, if permitted by SEC rules.

Suitability for listing

Suitability for listing is at the discretion of the exchange.

Other requirements and issues

The bid price must be at least US$4 and a company must have at least four registered and active market makers.

Other marketplaces

In addition to the Nasdaq Global Select Market, Nasdaq has two other marketplaces, the Nasdaq Global Market and the Nasdaq Capital Market. It is also possible to conduct direct listings on Nasdaq.

Source: © Copyright 2010, The Nasdaq OMX Group, Inc. Reprinted with permission.

Listing in New York on the NYSE

A summary of some of the principal initial listing requirements for foreign private issuers on the New York Stock Exchange (NYSE) is given below. A foreign private issuer must be a foreign (that is, non-US), non-governmental issuer with 50% or less of its outstanding voting securities held directly or indirectly by US residents. In cases where more than 50% are held by US residents, the majority of the executive officers or directors must not be US citizens or residents, more than 50% of the company's assets must not be located in the US, and its business must not be administered principally in the US. In addition to meeting NYSE requirements, a listing company must register its securities with the SEC before admission to dealings on the NYSE.

Financial requirements

Companies wishing to list on the NYSE must satisfy an earnings test or a valuation/ revenue/cash-flow test:

Earnings test: Pre-tax earnings from continuing operations and after minority interest, amortization, and equity in the earnings or losses of investees, as adjusted, must total at least US$100 million in aggregate for the last three fiscal years with a minimum of US$25 million in each of the most recent two fiscal years.

Valuation/ revenue/cash flow test: A minimum global market capitalization of US$500 million, with revenues of at least US$100 million in the most recent 12-month period, an aggregate cash-flow for the last three years of at least US$100 million, and a minimum cash-flow in each of the preceding two years of at least US$25 million; or

A minimum global market capitalization of US$750 million, with revenues of at least US$75 million in the most recent fiscal year.

In the case of companies listing in connection with an IPO (or an initial firm commitment underwritten public offering), the company's underwriter (or, in the case of a spin-off, the parent company's investment banker or other financial adviser) must provide a written representation that demonstrates the company's ability to meet the global market capitalization requirement based upon the completion of the offering (or distribution).

Public float and spread of shareholders

A minimum of 5,000 shareholders, holders of 100 or more shares, is required, with a minimum of 2,500,000 shares publicly held, representing a public market value of at least

US$100 million, each calculated on a world-wide basis. The calculation for shares publicly held excludes shares held by directors, officers, or their immediate families, and other concentrated holdings of 10% or more.

Operating history and management

See above.

A majority of directors must be independent.

Setting up an audit committee is compulsory.

The exchange has a free and confidential review process, where companies can learn whether or not they are eligible for listing and what additional conditions, if any, might first have to be satisfied.

Acceptable jurisdictions

There are no stated restrictions on jurisdictions, but listing is at the discretion of the exchange.

Accounting standards

The accounts must be audited and prepared in accordance with US GAAP or reconciled to US GAAP. But the NYSE also accepts financials prepared in accordance with IFRS, if permitted by SEC rules.

Suitability for listing

Suitability for listing is at the discretion of the exchange.

Other requirements and issues

New entities with a parent or affiliated company listed on the NYSE are subject to different thresholds and requirements. The shares must have a closing price of at least US$4 per share at the time of listing.

Other market

In addition to the NYSE, issuers can list on NYSE American, a market more particularly dedicated to small- and micro-cap companies. It is also possible to conduct direct listings on the NYSE.

Source: NYSE website.

Listing in London on the LSE

A summary of some of the principal initial listing requirements for the Premium Listing segment of the Main Market of the London Stock Exchange (LSE) is given below. Some of these requirements may be waived at the discretion of the exchange.

Financial requirements

A three-year trading record is normally required by the exchange. There are no financial requirements with respect to revenues or profit; however, at least 75% of the business must be supported by a revenue earning record of three years.

Market capitalization, public float, and spread of shareholders

A minimum of 25% of the shares must be in public hands.

Operating history and management

A clean annual report and a clean working capital statement are required. The issuer must also have had control over the majority of its assets for at least three years.

Acceptable jurisdictions

There are no stated restrictions on jurisdictions but listing is at the discretion of the exchange.

Accounting standards

The accounts must be audited and drawn up under IFRS or an equivalent standard for non-UK issuers.

Suitability for listing

Suitability for listing is at the discretion of the exchange.

Other boards

In addition to the Premium Main Market, there is a Standard Main Market segment, with no revenue criteria, and a High Growth Segment, with a lower free float (10%, with a minimum value of £30 million) requirement and a requirement for 20% CAGR in revenues over a three-year period. Companies must be UK or EEA incorporated. Young and growing companies may choose to list on the Alternative Investment Market (AIM), which has lower initial and ongoing listing requirements, subject to the appointment of a nominated adviser (or Nomad).

Source: London Stock Exchange website.

Listing in Amsterdam, Brussels, Dublin, Lisbon, London, Oslo, or Paris on Euronext

A summary of some of the principal initial listing requirements for Euronext is given below. Companies listing on Euronext benefit from a single, fully integrated trading platform and can choose their primary listing location, which may be either Amsterdam, Brussels, Dublin, Lisbon, London, Oslo, or Paris. Euronext is an EU-regulated market and, as such, companies listed on it are subject to a number of rules decreed by the EU, as well as certain non-harmonised rules. In particular, listing on Euronext requires a prospectus that is vetted by the relevant EU home regulator (e.g., the Autorité des Marchés Financiers or AMF for a listing in Paris or the FCA for a listing in London).

Financial requirements

A trading record of not less than three financial years (two years for SMEs) is required, although an exemption is available for investment funds. There are no financial requirements with respect to revenues or profit.

Public float and spread of shareholders

A minimum distribution of 25% of a company's share capital of €5 million is required (€1 million for a listing in Dublin).

Operating history and management

The accounts for the last three years (subject to exemption) must be audited.

Acceptable jurisdictions

There are no stated restrictions on jurisdictions, but listing is at the discretion of the exchange.

Accounting standards

The accounts for listing on Euronext must be audited and drawn up either under IFRS or local GAAP for certain segments of the market.

Suitability for listing

Suitability for listing is at the discretion of the exchange.

Other requirements and issues

Euronext is segmented into four compartments according to market capitalization, each with lower (or even no) free float requirements. In addition to Euronext itself, there is Euronext Growth, Euronext Access+, and Euronext Access.

Source: Euronext website.

Listing in Frankfurt on Deutsche Börse®

A summary of some of the principal initial listing requirements for the Prime Standard segment of the Frankfurter Wertpapierbörse (FWB®) EU Regulated Market is given below. These requirements follow the EU transparency standards. Some of these requirements may be waived at the discretion of the exchange.

Financial requirements

Generally, a trading record of not less than three financial years is required.

There are no stated financial requirements for revenues or profit.

Market capitalization, public float, and spread of shareholders

A market capitalization of at least €1.25 million is required.

A minimum free float of 25% is also required, although some exemptions are possible.

The exchange requires a minimum issuing volume of at least 10,000 shares.

Operating history and management

Normally, a three-year reporting history is a pre-requisite to listing.

Acceptable jurisdictions

There are no stated restrictions on jurisdictions, and the listing requirements are irrespective of the issuer's country or domicile.

Accounting standards

International Financing Reporting Standards (IFRS).

Suitability for listing

Suitability for listing is at the discretion of the exchange.

Other requirements and issues

Admission to the Prime Standard is a prerequisite for inclusion in the DAX®, MDAX®, TecDAX®, and SDAX® indexes.

Other segments and boards

A company may also list on the General Standard and on the Open Market for SME issuers.

The Neuer Markt, Germany's market for technology shares, closed in 2003. In addition, listings on the exchange's First and Second Quotation Boards were terminated in 2012.

Source: Various, including Deutsche Börse® website (www.deutsche-boerse.com), August 2010.

Note: Reprinted with permission of Deutsche Börse AG.

Listing in Zurich on the SIX

A summary of some of the principal initial listing requirements under the Main Standard segment of the SIX Swiss Exchange (SIX) is given below. Some of these requirements may be waived at the discretion of the exchange.

Financial requirements

A trading record of not less than three financial years is normally required. There are no financial requirements with respect to revenues or profit.

Market capitalization, public float, and spread of shareholders

A market capitalization of at least CHF25 million is required. The free float must represent at least 25%.

Operating history and management

A track record of three years is normally required.

Acceptable jurisdictions

There are no stated restrictions on jurisdictions, but listing is at the discretion of the exchange.

Accounting standards

IFRS or US GAAP. Other internationally recognized accounting standards may also be accepted.

Suitability for listing

Suitability for listing is at the discretion of the exchange.

Other requirements and issues

There are different listing criteria for domestic companies, investment companies, property companies, and collective investment schemes, as well as for DRs.

The listing application may be made in French, German, Italian, or English.

Source: SIX Swiss Exchange website.

Listing in Dubai on Nasdaq Dubai

A summary of some of the principal initial listing requirements for Nasdaq Dubai (formerly known as the DIFX) is given below. These criteria are set out by the Dubai Financial Services Authority (DFSA), the exchange's regulator.

Financial requirements

A trading record of not less than three financial years is required.

There are no stated financial criteria for revenue or profit.

Market capitalization, public float, and spread of shareholders

The issuer must have an expected market capitalization of at least US$10 million.

A minimum free float of at least 25% is also normally required. Generally, a minimum of 250 shareholders, each holding securities with a value of at least US$2,000, are required, although Nasdaq Dubai can permit a lower number at its discretion.

Operating history and management

The accounts must be audited. Management must have appropriate experience and business expertise for a listed company. Adequate systems must be in place to eliminate or manage material conflicts of interest. Proper systems must also be in place to enable the business to be run independently of the controlling shareholders.

Acceptable jurisdictions

There are no stated restrictions on jurisdictions and foreign ownership.

Accounting standards

IFRS and audited in accordance with the IAASB.

Suitability for listing

The DFSA has broad powers to determine suitability for listing and the ability to waive or modify some of the listing requirements. Waivers and modifications are most typically seen where there has been a restructuring or where the issuer is less than three years old.

Other requirements and issues

Shares must be freely transferable, fully paid, and free from any liens or restrictions on transfer. The shares must be duly authorised and validly issued under the laws of the jurisdiction where the issuer is incorporated. One or more market makers must be appointed.

In 2014, a REIT successfully listed in Dubai, the emirate's first IPO since the financial crisis of 2009.

Source: Nasdaq Dubai website and financial media.

Listing in Hong Kong on HKEx

A summary of some of the principal initial listing requirements for the Main Board of the Stock Exchange of Hong Kong is given below. Some of these requirements may on occasion be waived at the discretion of the exchange.

Financial requirements

A trading record of not less than three financial years.

One of three financial criteria must be met:

- a profit test: profit attributable to shareholders of at least HK$50 million in the last three financial years (at least HK$20 million for the last financial year and aggregate profits of at least HK$30 million in the two preceding years) and a market capitalization of at least HK$500 million at the time of listing (as of the first quarter of 2021, a substantial increase in the required minimum profit was under consideration); or
- a market capitalization and revenue test: a market capitalization of at least HK$4 billion at the time of listing and audited revenue of at least HK$500 million in the most recent financial year; or
- a market capitalization, revenue, and cash-flow test: a market capitalization of at least HK$2 billion at the time of listing, audited revenue of at least HK$500 million at the time of listing, and an aggregate, positive cash-flow from operating activities of at least HK$100 million for the three preceding financial years.

Market capitalization, public float, and spread of shareholders

At least 25% of the issuer's total share capital must at all times be held by the public (a lower percentage of between 15% and 25% may be acceptable for issuers with an expected market capitalization of over HK$10 billion).

A minimum spread of 300 shareholders under the profit and market capitalization, revenue and cash-flow tests, and under the market capitalization and revenue test (with not more than 50% of the securities in public hands owned by the three largest public shareholders).

Operating history and management

Management continuity for at least the three preceding financial years and ownership continuity and control for at least the most recent year are required.

A shorter trading record period may be accepted under the market capitalization and revenue test if the directors and management have at least three years of relevant experience in the same industry and if the issuer exhibits management continuity for the most recent audited financial year (this is particularly relevant for mineral and natural resources companies).

There are different listing requirements for new economy and biotechnology companies, which may also list with weighted voting rights (i.e., different classes of shares, in certain circumstances)

Acceptable jurisdictions

Historically, the exchange only accepted issuers incorporated in Hong Kong, mainland China, Bermuda, and the Cayman Islands. It changed its rules to accept for listing companies incorporated in a number of other jurisdictions, including Alberta (Canada), Australia, Austria, Brazil, British Columbia (Canada), the British Virgin Islands, Cyprus, England and Wales, France, Germany, Guernsey, India, Ireland, the Isle of Man, Israel, Italy, Japan, Jersey, Labuan (Malaysia), Luxembourg, the Netherlands, Ontario (Canada), the Republic of Korea, Russia, Singapore, and the US states of California, Delaware, and Nevada. Candidates must satisfy the criteria laid out in the listing rules and applications are assessed on a case-by-case basis. As of the first quarter of 2021, a few issuers had listed HDRs in Hong. REITs and business trusts can also be listed on HKEx, as can yuan-denominated IPOs.

Accounting standards

Hong Kong Financial Reporting Standards or IFRS are accepted, as are China Accounting Standards for Business Enterprises (CASBE). US GAAP and other GAAPs are acceptable under certain circumstances.

Suitability for listing

Suitability for listing is at the discretion of the exchange. An issuer whose assets are solely or substantially composed of cash or short-dated securities is not normally considered as suitable for listing, except for securities brokerage businesses.

Other requirements and issues

Automatic claw-back triggers exist for the re-allocation of stock from placement to public offer tranches in the event of over-subscription of the retail offering, normally as follows (subject to waivers that may be granted for very large transactions):

Over-subscription of the public offer tranche (times)	Initial amount	15x to < 50x	50x to < 100x	>100x
% allocated to the public offer	10%	30%	40%	50%

Producing a prospectus in both English and Chinese is required.

Other board

There is a second board called GEM in Hong Kong on which companies can also list with lower listing requirements.

Source: HKEx website.

Listing in Singapore on the SGX

A summary of some of the principal initial listing requirements for the Main Board of the Singapore Exchange (SGX) is given below. Some of these requirements may be waived at the discretion of the exchange.

Financial requirements

One of three financial criteria must be met:

- a minimum consolidated pre-tax profit of at least S$30 million for the latest financial year and an operating track record of at least three years; or
- profitability (based on consolidated pre-tax profit) in the latest financial year, an operating track record of at least three years and a market capitalization of not less than S$150 million based on the issue price; or
- operating revenue (whether actual or pro forma) in the latest financial year and a market capitalization of not less than S$300 million based on the issue price.

Market capitalization, public float, and spread of shareholders

For a market capitalization of less than S$300 million, at least 25% of the enlarged share capital must be in the hands of at least 500 shareholders.

For a market capitalization of between S$300 million and S$400 million, at least 20% of the enlarged share capital must be in public hands.

For a market capitalization of between S$400 million and S$1 billion, at least 15% of the enlarged share capital must be in public hands.

For a market capitalization of more than S$1 billion, at least 12% of the enlarged share capital must be in public hands.

In all cases, a minimum spread of 500 shareholders is required.

For a secondary listing, an issuer must have at least 500 shareholders world-wide. Where the SGX and the primary home exchange do not have an established framework and arrangement to facilitate the movement of shares between the jurisdictions, the issuer should have at least 500 shareholders in Singapore or 1,000 shareholders world-wide.

Operating history and management

There is no requirement for companies to demonstrate a particular length of trading history or time in operation.

Acceptable jurisdictions

There are no stated restrictions for listing in Singapore. A variety of companies from around the world are listed on the Main Board of the Exchange.

Accounting standards

Singapore Financial Reporting Standards (International), IFRS, and US GAAP are accepted.

Suitability for listing

The SGX considers whether the application satisfies the listing requirements and will decide whether a company is suitable for listing. Listing will not be permitted until all conditions set out on the eligible-to-list letter have been satisfied. In addition to shares, DRs, REITs, and business trusts can also be listed in Singapore.

Other requirements and issues

Moratorium:

Controlling shareholders and their associates and executive directors with an interest in 5% or more of the issued share capital at the time of listing (known as Promoters) are subjected to a share lock-up after listing. Main Board issuers who satisfy the profitability tests will have the entire shareholdings of the Promoters locked-up for a period of six months after listing. Main Board issuers who satisfy the market capitalization test will have the entire shareholdings of the Promoters locked-up for a period of six months, and at least 50% of the shareholdings will be locked-up for the next six months. For investors with 5% or more of the issuer's post-invitation issued share capital and which have paid for their holdings less than 12 months prior to listing, a prescribed cash formula will be applied to determine the proportion of shareholdings to be subjected to a six-month moratorium.

Directors:

Listing in Singapore requires the appointment of at least two non-executive independent directors. In addition, a foreign issuer must have at least two independent directors resident in Singapore.

Other board:

In addition to the SGX Main Board, which is for established companies with an earnings track record, SGX Catalist is a sponsor-supervised listing platform catering for fast-growing companies seeking to expand their business and presence into Asia and beyond. SGX Catalist has different listing requirements with, in particular, no quantitative criteria and lower requirements for shareholding spread and distribution. There is also a direct listing framework for Chinese companies.

Source: SGX website.

Note: Permission was sought and granted by Singapore Exchange or its affiliates for the reproduction of this material. Any error or omission in the reproduction of this material is not to be attributed to Singapore Exchange or its affiliates. Further, interpretation of this material is not to be attributed to Singapore Exchange or its affiliates.

Listing in Kuala Lumpur on Bursa Malaysia

A summary of some of the principal initial listing requirements for the Main Market of Bursa Malaysia is given below.

Financial requirements

One of two main financial criteria must be met:

- an uninterrupted profit of three to five financial years, with an aggregate profit after tax of at least RM20 million and a profit after tax for the most recent financial year of at least RM6 million; or
- a total market capitalization of at least RM500 million, based on the issue price.

In addition, infrastructure project corporations can list in Malaysia if the project cost totals not less than RM500 million, with a concession or licence from a government or state agency of at least 15 years. Positive cash flow from operating activities is required from listing applicants and there must not have been accumulated losses.

Public float and spread of shareholders

Twenty-five per cent of the shares sought for listing must be owned by at least 1,000 public shareholders, holding not less than 100 shares each. In addition, companies that derive more than 50% of their after-tax profit from operations based in Malaysia must allocate 50% of the free float (i.e., 12.5% of the total number of shares sought for listing) to *Bumiputera* (ethnic Malay) investors under a specific IPO tranche at the behest of the Ministry of Trade and Industry (MITI). The proportion of shares to be allocated to the general public varies between at least 2% and 5% of the enlarged issued and paid up share capital, depending on the amount of the latter.

Operating history and track record

There is a requirement for companies to have been in the same core business over the profit track record period. Alternatively, if listing under the market capitalization test, a company must have been incorporated and have generated operating revenue for at least one financial year prior to the application to listing (for primary listings only). Management continuity for at least three financial years is required.

Acceptable jurisdictions

There are no stated restrictions on jurisdictions, although a foreign company seeking to list on Bursa Malaysia must be incorporated in a jurisdiction with corporation laws and other laws and regulations that offer standards at least equivalent to those in Malaysia.

Accounting standards

Standards applied in Malaysia or international standards in auditing.

Suitability for listing

Prospectuses are approved by the Securities Commission while the admission of securities is approved by Bursa Malaysia.

Other board

In addition to the Main Market, the ACE Market of Bursa Malaysia (previously known as MESDAQ) is an alternative, sponsor-driven market offering early access to equity funding for emerging companies.

Source: Bursa Malaysia website.

Listing in Tokyo on the TSE

A summary of some of the principal initial listing requirements for foreign companies on the First Section of the Tokyo Stock Exchange (TSE) is given below. Some of these requirements may on occasion be waived at the discretion of the exchange.

Financial requirements

A trading record of not less than three financial years.

One of two financial criteria must be met:
- a profit test with a minimum amount of ¥2.5 billion in aggregate over the last two years; or
- a market capitalization and revenue test with a total market capitalization of at least ¥100 billion and a minimum turnover of ¥10 billion for the most recent year.

Market capitalization, public float, and spread of shareholders

A market capitalization of at least ¥25 billion is required.

At least 20,000 tradable shares are required (defined as excluding shares held by officers, treasury shares and shares owned by persons who individually own more than 10% of listed shares), with a market capitalization for such tradable shares of at least ¥10 billion. The ratio of tradable shares to listed shares must be at least 35%.

A minimum spread of 800 shareholders is required for a primary listing in Tokyo.

Operating history and management

A company must have continuously carried out its business for at least three years. The accounts for the last financial year must also be unqualified by auditors.

Acceptable jurisdictions

There are no stated restrictions on jurisdictions but listing is at the discretion of the exchange.

Accounting standards

Japanese GAAP or other accounting standards deemed acceptable by Japan's Financial Services Agency (FSA), as determined on a case-by-case basis. However, uncommon or more "exotic" accounting standards are unlikely to be readily accepted and may lead to considerable scrutiny and analysis on the part of the exchange.

Suitability for listing

Suitability for listing is at the discretion of the exchange.

Other board and market

There is a Second Section on the TSE on which companies can also list with somewhat lower listing requirements. In addition, there is a separate market dedicated to high growth and emerging stocks called Mothers. Transfers from the Mothers board or Second Section to the First Section are possible.

Source: Tokyo Stock Exchange website.

Listing in Sydney on the ASX

A summary of some of the principal initial listing requirements for the Australian Securities Exchange (ASX) is given below. Some of these requirements may be waived at the discretion of the exchange.

Financial requirements

Usually, a trading record of not less than three financial years. However, a shorter reporting period may, on occasion, be agreed to by the exchange.

One of three financial criteria must be met:

- a profit test over the last three years: a minimum of A$1 million in aggravated profit from continuing obligations over the past three years and exceeding A$500,000 in net profit over the last 12 months; or
- a net tangible asset test: a minimum of A$4 million in net tangible assets upon listing; or
- a market capitalization test: a market capitalization of a minimum of A$15 million upon listing.

Public float and spread of shareholders

A minimum of 300 investors, each with securities valued at A$2,000 or more and a free float of 20%.

Operating history and management

A three-year operating history is required for a company applying under the profit test, but not necessarily for companies applying under the asset test. Listing Rule 1.3.5 states that a company applying under the asset test must provide accounts for the last three full financial years (or for a shorter period, if the ASX agrees). In practice, a number of companies (mainly mining explorers) list without a three-year operating history.

Acceptable jurisdictions

There are no stated restrictions on jurisdictions, but listing is at the discretion of the exchange.

Accounting standards

Australian Accounting Standards, IFRS, Canadian GAAP, Hong Kong Financial Reporting Standards, New Zealand GAAP, Singapore Financial Reporting Standards, South African GAAP, UK GAAP, and US GAAP are all accepted by the ASX. Application may be made to the exchange for companies reporting under other accounting standards.

Suitability for listing

Suitability for listing is at the discretion of the exchange.

Other requirements and issues

Many of the ASX's ongoing listing rules do not usually apply to foreign companies listing pursuant to an ASX Foreign Exempt listing.

Mining and exploration companies are subject to additional reporting requirements.

In Australia, the Australian Securities and Investments Commission (ASIC) does not pre-vet, review, or approve prospectuses before they are lodged for an exposure period of normally seven days.

Glossary

A share: in mainland China, those shares listed and traded on the Shanghai or Shenzhen stock exchanges. A shares are quoted in renminbi.

accelerated bookbuilding (ABB): a form of follow-on equity transaction where a book of demand is gathered from investors over a short space of time. It may also be conducted pursuant to a hard underwriting.

accounting standards: the generally agreed accounting principles (GAAP), in conformity with which the accounts of a company are drawn up. Typically, listing requirements stipulate the accounting standard(s) that is/are accepted by the relevant regulator or stock exchange for the listing of a company. See also *generally agreed accounting principles.*

accredited investor: a type of investor in the US to which sales of securities may be made pursuant to an exemption from registration requirements. Accredited investors represent a wider universe of investors than the qualified institutional buyers (QIBs), which can be accessed through a Rule 144A private placement. See also *qualified institutional buyer.*

acrylic: see *deal toy.*

advertising name: the name used by an investment bank on the cover of a prospectus. The advertising name is generally shorter than the legal name.

aftermarket: the market once a newly listed company has started to trade.

aggressive growth investor: a type of institutional investment style in which investors focus on stocks that exhibit fast and increasing growth.

agreed-upon procedures letter: a lower standard of auditor comfort letter than an SAS 72 comfort letter. For example, an agreed-upon procedures letter may be delivered when 135 days or more have elapsed since the latest reviewed or audited accounts. See also *SAS 72 comfort letter* and *SAS 100 review.*

agreement among managers: an agreement between the underwriters of a particular tranche of a global offering, setting out their respective roles and responsibilities.

allocation: the amount of stock that a retail or institutional investor receives in an IPO.

alpha: a risk-adjusted measure of the active return (through skill) on an investment, equivalent to the return in excess of the compensation for the risk borne. Hedge funds in particular are said to focus on alpha.

alternative investment fund: a term often used to designate a hedge fund. See also *hedge fund*.

alternative investment market (AIM): the second board of the London Stock Exchange, with lower listing requirements than for a main board listing.

American depositary receipt (ADR): a security representing the economic interest in underlying shares, usually denominated in US dollars and normally traded in the US. ADRs can be sponsored or unsponsored. They may also be listed or unlisted.

American depositary share (ADS): an instrument that evidences American depositary receipts (ADRs). ADSs are traded by investors, whereas ADRs remain in the clearing system.

American Institute of Certified Public Accountants (AICPA): the national professional association for certified public accounts (CPAs) in the US. See also *certified public accountant (CPA) qualification*.

analyst: a junior, entry-level rank in an investment bank equivalent to business analyst or graduate trainee.

anchor investor: see *cornerstone investor* and *pre-IPO investment*.

anchor market: when a company is listed on more than one stock exchange, the exchange that is regarded as the "natural" listing location for the business and on which most of the trading volume takes place. See also *dual listing* and *multiple listings*.

appearance: how the names of the lead banks in a syndicate appear on the cover of a prospectus or in a tombstone advertisement. The top left position usually refers to the most senior bank in the syndicate, which often underwrites more stock than the others, or is paid a higher amount of fees (or both).

application form: a type of form used by retail investors to apply for shares in an IPO. For example, in Hong Kong, there are white applications forms for applicants who want shares to be issued in their own name through the delivery of physical shares; yellow application forms for applicants who want shares to be issued to them in the name of a wholly owned nominee subsidiary of Hong Kong Securities Clearing

Company Limited; and pink application forms for employee offerings. Applicants in Hong Kong may also apply for shares electronically through e-IPO application forms.

application to listing: communication to a stock exchange, usually by way of a prospectus and other documents, pursuant to which an issuer makes an application to list on that exchange. The application to listing is often primarily drafted by legal advisers with the help of investment banks.

ASIC exposure period: in Australia, a period of one to two weeks during which the market and the local regulator, the Australian Securities and Investments Commission (ASIC), can consider information in the disclosure document (or prospectus) before the issuer can accept applications for the shares on offer. The ASIC exposure period does not apply to offers of shares by companies that are already quoted. See also *Australian Securities and Investments Commission (ASIC)*.

asset manager: a generic term for an institutional investor. Through their portfolio managers (PMs), asset managers often manage collective investment schemes and invest across a spectrum of assets (equities or fixed income securities or commodities or real estate). When asset managers have a mandate to make investment decisions on behalf of their clients, they manage funds on a discretionary basis.

associate: a junior rank within an investment bank. Associates usually have between two and four years of work experience.

associate director: a mid-level rank within an investment bank, equivalent in some firms to the rank of vice-president. Associate directors usually have between four and six years of work experience. See also *vice-president*.

audit committee: a committee set up by the board of directors of a company tasked with oversight of financial reporting and disclosure. It is generally solely or mostly composed of independent, non-executive directors.

audited accounts: the accounts of a company, as audited and certified by auditors or reporting accountants. In some cases, the audited accounts can be qualified when the auditors have identified controversial (and disclosable) issues that may need to be remedied.

auditors: also called reporting accountants in the UK. A firm of accountants appointed by a company to audit and certify its accounts. For listed companies, the auditors are often one of the "big four". Also see *big four* and *audited accounts*.

auditors' report: a report written by a firm of accountants accompanying the accounts and certifying that they form a true and fair view of the affairs of the company. See also *auditor* and *audited accounts*.

Australian Securities and Investments Commission (ASIC): the Australian regulator for the securities industry.

authorized representative: a person (or a group of persons) authorized to handle communications with a stock exchange on behalf of a listed company.

*autocontrôle***:** shares in a company owned and controlled by that company or its subsidiaries, generally pursuant to a share buy-back programme. In most markets, *autocontrôle* (also called treasury stock) is limited to 10% of outstanding shares and such shares cannot be voted in a general meeting of the company. See also *share buy-back programme* and *Treasury stock*.

automated teller machines (ATMs): a popular method of application for retail investors for IPOs and other equity capital markets transactions with a public offering in Singapore.

Autorité des Marchés Financiers (AMF): an independent public body in France, established to safeguard investments in financial instruments and other savings and investment vehicles, and to ensure that investors receive material information and maintain orderly financial markets. The AMF, which was established in 2003, was formed from the merger of the Commission des Opérations de Bourse (COB), the Conseil des Marchés financiers (CMF), and the Conseil de Discipline de la Gestion Financière (CDGF).

average daily trading volume (ADTV): the average trading volume per day in the shares of a company, as measured over a period of time (typically 20, 30, or 60 days).

B shares: in mainland China, those shares listed on the Shanghai and Shenzhen stock exchanges but traded in foreign currencies. The B shares listed and traded in Shanghai are quoted in US dollars, while the B shares listed and traded in Shenzhen are quoted in Hong Kong dollars. B shares are now rarely issued.

back office: the operations department of an investment bank, in charge of the settlement of securities and of corporate actions.

backdoor listing: a mechanism through which a company obtains a listing by acquiring a listed shell company. Companies that obtain a listing through this method already have the required minimum spread of shareholders.

balloting: a mechanism through which shares are allocated to retail investors by a share registrar after the closing of the public offer in an IPO.

beauty parade: a formal process through which investment banks or other advisers are invited to pitch to act in a senior role in an IPO. See also *oral presentation* and *request for proposal (RFP)*.

best efforts underwriting: see *soft underwriting*.

big four: the four largest global firms of accountants: Deloitte, EY (formerly known as Ernst & Young), KPMG, and PwC.

bill and deliver: a mechanism through which shares are paid and delivered to investors by a senior underwriter on behalf of others. A senior bank in a syndicate (typically a bookrunner) will bill and deliver on behalf of more junior banks, assuming the latter have generated allocable investor demand.

bill voucher: a retail incentive typically used in the privatizations of utility (electricity, gas, or water) companies whereby retail investors receive a voucher to offset against their utility bills for owning shares in the company over a period of time. See also *retail incentives*.

blackout period: the period of time during which the members of a syndicate of underwriters can no longer publish equity research on an issuer, following the publication of pre-deal research. A blackout period typically lasts for 40 days after listing or the start of trading. The term "quiet period" is also sometimes used.

block trade: the rapid sale of a block of, usually, existing shares in a company. Block trades are often conducted at a fixed price over a few hours and may also be hard underwritten. See also *hard underwriting*.

blood letter: a letter issued by an investment bank confirming certain information included in an offering circular and for which it takes responsibility. Such information is typically very limited in scope and usually relates to the investment bank itself, such as how its name appears, or whether it may be conducting stabilization.

Blue Sky laws: State laws in the US, as opposed to federal securities laws.

BM&FBOVESPA: a stock exchange based in São Paulo in Brazil created by the merger in 2008 of the São Paulo Stock Exchange (BOVESPA) and the Brazilian Mercantile and Futures Exchange (BM&F). The BM&FBOVESPA is the fourth largest stock exchange by market capitalization in the Americas after the New York Stock Exchange and Nasdaq in the US and the Toronto Stock Exchange in Canada.[104]

board committees: committees set up by the board of directors of a company and usually mainly or solely composed of independent, non-executive directors. These normally take the form of an audit committee, which is usually compulsory, a remuneration committee, and a nomination committee.

board lot: the minimum number of shares in which a company is traded. For example, a company may be traded in lots of 1,000 shares. Trading shares in odd lots rather than multiples of the board lot usually attracts additional costs.

bonus share: a retail incentive often used in privatizations whereby retail investors receive additional shares for keeping their allocated holdings over a period of time. A typical ratio is one free share for ten held, after a period of 18 months. See also *retail incentives*.

book value: see *net asset value*.

Bookbuilder: an online, password-protected, electronic bookbuilding platform created by Dealogic, now called DealManager and widely used by equity capital markets teams to manage books of demand in IPOs and other equity capital markets transactions.

bookbuilding: the process through which shares are marketed to, and orders taken from, institutional investors in an equity capital markets transaction. In an IPO, bookbuilding is usually conducted simultaneously with the investor roadshow and follows pre-deal investor education (or pre-marketing) and the determination of a price range.

bookrunner: probably the most important level among underwriting banks in a syndicate. A bookrunner manages the book of demand and, importantly, determines allocations made to institutional investors. There can be more than one bookrunner in an IPO and a bank can also be appointed in other roles simultaneously with that of bookrunner, most commonly as a sponsor, global coordinator, and/or lead manager. In the US and some other markets, a distinction is sometimes made between "active" bookrunners (who actively run and participate in the process) and "passive" bookrunners (who, as the name suggests, principally have an underwriting role only).

bottom-up demand estimate: an estimate of the institutional investor demand for an IPO, in currency or in shares. A bottom-up demand estimate is made by guessing and adding up the amount of potential allocable demand for a number of key target investors in the jurisdictions where the IPO will be marketed.

bought deal: refers to an equity capital markets transaction that is the subject of a hard underwriting by one or more investment banks. IPOs are typically not structured as bought deals, although some follow-on transactions (especially block trades) sometimes are. See also *hard underwriting*.

bring-down comfort letters: subsequent comfort letters delivered by accountants and confirming the terms of earlier comfort letters.

bring-down due diligence: a short due-diligence session with management taking place at pricing and closing of an IPO. Its purpose is to confirm the results of earlier due diligence investigations and to identify any new material developments relating to the company. Bring-down due diligence may also take place upon exercise of the over-allotment option (if any).

broker firm offer: a type of retail offering frequently used in Australia, open to Australian as well as, usually, New Zealand, resident retail investors who have received firm allocations from their broker.

brokerage fee: a fee paid to a bank by an institutional or retail investor to buy shares issued or sold in an IPO or other equity capital markets transaction. Some IPOs and equity capital markets transactions do not carry any brokerage fee.

bulge-bracket investment banks: the name given to those large investment banks with global reach that typically dominate the league tables.

business analyst: one of the titles for entry-level investment banking staff. Equivalent to analyst or graduate trainee. See also *analyst* and *graduate trainee*.

business due diligence: the due diligence conducted by investment banks and legal advisers, usually by way of interviews with management, into the affairs of a company preparing for listing. Business due diligence focuses on the business of the company and serves to accurately describe it in the offering circular. Business due diligence also includes site visits and third party interviews and is supplemented by documentary and financial due diligence. See also *documentary due diligence* and *financial due diligence*.

business trust: a type of transaction whereby assets can be monetized through an IPO. A business trusts broadly follows the same format as real estate investment trust (REIT), but is not limited to the real estate sector. Typically, it involve investments in infrastructure assets, such as toll roads, ships, aircraft, telecoms assets, airports, tank farms (dedicated sites with large tanks for the bulk storage of oil), bridges, turnpikes, or wind farms in lieu of (or in addition to) property. This can also extend to "social" infrastructure, such as retirement homes, student accommodation, and even prisons. As with REITs, investors in a business trust own units in a vehicle that is publicly listed and traded on a stock exchange. A trustee-manager holds, manages, and operates the assets in which the trust invests for the benefit of all unit holders. A key difference is that business trusts enable the distribution (typically of 90% and up to 100%) of free cash-flow, rather than limiting distributions to accounting profits. In addition, business trusts have greater flexibility to acquire and own assets as compared with other trusts. Business trusts have mainly been issued in Singapore and, to a lesser extent, in Hong Kong.

buy-side research: research on securities conducted in-house by institutional investors or hedge funds. Often, buy-side research is either unpublished or not as widely distributed as sell-side research.

CAC 40 index: the most commonly used benchmark index for the French equity market, comprising the 40 largest companies listed on the Main Board of Euronext in Paris. The CAC 40 is a free-float-adjusted, market capitalization–weighted index.

cap (on fees): a mechanism through which fees that can be earned by a group of investment banks are capped at a certain level. For example, the selling concession that may be earned by the bookrunners of an IPO may be capped at 80% so as to incentivize more junior banks in the syndicate.

capital asset pricing model (CAPM): a model used to determine in theory the rate of return for an asset in a diversified portfolio, taking into account the level of risk inherent in such an asset (also called systemic or market risk). The CAPM takes into account the expected return of the market, as well as the expected return of a theoretical risk-free asset, generally a government bond.

capital structure: the proportion between equity and debt capital (minus cash and cash-equivalent securities) on the balance sheet of a company. The capital structure is sometimes adjusted prior to listing by increasing gearing to enable the payment of a special dividend to the issuer's pre-listing shareholders.

Catalist: the second board of the Singapore Exchange.

Central Provident Fund (CPF): a social security savings plan for citizens' old age in Singapore. Part of CPF funds can be used to invest in IPOs and other equity capital markets transactions through automated teller machines. See also *automated teller machines (ATMs)*.

certified public accountant (CPA) qualification: the statutory title of qualified accountants in the US and other countries, granted after examination. A US CPA is equivalent to a Chartered Accountant in the UK. Certain stock exchanges require that at least some directors or board committee members hold a CPA or equivalent qualification. See also *American Institute of Certified Public Accountants (AICPA)*.

chief executive officer (CEO): often the most senior executive position in a company, sometimes combined with the position of chairman. The CEO often takes an active role in the marketing of an IPO during the roadshow.

chief financial officer (CFO): the most senior financial executive position in a company. The CFO often takes an active role in the marketing of an IPO during the roadshow and is sometimes also involved in corporate finance aspects of the execution process.

Chinese wall: a barrier established between the advisory and financing, securities, and other departments of an investment bank. Chinese walls are set up to prevent and resolve conflicts of interest between the various activities carried out by an investment bank and are enforced by compliance departments.

circling (of accounts): the process through which the financial information included in an offering circular is sourced, verified and checked (or "ticked" or "ticked and tied") by a firm of auditors. A circled offering circular is appended to an SAS 72 comfort letter. See also *SAS 72 comfort letter*.

classes (of shares): in some countries, a company may have different classes of shares, for example Class A shares and Class B shares, each with different characteristics, values, privileges and voting rights.

claw-back: the process through which shares initially allocated to the placement (or institutional) tranche of an IPO are re-allocated to the retail (or public offer) tranche. Such claw-back can either be at the discretion of the bookrunners or be made automatically depending on the rules laid out by the stock exchange. Automatic claw-back triggers are a feature of IPOs in Hong Kong.

claw-forward: the process through which shares initially allocated to the retail (or public offer) tranche of an IPO are re-allocated to the placement (or institutional) tranche. Such claw-forward is generally made at the discretion of the bookrunners.

Clearstream: the custody and settlement division of Deutsche Börse®, based in Luxembourg. Previously known as Cedel.

closing: the final step in the IPO process, when shares are delivered to investors versus payment. Closing is usually subject to a number of conditions precedent, including the delivery of a number of documents.

club deal: an equity capital markets transaction that is marketed, and allocated, to only a small number of select institutions.

co-lead manager: a junior role in an IPO, usually confined to the writing of pre-deal research (outside the US, Canada, and Japan) and to investor education. Nowadays, co-lead managers are usually paid by way of fixed, pre-agreed economics.

co-manager: A junior role in an IPO, which generally does not require the writing of pre-deal research (outside the US, Canada, and Japan). In the US, co-manager is also a generic term used to describe all junior underwriters in an IPO below the rank of lead manager.

comfort letters: the letters delivered by a firm of auditors on the offering circular(s) and prospectus for an IPO to the issuer and to the underwriters providing comfort on the financial information included in such listing documents. International comfort letters usually take the form of an SAS 72 comfort letter, but a weaker standard of comfort (such as an agreed-upon procedures letter) may sometimes be delivered instead. Various domestic standards also exist. Bring-down comfort letters may also be delivered at later stages in the transaction. See also *SAS 72 comfort letter* and *agreed-upon procedures letter*.

Comisión Nacional del Mercado de Valores (CNMV): the Spanish regulator for the securities industry, equivalent to the Securities and Exchange Commission (SEC) in the US.

Committee on Uniform Security Identification Procedures (CUSIP): an alphanumerical code used to identify issuers and trades in securities. The first six characters of a CUSIP identify the issuer.

company benchmarking: the process through which an issuer is positioned against comparable listed companies to assess its performance, business and, ultimately, valuation. See also *comparable company*.

Company Share Option Plan (CSOP): A type of employee share ownership programme in the UK.

comparable company: a listed company against which an issuer is benchmarked in an IPO to assess its performance, business and, ultimately, valuation. See also *company benchmarking*.

compliance: a department in an investment bank tasked with ensuring that internal and external laws and regulations are followed and also with avoiding and resolving conflicts of interest that may occur between its divisions.

compliance adviser: an investment bank or broker that is appointed to advise a company on certain listing matters and disclosure after an IPO. In Hong Kong, compliance advisers must be licensed corporate finance advisory firms that are also eligible to work as IPO sponsors.

compound annual growth rate (CAGR): the annualized growth for a company, calculated over a number of years on a compounded basis. A CAGR is often calculated for revenue, cash-flow or earnings to express the performance of key profit and loss line items over a period of time.

concurrent retail offering: a retail offering that takes place concurrently with an institutional placement, generally during the last few days of bookbuilding. A concurrent retail offering is conducted at a maximum price, effectively equivalent to the top end of the institutional bookbuilding range, and subject to refund in the event that the offer price for retail investors is determined to be below the top end of the range.

conditions precedent: conditions required for the closing or underwriting of an IPO. Generally, these include, among other things, pricing, the signing of agreements, and the delivery of various documents such as legal opinions and comfort letters. See also *closing* and *underwriting*.

confidentiality agreement: in an IPO, an agreement signed by an investor pursuant to which it agrees to keep confidential certain advanced information given, for example, in connection with a cornerstone process. This can also apply to confidential information given to potential trade buyers in connection with a dual-track process. The term non-disclosure agreement (NDA) is also often used.

conflict of interest: in the context of an IPO, a conflict arising between the corporate finance and securities departments of an investment bank, or a conflict arising between the principal investment side of the bank and other departments. This may also apply to transactions entered into between shareholders and directors of a company, and the company itself. See also *related-parties transactions*.

connected-parties transactions: see *related-parties transactions*.

continuity of business: a listing requirement laid out by a stock exchange that the business of a company applying for listing has been substantially the same over a period of time.

continuity of ownership or management: a listing requirement laid out by a stock exchange that the main shareholders or senior management of a company applying for listing have been substantially the same over a period of time.

contractual rights: rights pursuant to which a company is able to enter into contracts with third parties. In the context of an IPO, it is important that such contractual rights are not held by a party other than the issuer.

contrarian investor: a type of investor that goes against established trends and believes that most other investors are wrong in their assessment of the market.

contribution to expenses: a mechanism pursuant to which the underwriters of an IPO are asked to contribute to some of the expenses associated with the transaction. Contribution to expenses is common in some privatizations and large, prestigious offerings. It is particularly frequent in South Korea.

control room: a part of the compliance department of an investment bank tasked with the control of pre-deal (or other) research prior to publication to ensure compliance with research guidelines and to avoid conflicts of interests, libel, or litigation.

conversion rate: (also known as hit rate) the ratio between one-on-one meetings held by a bank with investors during an institutional roadshow and the number of orders actually placed by those same investors in the book of demand. The hit rate can be computed on an overall basis, by region or by investor type. This information is commonly included in case studies of past transactions for IPO pitches.

convertible bond: a bond issued by a company and convertible into ordinary shares of that company, usually at a premium and pursuant to certain conditions, including the performance of the company's share price over a period of time. An exchangeable bond is issued by a company but is exchangeable into shares of another company, owned by the former, or exchangeable into Treasury stock owned by the issuer.

convertible preferred share: an instrument similar to a convertible bond but in this case preferred shares are issued instead of a bond. See also *convertible bond* and *preferred shares*.

core growth investor: a type of institutional investment style in which investors typically invest in companies that have good growth earnings potential.

core value investor: a type of institutional investment style in which investors typically invest in companies with a large market capitalization, below-average price-to-earnings ratios, price-to-book or cash-flow multiples, but usually higher-than-average dividend yields. Such investors often conduct significant, in-house fundamental analysis on the stocks they buy.

cornerstone investor: generally, a high quality institutional investor, hedge fund, or a tycoon that is allocated on a guaranteed basis prior to the start of bookbuilding, a significant amount of stock at the offer price, so as to provide momentum and leadership for the IPO. The names of cornerstone investors are disclosed in the offering circular(s) and prospectus and, in some (but not all) jurisdictions, they have to abide by a lock-up.

corporate governance: a set of best practice recommendations laid out initially in the Cadbury and Higgs reports in the UK to avoid conflicts of interest and abuses at senior management and board level for listed corporates. Stock exchanges encourage and sometimes include certain corporate governance practices as a condition to listing.

Corporate Information Handling Officer (CIHO): In Japan, foreign listed companies whose main market is not the Tokyo Stock Exchange (TSE) are required to designate a "Corporate Information Handling Officer" (CIHO) to remain in contact with the TSE and enhance timely disclosure. The CIHO can communicate with the TSE in Japanese or English, and is also generally in charge of corporate disclosure in the home country.

credentials: materials used by investment banks to pitch for new mandates to lead an IPO or other advisory or financing transactions. These typically include league tables, case studies of past transactions and testimonials by clients.

crib sheet: a short summary of the offer structure, characteristics, investment case, and valuation parameters for a new issue used by sales teams to verbally pitch a transaction to their institutional clients. Crib sheets are often double-sided and laminated for ease of handling or can also take the form of an internal email.

custodian: a financial institution, typically a bank, responsible for the safekeeping of financial assets. For example, in the case of depositary receipts, a depositary bank would use custodians around the world to hold and safeguard on its behalf the local shares underlying the depositary receipts issued by the depositary bank.

data room: in the context of an IPO, a room, usually at the offices of the issuer, where documents subject to documentary due diligence are kept for review by legal advisers. Increasingly, virtual data rooms (VDRs) are used nowadays, where documents can be stored on line with access through on a dedicated, password-protected website.

DAX index: a widely used total return stock market index of 30 companies listed on Deutsche Börse®, using free float in the index calculation.

deal captain: an equity salesperson tasked with coordinating the communication with, and collecting feedback from, sales teams around the world in an IPO. The deal captain also liaises with the equity syndicate desk. Different deal captains may be appointed to act in this capacity on subsequent transactions, so as to provide learning experience. Often, however, the deal captain will be a local or regional head of equity sales.

deal toy: a memento for an IPO, typically a lucite or acrylic paperweight, normally designed by junior members of an investment banking team, and usually presented at the closing ceremony or dinner to the issuer and senior third-party advisers as a souvenir.

death spiral: see *private investment in public equity (PIPE)*.

de-coupled transaction: a type of IPO whereby the price range is typically set after the first days or week of roadshows, so as to enable feedback from institutional investors to management presentations to also be taken into account when determining such price range. De-coupled transactions have recently gained popularity in Europe.

deep value investor: an institutional investment style in which investors typically use a strategy to invest in stocks with very low prices, often with a price-to-book ratio below one, or with a single-digit P/E. They use a variety of valuation methods to identify such investments and fundamentally believe that these stocks are under-valued and that their value will increase over time.

de-listing: the process through which a company decides to withdraw its listing on a particular stock exchange. This can be for a variety of reasons but is often because low trading volumes and a lack of research coverage no longer justify the additional expenses and disclosure required to maintain such listing. De-listing from certain stock exchanges can be difficult so long as a minimum number of local shareholders remain. A company listed on one stock exchange only and carrying out a de-listing effectively undertakes a privatization exercise.

delivery versus payment (DVP): a procedure whereby the delivery of the shares to investors (by the, or a, bookrunner) is simultaneous with payment for the shares (by investors) to that bookrunner, for onward payment to the issuer, net of fees. IPOs in most developed markets are now settled on a DVP basis.

deposit agreement: the agreement between a company and a depositary bank for the issue of global depositary receipts (GDRs) or level 1, 2, or 3 American depositary receipts (ADRs) or Rule 144A ADRs.

depositary bank: an issuer of depositary receipts (DRs) evidencing underlying shares to investors pursuant to a global depositary receipt (GDR) or American depositary receipt (ADR) programme.

depositary receipt (DR): a security usually denominated and tradable in US dollars evidencing underlying shares denominated in another currency. DRs themselves are evidenced by depositary shares.

depositary receipt (DR) programme: a programme usually set up by a company through a depositary bank for the issue of depositary receipts.

Depositary Trust Company (DTC): a company owned by The Depositary Trust & Clearing Corporation (DTCC) in the US that provides custody, safekeeping and other services. DTC is responsible for the settlement of global depositary receipts (GDRs) and American depositary receipts (ADRs) in the US.

designated market maker (DMM): see *specialist*.

designation: a mechanism through which an institutional investor can choose to reward an underwriter in an IPO syndicate through the allocation of sales credits by designating part of the selling concession payable on its allocation to certain members of the syndicate. In a US pot system, this is the only way syndicate members other than the bookrunner can effectively be paid for their marketing efforts since all institutional orders must be placed with the bookrunner. Often, a period of 24 or 48 hours after closing of the book is set aside for the more junior syndicate members to "chase" designations from investors.

dilution: a reduction in the value of a shareholding that occurs when new shares are issued by a company. Investors in an IPO experience immediate dilution if new shares are issued above the net asset value of the company.

direct listing: a type of listing that may conducted on the NYSE or on Nasdaq without the involvement of underwriters and also without a bookbuilding process. A direct listing may also include, in certain circumstances, a fund raising. In a direct listing, the shares are priced through an auction process. Also sometimes called *disintermediated IPO*.

director and officer (D&O) insurance: an insurance policy written to protect the directors and senior management of a company against liability arising from negligence, default, breach of duty, or (more rarely) fraud.

disintermediated IPO: see *direct listing*.

disclaimer: in the context of an IPO, a statement included in the inside cover of a pre-deal research report to bring investors' attention to the fact that the report has been drafted independently of the company and cannot be relied upon to purchase shares in the IPO. Disclaimers are also included on the front cover of, and within, offering circulars and prospectuses to warn potential investors about certain facts about the company or market in the shares.

discount (for DR trading): a depositary receipt (DR) that trades below the value of its underlying shares, taking into account the prevailing exchange rate. When a DR trades at a discount, this points to a lack of interest by investors in this instrument and to the fact that they prefer investing in the ordinary shares of the issuer instead.

discount to offer price: in some IPOs, the discount to which retail investors are entitled over the institutional offer price. See also *retail discount*.

discounted cash-flow (DCF) valuation: a theoretical valuation methodology most appropriate for businesses with good, long-term visibility, and predictable cash-flows. The value of a company calculated using a DCF valuation varies greatly depending on the assumptions used. A DCF valuation determines the value of a business using expected future cash flows, discounted at a rate that reflects the riskiness of such cash flows. This involves discounting the cash flows at a weighted average cost of capital (WACC) taking into account the company's capital structure, that is, the proportion between debt and equity capital, where such equity and debt are currently priced, how much of the debt is currently outstanding, and the company's tax rate.

discretionary fee: a fee payable by the issuer and/or the selling shareholders in an IPO in their absolute discretion to some or all of the underwriters to reward their execution and/or marketing efforts. An incentive fee may also be payable depending on some pre-agreed criteria, most commonly the valuation for the business achieved in the IPO. Discretionary fees can be structured in a number of ways, even including several components or tiers.

dividend per unit (DPU): a term equivalent to dividend per share, often used for real estate investment trusts and business trusts, where units rather than shares are marketed to investors.

dividend yield: the dividend per share divided by the price per share, expressed as a percentage.

documentary due diligence: a component of the overall due diligence process whereby legal advisers review contracts, agreements and other relevant documents relating to the issuer and its shareholders to ascertain their enforceability and authenticity. See also *due diligence*.

double dipping: the practice whereby a cornerstone investor in an IPO also places a separate order in the institutional book of demand. This is not allowed in Hong Kong.

dual listing: a listing by a company on two separate stock exchanges where the initial listing on the home market is usually referred to as the primary listing, home market or anchor market, while the other is referred to as the secondary listing. See also *anchor market*, *home market* and *multiple listings*.

dual-track IPO process: the process whereby the shareholders of a company attempt to sell the business by pursuing both a trade sale and an IPO at the same time. Eventually, only one of these options can be pursued as the IPO process nears completion.

due diligence: the process through which the parties involved in the execution of an IPO investigate the affairs of a company, so as to satisfy themselves with the adequacy of the business, financial, and legal aspects of the issuer and to ensure that all the necessary material information required by a reasonable investor to invest in the IPO has not only been accurately included in the prospectus, but also has not been omitted. Due diligence usually takes the form of business due diligence (including site visits, where appropriate, as well as third party interviews), financial due diligence, and documentary due diligence. Conducting appropriate due diligence provides the basis for due diligence defence against prospectus liability. See also *business due diligence*, *documentary due diligence* and *financial due diligence*.

due diligence report: a report compiled by a firm of legal advisers on certain due diligence aspects of a company. It typically covers a variety of issues pertaining to the issuer, such as shareholding arrangements; litigation; licences; banking facilities; insurance policies; intellectual property; sale and purchase agreements; subsidiaries and affiliated companies; joint ventures; corporate information; restructurings; and other relevant matters. Due diligence reports are usually largely finalized prior to the banks entering into an underwriting and sale and purchase agreement with the company and its controlling/major shareholder(s).

dummy order: an unethical practice in which a bookrunner includes a non-existent order for shares or depositary receipts (DRs), usually in its own name, in an institutional book of demand, in order to have more shares available to allocate to its own investors.

earnings per share (EPS): the net earnings of a company, divided by its number of outstanding shares.

ECM Manager: see *Bookbuilder*

Electronic Data Gathering, Analysis, and Retrieval (EDGAR): a database of documents issued and filed by companies with the regulator in the US, set up by the Securities and Exchange Commission (SEC) in 1984.

Electronic Disclosure for Investors' Network (EDINET): an internet-based system set up by the Tokyo Stock Exchange for the public inspection of corporate documents and financial reports by investors.

embedded value: a methodology used to value life insurance companies. The embedded value of a life insurance business is calculated as the sum of the company's net asset value (using current market prices for investments made) and of the present value of future cash-flows derived from life insurance policies currently in force (i.e., only insurance policies already sold and written by the company). A life insurer will generally be worth a multiple of its embedded value since this methodology does not take into account additional policies to be sold in coming years.

emerging market: a jurisdiction where financial markets are still at a relatively early stage of development.

employee share ownership programme (ESOP): a programme set up by a company to encourage and often subsidize ownership in its shares by its employees, generally through the use of price discounts, tax efficient investments or share grants.

engagement letter: the contract through which an issuer formally engages an adviser or bank for an IPO.

Enterprise Management Incentive (EMI): a type of employee share ownership programme in the UK.

equity capital markets (ECM): a generic term for financing transactions involving the issue or sale of equity capital. ECM transactions include IPOs; primary and secondary offerings; placements; public offerings; follow-on transactions; the issue of American depositary receipts (ADRs), global depositary receipts (GDRs) and their derivatives in other countries; accelerated bookbuildings (ABBs); block trades; convertible and exchangeable bonds; special purpose acquisition companies (SPACs); private investments in public equity (PIPEs); the issue of preferred shares; real estate investment trusts (REITs); business trusts; and other property funds and infrastructure funds.

equity capital markets (ECM) team: a specialist team within an investment bank, tasked with the origination and execution of equity capital markets transactions (including IPOs). ECM teams are often set up as a joint venture between both sides of the Chinese wall for revenue and cost allocation purposes.

equity corporate finance team: in some investment banks, a specialist team, tasked with the corporate finance execution aspects of equity capital markets transactions (including IPOs), particularly documentation.

equity story: similar to an investment case. The key attributes of a company, as marketed to investors in an IPO.

equity syndicate: a desk within an equity capital markets (ECM) team tasked with liaising with other banks and sales teams to coordinate the marketing of ECM transactions (including IPOs). Syndicate desks are particularly involved in coordinating pre-deal investor education (PDIE), roadshow schedules and bookbuilding, as well as pricing, allocations and stabilization.

Euroclear: the world's largest settlement system for securities transactions, covering both bonds and equities. Euroclear is based in Brussels, Belgium.

Euronext: a pan-European stock exchange active in Belgium, Ireland, France, the Netherlands, Norway, Portugal, and the UK. Euronext merged with the NYSE in 2007 to form NYSE Euronext. It was then acquired by Intercontinental Exchange (ICE), which subsequently spun off Euronext.

EV/EBIT ratio: the market capitalization of a company, plus its net debt (or minus its net cash), divided by earnings before net interest and tax.

EV/EBITDA ratio: the market capitalization of a company, plus its net debt (or minus its net cash), divided by earnings before net interest, tax, depreciation and amortization. This ratio is most appropriate to value cash-based businesses and to assess their cash generation ability.

EV/Sales ratio: the market capitalization of a company plus its net debt (or minus its net cash), divided by the company's turnover. This ratio effectively gives investors an idea of how much it costs to buy a company's sales.

exchange traded fund (ETF): a collective investment scheme that tracks an index comprising securities, and that can also be traded as a stock.

exchangeable bond: a bond issued by a company and exchangeable after a period of time and subject to certain conditions, into shares in another company owned by the former. Exchangeable bonds may also be convertible into treasury stock owned by the issuer.

executive director: a director who is also employed in an executive capacity by a company; also a relatively senior rank within an investment bank.

exempt list: in the context of an IPO, a list of investors that can only be contacted by certain members of a syndicate.

expert: see *specialist consultant*.

external growth: the growth achieved by a company through acquisitions. The opposite of organic growth.

F pages: pages usually located at the back end of an offering circular and where the accounts of a company are included. F pages are numbered F-1, F-2, and so on, hence their name.

Federal Open Market Committee (FOMC): in the US, a committee made up of 12 voting members (seven of whom are from the Federal Reserve Board and five of whom are chosen among the 12 Federal Reserve Bank presidents) tasked with overseeing the US's open market operations. The FOMC makes key decisions on interest rates and the growth of the US money supply. It must meet at least four times a year in Washington but in practice meetings are held more frequently. The release of FOMC minutes is usually eagerly awaited by market participants since it significantly influences trading in financial securities.

final offering circular: the version of an offering circular that includes the offer price, statistics based on the offer price, such as gross or net proceeds to be realized in the IPO, and any changes that have occurred and need to be disclosed since the publication of the preliminary offering circular. Nowadays, a simple pricing schedule is usually published instead.

Financial Conduct Authority (FCA): one of the regulators for the financial services industry in the UK, with particular responsibility for the oversight of IPO prospectuses.

financial due diligence: a component of the overall due diligence process for an IPO with a focus on the company's finances. See *due diligence*.

Financial Industry Regulatory Authority (FINRA): the successor to the National Association of Securities Dealers (NASD) in the US.

financial model: a model built by a company or an investment bank to compute financial projections or assess the value of a business using a discounted cash-flow methodology.

Financial Services Authority (FSA): the former regulator for the financial services industry in the UK, whose responsibilities were split in 2013 between the Prudential Regulation Authority, the Financial Conduct Authority (FCA), and the Bank of England.

financial sponsor: another name for a private equity firm.

firm shares: the shares issued by a company and/or sold by existing shareholders in an IPO or equity capital markets transaction, excluding shares that are the subject of an over-allotment option.

fixed-price IPO: an IPO where shares are, unlike in a transaction with a price range, offered at a fixed price to investors. Fixed-price IPOs, other than for retail tranches, are fairly rare.

flow-back: when shares (or shares and depositary shares) are traded in more than one market, the shift in trading from one market to another or from one type of security to the other. Shares generally flow back to the anchor market.

follow-on transaction: an equity capital markets transaction conducted after a company has become listed for the first time in an IPO.

football team: the manner in which the names of all the advisers working on an IPO are displayed on the back cover of an offering circular.

footsie index: also called FTSE 100. A widely used, free-float-adjusted, market capitalization–weighted stock market index of the 100 largest companies listed on the London Stock Exchange.

force majeure **clause:** a clause pursuant to which underwriting arrangements can be rescinded on the occurrence of extraordinary events such as war, terrorism, tsunamis, earthquakes, or other acts of God.

foreign-exchange restrictions: restrictions or controls imposed by a government banning or restricting the use of foreign currency or of foreign-currency-denominated financial instruments.

Form 6-K: a form used by non-US companies listed in the US to disclose material events to the Securities and Exchange Commission (SEC) and a US stock exchange.

Form 20-F: an annual report for non-US companies listed in the US (equivalent to Form 10-K for US companies) and filed with the Securities and Exchange Commission (SEC) and a US stock exchange.

Form F-1: a registration statement filed in the US with the Securities and Exchange Commission (SEC) and a US stock exchange by a foreign private issuer in connection with a sponsored level 3 American depositary receipt (ADR) programme.

Form F-6: a simple registration statement filed in the US with the Securities and Exchange Commission (SEC) by a depositary bank in connection with an unsponsored or sponsored American depositary receipt (ADR) programme.

Form S-1: the general form of registration statement with the Securities and Exchange Commission (SEC) in the US, equivalent to Form F-1 but for US companies.

free float: the amount or proportion of the shares of a company in public ownership.

free retention allocation: in an IPO, an amount of shares allocated to a member of a syndicate for it to allocate in turn to its own investors as it sees fit. Bookrunner banks also sometimes keep some free retention so as to be able to top up their own allocations.

frequent issuer: a company that frequently issues securities in the financial markets. See also *well-known seasoned issuer (WKSI)*.

front office: the client-facing side of an investment bank, as opposed to the back office.

generally agreed accounting principles (GAAP): a set of accounting principles, usually unique to a particular country or group of countries, pursuant to which the accounts of a company are drawn up. See also *accounting standards*.

global coordinator: a senior level or rank among investment banks in a syndicate of underwriters. A global coordinator is usually tasked with the overall coordination and execution of a transaction. More than one bank may be appointed in this capacity. This role is often combined with that of sponsor, bookrunner, and lead manager.

global depositary receipt (GDR): a security representing the economic interest in underlying shares, usually denominated in US dollars and usually listed either on the main board or the Professional Securities Market (PSM) in the UK, or in Luxembourg, Singapore, or other markets. GDRs are evidenced by global depositary shares (GDSs).

global depositary share (GDS): an instrument that evidences global depositary receipts (GDRs). GDSs are traded by investors, whereas GDRs remain in the clearing system.

go/no-go decision: a critical point within the timetable for an IPO when a decision may be made to no longer proceed with the transaction.

going-public convertible bond: sometimes also called pre-IPO convertible bond. A bond issued by a company and convertible into its shares upon listing of that company in an IPO on a stock exchange. Going-public convertible bonds are redeemed at a (usually) significant premium to par, together with accrued interest, in the event of non-conversion. A number of additional privileges are also usually granted to investors in going-public convertible bonds.

golden share: also sometimes called special share. A share retained by a government in the capital of a privatized company and to which special powers are attached. Golden shares enable governments to restrict foreign ownership that is deemed excessive in certain strategic industry sectors, for example in the capital of a company involved in the manufacturing of armaments or nuclear facilities.

grading (of investors): the process through which investors are ranked by quality in a book of demand prior to allocations being made. The grading of investors is done by the equity syndicate desk and is often extensively discussed between bookrunners when more than one house is appointed in this capacity.

graduate trainee: one of the titles for entry-level investment banking staff. Equivalent to analyst or business analyst.

Greenshoe: equivalent to over-allotment option. A mechanism through which additional shares beyond the firm shares are allocated to institutional investors in order to stabilize the share price, usually during the first 30 days of trading.

grey market trading: unofficial trading in securities in the over-the-counter (OTC) market prior to the start of official dealings, also called conditional trading in the UK.

gross fees: the fees paid by an issuer and/or selling shareholders to a syndicate of underwriters in an equity capital markets transaction.

growth at a reasonable price (GARP) investor: a type of institutional investment style in which investors typically look at both value and growth characteristics when selecting stocks.

guaranteed economics: fixed fees payable generally to a junior syndicate member and usually for producing pre-deal research and conducting (limited) investor education, and irrespective of any actual investor orders generated in an IPO.

Guide 2: guidelines issued by the Securities and Exchange Commission (SEC) in the US for the disclosure of oil and gas operations.

Guide 3: guidelines issued by the Securities and Exchange Commission (SEC) in the US for statistical disclosure by bank holding companies.

Guide 7: guidelines issued by the Securities and Exchange Commission (SEC) in the US for the description of property by issuers engaged or to be engaged in significant mining operations.

H shares: shares listed in Hong Kong and issued by, or sold in, a company incorporated in mainland China. H share companies are different from red chips, which have, after a re-organization, transferred their assets and liabilities to an offshore entity, usually a Cayman Islands company.

Hang Seng index (HSI): a widely used, free-float-adjusted, market capitalization–weighted stock market index currently comprising some 50 companies listed on the main board of the Stock Exchange of Hong Kong. In the first quarter of 2021, it was announced that the number of constituents in the index will gradually be increased to 100.

hard underwriting: the process through which one or more banks commit to buying, on a firm basis and at an agreed price, a number of shares from an issuer, or from a shareholder in a company, usually for onward sale to end investors. Hard underwriting is rare for institutional tranches of IPOs (although it is market practice in countries such as Indonesia) but more common in aftermarket transactions such as block trades. See also *bought deal*.

hedge fund: an unregulated type of investor managing money on behalf of high net-worth (HNW) or accredited investors (among others), subject to a lock-up, which can be for several years. Hedge funds generally focus on liquid investments across asset classes and can adopt a variety of investment strategies, often (but not always) hedging their investments using short selling or derivatives. See also *alpha*.

high net-worth (HNW) individual: a wealthy person with financial assets generally in excess of US$1 million.

home market: generally, the country where an issuer is incorporated or based. See also *anchor market*.

Hong Kong depositary receipt (HDR): a type of depositary receipt (DR) similar to an American depositary receipt (ADR) or global depositary receipt (GDR) listed and traded on the Stock Exchange of Hong Kong. HDRs can be traded in Hong Kong dollars or in US dollars. As of the first quarter of 2021, HDRs have not yet become popular with issuers, with only a few programmes issued.

house format or style (for a prospectus): the style and layout of the cover and inside pages of a prospectus used by a particular investment bank to make it recognizable to other parties as that for a "house" transaction.

IBEX index: (also called IBEX 35) a widely used, market value–weighted index of 35 companies listed on the Madrid Stock Exchange.

IFRS 8: the international financial reporting standard dealing with the segmentation of accounts under IFRS.

in-house research: see *buy-side research.*

incentive fee: see *discretionary fee.*

income investor: an institutional investment style in which investors typically look for stocks that have a high payout ratio and a significant dividend yield. This is one of the most conservative investment styles among the universe of institutional investors.

indemnity clause: a clause in an underwriting, subscription or sale and purchase agreement whereby one party agrees to indemnify another against misstatements in, or omissions from the offering circular, as well as against breaches of laws and of terms of the agreement such as representations and warranties. Indemnity clauses can also figure in engagement letters.

independent adviser: a bank, or boutique adviser or consultant not part of the syndicate of underwriters and separately advising the issuer and its shareholders on an IPO.

independent market research (IMR) report: a report, usually drafted by a specialist consultant or expert and included in an offering circular or prospectus that describes the industry in which the IPO issuer operates. The IMR report will include, among other things, information on market size and market shares.

index considerations: one of the considerations when deciding the stock exchange on which to list a company when there is a high likelihood that the issuer will eventually be included in one of the leading market indexes used by index investors to benchmark their returns.

Indian depositary receipt (IDR): a type of depositary receipt similar to an American depositary receipt (ADR) or global depositary receipt (GDR) listed and traded on a stock exchange in India. IDRs are traded in Rupees. Standard Chartered Bank was the first ever issuer of IDRs, with a significant capital raising undertaken in 2010.

infrastructure fund: a fund consisting of infrastructure assets such as airports, toll roads, or tank farms, either listed on a stock exchange or sold to institutional investors in a wholesale fund. Most common in Australia, in particular as issued by members of the Macquarie and (previously) Babcock & Brown groups, and in Singapore, through the business trust structure. See also *business trust*.

initial listing requirements: the requirements laid out by a stock exchange for the listing of a company in an IPO and at the time of the IPO. Distinct from ongoing listing requirements which must be met on a regular basis after the company has become listed.

institutional investors: investors that manage money on behalf of other parties, for example sovereign wealth funds, asset managers, mutual funds, charities, insurance companies, banks, pension funds, and hedge funds. In an IPO, institutional investors are distinct from retail or public investors and are accessed through the placement or placing tranche.

institutional offering: (also called placement or placing) in an IPO, an offering to institutions distinct from the retail or public offer. Institutional offerings are generally conducted on a bookbuilt basis, and using a price range, whereas public offers are often (but not always) conducted at a fixed price.

institutional pot: a system for computing syndicate fees when marketing to institutional investors in a US equity offering, in which all orders must be placed with the bookrunner. Investors can then choose to reward other syndicate members with part of the selling concession through designations.

intellectual property rights: rights pursuant to which a company is able to enter into contracts with third parties with respect to its intellectual property. In the context of an IPO, it is important that such intellectual property rights are not held by a party other than the issuer.

interim accounts: the accounts of a company published on a quarterly or semi-annual basis. Distinct from annual accounts.

Internal Revenue Service (IRS): the US government agency responsible for tax collection and tax law enforcement.

International Accounting Standards Board (IASB): an independent, privately funded committee based in London and comprising 16 members from different countries with the aim of developing global accounting standards. The IASB created and continues to promote the use of IFRS. The IASB was created in 2001 and is the successor to the International Accounting Standards Committee (IASC). See also *International Financial Reporting Standards (IFRS)*.

International Financial Reporting Standards (IFRS): widely used accounting standards, many of which have replaced the earlier International Accounting Standards (IAS). IFRS are most particularly used throughout Europe, although more than 120 countries have now adopted them. See also *International Accounting Standards Board (IASB)*.

International Organization of Securities Commissions (IOSCO): an association, created in 1983 and based in Madrid, comprising organizations that regulate the world's financial markets. The members of IOSCO, which are from more than 100 jurisdictions and regulate more than 95% of the world's financial markets, have, in particular, adopted common guidelines on disclosure standards for prospectuses.

International Securities Identification (ISIN) code: an alphanumerical code composed of 12 characters used to identify equity and other securities.

international wrap: pages added to, and usually around, a domestic prospectus for international distribution, and including information most particularly relevant to international investors. Such pages are typically numbered W-1, W-2, and so on. See also *US wrap*.

internet roadshow: a password-protected website that can be accessed by institutional investors not able to attend an IPO roadshow and where they can see (but not download) the roadshow slides and hear the roadshow script.

inter-syndicate agreement: an agreement between the underwriters in the placement tranche and those in the public offer tranche of an IPO. An inter-syndicate agreement includes, among other things, clauses on claw-back and claw-forward arrangements.

investment banks: banks that provide advisory, financing, and securities services to government, corporate, and institutional-investor clients. Sometimes the term "investment bank" may refer only to that part of a bank that provides corporate finance (including advisory, mergers and acquisitions, and financing) services to its clients, excluding sales, research, and trading departments.

investment case: see *equity story*.

investor conferences: conferences organized periodically by investment banks for the benefit of their institutional investor clients. These usually have a country, regional, or industry focus or theme, with corporates presenting on their business in a series of non-deal roadshows.

investor education: (also often called pre-deal investor education (PDIE). See *pre-marketing*.

investor relations (IR): how a corporate manages the information flow and interaction with (mainly) institutional investors, whether already shareholders in the company or not, as well as with sell-side research analysts after the company has become listed. Investor relations are usually handled by a dedicated executive and his or her team.

investor soundings: in an aftermarket equity capital markets transaction, refers to discrete soundings made to institutional investors after they have been made insiders by an equity syndicate or ECM team to assess their appetite and price sensitivity for the placement of a block of securities.

investor surveys: (usually) the ranking on an annual basis of sell-side research analysts for a defined region, country, or industry sector by institutional investors. Ranked research analysts are much in demand and can command a high compensation. Some investor surveys may also rank sales teams.

invitation telex: at the start of the marketing phase of an IPO, a telex, fax, or e-mail communication summarizing the key terms of the offering and sent out to invite junior underwriters into the syndicate.

IPO: an initial public offering. A type of equity capital markets transaction involving the listing of a company on a stock exchange for the first time.

IPO management team: the team appointed by an issuer and dedicated to the execution of an IPO throughout the transaction.

issue manager: the equivalent of a sponsor bank in Singapore. See also *sponsor*.

Japanese depositary receipt (JDR): a type of depositary receipt representing the economic interest in a company's shares that are denominated and traded in yen on the Tokyo Stock Exchange. A JDR is similar to an American depositary receipt (ADR) in the US, a global depositary receipt (GDR) in Luxembourg, Singapore, or the UK, a Hong Kong depositary receipt (HDR) in Hong Kong, an Indian depositary receipt (IDR) in India, a Singapore depositary receipt (SDR) in Singapore, and a Taiwan Depository Receipt (TDR) in Taiwan.

joint and several underwriting obligations: underwriting obligations whereby remaining underwriters are required to pick up the underwriting obligations of a defaulting underwriter in proportion to their initial underwriting amounts. Very rare in equity capital markets transactions, where several underwriting obligations are the norm.

jump ball: in the US, that portion of the selling concession that is variable and paid based on designations received from institutional investors. Distinct from the fixed portion of the selling concession, which is paid based on shares underwritten by a member of a syndicate of underwriters. Originally a basketball term.

Jumpstart Our Business Startups (JOBS) Act: a law signed in the US in 2012, which, among other things, facilitates the raising of equity capital through IPOs by smaller companies and businesses through easing securities regulations.

Kanto Local Finance Bureau (KLFB): a subdivision of the Ministry of Finance in Japan, where a securities registration statement (or SRS) must be filed in connection with a public offering without listing (POWL).

kick-off meeting: generally, an all-parties meeting held with the issuer at the outset of an IPO to introduce the working teams to each other and to communicate the key parameters of the transaction.

lead manager: a senior level among investment banks in a syndicate of underwriters usually combined with the role of bookrunner. However, a lead manager who is not also a bookrunner has little ability to perform in a marketing capacity in an IPO.

league table: a table compiled over a period of time, across a particular industry or jurisdiction and for a particular type of transaction, ranking investment banks, usually on the basis of the amount raised on behalf of their clients. League tables are compiled using a certain level of seniority attained in a syndicate of underwriters (e.g., bookrunner or lead manager league tables). League tables offer a lot of flexibility in the way they are devised, and it is often the responsibility of junior investment bankers to compile league tables that show the bank in a good light for use in pitches.

legal name: the name used by an investment bank within a prospectus and in a legal agreement. The legal name is generally longer than the advertising name. See also *advertising name*.

legal opinion: an opinion delivered at closing of an IPO by a firm of legal advisers to an issuer or to investment banks opining, among other things, on the due incorporation of the issuer, its power to conduct the IPO, and on the due execution and delivery of transactions documents. Generally speaking, one or more legal opinions are required from each of the legal firms working on the transaction, and specifically for each of the jurisdictions in respect of which they have been providing advice. In addition, various US legal opinions such as a no registration opinion, a 1940 Act opinion, a PFIC opinion, and a 10b-5 letter may also be sought when an offering is marketed in the US pursuant to a private placement.

Level 1, 2, 3 American depositary receipts (ADRs): types of sponsored ADR programmes. A level 2 ADR programme involves a listing in the US, while a level 3 programme also involves the raising of capital on a US stock exchange.

leveraged buy-out (LBO): a type of financial transaction, typically involving a financial sponsor, where the price consideration is financed mostly through leverage. See also *financial sponsor*.

like-for-like growth: the growth in certain line items of the accounts of a company using a constant structure for the business, that is, disregarding acquisitions made or newly opened production or distribution facilities.

limitations on enforceability of civil liabilities: limitations typically stated in a US wrap on the enforceability of civil liabilities for non-US companies, which usually have assets mainly located outside the US, effectively highlighting that it may not be possible in connection with an IPO to effect service of process, enforce in the US court judgments obtained against the issuer, its directors, or executive officers, or enforce through legal action abroad liabilities predicated upon US securities laws.

liquidity: a measure of the activity in the trading of a listed company. Liquidity is typically expressed as a daily average number of shares or currency amount traded, over a period of time, generally measured over 20, 30, or 60 days. See also *average daily trading volume (ADTV)*.

list of 49 investors (in Japan): a list of up to 49 institutional investors in Japan to whom sales of shares may be made by way of a private placement in an IPO or related transaction. Above that number, a registration statement (SRS) must be filed with the KLFB in Japan.

list of documents: A list of all the documents required to be produced, filed or reviewed for an IPO, typically compiled by one or more firms of legal advisers.

list of working parties: a list, usually in the form of a small, bound booklet, with contact details for the various parties working on an IPO, prepared and handed out to all parties by one of the lead investment banks at the kick-off meeting.

listing agreement: an agreement sometimes entered into between a company and a stock exchange governing the terms for the listing of the company, including initial and ongoing listing fees and requirements.

listing by way of introduction: a listing conducted by a company on a stock exchange independently of any sell-down or capital raising. This can also be done through the acquisition of a listed shell company and is predicated on the company already having a sufficient number of public shareholders, perhaps through a separate listing in another jurisdiction. Listings by way of introduction often result in poor trading volumes and in a lack of liquidity and coverage by sell-side research analysts.

listing committee: a committee of a stock exchange where decisions are made to admit candidates to listing.

listing costs: the costs usually borne by the issuer and selling shareholders and pertaining to the issue and listing of the shares in an IPO.

listing requirements: the requirements laid out by a stock exchange for the listing of companies on one of its boards. There are usually both initial—to be met at the time of the IPO—and ongoing listing requirements. Listing requirements can be both qualitative and quantitative.

lock-up: a period of time during which the issue of new shares by a company or sell-downs in its shares by one or more of its material shareholders (usually defined as owning more than 5% of the company's outstanding share capital) or cornerstone investors are prohibited. Lock-ups are typically for 180 days but can on occasion last for a year or more. The global coordinator or bookrunner of an IPO usually has the contractual ability (seldom used) to waive a lock-up. In Malaysia and Singapore, IPOs no longer feature lock-ups for cornerstone investors.

long-only: a type of institutional investor known for its stable, long-term investment horizon and for not using short-position hedging. Often the term "long-only investors" is used to distinguish these from hedge funds.

long/short: an institutional investment strategy often used by hedge funds whereby their investments in securities are hedged using short positions in other securities.

magic circle: a group of large firms of legal advisers in the UK comprising Allen & Overy, Clifford Chance, Freshfields Bruckhaus Deringer, Linklaters, and Slaughter and May.

main board: the main market of a stock exchange on which a company may seek a listing. Some stock exchanges have also established smaller boards or second markets with less stringent listing requirements and typically for the listing of smaller or emerging growth companies.

management commission: a component of the gross fees payable by an issuer and/or its selling shareholders to a syndicate of underwriters. Management commissions are payable on shares underwritten (rather than sold) and typically represent 20% of the gross fees. A *praecipium* payable to the global coordinator(s) (and sometimes lead manager(s)) only is often deducted from the management commissions.

Management commissions are also usually available to pay for unreimbursed expenses and stabilization losses.

management discussion and analysis of financial condition and results of operations (MD&A): the disclosure of financial information in a prospectus derived from market practice in the. An MD&A consists of a narrative discussion and explanation of changes in the principal line items in a company's consolidated profit and loss account and cash-flow statements for the periods under review. A similar analysis is also conducted of the company's capitalization and indebtedness. MD&As also include a summary of the company's principal accounting policies. See also *operating and financial review (OFR)*.

manager: a mid-level rank in an investment bank equivalent to associate or senior associate.

managing director: a senior rank within an investment bank. The primary responsibility of front-office managing directors is to originate new business.

mandate letter: a letter agreement pursuant to which an issuer appoints one or more lead banks for the execution of its IPO. Other advisers such as auditors are also usually formally appointed in this way. See also *engagement letter*.

market capitalization: the value ascribed by the market to a listed company. The market capitalization is equal to the number of outstanding shares of a company multiplied by the current market price for its shares.

market positioning: see *equity story*.

maximum price: in a concurrent retail offering, the price paid by retail investors, which, in an IPO with no retail discount, is equivalent to the top end of the bookbuilding price range. Retail investors are reimbursed the difference between the maximum price and the offer price in the event that the IPO is not priced at the top end of the range.

memorandum of association: the by-laws of a company.

memorandum of understanding (MoU): equivalent to rules of engagement. A memorandum drafted by investment banks working in a lead role in an IPO or equity capital markets transaction recording their respective roles and how they will work with each other on the offering. MoUs record, among other things, details of the banks' agreement on appearance; underwriting amounts; fees; expenses; investor education, roadshow, allocation and stabilization procedures; and advertising arrangements.

mergers and acquisitions: the corporate advisory activities of an investment bank.

momentum investor: (also aggressive growth investor) an institutional investment style in which investors are typically focused on stocks that exhibit fast and increasing growth. Can also refer to lower quality investors that place orders in the later stages of a bookbuilding process, once the news of a high subscription level have been released by the bookrunners or become known to the market.

money-back guarantee: a rather rare form of retail incentive, consisting of a partial money-back guarantee for a certain period of time in the event of a fall of the share price below the offer price.

multiple listings: the listing of a company on more than one stock exchange. See also *anchor market*, *dual listing*, *home market*, *primary listing*, and *secondary listing*.

naked short: a device used to stabilize an IPO above and beyond an over-allotment option. A naked short, where allowed, involves the stabilizing agent shorting shares using its own balance sheet without the "cover" of a borrowing agreement. This can prove to be a costly strategy if the share price rises in the aftermarket. Naked shorts for stabilization purposes are prohibited in many markets, although not in the US.

Nasdaq: a stock exchange in the US known especially for the listing and trading of technology stocks.

Nasdaq Dubai: a stock exchange in the United Arab Emirates (UAE).

National Association of Securities Dealers (NASD): a self-regulatory association in the US previously tasked with the regulation of Nasdaq and the administration of professional examinations for people working in the securities industry. The NASD merged with the NYSE's regulatory committee in 2007 to form the Financial Industry Regulatory Authority (FINRA).

negative assurance: language included in a SAS 72 auditor comfort letter whereby the auditors state that "nothing has come to their attention that would cause them to believe that any modifications should be made to the unaudited interim financial information for them to be in conformity to generally agreed accounting principles (GAAP) and that they comply as to form in all material respects with the applicable GAAP"; and that "nothing has come to their attention that would cause them to believe that there have been material changes in certain financial statement line items since the date of the last financial statements included in the offering circular". Such negative assurances cannot be given if 135 days or more have elapsed since the date of the latest audited or reviewed accounts, and may also require the reporting accountants to perform an SAS 100 review to review interim unaudited accounts. See also *SAS 72 comfort letter* and *SAS 100 review*.

net asset value (NAV): equivalent to book value. The net worth of a company, equivalent to its assets minus its liabilities.

net proceeds: see *proceeds*.

net profit: the profit of a company, after taxes, as stated in its profit and loss account. Net profit is used, in particular, to calculate a price to earnings ratio. Sometimes referred to as after-tax profit or profit after tax.

New York Stock Exchange (NYSE): the largest and most prestigious US stock exchange, located in Wall Street.

NIKKEI 225 index: a price-weighted average stock market index of 225 stocks listed on the Tokyo Stock Exchange.

1940 Act opinion: a US legal opinion whereby a firm of US legal advisers advises whether a company is an investment company as defined under the Investment Company Act of 1940 (also known as the 1940 Act). Investment companies may include conglomerates or holding companies, whose main business consists of investments in other companies. Complex tests may be required to ascertain whether a company is an Investment Company under the 1940 Act.

no registration opinion: a US legal opinion whereby a firm of US legal advisers advises on whether an IPO need not be registered with the Securities and Exchange Commission (SEC) in the US.

nominated adviser (Nomad): a qualified bank or broker appointed to act as adviser in connection with, and following, the listing of a company on the Alternative Investment Market (AIM) in the UK. Equivalent to brokers for companies listed on the main board of the LSE.

nomination committee: a committee of the board of directors of a company tasked with discussing the procedures and policies for, as well as the appointment of, directors.

non-deal roadshow: an investor roadshow that is made by a corporate irrespective of any capital markets transaction, for example in connection with the announcement of interim results or investor conferences.

non-disclosure agreement (NDA): see *confidentiality agreement*.

NYSE American: an American stock exchange formerly known as the American Stock Exchange (AMEX), and subsequently as NYSE AMEX Equities, and sold to NYSE Euronext in October 2008. NYSE American focuses on small- and micro-cap companies.

odd lot: a block of shares consisting of a number of shares smaller than in a board lot. Trading in odd lots generates additional costs. See also *board lot*.

offer price: The price that has been determined for the shares of a company in an IPO upon pricing, generally after bookbuilding has been completed.

offer structure: the way in which an IPO is structured between various tranches to access various classes of investors. IPOs most commonly include a placement tranche targeted at institutional investors and a public offer tranche targeted at retail investors but may, on occasion, also include additional tranches or further sub-divisions of the placement tranche in particular.

offering circular: the document published, registered and distributed to investors by an issuer in an IPO. Broadly equivalent to prospectus, offer document, offering document, disclosure document or, in the US, registration statement. An offering circular may be produced in different versions and in more than one language and includes all the information necessary for a reasonable investor to make an informed decision about buying the shares. An offering circular includes comprehensive information about the company, its business and its financials, as well as about the structure of the IPO and application procedures for investors. Generally, offering circular is the term used for the listing document produced for institutional investors, while the term prospectus is used for the disclosure document published for retail investors.

Offers and Prospectuses Electronic Repository and Access (MAS OPERA Public Portal): an internet-based, electronic information system established by the Monetary Authority of Singapore to display prospectuses and other information about issuers, IPOs, and other capital markets transactions.

Officer Responsible for Handling Information (ORHI): in Japan, listed foreign companies whose main market is the Tokyo Stock Exchange (TSE) are required to appoint a local Officer Responsible for Handling Information (ORHI). The ORHI, who plays the role of liaison for investors in Japan as well as with the TSE, must be selected among executives or officers fluent in Japanese.

offre à prix ouvert **(OPO):** a type of retail offering in France where orders by the public can be placed at various prices within a range.

on-margin borrowing: a mechanism whereby money is borrowed to buy shares using the investment as collateral. Popular with retail investors in Hong Kong IPOs.

one-on-one meetings: one of the components of an IPO roadshow. It consists of a series of meetings between the senior management of an issuer and individual institutional investors. One-on-one meetings are arranged by the bookrunners and reserved for the largest and highest-quality investors only.

ongoing listing requirements: requirements laid out by a stock exchange that must be met after a company has become listed in an IPO. Distinct from initial listing requirements, which must be met at the time of the IPO.

open-market property valuation: the valuation a property asset would realize if it were offered to all potential buyers in the market. Usually the basis on which property assets are valued by external valuers for the purpose of an IPO.

operating and financial review (OFR): the disclosure of financial information in a prospectus in Europe, and particularly in the UK, in a manner substantially similar to what is required under a management disclosure and analysis of financial condition and results of operations (MD&A).

oral presentation: usually, the second stage in a formal pitching process or beauty parade for investment banks for an IPO. Oral presentations generally follow written submissions delivered pursuant to a request for proposal (RFP), and may be conducted with a shortlist of banks only.

organic growth: the growth achieved by a company without external acquisitions. The opposite of external growth.

orphan stock: a company listed on a stock exchange where it does not really belong, which can be for a variety of reasons, or with no investor following. Orphan stocks exhibit poor trading volumes and no or little sell-side research coverage.

out of order: a lead investment bank usually displayed in the top left position among a list of banks on the front cover of a prospectus, irrespective of any alphabetical order. For example, when "Goldman Sachs" appears to the left of "Bank of America Merrill Lynch" on the same line and in the same role. An investment bank that is out of order often has a more senior role in the IPO, benefits from a larger underwriting, and/or receives more fees.

outsold: when a bank appointed in the same role and on the same basis as other houses has received a lower overall allocation for its orders from investors, either globally or for a particular region, or for a type of investor. An investment bank having outsold others in a particular deal constitutes a popular marketing argument used in pitches for IPOs and other related transactions. This can refer to demand generated as well as to allocations.

over-allotment option: see *Greenshoe*.

overhang: a term used when knowledge in the market that a block of shares owned by an investor may be available for sale depresses the share price of a company. Shares that are locked-up after an IPO often create an overhang nearer to the expiry of the lock-up.

over-subscription: when investor demand that has been generated for an IPO (or a tranche of an IPO) exceeds the number of shares available for sale or issue.

over-the-counter (OTC) market: a non-physical market for the trading of securities not listed on a stock exchange. For example, the pink sheets for American depositary receipts (ADRs) in the US constitute an OTC market. See also *grey market trading*.

P/E ratio: the most common financial ratio used to value companies. The P/E ratio is computed by dividing the price per share by the earnings per share. Alternatively, one can also divide the market capitalization of the company by its net profit. For an IPO, a P/E is generally computed on a forward rather than on a trailing basis. Equivalent to PER.

partly paid shares: a type of retail incentive popular in certain countries (such as Austria, the UK, Canada, and Australia), particularly in privatization offerings, whereby shares are paid for by retail investors in two or more instalments over a period of time, with no interest. Most instalment plans used in past privatizations had a period of 18 months and were not subject to a holding period, with partly paid shares separately tradable on the secondary market.

partner: in the context of an IPO, a partner in a firm of legal advisers or accountants, or a senior investment banking business title.

passive foreign income company (PFIC): PFIC tax rules, which are subject to interpretation by the Internal Revenue Service (IRS) in the US, impose additional tax liability on US investors on gains or dividends derived from investment in a PFIC. Holding companies, companies with significant cash holdings or start-up companies may sometimes be classified as a PFIC.

pathfinder: a term used for a preliminary offering circular in the UK. See *preliminary offering circular*.

penalty bid: in the US, when shares are sold by an investor brought about by one of the underwriters during the stabilization period and bought back by the stabilizing agent, such underwriter may be subject to a penalty bid by the bookrunners in the form of reduced commissions payable to it in connection with the IPO. Typically, such reduction in commissions consists in the selling concession payable on the order for that particular investor being reclaimed by the bookrunners. Penalty bids are defined under Regulation M, Rule 100 of the Securities Act of 1933 (as amended), and must be disclosed to the Securities and Exchange Commission (SEC). In effect, penalty bids are a way to discourage flipping of the shares by investors in the first days or weeks of trading.

penny share: a share with a particularly low denomination (e.g., a share price of, say, US$0.05) and perceived by retail investors in particular as having neither value nor prospects.

pension fund: a type of institutional investor that manages money set aside to pay for retirement liabilities.

PER: see *P/E ratio*.

per pop valuation: a popular valuation technique to value internet or mobile telecommunications companies. A per pop valuation puts a price on each individual customer or user for the market under licence and acts as a proxy for a discounted cash-flow (DCF) valuation of the business upon reaching maturity, taking into account market penetration, the revenue per subscriber, the business's profit margin, a cash-flow multiple, and a discount rate.

physical due diligence: a component of the due diligence process involving the visit of production sites and other physical facilities.

pilot fishing: in Europe, and in the UK in particular, the process through which the bookrunner banks target certain leadership investors at an early stage in an IPO.

pink sheets: an over-the-counter (OTC) market for American depositary receipts (ADRs) in the US.

pitch: a physical or written presentation made by an investment bank or advisory firm with a view to obtaining a mandate for an investment banking transaction.

placement tranche: a component of the global offer structure for an IPO. Equivalent to institutional offer tranche, institutional offering or placing. Part of an IPO targeted at institutional investors, often across multiple jurisdictions, through private placements and pursuant to selling restrictions. Placement tranches are underwritten separately to public offerings or retail tranches, and usually only after the offer price has been determined. See also *institutional offering*.

placing letter: a letter sent to an institutional investor formally informing it of its allocation in an IPO. Placement letters include details of relevant re-selling restrictions, as well as information on taxes, duties, levies and brokerage fees payable by the investor. Investors must sign and return to the bookrunners a confirmation included in the placing letter, together with details of their brokerage accounts for the settlement of the securities.

plain English: a style used for drafting an offering circular to make it more accessible to investors and reader-friendly.

plan of distribution: the section in an offering circular summarizing the key terms and arrangements for the underwriting of an IPO. Sometimes appears under the heading "Underwriting".

post-hearing information pack (PHIP): specifically in Hong Kong, the posting of a near final (but slightly redacted) prospectus for an IPO on the website of the parent company of the Stock Exchange of Hong Kong after the listing hearing and for the benefit of retail investors, so as to provide them with a level playing field with institutional investors. Similar to the posting of a prospectus on OPERA in Singapore, or on the website of the Securities Commission in Malaysia.

post-money valuation: the valuation of a company, including new money to be raised by it in an IPO.

praecipium: a component of the gross fees usually payable to the global coordinator(s) (and, more rarely, lead manager(s) only). A *praecipium* can either be deducted from the gross fees, in which case it represents a higher amount, or, more commonly, from the management commission.

pre-agreed allocation: a term commonly used in connection with cornerstone investors, who commit to buying an agreed allocation of stock at the offer price at an early stage in the IPO process, prior to the start of bookbuilding. See also *cornerstone investor*.

pre-agreed economics: an arrangement whereby the lead banks agree how they will allocate among themselves the gross fees payable to them by the issuer and/or the selling shareholder(s) in an IPO. Alternatively, the amount of fees payable to a junior member of an underwriting syndicate (such as a co-lead manager), irrespective of its performance in generating orders, and usually for producing pre-deal research and conducting investor education only. See also *guaranteed economics*.

pre-deal investor education (PDIE): see *pre-marketing*.

pre-deal research: a research report produced by an investment bank forming part of a syndicate of underwriters prior to the formal launch of an IPO. The issuance and publication of pre-deal research is generally subject to a number of guidelines and restrictions, and is prohibited in certain countries.

pre-IPO investment: an investment at an early stage in a transaction by a strategic or institutional investor in a company about to be listed. A pre-IPO investment is distinct from an investment by a cornerstone investor in that it is often made earlier, and at a significant discount to the offer price for the IPO.

pre-marketing: the process, also now commonly called pre-deal investor education (PDIE), which follows the publication of pre-deal research (outside the US, Canada and Japan), whereby sell-side research analysts meet with institutional investors across a variety of jurisdictions to convey the equity story with a view to obtaining feedback so as to be able to determine a price range for bookbuilding.

pre-money valuation: the valuation of a company, excluding new money to be raised by it in an IPO.

preferred shares: hybrid, usually perpetual, instruments that have both debt and equity characteristics. They rank ahead of shares in the event of liquidation, but below bonds, borrowings and other creditors. Preferred shares are usually non-voting. They usually pay a fixed rate, but sometimes a floating rate, dividend, prior to any dividends being paid to holders of ordinary shares. Preferred shares are sometimes also called preference shares.

preliminary offering circular: an early version of the offering circular distributed to investors, subject to completion and amendment and published without a price (and, more rarely, with a price range) at the start of the bookbuilding process. Also called pathfinder (in the UK), red, or red herring.

premium (for DR trading): a depositary receipt (DR) that trades above the value of its underlying shares, taking into account the prevailing exchange rate. When a DR trades at a premium, this points to interest from investors in this instrument and to the fact that they prefer investing in the DRs of the issuer rather than in its ordinary shares.

presentation to research analysts: a physical presentation made by the senior management of an issuer to brief the sell-side research analysts assigned by banks in the syndicate of underwriters to produce pre-deal research.

presentation to the syndicate: a briefing made by the global coordinators and bookrunners of an IPO to the more junior members of a syndicate of underwriters to inform them of the key terms and conditions and timetable for an IPO. Often, no physical presentation actually takes place.

price range: a range of share prices, usually in the order of 15 to 20%, determined at the end of investor education by the bookrunners and used to gather orders from institutional investors in a bookbuilding process.

price talk: the valuation parameters or approximate valuation discussed among market participants for an IPO.

price-to-book ratio: the share price of a company divided by its book value per share or net asset value per share. Can also be computed by dividing the market capitalization of a company by its net asset value. A popular valuation technique for banks and property companies in particular. Equivalent to price-to-net asset value (NAV) ratio.

price-to-net asset value (NAV) ratio: see *price-to-book ratio*.

pricing: a key step in an IPO when the offer price for the shares is determined, usually at the end of bookbuilding.

primary equity markets conditions: an assessment of the IPO and new equity issue market, on a global, regional, country or sector basis, made by an investment bank, in connection with a pitch or as part of a briefing to an IPO issuer.

primary listing: see *dual listing* and *multiple listings*.

primary offering: either an equity capital markets transaction in general, or, more specifically, the issue of new shares by a company.

principal adviser: the equivalent of a sponsor bank in Malaysia. See also *sponsor*.

printer: a commercial printing company specializing in documents of a financial nature, and tasked with printing and distributing to investors and other parties the preliminary and final offering circulars. Printers also often provide translation and virtual data room (VDR) services. See also *virtual data room (VDR)*.

private bank: a division of a, or a standalone, financial institution specializing in the management of assets, often on a discretionary basis, on behalf of high and ultra-high net-worth individuals.

private investigator: a firm of consultants specializing in assessing the existence, legality and legitimacy of a business. Often used by investment banks as part of their due diligence process for IPOs by issuers from emerging markets.

private investment in public equity (PIPE): a PIPE involves selling publicly traded equity to private investors, in the form of either ordinary shares, usually at a significant discount to the market price, preferred shares, or, more commonly, convertible bonds. PIPEs are common in the US and Japan and are particularly targeted at companies that would otherwise be unable to tap the public markets for financing. Their terms are often biased in favour of investors and may involve, among other advantages, downside protection against falls in the market price, often resulting in significant dilution and what has often been termed a "death spiral".

Private Offerings, Resale and Trading Through Automated Linkages (PORTAL): a platform in the US formerly for exclusive trading by market makers and QIBs of Rule 144A American depositary receipts (ADRs).

private placement: a placement to institutional investors, or certain types of institutional investors only, pursuant to an exemption from registration requirements. Institutional offerings are usually conducted across a variety of jurisdictions pursuant to private placements, most notably in compliance with Rule 144A in the US.

privatization: either the return of state-owned assets to private ownership through an IPO, another equity capital markets transaction or trade sale; or the de-listing of a publicly owned company by its majority owner.

pro forma accounts: the accounts of a company re-computed so as to show the financials as if the company structure today had been in existence in preceding years. It is often necessary to compute pro forma accounts when material mergers, acquisitions, or disposals have been conducted in the years immediately preceding an IPO.

proceeds: the amount of money raised by a company in an IPO. Can also be expressed as net proceeds, after deduction of the gross fees and expenses to be borne by them.

product banker: an investment banker specializing in a type of financial transaction, for example, debt or equity capital markets, mergers and acquisitions, or derivatives.

Professional Securities Market (PSM): a market established by the London Stock Exchange targeted at institutional investors only, and with less stringent listing requirements than the Main Market.

profit forecast: in the context of an IPO, a forecast made by a company of its net earnings for the reporting period immediately following an IPO. A profit forecast can sometimes be included in a domestic prospectus but more rarely in an offering circular that is given international distribution (and especially not in the US). Can also mean a forecast of net earnings made, for one or more reporting periods following an IPO, by a sell-side research analyst and published in a pre-deal research report.

project name: a code name given to a corporate finance transaction or an IPO for confidentiality reasons.

property valuers: a firm of professional consultants tasked with assessing the value of the property assets of a company. Valuation reports published by property valuers are included in offering circulars for IPOs when a company has material property assets.

proprietary trading desk: a desk within an investment bank using the bank's balance sheet to trade assets for the account of the bank itself, rather than on behalf of third-party clients.

prospectus: see *offering circular*.

prospectus drafting: the writing of a prospectus by legal advisers, investment banks and other parties. Traditionally, the first draft of a prospectus for an international IPO is produced by the legal advisers to the issuer.

public offering: a tranche of the offer structure for an IPO and an offering made to retail investors, usually in the jurisdiction where the shares are listed only. The main purpose of a retail offering is often to obtain at least the minimum number of public shareholders to qualify for listing. Also called retail offering.

public offering without listing (POWL): a mechanism whereby shares can be offered to a potentially large number of retail and institutional investors in Japan, without the need to secure a local listing. A POWL is conducted at a fixed price after pricing and involves, among other things, the filing of a securities registration statement (SRS) in the Japanese language with the Kanto Local Finance Bureau (KLFB), a subdivision of the Ministry of Finance.

public relations (PR): the process of promoting general awareness of a company and of its business through media and other third-party relations. Often used in connection with an IPO, subject to prevailing legal restrictions.

publicity guidelines: guidelines issued by a firm of legal advisers, usually at the outset of an IPO, setting out restrictions on communication with the press and other media (including websites and the internet), as well as in connection with public appearances by management.

pulling a deal: the action of discontinuing the execution or marketing process for an IPO or for another related transaction. Deals are often pulled as a result of adverse market conditions, poor reception by investors, or on low valuation grounds.

pure play: a company with a well-defined line of business and no peripheral activities, thereby providing potential investors with "pure" exposure to its industry sector (or sub-sector).

qualified institutional buyer (QIB): a type of US institutional investor that can be accessed by a non-US issuer through a Rule 144A private placement. This includes most US institutional investors with discretionary assets under management above US$100 million, smaller banks and savings and loan associations with an audited net worth of at least US$25 million, and registered brokers or dealers managing on a discretionary basis assets of at least US$10 million. There are several thousand QIBs.

qualitative market research: market research conducted by a specialized consultancy firm in connection with a mass retail offering, usually against the background of a privatization exercise. Qualitative market research generally uses focus groups to assess the public's views about, and knowledge of, a company or attitudes towards an IPO.

quantitative investors: investors that focus on trading statistics, stock performance trends and numbers almost irrespective of the business of a company. By definition, quantitative investors (also known as "quants") are not generally major buyers of IPOs since at that stage there is no trading history for these companies in the public markets.

quantitative market research: market research conducted by a specialized consultancy firm in connection with a mass retail offering, usually against the background of a privatization exercise and often used to assess, through statistical surveys, the public's sensitivity to various types of retail incentives.

real estate investment trust (REIT): a type of transaction whereby real estate assets can be monetized through an IPO. Through a REIT, the owner of property assets (also called sponsor) can transfer part of its ownership to institutional and public investors through the listing of a vehicle. The sponsor can then set up a REIT manager, which is paid management fees as a percentage of the value of the deposited properties owned by the REIT, as well as performance fees, either based on the net property income or on the performance of the REIT. Acquisition fees on the value of new property acquired as well as divestment fees on the value of divested property are also charged. REITs are now popular in many countries. See also *sociétés d'investissements immobiliers cotées (SIIC)*.

receiving bank: a commercial bank appointed in connection with the public offer of an IPO to distribute prospectuses and application forms and to receive completed application forms and application moneys from retail investors.

receiving bank agreement: an agreement entered into between the issuer, the lead banks and a receiving bank for an IPO covering the distribution of prospectuses and of application forms for the retail offering and specifying how the receiving bank will be paid. This often includes interest on money collected from retail investors to apply under the IPO.

recommendation: an opinion from a sell-side research analyst included in a research report as to whether investors should buy, sell or keep shares in a company. Pre-deal research reports do not include recommendations.

red: see *preliminary offering circular*.

red chips: companies from mainland China listed in Hong Kong which have, after a re-organization and prior to listing, transferred their assets and liabilities to an offshore entity, usually a Cayman Islands company.

red herring: see *preliminary offering circular*.

refreshing the shoe: a mechanism whereby shares allocated to institutional investors pursuant to an over-allotment option are bought back and subsequently re-sold to investors. Most jurisdictions now prohibit this practice.

Regulation D of the Securities Act of 1933 (as amended) (Reg. D): an exemption from registration for the re-sale of securities to accredited investors (as defined under Rule 501 of the Securities Act) in the US. In effect, this is a somewhat wider exemption from registration than that permitted under Rule 144A. It is used mainly for follow-on transactions such as block trades.

Regulation M of the Securities Act of 1933 (as amended) (Reg. M): see *penalty bid*.

Regulation S of the Securities Act of 1933 (as amended) (Reg. S): an exemption from registration for the re-sale of securities, enabling the sale of shares by a non-US issuer to offshore US institutional investors. When no listing in the US is being sought, the international portion of an institutional offering or placement is conducted either pursuant to Regulation S or to Rule 144A.

Regulation S-K of the Securities Act of 1933 (as amended): a regulation within the Securities Act that lists the information that must be included in a registration statement, with a focus on non-financial information.

Regulation S-X of the Securities Act of 1933 (as amended): a regulation within the Securities Act that explains the financial information that must be included in a registration statement.

regulator: a body established in most jurisdictions to regulate the securities or financial industry.

related-parties transactions: transactions with companies or persons connected to an issuer, sometimes made on preferential terms or not on an arm's length basis. In connection with an IPO, related-parties transactions are prohibited or must be disclosed in the prospectus after an exemption or specific waiver has been sought and obtained from the regulator or stock exchange. Also called connected-parties transactions.

remuneration committee: a committee of the board of directors of a company tasked with setting up a remuneration policy to attract, reward and retain executive directors and senior management and to balance their interests with those of shareholders and of the company.

remuneration consultants: a firm of specialist consultants appointed by a company to design and implement an employee share ownership programme, prior to, at the time of, or after an IPO. Also called human resources (HR) and performance consultants.

re-organization: in the context of an IPO, generally the transfer or sale of certain assets and liabilities with a view to creating an entity suitable for listing. Re-organization is a common feature of the red chips listed on the Stock Exchange of Hong Kong.

reporting accountants: a term for auditors in the UK.

representations and warranties: in the context of an IPO, usually contractual representations and warranties on the part of the issuer, and of the selling shareholders, with respect to their ownership of the shares (e.g., representations that these have not been pledged to a third party), information disclosed in the offering circular, maintenance of listing, and their ability to enter into the various agreements. They also warrant that they will abide by the terms of their respective lock-ups.

re-pricing: in an IPO, an adjustment made to the price range used for bookbuilding, either upwards or downwards, in order to respond to adverse market conditions or to poor (or strong) investor demand for the shares, as the case may be. Infrequent in Asia and Europe, but quite common in the US.

request for proposal (RFP): an invitation issued by a company and/or its shareholders to investment banks asking them to submit a proposal to act in a leading role in the proposed IPO of the company. RFPs can also be issued for follow-on transactions. See also *beauty parade*.

research analyst: usually, a sell-side equity research analyst employed by an investment bank, with a regional or country focus, or an industry sector specialty. Research analysts are assigned coverage of, and produce research reports on, companies for the benefit of their institutional investor clients. In the context of an IPO, research analysts produce pre-deal research and conduct investor education. See also *pre-deal research* and *pre-deal investor education (PDIE)*.

research analyst ranking: a ranking assigned to a research analyst by institutional investors in an annual survey generally devised by a financial magazine. Ranked analysts are much in demand and can command a high compensation.

research coverage: the universe of companies covered by one or more sell-side research analysts within an investment bank.

research guidelines: a set of guidelines, usually issued by the legal advisers to the underwriters in an IPO, setting out a number of restrictions relating to the drafting, publication and issue of pre-deal research.

re-set: a term used for a feature of certain convertible or exchangeable bonds (most particularly in Asia) when a downward adjustment to the conversion price is made in certain circumstances. A re-set usually encourages an issuer to re-finance the bond or perhaps to force conversion. Also called refix.

re-structuring: see *re-organization*. Can also sometimes refer to the re-negotiation of the terms of an outstanding financial instrument.

retail discount: a discount over the institutional offer price for the benefit of retail investors participating in an IPO. Retail discounts are now uncommon. See also *discount to offer price*.

retail incentives: mechanisms used to encourage the participation of retail investors in an IPO, particularly in the context of privatizations. Retail incentives can include discounts, bonus shares, partly paid shares, bill vouchers, money-back guarantees, and other devices.

retail investor: a qualifying individual investor targeted, and participating, in a public offering. Equivalent to public investor.

reverse roadshow: the process through which potential investors approach or visit an issuer directly (rather than the other way around), perhaps with a view to making an investment in the shares of a company, perhaps by way of a strategic or cornerstone investment.

reverse stock split: a transaction whereby the denomination of the share price of a company is increased, when the level at which it is trading is perceived to be too low compared to those of other companies listed on the same stock exchange. For example, a company with 10,000 shares trading at US$10 becomes a company with 1,000 shares trading at US$100, so that there is no loss in value for existing investors. See also *stock split*, which is the reverse of this form of transaction.

review (of accounts): a procedure performed by auditors to provide a level of comfort on (usually, interim) accounts of a company over a period of time. A review is less extensive in scope than an audit and therefore results in a lower level of comfort being provided.

right of first refusal: a right granted to a party similar to a call option and giving it the option to enter into a contractual arrangement before such an arrangement is opened to other parties.

rights issue: a fixed-price offering, which is generally fully underwritten at the outset by a syndicate of brokers and banks and provides certainty of proceeds to an issuer. In a rights issue, existing shareholders of a company are entitled (but not required) to exercise their right to buy shares in the company in proportion to their respective holdings at the time. This effectively gives them a right of first refusal to protect them for dilution. Rights may be taken up by such shareholders to subscribe to the rights issue or can alternatively be sold wholly or partly to other investors. Rights are traded separately from shares during the subscription period. Rights not taken up lapse and are automatically sold at the end of the subscription period by way of a "rump" placement.

risk factors: a key section of the offering circular, usually located in the first few pages of the document and providing investors with an extensive list of factors that could materially and adversely affect the financial condition or results of operations of the issuer or the performance of the shares if they were to occur. Risk factors, which are included for the protection of the company, can cover many pages and usually each take the form of a heading, followed by a detailed narrative.

roadshow: a series of meetings between a company and institutional investors set up by one or more investment banks. A roadshow may be organized irrespective of any capital markets transaction (see *non-deal roadshow*) or in connection with an IPO or another related transaction. A roadshow usually comprises large group presentations, small group presentations and one-on-one meetings. Sometimes, video or audio conferences may also be arranged, as well as an internet roadshow. See also *internet roadshow*.

roadshow coordinator: an in-house roadshow specialist within an investment bank. See also *roadshow consultant*.

roadshow consultant: a specialist consultant tasked with organizing the transport, hotel, room rental, and conference logistics associated with a company roadshow. Large investment banks also often have one or more in-house roadshow coordinators liaising with roadshow consultants.

roadshow presentation: the presentation delivered by the management of a company during a roadshow. The roadshow presentation for an IPO is usually drafted by one or more of the lead investment banks and includes a short video presentation, slides, and a script as well as a list of questions and answers, all of which are vetted by legal advisers. Management are usually introduced by a senior investment banker while another senior banker often coordinates a short questions and answers session, prior to delivering concluding remarks.

rule of law: a reliable system of well-defined and impartial laws. A stable rule of law is a pre-requisite for IPOs to take place in any jurisdiction.

Rule 12g 3-2(b): an exemption from full registration requirements in the US, whereby a foreign company issuing American depositary receipts (ADRs) can send information filed in its home market directly to the Securities and Exchange Commission (SEC) for the benefit of US investors.

Rule 144A American depositary receipts (RADSs): ADSs marketed to qualified institutional buyers (QIBs) in the US in connection with a Rule 144A private placement. RADSs are traded on the Private Offerings, Resale and Trading through Automated Linkages (PORTAL) platform.

Rule 144A of the Securities Act of 1933 (as amended): a set of rules enacted in 1991 in the US that enable the marketing of securities issued by foreign companies by way of a private placement to qualified institutional buyers (QIBs) in the US. See also qualified institutional buyer (QIB).

rules of engagement: see *memorandum of understanding (MoU)*.

safe-harbour rules for stabilization: a set of rules issued by a stock exchange setting out how the stabilization of a new equity issue may be conducted and offering a safe harbour for such stabilization activities from allegations of market manipulation. Most markets have explicit safe-harbour rules with respect stabilization, although certain emerging markets do not.

sale and purchase agreement: an underwriting agreement for the placement or institutional offer tranche of an IPO.

sales trader: see *trader*.

salespeople: employees of an investment bank tasked with selling securities to a portfolio of institutional investors and supported in their selling efforts by research analysts. Salespeople usually have a regional, country, investor type, or (more rarely) industry sector focus.

Sarbanes-Oxley legislation: a US federal law enacted in 2002 setting out demanding standards for the boards, management, and auditors of US companies or foreign companies listed in the US. It does not apply to privately held companies. Also called Sarbox or SOX.

SAS 72 comfort letter: the most common type of international comfort letter delivered by the auditors to an issuer and to the underwriters in connection with an IPO or related transaction where a prospectus is published. Importantly, an SAS 72 comfort letter includes a negative assurance clause. See also *negative assurance*.

SAS 100 review: a type of review for interim, unaudited financial information and accounts performed by the auditors of a company in order for them to include a negative assurance clause in their comfort letter for an international IPO. See also *negative assurance*.

Save As You Earn (SAYE) plan: a type of employee share ownership programme in the UK.

scrip issue: the issue of new shares to the shareholders of a company, in proportion to the shares they already own. Scrip issues (which are also called bonus issues, or capitalization issues) are made at no cost to the shareholders.

SEC-registered offering: an equity capital markets transaction registered with the Securities and Exchange Commission (SEC) in the US, and therefore targeted at US retail investors and institutional investors in the US (and, often, internationally).

second board: a market established by a stock exchange with less demanding disclosure standards than the main board and typically for smaller or fast-growing companies. See also *main board*.

secondary listing: see *dual listing* and *multiple listings*.

secondary offering: either the sale of shares by a shareholder in an equity capital markets (ECM) transaction (including an IPO) or a follow-on ECM transaction.

sector banker: an investment banker specializing in originating and executing advisory and financing transactions for companies in a particular industry sector.

Securities Commission Malaysia (*Suruhanjaya Sekuriti***):** the regulator for the securities market in Malaysia, which reviews and registers prospectuses for IPOs listed on Bursa Malaysia.

Securities and Exchange Commission (SEC): the US regulator for the securities industry, based in Washington.

Securities and Futures Commission (SFC): the regulator for the securities industry in Hong Kong.

securities registration statement (SRS): a document drafted in Japanese in a prescribed format, usually based on an international offering circular and filed with the Kanto Local Finance Bureau (KLFB) in connection with a public offering without listing (POWL) in Japan. See also *public offering without listing (POWL)*.

segmentation (of accounts): the breakdown of the turnover, operating earnings or assets of a company into several segments. Segmentation can be conducted on a geographical basis or pursuant to several lines of activities undertaken by the company. The segmentation of accounts provides investors with better visibility with respect to the financial performance of the company but is sometimes frowned upon by issuers as it can provide competitors with sensitive information or a competitive edge. See also *IFRS 8*.

sell-down: the sale of shares by one or more investors in an IPO or related transaction. Equivalent to secondary offering.

sell-side research: research on securities produced by research analysts employed by an investment bank or broker.

selling concession: a component of the gross fees, paid on shares actually allocated to investors and normally equivalent to 60% of the gross fees. In a US pot, part of the selling concession is paid on a fixed basis on the basis of shares underwritten, while the balance is paid based on designations received from investors in a jump ball system. See also *jump ball*.

selling group: a group of banks appointed to sell (but not to underwrite) securities in a syndicate.

selling restrictions: restrictions drafted by legal advisers and included in both the plan of distribution (or underwriting) section of a prospectus and the sale and purchase agreement. Selling restrictions set out the jurisdictions in which the securities on offer may be sold to institutional investors by way of private placements. On occasion, the selling restrictions include specific language or disclosure for the benefit of investors in a particular jurisdiction (e.g., for the benefit of investors in Ontario and Québec in Canada).

senior associate: a junior investment banking title, equivalent to manager.

senior co-lead manager: a junior investment bank in a syndicate of underwriters with a role and responsibilities similar to those of a co-lead manager but usually with slightly higher underwriting or higher fees.

senior manager: a junior to mid-level rank in an investment bank, similar to that of senior associate.

senior managing director: a senior rank in an investment bank.

senior vice-president: a high mid-level rank in an investment bank.

sequential retail offering: a retail offering that is conducted at a fixed price and after the institutional offer price has been determined. This generally implies a somewhat longer settlement timetable for institutional investors.

settlement: the payment of the consideration for the shares by investors to one of the lead banks, for onward payment, minus fees, to the issuer and/or selling shareholders, against the delivery of the securities, usually on a delivery versus payment (DVP) basis.

several underwriting obligations: the usual underwriting arrangement for equity capital markets transactions (including IPOs) whereby shares underwritten by an investment bank defaulting on its obligations are not taken up by the other underwriters.

Shanghai SSE 50 index: a free float-adjusted, market capitalization–weighted stock market index composed of the 50 largest companies listed on the Shanghai Stock Exchange in mainland China. A similar index exists for a larger group of 180 companies.

share buy-back programme: a mandate granted to a company by its shareholders pursuant to which it can buy its own shares in the market, either to be kept as Treasury stock, or to be cancelled. See also *autocontrôle*.

Share Incentive Plan (SIP): a type of employee share ownership programme in the UK.

share registrar and transfer agent: usually, a single institution undertaking both roles and tasked with maintaining a record of shareholders in a listed company to establish authenticity of ownership, ensure the accurate payment of dividends, and offer shareholders the opportunity to take up their rights in the event of a rights issue. It is also the responsibility of the share registrar to process and ballot applications from retail investors and to dispatch share certificates to applicants allocated shares in an IPO.

shelf registration: the procedure through which a prospectus for the issue of securities is split into various components, some of which are registered in advance with the competent regulatory authority or stock exchange, so as to facilitate and speed up the documentation process for offerings by frequent issuers.

shell company: a dormant company listed on a stock exchange that may be purchased by another company to execute a backdoor listing. See also *backdoor listing*.

Singapore depositary receipt (SDR): equivalent to a global depositary receipt (GDR) or Indian depositary receipt (IDR) but listed in Singapore and traded either in US or Singapore dollars.

***sociétés d'investissements immobiliers cotées* (SIIC):** The French version of a real estate investment trust (REIT), created in 2003. See also *real estate investment trust (REIT)*.

soft underwriting: the usual type of underwriting arrangement in an IPO, whereby the securities on offer are underwritten once the book of institutional demand has closed and the offer price has been determined. In effect, a soft (or best efforts) underwriting only underwrites the rather remote risk of one or more institutional investors defaulting on their settlement obligations. A soft underwriting is the opposite of a hard underwriting arrangement. See also *hard underwriting* and *bought deal*.

sovereign wealth fund (SWF): an investment fund set up by the government of a country. SWFs include revenue stabilization funds which are designed to temper the impact of volatile revenues (e.g., oil and gas revenues), and holding funds, which manage governments participations or direct investments in state-owned or other enterprises and savings funds, typically devoted to the funding of future pension liabilities. Some sovereign wealth funds are also set up to manage excess foreign reserves. A variety of investment styles, depending on the purposes of such funds, can be found among SWFs, but a number of names are well known as significant high-quality investors in IPOs.

special dividend: an extraordinary dividend paid by a company to its shareholders. In the context of an IPO, a special dividend is often a way for shareholders to pay themselves additional proceeds ahead of the listing, usually by first gearing up the company about to be floated.

special purpose acquisition company (SPAC): a shell or blank-cheque company that undergoes an IPO and is listed with a view to acquiring a business or company at a later stage. SPACs are sold on the basis of the experience of the management team, and also enable such management teams to use the proceeds of the SPAC's IPO to invest in these businesses or companies. SPACs became widespread in the US after the turn of the century, although a handful have also been listed in Europe.

special purpose vehicle (SPV): a company set up for the purpose of carrying out a financial transaction generally in a tax efficient manner, for example, the issue of a Eurobond or convertible bond. In this case, SPVs often benefit from a guarantee by their parent company.

special share: see *golden share*.

specialist (on the NYSE or NYSE American): a US broking firm responsible for establishing a market and providing liquidity in given stocks listed on the NYSE or on NYSE American (where prices are set by auction), effectively working as an auctioneer, matching buyers and sellers, resolving imbalances that may exist in the trading of a particular stock, and helping to maintain an orderly market. A specialist may need to trade for its own account, sometimes regardless of profitability, in order to achieve this. For an IPO and listing on the NYSE, between three and five specialists are generally interviewed in New York according to strict guidelines, prior to one firm being appointed to act in such a role. Specialists are called designated market markers (DMMs) since 2008.

specialist consultant: a consultant or expert that may be called upon to provide a report published in an offering circular for an IPO to help investors better understand the company's business. Specialist consultants may, for example, include mining consultants for minerals or natural resources companies to opine on the levels of resources and reserves of the mining assets, or shipping or traffic consultants in the case of companies in the transportation sector. They may also publish a report on the industry in which a company operates. See also *independent market research (IMR) report*.

spin-off: a financial transaction whereby an entire division or subsidiary of a company is listed as a stand-alone business.

split orders: separate orders placed by the same institutional investor with two or more investment banks in a syndicate of underwriters. Split orders are not always allowed, depending on the rules of engagement, and should always be allocated in the same way (as a percentage of demand).

sponsor: a bank, usually (but not always) an underwriter of an IPO, whose responsibility is to advise the issuer on listing matters and to liaise with the relevant regulator or stock exchange on documentation matters with a view to sponsoring the issuer for listing. This term can also be used to designate a corporate selling part of the ownership of some of its property assets into a real estate investment trust (REIT).

sponsored American depositary receipt (ADR): see *level 1, 2, 3 American depositary receipts (ADRs)*.

spread of shareholders: the number of public shareholders of a company. Usually, a minimum spread of shareholders (several hundred to several thousand) is required by a stock exchange for a company to be listed.

stabilization: the process through which a stabilizing agent or manager, appointed among the lead banks in an IPO, can resolve imbalances between short-term buyers and sellers in the first trading days or weeks of an IPO and support the share price when it falls below the offer price. The main tool used to stabilize an IPO is an over-allotment option. See also *Greenshoe, over-allotment option,* and *naked short*.

stabilization profit: the profit generated by the stabilizing agent or manager for the account of the syndicate as a result of stabilization activities, equivalent to the difference between the price of shares allocated to investors as a Greenshoe at the offer price and the lower price at which shares are bought back in the market.

stags: speculative investors with a very short-term horizon and largely driven by momentum.

steering committee: a committee usually composed of senior investment bankers and senior members of the management of a company about to be floated to oversee the execution of an IPO. The steering committee is usually concerned with ensuring that the timetable for the IPO remains on track, resolving critical issues and, potentially, strengthening the board of the company ahead of listing. When an independent adviser has been appointed by the company and its involvement disclosed to the lead banks, it should also participate in the steering committee.

Stock Exchange Daily Official List (SEDOL): a code of seven alphanumeric characters used to identify securities in the UK and Ireland.

stock exchange trading fee: a fee levied by a stock exchange on trades made by investors.

stock split: a transaction whereby the denomination of a stock is changed to a smaller amount so as to make it more easily tradable by investors (e.g., a company with 1000 shares currently trading at US$100 becomes a company with 10,000 shares trading at US$10 so that there is no loss in value for existing shareholders). A stock split may be undertaken prior to an IPO, so as to adjust the share price to a level more comparable to those for companies already traded on the same stock exchange. The reverse transaction is quite logically called a reverse stock split.

strategic investor: see *pre-IPO investment*.

strategist: a type of sell-side research analyst specializing in macro trends and in recommending allocations between markets, asset classes, or industry sectors.

sub-underwriter: in certain jurisdictions (such as Singapore), a junior member in a syndicate of underwriters. In others, an investment bank (or an investor) that agrees to underwrite, for a fee, part of the shares already underwritten by another.

subscription agreement: an agreement whereby a strategic or cornerstone investor agrees to purchase a specified number of shares in a company at an agreed price.

sukuk: an Islamic bond (or convertible or exchangeable bond) issued pursuant to *Shariah* principles. In particular, *sukuks*, which cannot be issued by companies involved in certain industry sectors, do not bear interest per se, although they are structured to replicate the cash-flows of bonds.

sum-of-the-parts valuation: the valuation of a company involving several distinct business activities, each of which may also be valued using a distinct methodology.

summary (of prospectus): a summary of the key information included in the prospectus for an IPO, including a short description of the issuer and its business, as well as key financial line items, operating data and statistics.

summary of principal differences between local GAAP and IFRS or US GAAP: a summary between the generally agreed accounting principles (GAAP) in which the company reports its accounts and International Financial Reporting Standards (IFRS) or US GAAP, included for the benefit of US or international investors, usually in the management discussion and analysis of financial condition and results of operations (MD&A) or, more rarely, in a US or international wrap. This is now less commonly included in IPO prospectuses, particularly in Europe.

syndicate: a group of investment banks or brokers formed for the purpose of marketing, selling and, generally, underwriting securities.

syndicate due diligence: a call or meeting with management arranged by the banks appointed to lead an IPO in order to offer an opportunity to those junior members of the syndicate of underwriters (i.e. co-lead and co-managers) to conduct limited due diligence.

syndicate structure: how a syndicate is organized, taking into account seniority levels among underwriters, tranches or jurisdictions in which defined classes or groups of investors may be accessed.

tail swallowing: in a rights issue, a practice whereby shareholders sell enough rights to buy new shares to allow them to take up as many shares as they can, without having to pay under the rights issue.

Taiwan depositary receipt (TDR): equivalent to a global depositary receipt (GDR) but listed in Taiwan and traded in New Taiwan dollars.

target investor: an investor identified by an investment bank or broker as a suitable candidate to invest in a particular transaction, usually because of its investment style or track record of investing in securities with a similar profile. See also *pilot fishing*.

target price: the price that a research analyst believes a security can attain within a reasonable time horizon, usually prominently stated on the front page of a research report. Target prices are prohibited in pre-deal research reports.

teach-in: a briefing, usually by a sell-side research analyst and an equity capital markets team, to salespeople about the equity story for, and structure of, an IPO about to be launched. See also *crib sheet*.

10b-5 letter: also called disclosure letter. A statement by US counsel addressed to the underwriters and stating that "upon reviewing the offering circular, and having conducted business and documentary due diligence, nothing has come to their attention to suggest that the offering circular contains any untrue statement of material fact or fails to state a material fact necessary in order to make the statements made, or in light of the circumstances under which they were made, not misleading". In short, a 10b-5 letter is a confirmation by US counsel that the prospectus does not omit any material information, and establishes a basis for due diligence defence against litigation in the US. 10b-5 letters are usually required from US legal advisers by investment banks for IPOs that include a Rule 144A private placement and in all cases for SEC-registered offerings.

tender offer: an offer made to investors to repurchase a security on certain terms. For example, a tender offer may be made in connection with a share buy-back programme, or to repurchase an outstanding convertible bond.

termination clause: a clause pursuant to which a subscription or an underwriting obligation might be terminated at the option of the investor or underwriter under certain circumstances, usually as a result of a breach of some of the representations and warranties made by the issuer. *Force majeure* clauses also provide for the termination of underwriting agreements in exceptional circumstances. See also *force majeure clause.*

theoretical ex-rights price (TERP): the theoretical price at which the shares are expected to trade after the launch of a rights issue. The TERP is calculated as the market value of the issuer before the rights issue plus the proceeds to be raised from the rights issues (ignoring fees and expenses), together divided by the number of shares after the rights issue. In effect, the TERP is an objective measure of the value of a company's shares after a rights issue. The TERP is "theoretical" in the sense that the percentage of shares that will be taken up under the rights issue by existing shareholders remains unknown until the close of the offer period. The calculation of the TERP therefore assumes that all the newly issued shares are taken up by existing shareholders. The subscription price and discount are selected at the start of the rights offering process.

ticker: a short alphanumerical identifier for a listed stock.

tombstone advertisement: an advertisement, usually made in the financial press, recording the "bare bones" of an advisory or financing transaction, chiefly the names of the lead investment banks that advised, underwrote and/or sold the deal.

top-down demand estimate: a theoretical estimate of investor demand for an IPO usually involving the use of market indexes. If a company and an IPO are large enough, then it is likely that the issuer will be included in one of the most commonly followed stock indexes. By estimating the company's weight in a country index, based on its likely valuation and free float as well as taking into account the weight of the country of listing in a global portfolio, for example by using the Morgan Stanley Capital International (MSCI) global indexes—probably the most widely used global equity benchmarks by institutional investors—one can in turn estimate the amount of passive, index-based demand for the stock.

TOPIX index: a widely used, free float–adjusted, market value–weighted index tracking the performance of all the domestic companies listed on the first section of the Tokyo Stock Exchange.

Toronto Stock Exchange (TSX): a stock exchange established in Canada in 1852 and part of the TMX Group, which also owns and operates the TSX Venture Exchange for early stage companies. The TSX is particularly well known for listings of companies in the mining and exploration sectors.

total return: the return on an investment in securities taking into account price appreciation, interest and any dividends or distributions.

total return swap (TRS): a financial contract that transfers, for a period of time, both the credit risk and market risk of an underlying asset. Investors in a security issued pursuant to a TRS receive dividends and have the benefit of any capital appreciation but, ultimately, do not have ownership of the asset.

trader: also called market maker. An employee of an investment bank or broker tasked with buying and selling securities in the financial markets either on behalf of clients served by salespeople, or for the account of the bank itself (in the case of a proprietary trader). By contrast, a sales trader talks directly to institutional clients to promote new investment ideas and also provides market execution.

trading: the level of buying and selling by investors in a particular security, as measured over a period of time.

tranche: a defined component of a syndicate of underwriters or offer structure for an IPO aimed at a particular region or type of investor.

transaction levy: a stock exchange trading fee levied by a regulator.

transaction team: in an IPO, the parties working on the execution of the transaction. The transaction team for an IPO includes members of the management of the issuer, investment bankers, several firms of legal advisers, accountants and, often, a variety of other advisers.

transparency: the amount, set by the bookrunners, above which the name of an individual end-investor that has placed an order in an IPO must be disclosed in the book of demand. Often set at around US$250,000, or the equivalent in other currencies.

treasury department: the department within the financial division of a company tasked with the management of cash and cash equivalent assets.

treasury stock: own stock bought in the market by a company or its subsidiaries but held as *autocontrôle*. See also *autocontrôle* and *share buy-back programme*.

triple-track process: Similar to a dual-track process but when an LBO is pursued simultaneously with an IPO and a trade sale.

trustee-manager: the manager of a business trust, which also acts as trustee. By comparison, a real estate investment trust (REIT) has a separate REIT manager and trustee (and also a property manager).

tycoon: a well-known, wealthy individual often chosen as a cornerstone investor in an IPO to provide early momentum and leadership. Most common in Hong Kong and other Asian IPOs.

UK listing authority (UKLA): an authority established under the Financial Conduct Authority in the UK that, among other things, previously reviewed and approved prospectuses for IPOs. It also monitored market disclosures by issuers and operated the UK listing regime. Its responsibilities were subsequently transferred to the Financial Conduct Authority itself. See *Financial Conduct Authority (FCA)*.

under-subscription: a situation in which demand generated from investors is below the number of shares offered in an IPO (or in a tranche of an IPO).

underwriting: a contractual arrangement whereby one or more investment banks or brokers commit to purchasing shares in a company at an agreed price. Underwriting may be subject to conditions precedent. See also *best efforts underwriting, conditions precedent, hard underwriting, soft underwriting,* and *sub-underwriter*.

underwriting agreement: an agreement evidencing an underwriting arrangement. Often called a sale and purchase agreement for a placement or institutional offer tranche.

underwriting commission: a component of the gross fees payable by an issuer and/ or selling shareholder(s) to a syndicate of underwriters. Like management commissions, underwriting commissions are payable on shares underwritten (rather than sold) and typically represent 20% of the gross fees.

underwriting committee: a committee, sometimes also called commitment committee, within an investment bank composed of senior bankers, market professionals, and risk management and compliance staff, and tasked with taking decisions to underwrite capital markets transactions led by the bank.

unsponsored American depositary receipt (ADR): an ADR programme not initiated (or controlled) by the issuer, but instead created at the initiative of a broker working with a depositary bank in response to US investor demand. It involves the filing by such depositary bank of a simple registration statement called Form F-6 with the Securities and Exchange Commission (SEC). Such programmes, many of which are illiquid, trade on the over-the-counter market on what is called the pink sheets. Because the company has no control over an unsponsored ADR, the programme can sometimes be duplicated by more than one depositary bank, without the company's consent.

upsize option: an option, normally at the discretion of an issuer and/or of its selling shareholders, to increase the size of an IPO or of an equity capital markets offering in light of investor demand.

US wrap: similar to an international wrap but with additional information included specifically for the benefit of US investors. See also *international wrap*.

Valor number: a number (incorporated in the Swiss ISIN number) used to identify securities in Switzerland.

valuation: the theoretical or actual value of a company in connection with an IPO. Also one of the working group modules for the execution of an IPO, more particularly concerned with determining an appropriate valuation methodology and level for the business.

verification notes: a set of notes compiled by a firm of legal advisers to check, source and verify every statement or narrative included in an offering circular. Verification notes are updated throughout the execution of a transaction.

vice-chairman: a particularly senior investment banking title and rank.

vice-president: a mid-level investment banking rank, equivalent to associate director.

virtual data room (VDR): see *data room*.

volume-weighted average price (VWAP): a measure of the average price relative to the volume traded in a given stock over a period of time. A VWAP is calculated by multiplying the number of shares traded by the share price for each transaction undertaken over a period of time (e.g., over a single trading day) and by dividing the result by the total number of shares traded over that period.

voting rights: rights attached to the ownership of shares pursuant to which the owner of such shares may vote at an ordinary or extraordinary general meeting of a company.

When a company has different classes of shares, these may have different voting rights.

W pages: the pages of an international or US wrap, usually numbered W-1, W-2, and so on.

waiver: in the context of an IPO, the permission granted to an issuer by a regulator or stock exchange to undertake certain transactions otherwise prohibited by the listing rules. Also used where a bookrunner waives the lock-up adhering to shares owned by an investor or shareholder.

wealth management: see *private bank*.

weighted average cost of capital (WACC): the discount rate used in a discounted cash-flow (DCF) valuation.

well-known seasoned issuer (WKSI): in the US, a frequent issuer of securities as defined under the Securities Act with, inter alia, US$700 million in public float. WKSIs represent about 30% of all listed companies in the US and about 95% of market capitalization. Also see *frequent issuer*.

Wertpapierkennnummer (WKN): a number used to identify issuers and securities in Germany.

"white shoe" firms: the US equivalent of "magic circle" firms in the UK. "White shoe" firms are said to generally include, among others, Cleary Gottlieb Steen & Hamilton, Cravath, Swaine & Moore, Davis Polk & Wardwell, Latham & Watkins, Shearman & Sterling, and Sullivan & Cromwell.

working group modules: the working groups set up among the working parties in an IPO to organize the execution of the transaction. Usually, defined groups are set up to focus on documentation, valuation and marketing issues. The working groups are generally coordinated by a steering committee, which meets periodically.

yield investor: an institutional investment style whereby investors typically focus on investments that offer a pick-up in yield, such as real estate investment trusts (REITs), business trusts, infrastructure funds, or utility stocks.

Notes

Chapter 1: Defining the parameters

1. *South China Morning Post*, 30 October 2010.
2. Economist.com, 8 July 2010.
3. Berkshire Hathaway website, memo from Warren Buffet dated 20 January 2010.
4. WSJ.com, 4 April 2014.
5. Bloomberg.com, 30 June 2010.
6. Dow Jones Newswires, 11 April 2006.
7. FinanceAsia.com, 3 July 2006.
8. IFLR.com, 1 November 2006.
9. Bloomberg.com, 6 February 2008.
10. FT.com, 24 September 2010.
11. WSJ.com, 14 December 2010.
12. Forbes.com, 17 January 2006.
13. Vivendi website, memo dated December 2008.
14. Information sourced from the respective companies' websites in September 2010.
15. Correspondence between the author and the company.
16. Correspondence between the author and the company.
17. China Daily.com.cn, 16 July 2010.
18. Bloomberg.com, 29 November 2012.
19. Tokyo Stock Exchange website, consulted in August 2010 and April 2014.
20. Company website, consulted in August 2010.
21. Filing with the Stock Exchange of Hong Kong, 4 March 2014.
22. Reuters.com, 23 June 2010.
23. Dow Jones Newswires, 3 June 2010.
24. Bloomberg.com, 18 and 19 November 2010.
25. Freud D. (2006), *Freud in the City*, Bene Factum Publishing.
26. Lilja R. (1997), *International Equity Markets: The Art of the Deal*, Euromoney Books.

27. *Financial Times*, 4 October 2010.

28. FT.com, 16 July 2010.

29. FinanceAsia.com, 7 April 2010.

30. Bloomberg.com, 16 August 2010.

31. Bloomberg.com, 7 October 2010.

32. News.sky.com, 31 March 2014.

33. IPO registration statement displayed on the SEC's EDGAR database, consulted in July 2010.

Chapter 2: Getting ready

34. New York Stock Exchange website, consulted in July 2010 and April 2014.

35. IR Web Report, 5 January 2011.

36. Information sourced from the banks' respective websites, consulted in July 2010.

37. Keloharju M., S. Knüpfer, and S. Torstila (2006), "Do Retail Incentives Work in Privatizations?", *The Review of Financial Studies*.

38. Cadbury A. (1992), *The Financial Aspects of Corporate Governance*, Gee.

39. Higgs D. (2003), *Review of the Role and Effectiveness of Non-Executive Directors*, DTI.

40. Herbert Smith (2006), *Hong Kong IPO Guide*.

41. Tokyo Stock Exchange website, consulted in July 2010.

42. Website of the Stock Exchange of Hong Kong, April 2014.

43. Bloomberg.com, 27 January 2010.

44. Announcement by United Company RUSAL PLC, 12 November 2010.

45. *Financial Times*, 4 October 2010.

46. GlobalCapital.com, 27 March 2014.

47. *The Baltimore Sun*, 2 July 2004.

48. Akin Gump Strauss Hauer & Feld LLP (2003), *Insights*, Aspen Publishers.

49. Bloomberg.com, 23 January 2014.

50. Dewey & LeBoeuf (2008), "SEC Accepts IASB IFRS Financial Statements from Foreign Private Issuers without U.S. GAAP Reconciliation", Client alert.

51. IPO registration statement displayed on the SEC's EDGAR database, consulted in July 2010.

52. IPO registration statement displayed on the SEC's EDGAR database, consulted in July 2010.

53. IFRS website, 28 September 2010.

54. HKEx website, November 2010.

55. IOSCO website consulted in October 2010.

56. Slaughter and May (2004), *The New EU Prospectus Directive*, Client publication.

57. Herbert Smith (2006), *Hong Kong IPO Guide*.

58. CLM Associates (2005), *Corporate Treasurers' Seminar Slides on the Investment Company Act of 1940*.

59. Testa, Hurwitz & Thibeault (2002), "PFIC Means Taxes on Foreign Investments", AltAssets Knowledge Bank.

60. JPMorgan (2008), *Sovereign Wealth Funds: A Bottom-Up Primer, various media and fund websites, consulted in January 2021.*

61. *Financial Times*, 4 November 2013.

62. Forbes.com, consulted in August 2010.

63. Press release by Chaowei Power (Holdings), 23 June 2010.

64. IPO prospectus dated 30 June 2010.

65. Information sourced from the issuers' respective IPO prospectuses.

66. Bloomberg.com, 5 October 2010.

67. Freud D. (2006), *Freud in the City*, Bene Factum Publishing.

68. Conversation between the author and some of the bookrunner banks.

69. FinanceAsia.com, 25 October 2010.

70. Press release issued by Standard Chartered, 13 May 2010.

71. Press release issued by the Taiwan Stock Exchange, 8 September 2010.

72. Whitmore J. (2010), "REITs 'Destroy' £24bn of Value", *Property Week*.

73. Ernst & Young, "Global perspectives 2013 REIT report".

74. Real Capital Analytics (RCA), "Global capital trends, 2012 year in review and mid year review 2013".

75. Bloomberg.com, November 2007.

76. Marchal G. (2010), "Les Reits respirent à nouveau après avoir subi la crise de plein fouet", *L'Agefi Hebdo*.

77. Reuters.com, 6 April 2014.

78. IFRAsia.com, 19 April 2014.

79. Freshfields Bruckhaus Deringer, "Business Trusts in Hong Kong and Singapore", August 2013.

Chapter 3: Marketing the deal

80. Freud D. (2006), *Freud in the City*, Bene Factum Publishing.

81. *The New York Times*, 18 May 2012.

82. FinanceAsia.com, 11 June 2010.

83. Freud D. (2006), *Freud in the City*, Bene Factum Publishing.

84. Worldbank.org, Labor Tool Kit, "Key Elements of a Labor Program", consulted in June 2010.

85. Businesslink.gov.uk, "Practical Advice for Business, Set up Employee Schemes", consulted in June 2010.

86. Businesslink.gov.uk, "Practical Advice for Business, Set up Employee Schemes", consulted in June 2010.

87. WSJ.com, 31 March 2014.

88. Jenkinson T. and A. Ljungqvist (2001), *Going Public: The Theory and Evidence on How Companies Raise Equity Finance*, Oxford University Press.

89. Herbert Smith (2006), *Hong Kong IPO Guide*.

Chapter 4: After the IPO

90. IPO prospectuses.
91. Company filing with the Singapore Exchange.
92. FinanceAsia.com, 17 October 2007 and *The Standard*, 17 December 2007.
93. Various press releases available on the group's websites, consulted in July 2010.
94. FinanceAsia.com, 27 July 2010.
95. IFRAsia.com, 29 July 2010.
96. Press release issued by the Tata group, 21 June 2007.
97. *The Indian Express*, 22 August 2012.

Appendix 1

98. FinanceAsia.com, 28 September 2009.
99. *Financial Times*, 17 November 2010.
100. Reuters.com, 27 May 2010.
101. FinanceAsia.com, 14 April 2010.
102. FinanceAsia.com, 3 May 2010.
103. Bloomberg.com, 14 April 2014.

Glossary

104. World Federation of Stock Exchanges, 31 December 2009.

Further reading

On IPOs generally and on the execution process

Draho J. (2006), *The IPO Decision: Why and How Companies Go Public*, Edward Elgar.

Espinasse P. (2014), *IPO Banks: Pitch, Selection and Mandate*, Palgrave Macmillan.

Espinasse P., and S. Johnstone (2013), *Study Manual for Paper 15 Sponsors (Principals) and Paper 16 Sponsors (Representatives) of the Licensing Examination for Securities and Futures Intermediaries*, Hong Kong Securities and Investment Institute.

Espinasse P., and others (2012), *The Hong Kong IPO Guide 2013*, LexisNexis.

Espinasse P., and others (2012), *The IPO Guide 2012*, LexisNexis.

Geddes R. (2003), *IPOs and Equity Offerings*, Elsevier Ltd.

On IPOs in the UK in particular

Reuvid J. (2007), *Floating Your Company: The Essential Guide to Going Public*, Kogan Page.

On US and SEC-registered IPOs in particular

Blowers S. C., P. H. Griffith, and T. L. Milan (1999), *The Ernst & Young Guide to the IPO Value Journey*, Wiley.

Bragg S. M. (2009), *Running a Public Company: From IPO to SEC Reporting*, Wiley.

Lipman F. D. (2008), *International and US IPO Planning*, Wiley.

Westenberg D. A. (2010), *Initial Public Offerings: A Practical Guide to Going Public*, Practising Law Institute.

On convertible bonds

Cazaubieilh F. (2004), *Théorie et Pratique des Obligations Convertibles en Actions et des Produits Assimilés*, Maxima Laurent du Mesnil.

Connolly K. B. (1998), *Pricing Convertible Bonds*, Wiley.

On REITs

Block R. L. (2006), *Investing in REITs: Real Estate Investment Trusts*, Bloomberg Press.

Whiting D. (2006), *Playing the REITs Game: Asia's New Real Estate Investment Trusts*, Wiley.

On privatizations

Letwin O. (1998), *Privatising the World*, Cassell.

Lilja R. (1997), *International Equity Markets: The Art of the Deal*, Euromoney Books.

On IPOs in China and associated pre-IPO restructuring transactions

Clissold T. (2004), *Mr. China: A Memoir*, Constable and Robinson.

Walter C. E., and F. J. T. Howie (2003), *Privatizing China: The Stock Markets and Their Role in Corporate Reform*, Wiley.

On investment banks and their practices

Alletzhauser A. (1990), T*he House of Nomura*, Bloomsbury.

Augar P. (2005), *The Death of Gentlemanly Capitalism,* Penguin.

Augar P. (2006), *The Greed Merchants*, Penguin.

Augar P. (2009), *Chasing Alpha: How Reckless Growth and Unchecked Ambition Ruined the City's Golden Decade*, Penguin.

Charters D. (2002), *No Tears: Tales from the Square Mile*, Elliott & Thompson.

Chernow R. (1990), *The House of Morgan*, Touchstone.

Cohan W. (2010), *House of Cards: A Tale of Hubris and Wretched Excess on Wall Street*, Anchor.

Ellis C. D. (2008), *The Partnership: The Making of Goldman Sachs*, Penguin.

Endlich L. (1999), *Goldman Sachs: The Culture of Success*, Warner Books.

Ferguson N. (2010), *High Financier: The Lives and Time of Siegmund Warburg*, Penguin.

Freud D. (2006), *Freud in the City*, Bene Factum Publishing.

Reid M. (1988), *All-Change in the City: The Revolution in Britain's Financial Sector*, Macmillan.

Roberts R. (1992), *Schroders: Merchant & Bankers*, Macmillan.

Sabouret A. (1987), *MM Lazard Frères: Une Saga de la Fortune*, Olivier Orban.

Tett G. (2010), *Fool's Gold: The Inside Story of JPMorgan and How Wall Street Greed Corrupted Its Bold Dream and Created a Financial Catastrophe*, Free Press.

Walter I., and R. Smith (1997), *Street Smarts: Linking Professional Conduct with Shareholder Value in the Securities Industry*, Harvard Business School Press.

On institutional investors, hedge funds, investment in IPOs, and the performance of IPOs

Chechile R. A. (2004), *The ABCs of IPOs: Investment Strategies and Tactics for New Issue Securities*, iUniverse Inc.

Gregoriou G. N. (2005), *Initial Public Offerings: An International Perspective*, Butterworth-Heinemann.

Jenkinson T., and A. Ljungqvist (2001), *Going Public: The Theory and Evidence on How Companies Raise Equity Finance*, Oxford University Press.

Khurshed A. (2010), *The Investor's Guide to IPOs: How to Profit from Initial Public Offerings*, Harriman House.

McCullough K., and R. Blake (2010), *Diary of a Fund Manager: From the Top, to the Bottom, and Back Again*, Wiley.

Walter I., and R. Smith (2000), *High Finance in the Euro Zone*, Financial Times Prentice Hall.

Zuckerman G. (2009), *The Greatest Trade Ever: The Behind-the-Scenes Story of How John Paulson Defied Wall Street and Made Financial History*, Crown Business.

On valuation

Antill N., and K. Lee (2005), *Company Valuation under IFRS: Interpreting and Forecasting Accounts Using International Financial Reporting Standards*, Harriman House.

Brett M. (1995), *How to Read the Financial Pages*, Random House.

Smith T. (1992), *Accounting for Growth*, Century Business.

In addition to the above books, a wealth of information on IPOs can be found on the websites of the stock exchanges listed in Appendix 8 (and on those of other stock exchanges), generally in the form of short guides detailing the listing process. The websites of some of the larger law and accounting firms and of the major financial printers also include high-level, general, or country-specific guides to IPOs and listing.

The following newspapers, magazines, and websites also include regular or occasional columns on IPO transactions and are worth researching: *Financial Times*, *Wall Street Journal* (including its European and Asian editions), Reuters, Bloomberg, Dow Jones Newswires, *Financial News*, *Australian Financial Review*, *International Financial Review*, *Nikkei Asian Review*, *Global Capital*, *FinanceAsia*, *Asiamoney*, *Euromoney*, *The Asset*, and *Institutional Investor*.

Index